boo hoo

$135 million, 18 months . . .

a dot.com story from

concept to catastrophe

boo hoo

$135 million, 18 months . . .
a dot.com story from
concept to catastrophe

Ernst Malmsten
Erik Portanger
Charles Drazin

arrow books

Published by Arrow in 2002

7 9 10 8 6

Copyright © 2001 by Ernst Malmsten, Erik Portanger, Charles Drazin

Ernst Malmsten, Erik Portanger and Charles Drazin have asserted their right under the Copyright, Designs and Patents Act, 1988, to be identified as the authors of this work.

First published by Business Books in 2001

Arrow
The Random House Group Limited
20 Vauxhall Bridge Road, London SW1V 2SA

Random House Australia (Pty) Limited
20 Alfred Street, Milsons Point,
Sydney, New South Wales 2061, Australia

Random House New Zealand Limited
18 Poland Road, Glenfield,
Auckland 10, New Zealand

Random House (Pty) Limited
Endulini, 5a Jubilee Road, Parktown 2193, South Africa

The Random House Group Limited Reg. No. 954009

www.randomhouse.co.uk

A CIP catalogue record for this book
is available from the British Library

Papers used by Random House are natural, recyclable
products made from wood grown in sustainable forests.
The manufacturing processes conform to the environmental
regulations of the country of origin.

ISBN 0 09 941837 1

Typeset in Bembo by MATS, Southend-on-Sea, Essex
Printed and bound in Great Britain by
Bookmarque, Croydon, Surrey

To everyone who believed in boo

Preface

WHEN BOO COLLAPSED that fateful day in May almost a year and a half ago, I felt a strong urge to tell the story of its brief but intense life. By writing a book, I hoped to come to terms with the overwhelming sadness and emptiness that follows such a great loss. As a sort of therapy, I would work out what had gone wrong and what mistakes I had made. But there were also all those questions from close friends, relatives and just about everyone I met. Was it true? Did you really spend all that money? It was obvious that with just the newspaper accounts to depend on, some rather wild and fanciful ideas had been formed. boo had become a myth, a legend. People seemed to assume that all I did was party, meet beautiful girls, drink Krug and fly everywhere first class with my private chef and bodyguards.

While I was amused by this other self, I was even more concerned to set the record straight, to tell the true story as honestly as possible. So, I decided to write a book that would be not just a distanced reconstruction, but a personal account of boo from first inspiration to its bitter end. I wanted to record the events, but also to capture how I and everyone else involved in the boo story actually felt at the time.

Then, as around me other internet companies went bust and the legions of the dot-com dead swiftly grew, I began to realize that boo had a much broader significance. It could serve to capture all the fever, glamour and broken dreams of the dot.com era. As the first big casualty, boo was a convenient scapegoat, but our collapse was only part of a much larger story involving business people, the media, banks and individual investors.

It would have been natural to write the story with my co-founder Kajsa Leander, who had been my close partner in not only boo but also several other ventures over the last decade. But, while in every other way she gave what help she could, it was not possible because she had returned to Sweden and, what was more, had just given birth to her second child. So with some nervousness I set out on my own, receiving enormous encouragement and practical advice from my agent Lesley Shaw at Gillon Aitken Associates. Over the next year, whether it was negotiating with publishers, newspapers and film companies, or sorting out countless other problems, she proved to be an invaluable support.

As English is not my native tongue, I realized that I would have to find someone to help me and, after reading a piece about boo that Erik Portanger and a colleague had written in the *Wall Street Journal*, I invited him to be my collaborator. I was impressed by how well written and researched his piece had been. He was not only deeply familiar with the boo story, but also, as a writer for the *Wall Street Journal*, well placed to give the transatlantic perspective on what was always intended to be an international company. Together we wrote a proposal which Random House agreed to publish. Erik received extended leave from the *Wall Street Journal* and we began to work on the book in November 2000.

From the outset I had always wanted to give as full an account as possible, but I had under-estimated just how huge that task would be. boo's existence may have been a brief one, but it touched many lives around the world. With tireless persistence, Erik undertook the time-consuming task of tracking them down and conducting often exhaustive interviews in an effort to recreate the many events, meetings and conversations as they actually happened. All together, he spoke to well over 200 people in the course of his research. But it was also a story that passed through many different areas – from business and high finance to marketing, fashion and even poetry. It soon became clear that the six months we had originally allowed ourselves to tell this story was absurdly optimistic and that if we were to make our publication date we would need some extra resources.

So in May of this year, we asked film writer and editor Charles Drazin, who had by a lucky coincidence just finished writing his own book, to join our team. As all three of us then raced ahead to make the publication date, with Erik as lead co-author, there was an increasing sense of the spirit of boo – which requires round-the-clock effort and total dedication – coming alive again. Indeed, I was struck by how similar the creative process of putting together a book was to being an entrepreneur. I depended on the efforts of not just my partners, but also editors, proofreaders, designers, typesetters, lawyers and so on.

It is not usual for a book like this to be commissioned, researched, written and then published within the space of a year. I owe an enormous debt of gratitude to my editor at Random House, Clare Smith, who coped with the resulting pressures and my often unreasonable demands with good humour and extreme flexibility. Others who have put up with me at Random House include publicity manager Sarah Harrison, marketing director Mark McCallum, rights director Jonathan Sissons, sales director Ron Beard, production director Barry Featherstone, art director Dennis Barker and editorial assistant Tiffany Stansfield. I am also grateful to Sohail Sahi, who spent three months conducting research, Beth Humphries and Donna Poppy, who gave some excellent editorial advice. Over the past twelve months many other people, including investors, bankers, suppliers and employees, have helped to put together this story, often giving up countless hours of their time. To all of them, I would like to express my deep gratitude.

In the last stages of completing this book I began to worry about the prospect of its publication. I wanted to be honest, but at the same I knew that in telling the truth I risked upsetting many people. If I now take this risk, it is because I believe history will judge the dot.com revolution of the late 1990s to have been a golden age, in which boo's part is too important to be left untold.

Ernst Malmsten
October 2001
emalmsten@hotmail.com

Prologue

boo.com, the online sportswear retailer, was on Tuesday night on the brink of collapse as attempts to secure additional funding from investors seemed doomed to failure.

People close to the company conceded that unless it secured the $30m of extra funding needed to take the business forward within 48 hours it would be forced to call in receivers.

If boo fails to win a last-minute reprieve, it will be the highest profile casualty among European e-tailing start-ups.

Financial Times, 17 May 2000

THE SHEET OF PAPER that has just been handed to me is covered with little yellow Post-Its. On each is scribbled a name and contact number, along with the media group they represent. There's CNN, BBC, *Le Figaro* and just about every other broadsheet, tabloid, online news site and TV station you can think of. 'All the big ones,' I say, lifting one of the Post-Its to reveal more numbers underneath. 'What do they want?'

Dina Cholack, who heads up public relations for boo.com, looks exasperated. 'Ernst,' she says, waving at the *Financial Times* spread across her desk. 'They all want to know if it's true.'

I leaked the story to the *FT* last night. Our investors needed to know that things really were serious this time. Right now, in a little room hidden away on the other side of our office in London's Soho, boo's co-founder Kajsa Leander and two of our senior managers are ringing around for money. Unless we raise $20 million by midnight boo.com is dead.

'Just tell them nothing has been decided yet – and don't answer the telephones any more.'

I'm trying to speak softly and to appear calm. Around Dina's desk, rows of young, casually dressed staff are tapping away at their computers with cool efficiency, but I sense their eyes on me, looking for hints of what the day will bring. Is he worried? Are things really that bad? After all, boo's sales in just the past fortnight have already hit $500,000, compared with $1.1 million for the entire first quarter. The whole building is humming with the energy of a healthy, thriving business. On the far side of the office I can see dozens of people working on Version 2.0 of our website. We're looking to the future, trying to put boo's reputation as the ultimate online shopping experience beyond doubt.

Dina looks impatient. 'It's not quite as easy as you think,' she says. 'We've got journalists cold-calling the staff. I don't know where they're getting the numbers from.'

Kajsa's assistant just got a call from a reporter pretending to be Christina Preisler, boo's head of PR in Stockholm. With no official comment from the company itself, the media are scenting blood and starting to get creative.

'The BBC are pushing really hard for an interview with you and Kajsa,' Dina continues.

'Did you speak to them?'

'No. We didn't call back, so they just showed up. They tried to set up their cameras in the lobby.'

'What? You didn't let them, did you?' If things weren't so desperate, this would almost be funny.

'Of course not. The Gurkhas threw them out. But I think they're still outside.'

I walk to the window and peer through the blinds. In the narrow alley below, I can see a few people loitering around and telephoto lenses trained on our windows.

'Shit.'

'Right,' Dina says, giving me a 'Told you so' look. 'There's also the John Cassy problem,' she adds, gesturing back over her shoulder.

Cassy, a reporter from the *Guardian*, has been sitting in our first-floor reception now for over an hour. He's refusing to leave until someone speaks to him. Kajsa and I had coffee with him a week ago. Now he's probably upset because we didn't keep him in the loop.

Dina lowers her voice to a whisper. 'We're going to have to speak to him soon.'

Dina's colleague, Alison Crombie, walks over, holding up a faxed article from the *New York Post*. 'Ernst, have you seen this?' 'CONFUSION REIGNS AT BOO.COM,' reads a giant headline. I shut my eyes tight for a few moments and walk away without comment.

The airless, claustrophobic cubicle that we have set aside as our war room is wreathed in cigarette smoke. The table in the middle is littered with overflowing ashtrays, Mars Bar wrappers and empty cans of Diet Coke. On the wall, someone has pinned up an email that arrived this morning from the German office.

> From: BooCrew@de.boo.com
> Subject: keep fighting
> Hi, this is the munich office . . . and we will fight

As I enter, I hear a voice on the speakerphone. 'I'm sorry. It's too late. It's just too late . . .'

Kajsa looks up with a tired smile. 'Prince Faisal's backed out,' she says. 'And now – well, you heard.'

We've raised only $9 million so far. It's mid-afternoon and we're not even halfway there.

Too late . . . For probably the first time it hits me that in just a few hours boo, which has been the focus of our lives for so long, which has inspired in so many of us a devotion bordering on love, might no longer exist. I try not to panic, but I feel numb. In my head I see images of all boo's employees, who worked day and night with such enthusiasm; and the investors who were so confident of our future that they had put $130 million into the company. Two years' work, five overseas offices, 350 staff. All these people trusted me and now I have failed them. What have I done? How could things have gone so wrong?

1

Spring 1992.

A T FOUR IN THE MORNING, the queue outside Les Bains
was thinning out. Marilyn, the bouncer at this most chic of
Parisian nightclubs, was less menacing now than bored. 'Va t'en' she
muttered – 'Get lost' – as we slipped out on to the street.

I was with Ascer, an old schoolfriend who was studying at L'École
Spéciale d'Architecture. We'd spent the last few hours staggering
from one packed bar to another. Les Bains, with its impossible
assemblage of beautiful people, was the high point of the evening.
This was the former Turkish bath-house that Roman Polanski had
used in his films *Frantic* and *Bitter Moon*. We'd sipped cocktails in the
lower bar, our eyes roving happily across the young, Gaultier and
Versace-clad bodies crowding the dance floor.

Now we were trying to decide where to go next. Ascer looked
miserable. 'I don't have much money left – just over 100 francs,' he
said, fingering the envelope that had arrived that morning from his
parents.

'We should probably save that for the taxi,' I said wearily.

As we stood on the kerb, I heard someone calling out to us and
turned to look. There was a tall girl striding purposefully across the
road towards me. 'Ernst Malmsten?' she said, with a grin.
'Remember me?' I was drunk and not a little surprised. 'It's Kajsa,'
she prodded. 'From kindergarten.'

Although I had trouble placing Kajsa at first, things started coming
back when we sat down for a *café au lait* at a bistro around the corner.
Both of us had grown up in Lund, a small town at the southern tip
of Sweden. I was now in my second year at the university there,

studying history and political science. But Kajsa remembered me as
the child tyrant who organized digging events in our kindergarten
sandpit. I was sent home for a few days because all the other children
were so scared of me, and soon afterwards the teachers had the
sandpit filled in. Kajsa was briefly at the same high school, but we had
lost touch over the years, catching only fleeting glimpses of each
other on the street. I vaguely recalled hearing that she was modelling
in New York. It wasn't something she seemed terribly proud of.

'I'm here on a fashion shoot,' she admitted, flushing slightly. As
a teenager Kajsa had been spotted by a talent scout but didn't follow
it up until she was seventeen: she was in Paris with a friend on the
last leg of a backpacking tour around Europe and they were getting
pretty low on funds. Elite found her work straight away and she
continued to work in the fashion industry for another three years.
Although she had never planned it like this, the attractions of being
a model were obvious – it was an opportunity to get away from
Lund, see the world and make a lot of money in the short term.
After a year in Paris she spent another year in Madrid, where she
was able to continue modelling and attend a Swedish school to
complete her high school education. She spent the next two years
working in Milan, Paris and New York (where she now had an
apartment) and, besides making the covers of top magazines like
Elle and *Vogue*, became one of the faces of Benetton's global
advertising campaign.

It taught her a lot about fashion and even more about how to look
after herself. But now, at the ripe age of 21, she was thinking about
what to do next. She had started a course in film and art history at
New York University, and was planning to return to Sweden.

My life had been nowhere near as cosmopolitan, but nor had it
been dull.

At Lund University, whatever there was to organize, I would do it.
I put on literary evenings and I arranged celebrity visits from writers
and politicians. I wrote for a student paper and, through the contacts
I'd made, began to contribute book reviews to one of the largest
morning papers in Sweden, *Arbetet*.

Above all, I loved poetry – I had always been fascinated by the way
it could compress complex thoughts and emotions – and wanted to

do what I could to make it accessible to ordinary people. So I organized a festival of Nordic poetry at the university. I managed to raise a lot of money and sixteen poets attended. The event was a huge success and attracted enormous coverage. I had been motivated by a mixture of idealism and a thirst for attention, but what I loved even more was the thrill of creating something big out of a simple idea.

It was already dawn when we gathered our coats to leave. With a smile, Kajsa said, 'Do you remember when you were stuck up the tree?' I took this for some kind of philosophical joke. 'You were probably only four years old,' she went on, looking thoughtful. 'You were really scared. The teachers wanted you to come down but you wouldn't.' I remembered now. It was Kajsa who had coaxed me down. 'I called you a coward,' she recalled.

As we walked out into the chill early morning air, Kajsa wrote her phone number on a scrap of paper before jumping into a waiting cab. I was almost surprised to find that Ascer was still with me, looking drowsy but impressed. I spent that night curled up on the wooden floor of his cramped bedsit in Montparnasse, already planning my trip to New York.

A year later Kajsa and I were living together in an apartment on East 83rd Street, next to Central Park. A lot had happened since our springtime meeting in Paris. We had started seeing each other, and I had dropped out of university at the end of the academic year to organize an even larger poetry festival in Lund than the last. This time there were forty poets and over 2,000 people attended. I became something of a celebrity. Newspapers wrote profiles of the 'young poetry promoter'. But now I wanted to go one better. I wanted to introduce Nordic poetry to the world. More than that, I wanted to stage the event in New York, the capital city of the world.

Kajsa, who was extremely sceptical at first, agreed to join me in what most people would probably have regarded as a pretty mad venture. But it quickly became obvious that we made a great team. While I possessed unflagging enthusiasm and persistence, Kajsa had a sense of style, which I sorely lacked. I was a lanky six foot five, with thick-rimmed glasses and a student wardrobe. 'You know, you really can't keep wearing these slacks everywhere,' she said over lunch one day, before dragging me around designer stores for the next two hours.

We had support and funding from all the Nordic governments, and were given an office in the Finnish consulate on Madison Avenue. They regarded our festival as just the sort of initiative they had been looking for to promote Scandinavia abroad. We took on a couple of staff and somehow our plans, which had started out quite modest, just grew and grew. Soon, we also had sponsorship from some of Scandinavia's biggest companies – Ericsson, Saab, Ikea, Carlsberg, Absolut Vodka. We were never afraid or too embarrassed to ask for money. In New York we sent out flyers to all the literary associations and put up posters in universities, libraries, theatres. We called up writers, who introduced us to other writers, and soon we found that we had infiltrated New York's literary set. We became the talk of the town, the crazy Swedes that everyone wanted to hang out with. Even *Esquire* wrote a piece on us. 'All this wasn't particularly difficult to pull together,' I was quoted as saying. 'Everyone was so friendly. Americans have so many friends – friends, very good friends, best friends.' The tone of the article was one of amused astonishment that a poetry festival should have taken New York by storm.

A few weeks before the festival took place, we went on a tour of all the Nordic countries to promote the event. We were surprised by the excitement that greeted our arrival. Everyone thought it was a fantastic idea. All the newspapers and TV stations were clamouring for interviews. It's hard for a person from a large country to understand, but there had never been such a high-profile platform for Scandinavian culture. For the first time in years our contemporary literature was being shown off to the world. Our first interview was with *Dagens Nyheter*, the biggest newspaper in Sweden. Kajsa had been used to seeing photos of herself in fashion magazines around the world, but this was a new kind of limelight. It was nerve-racking for both of us.

In those few months Kajsa and I had a crash course in publicity, marketing, fund-raising, diplomacy, logistics – in fact just about everything you need to run an effective business. It was an exhilarating time. There was also the satisfaction of developing a partnership in which each of us seemed to have an instinctive understanding of the other. Together we sparked off ideas that we wouldn't have had alone and gave encouragement to each other when things weren't going so well.

The two-day festival took place on 30 – 31 October 1993 in the historic Cooper Union Hall, East Village, where Abraham Lincoln had made the speech that won him the presidency. Fifty poets had been flown in not just from Sweden, Norway, Denmark and Finland, but from Iceland, Greenland, the Faroe Islands and other remote Arctic places that people outside Scandinavia probably hadn't even heard of. We also had as many of their American counterparts read their work in English. Those who presented English translations included John Ashbery and the Nobel prize-winner Derek Walcott. All in all, we had to arrange flights and accommodation for 300 guests, including dozens of foreign journalists.

We made sure that the poets had a good time. There were drivers to pick them up from the airport, they stayed in the best hotels, and we laid on a VIP room where they could drink as much vodka as they liked. Dealing with their eccentricities gave us a challenging time. My favourite was the Icelander who hated flying. 'I'll sail,' he insisted, on a crackly line from Reykjavik. It took us almost a week to arrange. His trip turned into a Homeric voyage, with stops at the Faroe, Shetland and Orkney islands. From the Scottish mainland, he caught a train down the full length of Britain to Southampton. The *QE2* then took him across the Atlantic to New York, where we found him standing on the docks looking bewildered. A week later, when everything was over, we put him back on the boat again.

About 3,000 people turned up over the two days, each paying $10 a ticket. Most of them were people who would not normally have been listening to poetry in their own language, let alone in Swedish, Finnish or Norwegian. We had a stylishly designed anthology of poems published, copies of which were handed out to the festival visitors. Among the glossy full-page adverts was an August Strindberg poem in the shape of a bottle with the caption 'Absolut Poetry': 'Where ancient hovels stood abreast / And shut out light from every nook, / A crowd of youngsters, full of zest, / Came bearing axes, bars and hook. / Soon chaff and dust / Flew in the air as crowbars thrust / Through floor and stair . . .'

We tried to make a similar impact on the cultural scene. We attempted to show that at the end of the twentieth century poetry still mattered. The event was such a success that the United Nations Society of Writers presented us each with a bronze medal. On one side was the UN building in New York, on the other a globe flanked by two quills with the words: AWARD OF EXCELLENCE: EX MENTE ORBIS (from the spirit of the world). 'You have made a major contribution to the world of the arts and brought people together in the spirit of brotherhood, peace and understanding,' declared the president of the UN Writers Society, Hans Janitschek, at a special ceremony. We were both still only 23.

What to do next? The obvious thing was to start a publishing house, to make use of all the contacts and experience that organizing the festival had brought us. We thought we could bring to books the same enthusiasm and style that had made such a success of the festival. The conservative firms that dominated Swedish publishing tended to stick to safe bets and established names. No wonder people were reading less, we thought. Our idea was to promote literature to a broader audience, while supporting new, young writers. Calling our new company LeanderMalmsten, we set up in Lund in the summer of 1994. As a university town, it was convenient for translators and editors.

Besides the Swedish writers on our list, the foreign authors we published included Esther Freud, Alex Garland, John Ashbery and Walter Mosley. In contrast to the rather staid world of Swedish publishing, we saw ourselves as more like a record label. The book covers of the conventional publishers were dull and grey. We made ours stylish and vibrant. We thought a lot about typography and even about the feel of the paper. We wanted our books to be beautiful – because then, we thought, people in bookstores would be more likely to pick them up. We took the promotion of our books just as seriously. Apart from the occasional book signing, most publishers didn't devote a lot of energy or resources to marketing. We treated our authors like rock stars, arranging readings in night-clubs.

LeanderMalmsten caused a sensation at the Gothenburg Book Fair in 1995. This was a major national event, an opportunity for publishers to showcase upcoming titles. As usual, most of them hired small, off-the-shelf, display stands. We had ours purpose built in the shape of a minimalist living room, with designer armchairs and coffee tables. We held large readings, which were introduced by Alan Jenkins of London's *Times Literary Supplement*, and hired models to serve free drinks provided by our sponsors Pripps Beer. Our guest speakers included the writer Al Alvarez and Elizabeth Wurtzel, the best-selling author of *Prozac Nation* – a book we published in Sweden. The media loved it.

But all this style and glamour, with our hunger for perfection, cost money, and we always seemed to be in financial trouble. I borrowed from my parents, and Kajsa dipped into what she had saved from her modelling career. Behind the scenes it was a seat-of-the-pants operation. Our office was my apartment. Books were stacked to the ceiling and the floor creaked ominously when we walked across it. Neither of us had a driver's licence, so we bought rail passes and travelled back and forth to bookstores across Sweden to market our titles.

Help arrived in the form of Sarah Skansing, a student who was doing a publishing course at Lund University. She had read a lot about us, and asked if she could work with us for the five-week internship required by her course. She stayed on as our first full-time employee. Another intern, Annica Mattsson, who was studying at Stockholm University, joined us the following year and she too stayed. Yet still there was more to do than we could possibly cope with, and normality for us was one continual crisis. When a couple of poetry books flopped, our electricity was cut off. Then bailiffs started turning up at the door. 'Take what you want,' I smiled, almost hoping they'd cart off some of our books. Instead, they put us on payment plans with mind-bending interest rates.

Our very survival depended on delaying what payments we could. In itself, the situation wasn't that extraordinary – how many small businesses aren't strapped for cash at some time or another? But the *Svensk Bokhandel*, the magazine of the Swedish book trade, still ran a campaign against us, deploring the way we could throw money into lavish publicity campaigns, yet fail to pay our printers. As criticism mounted it became a very unpleasant, difficult time, but we learned the invaluable lesson of how to stay calm while living continuously on the verge of bankruptcy.

With all the pressure, our personal relationship began to suffer. Kajsa and I had always argued a lot. It was part of the creative process. But now something larger seemed at stake. We had become more like siblings, so we decided to end our romantic involvement – instead securing a long-term friendship and business partnership that carried us through heated rows and differences of opinion, both of which we continued to have. We both moved on to new relationships.

It was September 1996. The Western world was enjoying probably the longest economic boom in its history. Markets were soaring, inflation was low ... but Kajsa and I were still broke. What we needed were new ideas, new ways to unlock the full potential of our publishing business. This was where the internet came in.

Kajsa and I were exceptional in that neither of us had ever actually used the internet, but, living in Sweden, we could hardly help knowing about it. As citizens of a small country, we were made constantly aware of the need to be adaptable and to make the most of new technologies. The government has always encouraged a sort of national paranoia about falling behind. Its message, through subtle advertising and teaching in schools, is simple but persuasive: 'Technology is important. If you don't know about it, you'll be a second-class citizen.' In 1996, there were more people in Sweden with access to the internet than in France, a country seven times its size. To my eyes, it was an almost miraculous way of reaching a mass market at minimum expense. It was also clear that, in Europe at least, the concept hadn't been properly explored.

A catalyst for our thinking was an offer from Mikael Karlsson, the founder of a software company called Axis Communications, to buy a stake in LeanderMalmsten. But our ideas needed more money than he alone was able to invest, so he introduced us to a possible partner, an extremely clever Swedish aristocrat named Dag Tigerschiöld who ran a venture capital firm – although this was not a term that

Tigerschiöld liked to use. 'I'm an industrialist,' he explained. 'I help build companies.'

In his lavish office overlooking Stockholm's Royal Opera House, we talked about how the internet might be used to release the full potential of LeanderMalmsten. One idea Kajsa and I had often discussed was starting an internet bookstore to sell books to students. Our initial target market would be Sweden's 350,000 students who, we felt, were paying exorbitant prices for imported English-language textbooks. If we could hook them with low prices and free delivery, we figured they'd soon spread the word to their friends and family. Tigerschiöld wasn't at all technical but he could envisage the huge importance that e-commerce would have. He liked the idea and suggested that we write a business plan. In the meantime, he and Karlsson invested 25 per cent each in LeanderMalmsten.

Passionate and creative, Tigerschiöld would give us an invaluable early training in business and finance. 'Whenever I'm entertaining candidates for CEOs,' he told us at one of our early meetings, 'I always see how much time they take over the menu. If they have difficulty choosing their courses, then they're likely to be just as poor decision-makers in business.' With his razor-sharp intellect and hard-working enthusiasm, Tigerschiöld was many of the things I aspired to be. He wasn't content just to find the finance, but often came up with inventive ideas and gave the impression that he would have liked to have been an entrepreneur himself. He was sociable and enjoyed dining out, although with his professorial and somewhat distracted manner he could occasionally seem rather eccentric. Like me, he hated to lose. Shortly after our first meeting we played each other at chess. He lost and got very upset. Kajsa was afraid he would change his mind about investing.

The highlight of our newly financed publishing programme was a book written by stage director Lars Rudolfsson in collaboration with Björn Ulvaeus and Benny Andersson, the male half of ABBA. The previous year Ulvaeus and Andersson had produced *Kristina from Duvemåla*, an enormously successful musical about nineteenth-century Swedish emigrants to America. It was a sellout across Sweden. Now they wanted us to publish the book of the musical. Impressed by the efforts we put into design, they thought we would best be able to produce for the book they had in mind.

Our lavish volume, with lots of pictures printed on expensive paper, appeared in November 1996. As just about everything else the pair did turned to gold, we were convinced that we had an enormous success on our hands. But the book turned out to be far too expensive for most people and came nowhere near to selling the 10,000 copies we needed to break even. Of the 2 million kronor our new investors had put into the company, a million was instantly spent on covering the losses of that one book, and another half a million on clearing our backlog of debt.

It was a disappointing start, and it hardly seemed the time to ask for more money to develop our idea for an online bookstore, but Dag Tigerschiöld suggested that we should set it up as a separate company and he would then help us find investors on this basis. Eventually we managed to raise around $700,000 – more money than either of us had ever seen or ever expected to see. It was becoming increasingly obvious that we were on to something big.

We called our new company bokus, which wasn't a real word in Swedish but sounded similar enough to the word meaning 'book' to suggest the association. As we were putting together our plans, Kajsa and her boyfriend Joel Berg (the art director at *Harper's Bazaar* in New York) announced that Kajsa was pregnant. I was really pleased for them, but what I wanted to know was how this sudden turn of events would affect our plans for bokus. 'Are you sure you still want to do this?' I asked. 'Of course,' she said, looking vaguely irritated. 'I'm not dying.'

bokus wasn't an original idea. Amazon.com had already been selling books online for three years before we came along. In April 1997 Kajsa and I decided to pay them a visit in the hope of picking up some useful tips. Our trip, arranged through a friend of a friend who knew Amazon's founder and CEO Jeff Bezos, didn't start off too well. Amazon had just moved and we turned up at the wrong office, in one of Seattle's industrial zones. When we found their new office, in the city centre, it looked more like an old apartment building than the headquarters of a pioneering new economy business.

It was our first exposure to the start-up culture. The staff, working on desks that had once been doors, looked more like roadies for one of the local grunge bands than leaders of the future. We had been hoping to meet Bezos himself, but he was out of town for the day. So instead we sat down in a small room with David Risher, Amazon's head of product development. Risher gave us a quick rundown on the Amazon story, pulling out a thick folder with recent press clippings. He agreed to give us a tour of the office and one of the company's warehouses. But this was a sensitive time for Amazon. It was one month away from its initial public offering (IPO) of shares on America's Nasdaq market for technology stocks, and couldn't say too much.

The person assigned to show us around looked and acted a bit like a CIA agent. In fact, he probably was.

'I used to work for the State Department in Kiev,' he told us. He looked suspicious at even the most innocuous questions.

'What kind of servers are you using?' I asked one guy in the tech department.

'Don't answer that,' the CIA agent barked.

In the end, we learned a bit of everything but not too much about anything.

Back in Sweden a welcome break for us that summer was an event which Annica and Sarah had organized to promote LeanderMalmsten's authors. We hired a huge tent in the market of a small town called Kivik and put down sawdust on the ground like at a circus. We invited a famous soap opera star, an ex-Miss Sweden, to introduce the six writers who were giving readings, while my old friend from Paris, Ascer, turned up with his jazz band. Outside loudspeakers pulled in the crowds: 'Roll up, roll up, buy tickets now. Come and hear Miss Sweden introduce LeanderMalmsten's great new authors . . .'

But bokus inevitably commanded more and more of our time. 'You're going to need a camp-bed in your office,' Tigerschiöld had warned. And he was right.

Unlike America, where most books could be sourced from two major wholesalers, Europe was a fragmented mess. This was one of the reasons why Amazon hadn't come over yet. Kajsa and I spent weeks negotiating deals with dozens of different British publishers. There was a lot else to be done besides. While I talked to Swedish Post about logistics, Kajsa planned our marketing strategy and worked with Me Company, a British design company in Camden, on developing our corporate image. The job of building our website was given to a small start-up in Lund called Netch Technologies. Half owned by Mikael Karlsson's company Axis Communications, it had recently set up an e-commerce site for a department store in Stockholm. Kajsa had to worry not just about bokus, but the imminent birth of her first child. Everyone was impressed by how hard she worked even when she was heavily pregnant. As our launch date approached, we had to implore her to take it easy.

For our staff, we recruited a workforce of about thirty students. They were part-timers, but had the advantage of being highly skilled and belonging to our target group. At Tigerschiöld's suggestion we also recruited a managing director, who had worked for a Swedish wholesaler. As it was before internet fever had erupted in Europe, we were able to hire him without offering the share incentive schemes that just a few months later would become a standard feature of executives' contracts. He could have a bonus, Dag Tigerschiöld suggested, once the company had made a profit.

We told only a handful of people about bokus. Even our closest friends were kept in the dark. A couple of days before the launch I invited Ascer to come up and see our new office, in a loft above a freemason's hall in Lund's old town.

'What do you think?' I asked, leading him into a room where the students were tapping away at their computers.

His jaw dropped. 'These people work for *you*?'

On 18 August 1997 at 12.23 p.m. – just 23 minutes behind schedule – bokus finally launched. Four days later, Kajsa gave birth to a baby girl. To make the hat-trick and round off an already remarkable week, *Elle* magazine named Kajsa Sweden's best-dressed woman. A little later we won a prize for Sweden's best website.

bokus was offering 1.5 million titles, with average discounts of 25 per cent. By Christmas 1997, just four months after launching, we had

60,000 customers and daily revenues of \$20,000 – \$40,000. I felt a surge of satisfaction at what we had managed to create after all the months of hard work. But there was still a lot to do and I was impatient to get on with it.

The website was simple and would need to be upgraded. It also seemed obvious – to Kajsa and me at least – that bokus would have to expand into other parts of Europe if it was going to succeed in the long term. Sweden wasn't a huge market. If we didn't move quickly, someone else would get there first. In fact, it was already starting to happen. Amazon had just snapped up a small UK business and Germany's Bertelsmann was making loud noises about its internet ambitions. bokus would need a lot more money. As with Amazon, the best solution was probably an IPO.

Kajsa and I talked about it for a couple of weeks before deciding to raise the issue at a board meeting. The events that followed would teach us a lot about business and shape our attitude towards investors. The problem was, our grey-haired venture capitalist (VC) shareholders couldn't seem to get their heads around the prevailing internet logic of 'grow now, make profits later'. When I told them what we were thinking, their reaction was a mix of surprise and amusement.

'You can't take a company public before it's profitable,' one of them declared.

'What about Amazon?' Kajsa asked.

'Amazon!' he scoffed. 'That company is never going to make any money.'

Tigerschiöld took the investors' side. The key thing, he said, was to break even as quickly as we could. Then we could start thinking about expansion.

As we struggled to convince our shareholders, we began to turn elsewhere for advice. My assistant Peder Wickström had a brother who worked for a small Swedish investment bank, Chevereux de Virieu Nordic, owned by Crédit Agricole. One day, just a couple of months after the launch, Fred Wickström turned up with his colleague Patrik Hedelin, the bank's director of corporate finance. Striding into our office in a heavy cashmere coat, pinstriped suit and galoshes, Patrik, with his self-assured manner, made an impression

beyond his 29 years. They would like to help us with the IPO whenever we were ready, he explained. They had already worked with
another Swedish start-up, an online recruitment agency named
Plenja.

But it pretty quickly became clear that we would not get the
support of our board for such a step, and in the meantime we had to
deal with a more urgent problem. bokus was running out of cash and
needed a top-up. Tigerschiöld had already agreed to put in a chunk
of money. But there was a catch, which we didn't really become
aware of until it was too late. His investment would be at the same
valuation as when he had first invested almost a year earlier. We were
being exploited. bokus was a real company now, with real sales. If we
let him do this, our own shareholdings would be diluted. But there
was no time to argue, so reluctantly we accepted his offer.

We became so fed up with the difficulties we had in running our
own company and the never-ending conflicts with our shareholders
that we decided to sell our stake, asking Fred and Patrik to help us in
our dealings with potential buyers. Eventually we decided to negotiate with KF, the giant Swedish co-operative that owned industrial
manufacturers, supermarkets, publishing companies and, not least, a
chain of bookstores. Their media division had particular reason to be
interested, because bokus had cut into their market share. They knew
what a threat we were likely to become. And as they had just hired
someone to handle their internet strategy they saw bokus as an
obvious gateway into the online world.

As our talks entered their final, legally baffling stages, we became
hugely appreciative of Patrik Hedelin's hard-headed presence. He
possessed a tireless and assertive style that seemed capable of sur-
mounting any obstacle. In love with his mobile phone, which
seemed almost glued to his ear, one of his tactics was to call people
over and over again until they agreed to meet us. He simply wore
them down.

'If we sell you our shares, the other investors will probably do the
same,' I assured KF. At last they went for it and I called Tigerschiöld
to break the news. 'We have an offer on the table that we've decided
to accept,' I said. It was like winning another chess match.

He was astonished. It was a major coup for a start-up that had been in business for less than a year to be bought by one of Sweden's biggest concerns – and we were still just a couple of kids, after all. Like the other investors he was also very pleased and, as we expected, no one had any difficulty in accepting the extremely favourable terms.

The arrangement was that KF would buy half the company with an option to buy the remainder at some time in the future. Kajsa and I had to sign a golden handcuffs agreement preventing us from working for any competitors. We stayed on as consultants, helping to develop the business in other Nordic countries, and I continued to have a seat on the board. As a large co-operative, KF had very different values from its new partners, and this changeover period was a fascinating time, which taught me a lot about how large corporations work.

Even after the dilution of our shares, Kajsa and I had been transformed into overnight millionaires. This fact didn't really sink in until a few days later, when I used my card at a local cashpoint. I had never seen so many zeros.

It was March 1998. Kajsa and I had money and a track record as internet entrepreneurs – something almost nobody in Europe could claim at the time. Now we were ready for something really ambitious.

2

BUILD IT AND THEY WILL come. If there was a catchphrase that summed up the American attitude to the internet in 1998, this was probably it. It was the year of e-tailing, when everyone you spoke to was either talking about opening an online store or knew someone who was. There were now more than 400,000 commercial websites in the US, up from just 2,000 in 1995. Amazon.com, whose philosophy of discounting and first-rate customer service was seen as a blueprint for the industry, had now been joined by a host of other prominent names, from eToys to eBay. Below them, a virtual galaxy of smaller companies were peddling everything from toasters to diamond tiaras.

It was still a very different story in Europe, for a variety of reasons. To start with, fewer people were connected to the internet. In some countries, like Spain and Italy, only around 2 per cent of households had internet access, and those that did often had to pay hefty bills from the local phone companies. In Germany, for example, twenty hours of online use cost around $75, more than double what US users were paying. But these were temporary obstacles. Things would change, I suspected, very quickly. Europe's borders were fast melting away. More people were travelling, working and studying abroad than ever before. In less than two years the region would even have a single currency – the euro. All these developments would encourage rapid internet growth.

The question on my mind, in the weeks after selling bokus, was how Kajsa and I could best position ourselves for the coming boom. One of the things that struck me was how few companies could claim a truly pan-European presence. One reason for this was the spider's web of different legal, tax and regulatory systems throughout the region. Then there were all the cultural and language issues.

Kajsa and I had no special skills to cope with the first problem. But, as Swedes, I felt that we were well equipped to understand Europe's cultural nuances, having had long practice of adapting to the ways of larger countries. I realized, for example, that launching one English-language website for all of Europe, as some American companies had done, wouldn't get us very far. People in Sweden or Holland might speak English, but they'd still rather shop on a website that was in their own language and gave them alternatives when it came to paying for goods. In America the credit card was king, but a lot of Europeans were uncomfortable with credit cards, especially on the internet. It was one reason why e-commerce had been slow to take off on this side of the Atlantic. The great strength of our site would be its responsiveness to the varying needs and likes of European consumers. Here was a real challenge, I thought. It would be difficult, no doubt, but I felt confident that we could pull it off.

In early March 1998 Kajsa and I moved LeanderMalmsten to Stockholm. With the money we had received from KF we had had the satisfying experience of being able to regain control of our publishing company from the other investors and establishing it on a more secure financial footing.

The office we chose was small but central and just a short walk from one of Stockholm's biggest parks, Humlegården. Most afternoons I'd go for brisk walks along the icy path through the park to clear my head and try to flesh out my ideas.

Quickly I realized that if we were going to build a company that would dominate Europe, then we would have to establish a presence in the US too. The global nature of the internet meant that the only way to protect your lead in one market was to take on markets everywhere. This wasn't something that I had dreamed up myself. Analysts and other industry commentators believed that the e-commerce winners would be those companies able to capture new markets with the greatest speed. It was, as some liked to call it, Survival of the Fastest.

To make sure we stood out among the multitude of other e-commerce start-ups, we'd also have to create a strong brand. It would be a European brand. One that somehow captured the culture and style of the region rather than copying the efficiency-obsessed American offerings.

This notion of a European brand with global appeal was an idea with which Kajsa felt particularly comfortable: it had been a striking aspect of the fashion world that she already knew so well. She was fascinated by the way in which a single fashion brand worked in a lot of different markets. The nature of contemporary culture was such that, say, a Lacoste T-shirt or a pair of Adidas trainers had the same appeal to people whether they lived in Rome, Rio, Tokyo or New York. Indeed, as a commodity with which to exploit the global reach of the internet, fashion items, free as they were of language barriers, actually made far more sense than books.

Kajsa had often discussed the possibilities of a fashion website with both me and Joel. But there had been too many other things to think about for her to explore the idea much further. She not only had a baby daughter to take care of, but also, after our recent move to Stockholm, a new office to organize. On top of this there was our agreement to act as consultants to the new owners of bokus, which involved helping to expand the business into Finland and the other Nordic countries. So now was not the best time to press her on a new business venture, but I knew that if we were going to start another internet company we'd have to move fast.

Saturnus was a small but lively café, a short walk from our office. Its small wooden tables were pushed together so tightly that it required gymnastic agility for Kajsa and me to get in and out of our chairs.

This was our favourite venue for discussing private matters. It was so noisy that nobody could overhear us, even if they wanted to. Kajsa had to lean forward just to catch what I was saying. 'We really have to do it soon,' I repeated.

'Sure. But why do we have to do it right now? I feel like I need some time out with my family.'

It was true. After a long Swedish winter, we could both do with a break. It had been almost two years since my last holiday, a weekend in Spain. But my mind was running wild with ideas now and I was impatient to get started.

'We didn't sell bokus to take it easy,' I said, a little too abruptly.

'I know,' replied Kajsa, 'but we're doing so much as it is. We need a rest.'

'Look,' I continued in a more conciliatory tone, 'I'm really worried about this. It's an amazing opportunity, but if we wait, other people are going to work it out.' I was starting to wave my arms around. 'In a few months, there'll be internet companies all over the place.'

'I suppose you're right,' Kajsa sighed.

After ordering a second coffee and one of the café's giant homemade pastries, we began to discuss the possibilities.

'Whatever we do,' I stressed, 'it's got to be something nobody is doing yet.'

It was the key to success. If we were really to achieve the global impact we hoped for, then we had to exploit 'first mover' advantage. If you're first, then you achieve vital recognition as you become identified with whatever you're selling. You get a lot of free publicity and customer confidence because you're the leader. It's then very difficult for the second wave to compete. Amazon.com was a shining example of that. Here was a company that spent almost nothing on marketing before its IPO, but still managed to create one of the best-known brands in the world.

Whatever else we thought about, we always seemed to find ourselves returning to the fashion idea. People spent far more money on clothes than they did on books or CDs, and the margins were a lot better too. Fashion brands had the added attraction of being immune to the price wars that affected other retail sectors, since most suppliers of high-end clothing wouldn't allow their products to be discounted. It made them less exclusive and damaged their brand.

A crucial question was how to convince people to buy clothes they couldn't try on. The answer wasn't clear, but we had a few ideas. Both of us had read a newspaper article about experiments using 3D photography to create the online sensation of being in a real shop. The idea was to make it possible for you to spin products around and to zoom in on them. Another new technique, called body scanning, could create a computer-generated replica of the customer's body, which might then 'try on' clothes for itself. These developments represented an incredible advance on the largely text-based e-commerce sites that then dominated the Net.

Our early research served only to sharpen our resolve. 'Take a look through this,' Kajsa said the following afternoon, tossing over a copy of American *Vogue*. 'Now try to find something that's actually for sale here in Stockholm.'

It was an interesting point. The global nature of the media meant it was now possible to read about all the latest fashions, no matter where you lived. In some Russian towns, you could find a copy of *Vogue* more easily than a loaf of bread. But the fashion industry had failed to keep pace. To buy many of these clothes usually involved travelling to a major city. I'd seen the effects of this at first hand while on overseas trips with Kajsa. On the way out, she'd walk with a light step, one suitcase trailing smoothly behind her. On her return, she would be weighed down with several designer carrier bags of hard-to-find clothes for herself and her friends. By drawing together these niche brands, our site would do the travelling for you. The point was not to sell clothes which were necessarily that expensive; on the contrary, we hoped to democratize the world of fashion by putting people in touch with the latest trends no matter where they happened to live.

Some internet surfing in the next few days revealed the potential competition. At first, I was worried. There seemed to be dozens of fashion-related websites. But a closer look showed that most were just information providers, like Fashion.Net, which published schedules and photos of New York designer runway shows, or @fashion, a sort of industry gossip site. A second group was made up of catalogue companies like L.L. Bean and high-street retailers such as Gap and Esprit that had simply moved their products online.

What we planned to do was very different. We would create the first fully branded shopping experience on the Net. There wasn't really any direct equivalent in the old world of retailing, but what we had in mind was a virtual hybrid of a department store like Harvey Nichols in London or Bloomingdales in New York, where the name of the store itself was as significant as anything you could buy in it. This was still a pretty new idea. Most of the early American internet companies had sprung from the minds of technologists. All they cared about was functionality and cost.

By now it was obvious that our idea had potential, but a few practical issues still had to be ironed out. If it was to be a global company, then we would have to go to a city like London or New York, where we would be able to attract top international talent. In Stockholm, we'd always be just another Swedish internet company. There was also the problem that in Sweden we had become too well known. In a more international environment it would be easier to be anonymous and to take steps without comments in the press. New York had obvious attractions. It was a major financial centre and we both felt comfortable there, but finally we agreed that London made more sense. We were Europeans. Therefore we had to be based in Europe.

The more difficult question was money. How much would a company like this cost to build? $10 million? $20 million? We had no idea, but we knew it would dwarf anything we'd done so far. This was a worrying thought. We lacked financial expertise, as our experiences with LeanderMalmsten and bokus had shown. 'Maybe we should bring someone in,' I suggested. 'Someone that can talk to investors and handle the finances. A bean counter.'

'You mean someone like Patrik?' Kajsa asked.

I nodded. Patrik Hedelin, the investment banker who had helped so much during the bokus sale, was an obvious choice. He knew the direction our thoughts were taking, and indeed had already expressed his interest in joining us in such a venture.

Kajsa seemed a little uncertain. 'Do you really want to be partners with a banker?'

'We don't all have to be the same,' I replied. 'In fact it's probably better if we aren't. Let's at least give him a call.'

Patrik showed immediate interest when I called him at his office. He didn't want to talk over the phone in case the call was being tape-recorded – a common practice in investment banks – but agreed to meet us the following afternoon to go over things in more detail. In the meantime, having offered to bring him into the new company, we had to decide whether he should have as many shares as us. Kajsa, who had been a bit dubious about bringing him in at all, found the prospect hard to take.

'We're the ones with the idea,' she argued. 'We have the track record. What does he bring?'

I saw her point, but was worried about starting a partnership on the wrong footing. 'He'll resent it later on,' I said. It also seemed unlikely that he would quit his job unless there was something substantial in it for him. Investment bankers aren't known for their altruism and Patrik, despite a certain appetite for risk-taking, was a pretty typical example of the species. In the end, we agreed an equal partnership was the only solution.

'I guess this way, he'll do everything to protect his own investment,' Kajsa observed, 'which will be good for us as well.'

We met Patrik in a small square near my apartment. It was a brooding, icy afternoon and the three of us huddled together with our coats tightly buttoned. Patrik was excited, but kept looking furtively over his shoulder as if worried about being seen with us. It was only when Kajsa began talking him through the plan that we got his full attention.

'It's still just an idea,' she cautioned, 'but we'd like you to help us.'

'We want to offer you a third share of anything we do,' I said, adding quickly for form's sake, 'if you're still interested.'

Patrik tried hard to look serious, but couldn't stop a smile creeping across his face. 'I'm definitely interested,' he said.

It was liberating to have someone else at last to share the huge load of what we were planning. Patrik could deal with banks and lawyers and worry about our finances while the two of us focused on strategic issues. I wondered briefly whether perhaps we shouldn't also involve Fred Wickström, the other banker who had worked with us on the bokus sale, but, as Patrik was quick to point out, we only really needed one finance guy.

Patrik was already running things through in his head. 'We're going to need an investment bank,' he said. 'Probably one of the big ones.' This was the validation he'd need before officially quitting his job, he told us. It made sense, anyway. A bank would help us find investors.

'Have you thought about your exit strategy?' Patrik continued.

We were a little thrown by this question.

'We've only just come up with the idea,' Kajsa said.

'Sure,' he replied. 'But you'll want to do an IPO at some point, right?' He seemed surprised that we hadn't already thought this through.

'I guess so,' I replied.

He nodded, apparently satisfied.

The next few weeks were spent in heavy research. Patrik, who slipped away from the bank to help us whenever he could, had a desk in our office. We began to haunt the shopping malls, noting down what people were buying and also what they were wearing. It became an obsessive habit which we indulged even on the subway. 'Look at that guy's shoes. Probably worth $200. He's the sort of person who would visit our site. Young, well off and fashion-conscious . . .'

One guy in particular caught my attention. He looked a bit like a tourist, with a checked Gap shirt that stretched tight over the flabby mass of his stomach. I doubted if he could see his own feet. But I could. He was wearing Reebok basketball boots. This wasn't so unusual in itself. But it made us think about the market for sports clothes. Who really bought this stuff? Athletes? Or average people trying to make a fashion statement? We spoke to some shopkeepers. Their response was emphatically the latter. So why were these clothes sold only in specialized sports stores? It seemed a glaring oversight. Our website, we decided, would sell sports and fashion brands alongside each other. Sports clothes for people who don't sweat, as someone later described it. Sportswear also made sense because the sizes were more standardized than with designer clothes, where the fit mattered more.

The next step was to get price lists from suppliers and to figure out the margins. Patrik did the telephoning because Kajsa and I were too well known, and, even more than with bokus, secrecy was crucial. The early responses were a bit of a shock. 'I'm thinking of setting up an internet store,' Patrik would say as he asked for a price list. Most of the suppliers curtly explained that they didn't deal with internet companies and hung up.

So we tried another tack. 'I'm about to open a sports store,' Patrik said. 'Can you send me a price list?' This time a few suppliers did, but as many asked to see details of his finances and even a sketch of the store. It was clear that in the months ahead getting suppliers was going to be a real challenge. It wasn't like books, where publishers were only too happy to sell to anyone who came along.

In some ways, though, the suppliers' attitude was encouraging. If it was hard for us to make them like the internet, it would be hard for everyone – and we would have a huge advantage when we were the first to persuade them to change their minds.

It was Easter 1998 and I decided we should use the time off to make a quick trip to New York. 'We've got to start thinking globally,' I said. From past experience, I also knew the importance of just going out and meeting people – building up a base of contacts. This was something that Kajsa and I had a talent for. Put us down in any strange town and we quickly managed to meet the people we needed to see. It was a pretty spontaneous process. Just days before we set off, for example, we read a piece in the *Wall Street Journal* about a company that was designing software to make shopping over the internet work more like it does in the real world, with communication in real time between real people. You would be able to order things on a site, but also, if you wanted, summon the immediate assistance of a customer service team. This was a major preoccupation of ours, so we rang the company and also the journalist who wrote the piece, in case she knew of other software companies we ought to be talking to. She was one of several people who agreed to meet us.

New York was the perfect place to spark off important ideas and had just the sort of expertise we needed – in international finance as much as internet technology. But at the same time, the trip was a bonding exercise. Kajsa and I had seen quite a bit of Patrik in the last few weeks, but it's when you travel with people for a few days that you really get to know them. Although we got along with Patrik, it was obvious that we didn't have a lot in common with him. Patrik was a capitalist to the core. His first experience of trading shares, he told us, had been when he was just 12 years old. In the years when Kajsa and I were organizing the poetry festival and building a publishing business, Patrik had been putting himself through a gruelling study regime, starting an MBA at the Stockholm School of Economics while he was still halfway through a master's in law at the University of Stockholm. And now he was married with a middle-class house in the suburbs, a young child and another on the way. It seemed to me that he had never really had a chance just to enjoy life, and I hoped that the trip would be an opportunity to get him to loosen up a little.

'Here. Try this,' I said, pouring him a vodka and tonic after we'd been in the air for about half an hour.

Patrik crossed his arms defensively. 'I don't really feel like it,' he said.

I unfastened his tray table and plonked the drink in front of him. 'You need to start adapting to your new lifestyle,' I replied.

Patrik had wanted to stay safely midtown at the Waldorf Astoria, a haven for politicians and middle-aged heiresses. We convinced him to join us at the SoHo Grand, with its young media and entertainment crowd. The first new hotel to be built in downtown SoHo in over a century, it was close to some of the city's coolest night-spots and, we reassured Patrik, not such a long walk from the banks on Wall Street. A steel staircase embedded with bottle glass led upstairs to a magnificent lobby with tall, square columns supporting a high ceiling. In the Grand Bar close by you could sit back in a comfortable lounge sofa with a cocktail and help yourself to 'day & nite bites' until three in the morning.

I felt the usual thrill from being back in New York. It was something in the air – an invisible energy. Mildly time-confused that first evening, we visited some SoHo bars, then polished off a bottle of wine at Indochine, an Asian restaurant on Lafayette Street. It was all too much for Patrik. By the time the meal arrived, his eyes were already glazing over.

'He'll get used to it,' I said, just hoping he would wake up in time for our first meeting the next morning.

*

'You want to raise *how* much?' The stocky financier at the end of the table almost sprang out of his chair.

'About $2 million,' Patrik repeated, looking uneasy. It was the first time we'd discussed money with an outsider and I now wondered if maybe we should have started lower.

'Listen,' the man said, in the kind of tone usually reserved for small children, 'I could throw a stone out the window right now and hit someone who would give you $2 million.' He paused to let this fact sink in. 'If you want people to take you seriously you can't go looking for unserious money.'

Dressed in jeans and an open collar shirt, Jeffrey Leeds didn't look like a typical financier, but he ran his own investment company from a fifteenth-floor office on Madison Avenue. He was a friend of James Linville, who had written the original *Esquire* article about us and the poetry festival back in 1993. 'You have to meet this guy,' James had insisted. 'He's street smart and knows a lot of people.'

Leeds's credentials were impressive. He'd graduated from Harvard with the best law degree in his year, worked as a clerk to US Supreme Court judge William J. Brennan, and spent seven years as an investment banker at Lazard Freres. He now had tendrils that wound through New York's social and financial scenes. Among the names in his Rolodex were people like Henry Kravis, architect of the daring $25 billion takeover of R.J.R. Nabisco in 1989; John Fisher, whose family owned the hugely successful Gap clothing chain; and Ian Schrager, co-founder of the legendary Studio 54 nightclub and now owner of the Paramount and Mondrian hotels.

Leeds, after recovering his composure a little, leaned across the large oval table in his office and tried to explain himself a bit better. 'I'm not an internet expert,' he admitted, 'but, come on, look around you. Read the newspapers. The market loves the internet right now.'

Venture capitalists were clamouring to invest in dot.com start-ups. Just a couple of days earlier, on 9 April, internet search engine Yahoo had delivered a first-quarter profit of $4.3 million. It was a measly sum compared to its $5.2 billion valuation, but its shares had actually jumped more than 16 per cent on the news. Recent internet IPOs were also racing ahead. Shares in Doubleclick.Inc, an online advertising company, had almost doubled in their first week of trading. The

Nasdaq index, on which most internet stocks were listed, was on the verge of a record high.

'What's great about you guys is that you're different,' Leeds observed. 'You're the first serious thing to come out of Europe.' By aiming high, we'd get noticed by all the right investors. People who wouldn't waste their time on small projects. People like Bob White, a managing director at Bain Capital, the giant US private equity fund based in Boston. 'This guy probably makes $100 million a year,' Leeds told us. Even better, he loved the internet. Bain was one of three investors that had, a few months earlier, put $40 million into Doubleclick.Inc. That investment was now worth closer to $80 million. 'I'll give him a call and put in a good word,' Leeds said. He also suggested we talk to more strategic investors, like John Fisher at Gap. These were people who knew something about building brands.

The meeting lasted only an hour, but when it was over I felt that we had taken a huge step forward. Leeds had grasped at once what we were trying to do and knew exactly the people we needed to talk to. As we waited for the elevator, he tossed out one last piece of advice. 'Just remember,' he said, with what would later seem like uncanny foresight: 'No matter what happens, the investor is always your enemy.'

We had a couple of hours to kill before our next meeting, with an analyst from investment bank Goldman Sachs. So the three of us decided to continue the street research we had begun in Stockholm. We started by browsing in some of the flashy designer stores on Madison Avenue – Prada, Calvin Klein and Polo Ralph Lauren – before visiting upmarket department stores such as Barneys and Bloomingdales. We checked prices, but also questioned senior staff about logistics. How did these stores get their stock delivered? Did they have warehouses nearby? What was it like dealing with suppliers?

We also looked around sportswear outlets. In the vast Paragon store, two blocks north of Union Square, you could get anything from golf balls to kayaks. Patrik told the staff we liked the place so much that we were thinking of opening up a similar store in Sweden, and could we talk to the manager? But he couldn't be found and so we contented ourselves with jotting down prices and the names of cool brands that weren't available in Europe at the time.

But it was one thing to look through stores and another to understand how the industry actually worked. This was where David Bolotsky came in. He was a retailing analyst at Goldman Sachs, whose name Patrik had got from a friend who worked for Goldman in London. Bolotsky had agreed to meet us in the SoHo Grand bar so we could run our idea past him. I'd expected some kind of driven Wall Street type, and was surprised by the tall, casually dressed figure that joined us at the table.

Bolotsky flicked through a small packet of press clippings that we handed him. Inside was a selection of articles about the poetry festival, LeanderMalmsten and bokus.

'Oh yeah,' he said. 'I had a look at the bokus website after you called.'

'Do you speak Swedish?' I asked.

He laughed. 'No. I didn't understand a word. But it looked pretty good.'

After getting Bolotsky to sign a confidentiality agreement, we ran him through our plan. Bolotsky sat quietly, nodding occasionally and sipping a Coke.

'It's all very interesting,' he said, when we had finished, 'and you've obviously put a lot of thought into it, but what worries me is the suppliers. They're never going to go along with something like this.'

'Why not?' I asked.

After Patrik's experience of contacting suppliers in Stockholm this wasn't exactly a surprise, but Bolotsky was the first person able to explain to us exactly what we were up against. Leaning across the table, he said, 'Well, let's say you run a profitable fashion business and you've got thousands of little retailers around the country, or even the world, that sell your products. Why would you be in a hurry to change the rules? These companies aren't visionaries. They're closing their eyes and hoping the internet will go away.' There were a few reasons for this. So far, most internet companies had based their strategies on being cheaper than physical stores. 'That pisses off the retailers,' he said. It was also damaging to brands. No high-end fashion label wanted to see its products sitting in a discount bin.

'What if we don't discount?' I asked.

'How are you going to get the customers, then?'

'We'll give them free delivery,' I replied. 'And it'll be a cool site.'

Bolotsky tilted his head sceptically. It would be hard enough to sell clothes on a national basis. But globally? 'Retailing is a local business,' he said. Clothing suppliers sold their products at different prices in different countries, depending on how competitive each market was. It was called *zone pricing* and was a source of easy profits. Bolotsky's point was this: if we were going to sell globally we'd probably have to create separate websites, with separate prices, for every country we sold into. Without this sort of protection, suppliers wouldn't let us through the door. So be it, I thought. If that's what was needed, that's what we'd do. I wasn't exactly sure how, but we'd worry about that later on.

On the even bigger question of whether people would actually buy clothes online, Bolotsky was a little more upbeat. The top selling category for catalogue retailers was clothing, he pointed out. The often-repeated argument that people liked to be able try things on before buying them was specious. Mail order clothing catalogues were a multi-billion dollar business. There was also evidence to show that price wasn't the only issue for consumers. Books.com was a case in point. It often sold books more cheaply than Amazon.com but had only a fraction of their revenues. Why? Because Amazon was easier to use and reliable. 'What you're talking about is possible,' Bolotsky told us. 'It just won't be easy.'

Our final scheduled meeting was with Tom Kennedy, a partner at law firm Skadden Arps, Slate, Meagher and Flom. Patrik had set it up through a lawyer Fredrik von Baumgarten, who worked for Vinge, a leading law firm in Sweden. As we waited in the bar for Kennedy to show up, Patrik could barely contain his excitement. It was a coup to get this meeting and he wasn't shy about letting us know it. Skadden was one of New York's oldest and most formidable law firms. It had been a central player in the 1980s mergers and acquisitions boom, representing one side or the other in virtually every major hostile takeover. It was about the most prestigious law firm you could hope to have. We were going to need expert advice on our company structure as well as tax issues in the US, but Patrik pointed out that such a blue-chip organization would also give us huge credibility with the banks and suppliers. 'It'll make people take us seriously.'

Kennedy headed up the firm's technology business in between advising companies on multibillion-dollar takeovers. When United Airlines sold 55 per cent of its stock to employees in 1994, it was Kennedy who was brought in to help structure the deal. Indeed, everything about him seemed to suggest a heavyweight. As he strode into the SoHo Grand bar, it was impossible not to be impressed by his sheer physical presence. 'At Skadden Arps, we come in all shapes and sizes,' he said, as if he could read my thoughts.

He seemed to enjoy mixing with entrepreneurs and regaled us with some of his favourite corporate stories. Like his encounter with Robert Maxwell, the late billionaire media tycoon and pension-fund fraudster. 'I was flown to London on Concorde,' he said. 'Then a helicopter picked me up and dropped me on the roof of his building. The first thing he asked me was "Do you want Dom Pérignon or Krug?"' Patrik, who loved dealing with lawyers, was mesmerized.

When we finally got down to business, Kennedy seemed surprised by our plans for a fast, global rollout. 'Over here, the process goes like this,' he said, drawing on a table napkin. To start with, a company's founders would get their business plan into shape. Then they'd go looking for 'angels'. He noticed our confusion. 'Friends and family,' he said. The angel money was often used to get the company's technology sorted out. 'Most VCs won't go near a start-up before then,' Kennedy noted. After this would come several rounds of VC funding before the company either got sold or went public a few years later.

'We don't have that kind of time,' I explained. The whole point was to bury the competition by cornering the market right from the start.

Kennedy shrugged. 'It's your company.'

'Can you help us?' I asked. 'We can't pay you anything until we've raised some money.'

This didn't seem to surprise him too much. 'Sure. Why not?'

Like other law firms, Skadden had been taking on a few start-ups a month. It would be able to advise us on all the legal issues that needed to be thought about when a company is born, such as the agreements with investors, the corporate structure, and so on. It was low risk and high reward. Big shots like Kennedy could do this sort of work in their sleep. But it was something they could brag about when pitching for the internet business of serious clients like Citigroup or Kmart. At that moment, though, none of us really cared much about his reasons. We didn't even have a company yet – but we had Skadden Arps as our lawyer.

We spent the day before our flight home relaxing a little. While Kajsa went off to catch up with a few old friends, Patrik and I sipped strawberry daiquiris at the Boathouse café by the pond in Central Park. The sun was warm on our backs and neither of us felt much like talking. It was an opportunity to reflect a little on what we'd learned and the challenge that lay ahead.

I was just about to nod off when Patrik gave a sharp whisper. Some friends of his from Stockholm were walking towards the Boathouse.

'What are we going to do?'

Our trip to New York was supposed to have been a secret. Some absurd instinct made us look around for a bush we could hide behind, but it was already too late. They were waving to us now.

'Tell them that you're doing some work for LeanderMalmsten,' I murmured as they approached.

Their beaming smiles signalled their awareness of having caught us out in something illicit. Awkwardly, Patrik introduced me. It wasn't really necessary as I had been all over the Swedish newspapers just a few weeks ago with the sale of bokus.

'The sooner this is up and running and I can leave the bank the better,' said Patrik after they had gone.

'Well, let's start work on the business plan.'

After slurping down the last of our daiquiris, we went looking for a Kinko's, one of a chain of copy centres that also rented out computers. We found one nearby and spent the next hour drafting the basic structure for a business plan and working out our respective responsibilities. We agreed that I would be CEO and also handle the business concept, logistics and technology platform. Kajsa would do marketing and design, while Patrik, the money man, would take responsibility for the company's financial and legal issues. It felt great finally to have something on paper.

The following afternoon, as we took off from Newark and headed into the dusky sky, I began slowly to grasp the full magnitude of what we were trying to do. This was going to be something innovative and daring, but also immensely complicated and difficult. I felt ready to push the limits. Right now, we were just on the starting line. We'd need the best people in every field if we were going to make this work. I remembered a documentary I'd seen about the Apollo space programme. Something that John F. Kennedy had said back in the early 1960s rang in my ears: 'We choose to go to the moon in this decade and do the other things, not because they are easy but because they are hard . . .'

3

'I'VE NARROWED IT DOWN to the big ones,' said Patrik, looking at the special banker's notebook in which he wrote everything down. 'We should start with Goldman Sachs, then Morgan Stanley and Deutsche Morgan Grenfell. They're doing most of the internet work right now.' The three of us were sitting in the kitchen of Kajsa's apartment in Stockholm. The rough, three-page business plan we'd typed up in New York a few days earlier was laid out on the table. It needed a lot more work, but we knew we had to start thinking about other things as well.

A good investment bank would bring us credibility, it would offer us vital guidance on how to establish a global company, but above all it would help us to get money. After our meeting with Jeffrey Leeds, we had raised our sights. Instead of $2 million for our first round of funding, now we wanted $15 million.

'We'll need a Wall Street bank if we're going to raise that kind of money,' said Patrik. The European banks had fewer contacts with the leading US investors and, as Patrik pointed out, they didn't know anything about the internet. As we were paranoid about secrecy, it was also somehow reassuring to be dealing with people who were 10,000 kilometres away.

Over the next few days, Patrik began trying to set up meetings with bankers in San Francisco and New York. He sent out letters in which he explained our backgrounds, gave a brief description of our business idea – 'a totally new concept of online shopping' – and laid out our funding strategy. He took care to emphasize our experience with bokus and included articles about Kajsa and me that had appeared in magazines familiar to Americans, such as *Esquire* and *Elle*. After our first round of $15 million, we planned to raise $25 million a few months later, and a further $40 million through an IPO on the Nasdaq market.

A few days later, he followed up with phone calls. The initial reaction wasn't exactly overwhelming. 'We've only got two appointments so far,' he admitted after he had rung everyone on his list.

'What's the problem?' I asked.

Patrik sighed. 'I don't know. They just don't like start-ups.'

His thick Swedish accent probably didn't help, but in most cases the bankers weren't even taking his calls. Not that Patrik was deterred. Formidably confident, he was prepared to try the same bank again and again until finally he found someone who would talk to him. He never seemed disheartened. 'Don't worry. I've got the names of all the secretaries now,' he said.

Kajsa and I left him to it. From our now fully furnished office, we began fleshing out the business plan from three pages to more than thirty. Once the meetings with the banks had been set up, we'd need something credible to show them. We didn't have a name yet for our company, so we called it LMH – an acronym for Leander, Malmsten, Hedelin.

'The business idea is to become the world-leading internet-based retailer of prestigious brand leisure and sportswear names,' we wrote on the first page. An enticing list of names followed: Polo Ralph Lauren, Tommy Hilfiger, Nike, Fila, Lacoste, Adidas, and so on. It seemed so simple. But, after our meeting with Bolotsky, we knew that to get these names on board would be as much of a challenge as finding investors.

Our website would be 'pleasant to navigate' and tailor-made for each country, using the local language and currency, as well as local prices and tax rates. As part of our branding strategy, we came up with the idea for a virtual salesperson that would guide users through the site and give helpful tips. We were thinking of calling her Jenny.

Our marketing plans were sketchy but ambitious. 'When we start to sell over the internet, an extensive "high impact" marketing campaign will begin, so that our business establishes itself rapidly and increases its sales volumes.' We were planning to hire public relations agencies in Germany, the UK and the US. This, we wrote, would lead to coverage in all the major daily newspapers, magazines and TV stations.

By the time our business plan was ready at the end of April, Patrik's persistence had paid off. He had flattered secretaries and used his connections with Swedes at several of the American banks. The result: almost a dozen meetings. Just three weeks after our last visit, we were going back to the US again.

It was a balmy spring evening, with just the hint of a breeze wafting in off the sea, when Patrik and I landed in San Francisco. Kajsa, who had a few things to sort out back home, was to meet us in New York two days later.

In the short history of the internet, San Francisco was a legendary town. This was where companies like Yahoo, Netscape and eBay had sprung up. When I had last visited the city on a holiday six years before, the billboards along the airport road had advertised old economy companies like Coca-Cola or McDonald's. Now, all the signs were for dot.coms.

Patrik was pleased to discover that our travel agents had booked us into the Ritz Carlton, one of the most exclusive hotels in town. 'It'll sound good when we leave messages for bankers,' he said. But practically the first thing we did after checking in was to head for the local branch of Kinko's, which was beginning to feel like a home away from home, to make some final amendments to the business plan.

We probably shouldn't have bothered. Our first meeting the following day, at Montgomery Securities in the city centre, lasted all of fifteen minutes. The banker we met, although polite, seemed distracted. 'We don't really deal with start-ups,' he said. When I asked why, he just shrugged. 'That's not how things are done here.'

It was at our next meeting, a short walk down the road at Hambrecht & Quist, that the reasons began to emerge. Genni Combes, an internet retail analyst, was pleasant but blunt. 'Working with start-ups means only two things to an investment bank,' she explained. 'Lots of work and puny fees.' Most banks waited until a company was off the ground and thinking about an IPO. Then they stepped in, helped the company go public, and collected million-dollar payments. 'You should really think about talking to some VCs instead of banks,' she suggested. She also warned us that we weren't the first ones to think of selling clothes online. 'I've seen other ideas like this before,' she said. 'but they all fizzled out.'

When we asked her why, her answer had a familiar echo.

'Suppliers,' she said. 'They don't like the internet. If you can't get the clothes, you don't have a business.'

There was one encouraging moment. Ted Smith, a banker from Deutsche Morgan Grenfell in Palo Alto, whom we met in Menlo Park, pored over our business plan for a good ten minutes, took a few notes and looked thoughtful. 'It'll probably take at least three months to raise the money,' he said. But it wasn't to be. A short time later, he joined about 100 of his colleagues in a mass defection to Crédit Suisse First Boston.

It had been a disappointing couple of days. New York, I hoped, would be different, and it was good to meet up with Kajsa in the familiar surroundings of the SoHo Grand. This at least was a city with no shortage of banks, and a lot of the Wall Street firms, although slower off the mark than their rivals on the West Coast, were starting to pay attention to internet companies.

'The bankers here will be hungrier,' Patrik said. They were certainly better fed, I thought, as the three of us ploughed our way through a four-course meal in a top-floor dining suite at Bear Stearns. We had come to the bank's Park Avenue headquarters to meet Steve Tishman, head of its technology division. Tishman, tall and sporty-looking, was in a chatty mood. While tuxedoed waiters scurried in and out with silver platters, he told us about his family and the occasional coaching he did for his son's baseball team. We were halfway through the salmon and baby potatoes before the conversation finally turned to business.

As we talked Tishman through the concept, he began to look a little troubled. 'Who did you say arranged this lunch?' he asked. 'Was it someone in my team or a different part of the bank?'

'We went through the switchboard,' said Patrik, helping himself to some more salmon.

Tishman coughed. I couldn't tell if he was laughing or choking. But we didn't do any deals with Bear Stearns that day.

Nor did we have any better luck with André de Baubigny, a technology banker at Morgan Stanley who counted AOL and Amazon.com among his clients. He was encouraging but practical. 'Your idea has potential,' he said. 'But we're just going to cost you a lot of money. Why don't you call us when you're ready to do an IPO?' In the meantime, he'd be happy to give us informal advice whenever we needed it. 'That's the Morgan Stanley way,' he said. 'We like to build relationships for the future.'

We ended the day with a 25-year-old salesman from Alex Brown. 'I have a credit card and it's my job to use it on people like you,' he said, taking us on a bar crawl around SoHo. We barely even talked about the business plan. I have two lasting images from that evening – a tipsy Patrik setting fire to a lampshade with his cigar, and the banker, at about 2 a.m., clanging uncertainly down the iron stairway of the SoHo Grand. I still wonder if he made it home.

It was late on the following day, after another series of fruitless meetings, that the three of us trundled, worn out and demoralized, into the vast entrance hall of the Wall Street headquarters of J.P. Morgan. Everything about the place exuded power and wealth, from the stone columns to the gold mosaic ceiling. This was the bank that had financed General Electric, AT&T and General Motors. Like the others, it wouldn't normally have looked twice at a start-up. But it had recently helped raise money for StarMedia Network Inc., a Latin American internet company. Although just a small deal, it generated enough attention to make J.P. Morgan realize what it was missing out on. Kajsa and one of the two bankers we met also had mutual friends.

Even so, John Littlefield, head of private placements at the bank, seemed hesitant. 'This is a bit too early for us,' he said. 'But we have some people in the London office that you should speak to. I'll try and set something up.' It was a glimmer of hope, but not enough to ease the realization that we had seriously underestimated the job ahead of us. Patrik, as the money man, seemed especially conscious of this. Getting a bank was supposed to be his responsibility. Even so, he tried to put a positive spin on things. As we headed for the airport in a cab, he said, 'I'll call them all back in a week or so. Maybe one of them will change their minds.'

★

If the bankers played hard to get, at least now they were talking to us. The same couldn't be said for suppliers. When we got back from New York, Kajsa and Patrik started calling companies like Fila and Adidas, but usually couldn't even get past the receptionists. And when they did, the response was always negative.

A fax from the Boston-based running-shoe and sportswear company New Balance was pretty typical. 'Thank you for including New Balance in your consideration of desirable brands for your proposed global distribution company,' wrote its vice-president Martin Walter:

> New Balance does business in almost all the countries of the world. The form of our representation may be a wholly-owned subsidiary, distributor, licensee or joint venture, but each representative has been granted the exclusive right to handle New Balance shoes in a particular country. Given that situation, New Balance actively curtails and opposes efforts by un-authorized third parties to sell New Balance product in countries where we have representation.

It was ridiculous. We clearly had to find some other way of getting to talk to these people. On the internet we discovered that there was an organization called the World Federation of the Sporting Goods Industry, to which all the big suppliers belonged. We arranged a conference call with its chairman, Andre Gorgemans, who was based in Verbier, Switzerland. 'Do you know any consultants who work with suppliers?' we asked. 'I can't recommend anyone,' he replied, 'but I'll be happy to send you a list.'

The first person we contacted was Walter Loeb, a fierce septuagenarian who ran a consultancy based in New York. The names on Gorgemans's list were scattered all over the world, and, as we set off on yet one more trip across the Atlantic, we began to realize that almost continuous travel was going to be the price of building a global business. We would end up catching jets as casually as other people hopped into taxis.

'You're twenty minutes late!' Loeb snapped when we turned up at his midtown office in Manhattan. Patrik immediately excused himself to go to the rest room, which seemed to make the old man even more irritable. He studied us with gimlet eyes as we explained our concept.

'I want to know more about you,' he said, once we'd finished. 'Can you show me your CVs.'

Another few minutes went by as he peered critically at our press clippings and other assorted documents. Then, apparently satisfied, he said, 'I can help you, but you'll have to give me a stake in the company.' And that was the end of that. Pretty soon afterwards we were heading back to the airport again.

Back in Stockholm, Patrik called Kurt Salmon Associates, another consultancy on our list that had strong connections in the fashion and sporting-goods industries, and we set off to see them in their London office. This time we struck lucky. KSA didn't want shares. It didn't even want money, to start with at least. It was happy to work on a 'success fee' basis. If the internet was going to revolutionize retailing, KSA figured, then working with a company like ours was the best way to prepare. Having already helped to design the logistics infrastructure for eToys in the US, it was looking for a similar project in Europe.

Tony Barsham, the KSA consultant assigned to work with us, was a prematurely grey-haired and rather tense Englishman. He had just joined KSA from Andersen Consulting, and we represented an opportunity for him to make an early impression in his new job, a challenge that he took very seriously.

'The first thing you need to realize is that you don't know anything,' he said to us soon after we had sat down with him in KSA's tiny office in Cannon Street. This became increasingly obvious as our meeting progressed.

'We don't want to have any inventory,' I told him. At bokus, we had never bought any of the books we sold. We simply bundled all the orders together each evening and sent them off to book suppliers. That kept our overheads low and meant we didn't have to build warehouses to store products in.

Barsham shook his head. 'You can forget that right now,' he said. 'Very few suppliers are going to sell on an order-by-order basis.' For a start, the fashion industry was largely organized around seasons. No supplier wanted to get stuck with warehouses full of last season's fashions, so most insisted on taking advance orders from retailers. Some were more sophisticated than others. Patagonia, the rugged US outdoor-clothing brand, was one of the most high-tech. It could ship in 24 hours. Others, like Fila in the US, took more than a week.

'You'll have to be very flexible,' Barsham said.

There were other issues we hadn't thought through. We knew a lot of people would probably be reluctant to buy clothes that they hadn't tried on, so we wanted to offer free returns if they weren't satisfied. Barsham looked sceptical. 'That could be a real problem for you,' he said. Some catalogue retailers had return rates as high as 35 per cent, he pointed out, because customers ordered the same item in five different sizes, tried them all, then sent four back. 'We'll have to think of ways to minimize that, otherwise you'll go broke pretty quickly.'

Barsham agreed to help us put together a presentation for suppliers. This would take at least a few weeks. Then he'd arrange a couple of test runs with 'friendly' suppliers. 'They'll tell you pretty quickly if they don't like what you're doing,' he said. If they didn't, I knew, we'd be back where we started.

Kajsa thought she had it. 'Bo,' she said. 'You know. Like Bo Derek.'

'What does Bo Derek have to do with anything?' I asked.

'She's so retro. You remember that movie *10*? With the braids, running on the beach?'

'Hmm. Maybe.'

It was late May. We were back in Stockholm, sitting on the sofa in Kajsa's apartment and trying to come up with a name for our company. On the floor, near my feet, Kajsa's daughter, Alva, was playing happily with coloured blocks. The problem we had was that every name sounded a bit silly until you'd seen it in an appropriate context. So I tried to imagine 'bo.com' on our website, on billboards and on television ads. It wasn't too bad. Certainly no worse than the other company names we'd thought of. One of Kajsa's early ideas was 'sneaky.com'. But that sounded too much like sneakers. We needed a name that was universal. Who knew what we might end up selling on our website? Amazon.com, for example, could start selling everything from toys to airline flights if it wanted to. CDNow or eToys, on the other hand, didn't have a lot of room to manoeuvre.

The good thing about 'bo' was that it was short and easy to remember. But after a quick search on the internet, I discovered that someone else had got there first. Rainbow Pet Supplies of Ballwin, Missouri, to be precise.

Maybe we can add an 'o'?' Kajsa suggested. 'boo.'

I shrugged. Why not? I did another search and this time we were lucky. The page that came up told us that boo.com was owned by a web domain dealer and for sale at the right price.

I rang Patrik on his mobile. 'What do you think of boo?' I asked.

'What does it mean?'

'Nothing. That's the point.'

'I like it,' he said.

But the following morning Kajsa sought independent advice from Me Company, the London web design agency that we'd worked with on bokus. We were planning to use them again to design our logo and virtual salesperson.

'What do you think of boo.com?' she asked one of the directors.

'It's too childish,' he said. 'You're not targeting 5 – 10-year-olds, are you?'

'I think it's quite catchy,' Kajsa said.

'Look. You're Swedish. You wouldn't understand.'

Meanwhile, I did some research of my own. In Holland, I discovered, boo was a street name for marijuana.

The three of us talked it over that night. The web domain dealer was prepared to sell us the name for $3,500. Patrik and I liked it and doubted we'd get anything better. But Kajsa wasn't quite sure yet. 'This is important,' she said, scribbling the name over and over again on a piece of paper to see how it looked. Late the following afternoon, boo.com was born.

It was a couple of weeks later, in mid-June, that Patrik got the call. 'J.P. Morgan wants to meet us in London,' he said with a note of pride in his voice. At last, just as we had begun to question our early optimism about finding an investment bank, one of them had been interested enough to call us.

J.P. Morgan wasn't like the other US banks that had moved into Europe back in the 1980s. It had actually started life as a small merchant bank in London's financial district in 1838. Although later it would shift its headquarters to Wall Street, becoming probably the most influential of all US investment banks, it always kept a strong presence in Europe.

In contrast to the glitz of its New York headquarters, the J.P. Morgan building in London was all oak panelling and giant paintings. Perched on the banks of the Thames, it had previously been the City of London Boys' School. The names of its brightest students could still be seen, engraved on plaques, in what was once the 'great hall'.

The three of us were led into a small, dimly lit room in the basement, where two bankers were waiting to meet us. They were young – in their late twenties, I guessed – and wearing matching dark suits. Thomas Paulmichl worked in J.P. Morgan's telecommunications, media and technology, or TMT, division. He was Italian, but had light ginger hair and a pale complexion, and turned out to come from a German-speaking area near the border. His colleague, Andreas Tenconi, on the other hand, with his dark hair and olive skin, was typically Italian. He was from Morgan Capital, the private-equity arm of the bank, and had come along to analyse our plan from an investor's perspective – the bad cop, I thought, as we all took our seats around a large oval table.

'So we've looked through your . . . uh . . .' Tenconi paused, as if searching for the right word – 'business plan.'

'What do you think?' I asked.

'It's quite thin,' he said. 'Let's go through it one step at a time.'

What followed felt like an interrogation.

Even Paulmichl, who had come across as friendly and even a little shy at first, seemed sceptical about almost everything we said. 'So you're saying that you can deliver products anywhere in the world in 48 hours?' he asked.

'Sure,' I said. 'We learned a lot about this from bokus.'

'Do you realize how expensive that's going to be?' Paulmichl retorted.

Tenconi weighed in. You can't have it both ways.' As far as the bankers were concerned, the faster we delivered the more it was going to cost. They seemed to think that there was no such thing as fast, cheap delivery.

I disagreed, but didn't press the point.

The questions continued at break-neck speed for the next half-hour. The tone felt aggressive and patronizing. Kajsa folded her arms and glowered. Patrik and I became snappy. This wasn't the first time we'd had problems dealing with people our own age, and in this case I couldn't help feel that the bankers' toughness was an attempt to compensate for their lack of knowledge. I doubted if they had ever worked with an internet company before.

Paulmichl's next question confirmed my suspicions. 'Have you done any market research?' he asked.

Market research? That was something Colgate did before it launched a new toothpaste. The internet was something you had to feel in your fingertips. There were only really a few questions worth asking. Is the market big enough? Can it work on the internet? Is anyone doing it already? As far as I was concerned, we had answered them all.

'So much for J.P. Morgan,' Patrik said afterwards. 'Why did they even bother to call us in?'

'Let's call them before they call us,' I said. 'Tell him his people have no idea about the internet.'

Patrik got on the phone to John Littlefield at J.P. Morgan in New York. It was early morning there, but Littlefield was already at his desk. 'That was ridiculous!' Patrik yelled down the line with characteristic bluntness. 'What's the point of putting us together with two office juniors?'

'Just take it easy,' Littlefield said. 'I'll check it out.'

As hard as we tried to forget about it, we couldn't pretend to ourselves that it hadn't been a deeply dispiriting meeting. It just seemed to underline the fact that after a month of looking we had got nowhere in our hunt for a bank. Back in Stockholm, Patrik kept calling all the investment bankers we'd met in San Francisco and New York. 'Don't worry. It takes time,' he told us at the end of another fruitless week, although the lack of a positive response had clearly dented his self-confidence.

After yet another week had gone by, the three of us got together at Prinsen, one of my favourite restaurants in Stockholm, to talk through the options. Maybe we had got too used to the idea of working with a reputable bank. But the only realistic alternative was to bring in a big venture capital investor, which could mean losing control again as had happened to us with bokus. It would also make it more difficult for us to raise the kind of money we were now thinking about. So it seemed clear to us that we had to persevere with the banks.

'We might have to make a few more trips to the States,' Patrik said.

Kajsa looked doubtful. 'They aren't interested,' she said. 'Maybe we should talk to the European banks instead.'

It was hard to see why they should be any more interested. I knew that somehow we had to struggle on, but as we left Prinsen that night there was a depressing sense of having reached a dead end.

Then one day in early July Patrik received the news we had all been waiting for. He was reading a newspaper in the garden of his country house in northern Sweden. He may have been on holiday, but as usual his mobile was close by. We used to joke that he would get withdrawal symptoms without it.

Patrik reached me while I was in a cab, coming home from Stockholm's Arlanda airport. 'I just spoke to Paulmichl at J.P. Morgan,' he said. 'They want to work with us.'

The radio in my taxi was blaring an obscure Swedish pop song and it took a few seconds for Patrik's words to sink in.

'Why?' I asked finally.

Patrik laughed. 'I don't know. They just do.'

It wasn't until later that we learned of the fierce debate that had been raging within J.P. Morgan. In spite of our ill-tempered first encounter, Paulmichl had emerged as our biggest champion. He was still only a first-year associate – about three rungs up a long ladder – but a lot sharper than we'd given him credit for. He had spent the past few months working on a joint venture between British Telecommunications and AT&T. In comparison, boo was like being given a toy. Almost immediately after our meeting, he had done some digging around. This included visiting Sweden to talk to people about bokus and LeanderMalmsten. The reactions must have been positive, because he then took our idea to Chris Bataillard, a Frenchman who ran J.P. Morgan's TMT division in Europe.

'I think there's enough cannon fodder here to sell this story to investors,' Paulmichl said.

Working with a start-up was a new thing for J.P. Morgan, which still focused on 'elephants' – large corporations with deep pockets – but Bataillard had agreed. Even as we were giving up hope of ever finding a bank, Bataillard was building a case internally to take us on as clients. No investment bank in Europe had yet claimed a leading position in the internet sector, he argued to Joe Walker, global head of TMT. If J.P. Morgan could tap into the local entrepreneurial market by working with a company like boo, it would have a head start over other banks when the internet really took off. What made boo especially interesting was the scope of its vision. 'I liked the fact that it was bold,' Bataillard later told us. 'E-commerce was supposed to be global, but most internet retailers were still national.'

We were probably more relieved than euphoric at the news. We didn't have time to celebrate. A couple of days later, the three of us were back in London to meet some of J.P. Morgan's senior bankers. These included Bataillard himself, tall and athletic, with a permanent friendly smile on his face, and Vincent Mulliez, another Frenchman, and Bataillard's second in command. The message from them was simple. 'This needs to be a partnership,' Bataillard told us. 'Our job is to work for you and find investors. Yours is to make sure the company is something that people will want to invest in.'

On 22 July, we returned for a meeting to discuss the fund-raising strategy. This time a wonderful smell wafted up to greet us as we headed down into the basement. 'Maybe they're going to give us lunch,' I said hopefully. When we entered the room, though, the only food I could see was a bowl of fruit. The attitude here was definitely business first.

Paulmichl, joined this time by a young-looking analyst, Jaime Hugas, greeted us enthusiastically. 'Here,' he said, handing over a thin green folder with J.P. Morgan's silver-embossed logo on the cover. On the first page, the words KICK OFF MEETING and HIGHLY CONFIDENTIAL were written in big letters. Further in, I noticed a chart showing the build-up to our fund-raising. Preliminary talks with investors would start immediately. Our first round of funding would be completed within four months. My pulse quickened.

Paulmichl got to the point quickly. 'What we want to do is raise $100 million over the next year and a half,' he said. This was even more than we had planned. The reason was speed. 'You have a real opportunity,' Paulmichl said. 'You're the first ones planning anything like this. But you've got to stay that way.'

J.P. Morgan also had other reasons for aiming high. Its fee for introducing us to investors and acting as our advisers would be 7 per cent of any money we raised – a healthy $7 million if we reached our target. J.P. Morgan also wanted the option of transferring these fees into boo shares, which would result in an even larger windfall for the bank if our IPO was a success. That was fine with us. Having J.P. Morgan as an adviser was great, but having it as a shareholder too was an unexpected bonus.

At this point, another more senior banker joined us in the room. Samer Salty was Lebanese with an expressive face that could jump from morose seriousness to cherubic jollity in the blink of an eye. He had more experience in raising money than Paulmichl and would play an important role in introducing us to investors over the coming months. His contacts included a number of wealthy investors from the Middle East.

'Do you think we'll have any trouble getting the money?' I asked him.

Salty was careful in his choice of words. 'A lot depends on the markets. This is an all or nothing concept. If it works, it'll be big.'

We spent the next half-hour going over the timeline. boo would launch in May 1999. Our IPO would come six to nine months later, once revenues hit $5 million on an annualized basis.

'We'll also need to draw up a contract,' Paulmichl said. 'What's the proper name of your company? Is it boo.com Ltd?'

'We haven't actually set up a company yet,' Patrik said. 'All we have is the name.'

Paulmichl's eyebrows shot up. Here they were about to raise $100 million for a company that didn't even exist. 'That's one of the things you'll have to sort out soon,' he said.

There were a lot of other things that needed to be done as well.

'Before we go out to investors,' Salty said, 'we need to produce a private placement memorandum.' He passed us a heavy ring-bound folder, with more than 100 pages in it, to illustrate the point. It was like an extended, incredibly comprehensive, version of our business plan, containing all the information needed to win the support of investors. 'It's up to you exactly what we put into it,' he continued. 'But you'll have to address important areas like technology and logistics.'

The meeting lasted almost two hours. The three of us left on a high, laughing and talking across each other, as we walked out into the bright, mid-afternoon sun. In a bookstore on nearby Fleet Street I bought *The House of Morgan*, an 800-page history of the bank. It felt reassuringly heavy in my hand. This was the bank that, during its pre-1935 heyday, had 'stopped panics, saved the gold standard, rescued New York City three times and arbitrated financial disputes'. At one time, it boasted that 96 of America's top 100 corporations were clients. And now it was working for us. If there was a defining moment in boo's creation, this was probably it.

Meanwhile Tony Barsham at KSA had set up the two trial meetings he had promised with 'friendly suppliers'. Ironically, the first of these companies was New Balance, whose US office had responded so negatively to our overtures only a few weeks earlier.

For some strange reason the world's coolest fashion brands seem to be situated in the least glamorous of places. If you want to pay Adidas a visit, for example, you'll have to trek down to Herzogenaurach, a small German town outside Nuremberg. Nike's head office is in Beaverton, Oregon. New Balance was no exception. The US company's English headquarters was situated in the northern town of Warrington near Manchester. Until recently it had been questionable whether New Balance was a fashion brand. Its lead colour was grey and it proudly boasted a wider range of shoe widths than any of its rivals. But it was enjoying a bit of a renaissance. One of its older models – the suede, retro-looking 576 running shoe – had inexplicably become cool. They were now being snapped up by nightclubbers in London and Paris and worn by the likes of Naomi Campbell and Catherine Deneuve.

A few hours after our meeting at J.P. Morgan, the three of us flew up to Manchester where KSA's UK headquarters was located. We spent the evening going over our presentation with Barsham and his colleague Robert Blythe, who had even more retail experience. 'Make sure you tell them early on that you won't be discounting,' Blythe stressed. 'They need to feel confident that you won't be damaging their brand.'

The next day we felt well prepared as we set off in good time for our meeting, but still managed to be late, as Barsham, who claimed to know where he was going, ended up taking us down a succession of industrial-looking back streets. Fortunately Russ Lucas, the middle-aged American who headed up New Balance's UK operations, seemed much too pleased to see us to mind.

'We don't get that many visitors,' he said, leading us into a small room with shoes stacked on shelves around the walls.

The presentation took about twenty minutes, with each of us taking turns to speak.

'Why should suppliers be partners with boo.com?' Kajsa asked before going on to answer her own question. 'Because the internet is global and can reach customers anywhere, anytime. We will jointly market with suppliers to help strengthen their brands . . .'

And what about the customers? Why should they use boo? Well, I explained, because 'we will offer an unlimited selection of products and aggressively market the site as a hip and trendy retail outlet . . .'

Patrik, slipping into his thoughtful banker's persona, rounded things off with an overview of our financial situation. 'J.P. Morgan has been appointed as our financial adviser,' he said, clearly enjoying the way that sounded. 'It will raise $15 million during autumn 1998, with the further objective of raising $100 million of equity over the next eighteen months.' We drove our advantage home with more shameless name-dropping, as we mentioned some of the other blue-chip companies that we had already begun to work with: Skadden Arps, UPS, Ernst & Young . . .

It was a slick and professional pitch. Everything went perfectly.

Lucas rubbed the back of his hand absently. 'So each country will have its own website, with its own prices, right?'

'Right,' I said, glad that we'd recognized this as a key issue. 'No discounting.'

'I like the fact that you're going out to all of the European markets,' Lucas continued, almost to himself.

'We're going out to the world,' Kajsa noted.

'Even better.'

Naturally, we said nothing about the negative response we had received from New Balance's Boston headquarters two months earlier. It just didn't seem relevant now. Anyway, things had moved on a lot since then. In recent weeks, the company had at last begun to take the internet seriously. Lucas explained that he'd been approached by a few catalogue retailers that were looking to go online. 'But this is the most comprehensive plan I've seen so far.' New Balance might be interested, he added, on certain conditions. 'We don't want to be the only major supplier you sign up. You've got to have a good mix of brands.' Even then, the final word would have to come from Boston.

None of this really mattered, though. If this was the response to our first presentation, how would people react once we had had some practice? We were euphoric. At last, we thought, we had cracked the suppliers.

Our next meeting was back in London. The Pentland Group was a family-controlled business, whose brands included Speedo, Ellesse and Kickers. KSA had done a lot of work for them, Barsham told us. Not only that, but the group's new chief executive Andrew Rubin had just taken over from his father. He was a smart young guy, said Barsham, who would be keen to make his mark and would be more than usually receptive to the internet. 'We should get a friendly reception here.'

The meeting took place in Rubin's office in the run-down London suburb of Finchley. Still only in his thirties, Rubin had certainly shaken things up. One of his first acts on succeeding his father had been a deep restructuring of Pentland's unprofitable US business.

Confidently we launched into our presentation. When it was finished, Rubin was silent and unsmiling. Finally he said, 'Did you buy that suit on the internet?'

'No,' I replied.

'Well, what makes you think other people will?'

That was just the start. He didn't think much of our logistics, doubted our ability to get other suppliers and seemed confused about who our customers would be. 'I don't understand where you're taking this brand. Is it fashion? Is it sports? What is it?'

Pentland's head of technology, who had joined us in the room, had a suggestion. 'Why don't you sell something else,' he said, 'like office furniture?' None of us knew what to say. Barsham tried to brush it off as a joke. But they definitely weren't joking.

'You should really do some more homework before you come back to us,' Rubin said.

It was torrid, but educational. There would be more meetings like this. We couldn't let ourselves get demoralized if people didn't believe in what we were doing. boo wasn't an ordinary start-up. As far as I was concerned, it was a billion-dollar start-up. If we didn't believe this ourselves, how could we expect others to?

Even so, it had been hard to take. 'What the hell was going on in there?' Patrik said as we piled into a black cab. 'I thought he was supposed to be a "friendly" supplier.'

'Maybe he was having a bad day,' Barsham said, looking sheepish. Over the next few weeks, he promised, we'd have meetings with suppliers all over Europe and the States. 'Everyone talks to each other in this industry,' he said. 'Even if only a few of them like what you're doing, others will follow sooner or later.'

The next few weeks would be among the toughest that any of us had ever experienced. We were trying to build a multinational business from scratch and we had to do it fast – faster than anyone had ever attempted before. There were no precedents. We'd just have to work it out as we went along.

We started by trying to get our lives in order. Patrik, with J.P. Morgan on board, finally quit his job and all of us began spending at least a couple of days a week in London. I stayed in a house my parents owned in Notting Hill, while the other two alternated between the Metropolitan Hotel and Blakes. Kajsa and Joel hired a nanny back in Sweden to look after their young daughter while Kajsa was away. None of us knew London very well so we used J.P. Morgan shamelessly, transforming one of its meeting rooms into a makeshift office. The room had a desk with a speakerphone and each morning a friendly, uniformed waiter delivered a pot of steaming coffee and a fresh batch of chocolate chip cookies. We took advantage of the bank's courier and Fedex services and even the bankers themselves were scurrying around doing odd jobs.

Thomas Paulmichl had started working on our private placement memorandum. Helping him with research and paperwork was an analyst called Felix von Schubert, a slight, pale German, who seemed to work around the clock. In the background was the more senior Samer Salty, ready to step in when it came to dealing with investors. All three were incredibly dedicated. 'Let's meet on Sunday at 6 a.m.,' I said once, and to my amazement they actually showed up. They also wrote us recommendation letters to help with estate agents as we began to hunt for office space. All three were fascinated by the opportunities being thrown up by the new economy: boo was their first exposure to this world.

At our first strategy meeting, the bankers stressed the importance of quickly putting in place the key partnerships that would help us to build the business. These included headhunters, tax consultants, technology providers and not least an advertising agency.

Leagas Delaney was one of three that we approached in late August. All seemed excited at the prospect of working with what was obviously going to be a high profile and extremely well funded start-up, but Leagas Delaney, whose clients included Adidas and Harrods, made the most impressive pitch, and offered the added attraction of a digitial division that could build a prototype of our website.

But Leagas Delaney's chief asset, we felt, was its chairman Jerry Fielder. With his grey-flecked hair and restless eyes, he was a bundle of energy. According to office gossip, he got up each morning at 4.30 and ran 10 kilometres to work. He was often still there late in the evenings.

We had been impressed by the way Fielder's presentation during the agency's pitch had helped to focus our identity as a company and also the overall strategy we should be pursuing. The help he was able to give extended far beyond simply organizing an advertising campaign. In the weeks that followed, Fielder was not afraid to be brutally upfront in his attempts to educate us.

'You have no idea about who you are targeting,' he said, when we got together for our first proper meeting.

The three of us had a vague notion that our customers would be 25–40 year-olds. That was fine, Fielder said, but we should be aiming for the 18–24 year-olds. Why? Because this was 'the primary centre of influence' – the age group that defined trends. Fifteen-year-olds want to look as if they're 18, while 30-year-olds dress as if they're 24. Fielder also gave us ideas about which sorts of brands to stock. We wanted a mix of big name and niche brands. But how would we get the balance right? The answer, he said, could be found by visiting a department store. There, in the window, would be clothes from the most hip and exclusive young designers. These brands gave credibility. They got people into the store. But they were also expensive and didn't sell in large volumes. That's why most of the racks were actually filled with mainstream labels like DKNY, Calvin Klein and Nike.

Our plan to sell sports and designer clothes alongside each other was the cause of considerable debate. The sports brands, Fielder said, were very specific in their marketing. 'All their ads are about sports. Their clothes are only sold in sports stores.' They might not care what their clothes would be used for, but they wanted to be known for only one thing. 'It's a simple and very effective branding tool.'

It meant, Fielder warned us, that we had to be very careful about how we were going to position ourselves.

'Are you going to call yourselves a sports company or a fashion company?'

'Both,' I said.

He shook his head. 'It won't work. The sports brands won't go for it.'

It would become a growing cause of contention.

★

By far the most pressing issue was technology. Most internet companies before now, including the big ones like Amazon and eBay, had built their technology platforms in-house. This was partly for cost reasons and partly because they had started off small and expanded gradually. On bokus, our consultants Netch Technologies had helped us to build everything from the ground up. It was relatively simple. bokus needed almost no 'back end' – the part of an e-commerce platform that manages things like financial accounts, stock inventory and logistics. But boo.com would be global from day one, with all the complexities that this entailed. We would need to provide individually tailored versions of our website to accommodate the different languages, postal systems, prices and taxes of the countries we operated in. There was the further challenge of showing all our products in 3D, and creating our virtual salesperson, which we now planned to call Miss Boo.

There was no way we could handle this ourselves, especially in such a short amount of time. Besides, our goal was to build an online retailer, not to be a software company. The answer was to outsource the project to a large technology firm that could handle everything itself or bring in specialist firms to build specific parts of our platform, before pulling everything together in time for our launch. But which one? Up to this point, few of the big technology companies had done this kind of work and even fewer start-ups could afford them if they did. These were the guys that built technology solutions for billion-dollar companies.

Around the time that contracts were being signed with J.P. Morgan in early August, we found someone to guide us through the technology maze: Jan-Erik Gustavsson, a jovial Swede who ran his own small internet consultancy in Stockholm. In his navy jacket with gold buttons, he looked a bit like a hotel porter, but he knew his stuff and was fascinated by what we were doing – it was a lot more interesting than his usual work for big corporations. Even better, he was prepared to forgo any fees until our first round of funding had come through.

Over the next few days we drew up a basic specification of what we were trying to achieve, then tried to think of potential candidates. Our first meeting was with IBM at its research labs in Hursley about

70 kilometres south-west of London. This colossus had managed to lose $8 billion in 1993 after somehow failing to capitalize on the PC revolution, but after some lean years it was making money again and trying to reinvent itself as a champion of new-economy businesses. Its ads at the time were everywhere: 'The work matters. The people matter. The tools matter.'

Maybe we could do some kind of co-advertising with them, I thought, as we pulled up outside what looked like a castle, complete with ivy climbing the walls. It was actually an eighteenth-century mansion that IBM had bought in the 1960s for the purpose, I assumed, of imbuing visitors with a sense of awe.

But the discussion that followed was strangely disconnected. We wanted IBM as a project manager. The five-strong IBM delegation, a dry-humoured bunch, seemed more interested in selling us their products. Like two of their RS/6000 servers. 'Isn't that Deep Blue?' Gustavsson asked, beginning to smile. Deep Blue was the name IBM had given to its chess-playing supercomputer. Capable of calculating 200 million moves per second, it had recently defeated world chess champion Garry Kasparov. One of the IBM salesmen nodded. 'It's very similar,' he said.

At this point, I felt an explanation was needed. 'We want to be able to mix and match,' I said. 'We don't want you just to sell us your machines. We want you to manage the best available systems wherever they come from.' I got up and drew a diagram on a whiteboard to illustrate my point. It had IBM at the centre, as project manager, with arrows fanning out to other technology providers. 'We'll pay you more to do it this way.'

The room went silent. Gustavsson looked mortified. I was conscious of having said something wrong, but wasn't exactly sure what it was. So I just kept talking. 'If we work together, we'd also really like to get some of your American experts . . . your gurus . . . in to help.' As far as I was concerned, this was vital. IBM in Europe had designed the website for the English retailer Sainsbury's, but hadn't done much else that I could see. Its US team, on the other hand, had just built an e-commerce platform for Borders Books (a leading chain of US booksellers).

'We often work closely with other teams,' one of the salesmen said. 'But don't worry. We have all the skillsets to handle a project like this from Europe.'

'That's great. But we want to feel that the company as a whole is committed to us.'

More meetings followed, they even began work on developing a prototype of our website, but because they were so reluctant to introduce us to their key people in the US it was impossible to feel – whatever their slogan may have been – that our work mattered or that we mattered, and the relationship quickly fizzled out.

The good news was that, with the help of Jerry Fielder and Tony Barsham, we were now starting to make real headway with suppliers. By mid-September three had tentatively agreed to work with us: New Balance, Converse and North Face. Others were on the way. But the punishing schedule required to secure such deals did not make our quest for the ideal technology partner any easier. When Gustavsson set up a meeting with Oracle, the world's second-biggest software company after Microsoft, we had to put it off three times. Eventually, his contact there, Dave Pearson, told him that Oracle wasn't interested in going any further unless we provided a plan, showed 'professionalism' and 'respected meeting times'. We obviously hadn't made a great impression, but there was very little that could be done, given the enormous work-load. Whenever I arrived at an airport I had the feeling that there were two different jets I could catch to two equally vital meetings.

Ericsson, the company Gustavsson urged us to consider in place of IBM, didn't at first seem an obvious technology partner. Its main business was telecommunications, but it was looking to diversify. Ericsson's new CEO, Sven-Christer Nilsson, had ambitions to transform it into a full technology solutions provider, as Louis Gerstner had done for IBM a few years earlier. A division within the company, Ericsson Data, which had been responsible for looking after internal technology needs, was now encouraged to sell its services outside. But its only contract so far, to build an e-commerce platform for French retailer Carrefour, had just fallen through. boo represented an opportunity for managers at Ericsson Data to redeem themselves and they threw everything they had at us.

During the last two weeks of September, Kajsa, Patrik and I

attended two workshops at Ericsson's Stockholm headquarters. These were informal sessions at which six of the company's excited-looking senior technology staff asked us questions about our concept and requirements in advance of an official pitch at Ericsson's recently opened 'Cyberlab' in New York.

Cyberlab, just a short walk from the New York Stock Exchange on Broad Street, was a classic illustration of Ericsson's efforts to reinvent itself. It was described in the company's internal PR as a 'project station . . . where an impudent enterprising spirit will be cross-pollinating with Ericsson's 122 years of wisdom and business success'.

The pitch was to take place on my birthday, 5 October. Thomas Paulmichl from J.P. Morgan, who was becoming an invaluable member of our team and showing signs of becoming almost as obsessed with the project as we were, flew out for the occasion. He had taken to sending me daily emails with assorted newspaper articles about new technology or retailing trends. He had the entrepreneurial bug. It wouldn't be easy for him to go back to normal banking.

Cyberlab's open-plan office, with its steel door, concrete floors and staff of laid-back internet types, might easily have belonged to a start-up. The message was clear, if a bit lacking in subtlety: Ericsson is cool.

There was a charged atmosphere in the conference room when we entered. Ericsson had pulled together half a dozen people from different parts of the world and they lined up to introduce themselves and shake hands. Among these were Per Hedberg and Ann-Catrine Appelquist, two executives from Ericsson Data who had flown in from Stockholm, and Donna Campbell, the head of Cyberlab, who was spearheading Ericsson's charge into the internet.

The presentation was impressive. Ericsson would do what IBM couldn't, Campbell assured us. They would find the best products in every category, regardless of who made them, and commit the full resources of the company. 'We'll give you a global team,' said Per Hedberg. Specialists from PSINet in Canada, with which Ericsson had recently formed an alliance, would develop the website; Ericsson's consumer-testing lab in Sweden would then assess the market reaction to the site before it was launched. 'We also have a close relationship with companies like Hewlett Packard and Sun,' Hedberg added. 'We can bring in some of their specialists if necessary.'

When the meeting ended, almost two hours later, I was sold. Ericsson was a name I had grown up with. It represented stability and integrity. It might also be able to give us useful access to mobile technology. The mood in the room was upbeat and excited.

'We're going to take this very seriously,' Hedberg said as we left the room.

'So are we,' I replied, feeling I had just been given the perfect birthday present.

By late October, the three of us were at the point of collapse. We'd been living in hotels and getting by on minimal sleep. It felt as if we'd spent more time in the air than on the ground. It was pretty tough too on people like Paulmichl, Barsham and Gustavsson, whom we often dragged along with us – although Gustavsson seemed more bemused than stressed by his new whirlwind lifestyle. We brought him to one meeting, with a consultant, in the all-pink bar of the Beverly Hills Hotel. Then we went to the consultant's home in celebrity-packed Bel-Air and drank champagne. Gustavsson called his wife that night. 'It's like being in a *Star Trek* movie,' he said. 'Today, we were in the Delta quadrant.'

But we were proud, and a little amazed, by what what we'd achieved. Deutsche Post had expressed strong interest in managing our complex European logistics – the process of shipping products to each country. We were thinking of using Federal Express or UPS in America.

Patrik, meanwhile, had managed to design a dizzyingly complex company structure with the help of accountants at Ernst & Young. Our parent company would be based in Holland because of that country's attractive tax environment. An Irish company would hold boo's intellectual property rights, while a string of companies in France, Germany, Sweden, the US and Britain would hold our assets in each of those countries. Patrik loved this sort of work, but Kajsa and I weren't so sure.

'Is this really necessary?' we asked, when he showed us an elaborate chart with a dozen company names and interconnecting lines.

'We've got to get this right now,' Patrik insisted. 'It won't be possible to change it later.' Then he added after a pause, 'and do you really want to pay 50 per cent tax if one day you decide to sell your shares?'

This prospect actually didn't bother Kajsa and me. It seemed fair enough. Whatever we might pay in tax, there would still be plenty left over. But Patrik, capitalist to the core, didn't share our social-liberal instincts. He wanted to hold on to every penny he could of what he had earned. But there were, nonetheless sound business reasons for what he was proposing. If investors could see that we had done everything possible to ensure that they saved tax, the company would seem a more attractive prospect.

At the same time, Ericsson was now unofficially on board and had started helping us fill out the technical sections of our information memorandum. Its fee for overseeing the project would be $10 million, but the precise terms still had to be settled. Just before the end of the month the three of us, together with Paulmichl and Samer Salty, headed over to Ericsson's Stockholm office for the negotiation. 'This deal is important for Ericsson,' Paulmichl pointed out on the flight over. 'I think we can push them.'

The Ericsson complex was in Kista, a quiet suburb of Stockholm. We were greeted by Haijo Pietersma, a tall, reserved Dutchman who headed up the company's enterprise solutions division. He was one of a handful of senior executives who reported direct to the chief executive. Also in the room was Ann-Catrine Appelquist, who had been at the pitch in New York.

Quickly the bankers set the tone for the discussion by stressing the need to move quickly. 'We want the website to go live on 1 May next year,' Paulmichl said. 'We'll need you to deliver everything at least a month before that so we can start testing.'

'That should be possible,' Pietersma said, 'but obviously we'll need to do a feasibility study first. This is a complicated platform.'

'We'd like to include a penalty clause in the agreement,' Salty said.

'What kind of penalty?' Appelquist said, a little taken aback.

'If you don't deliver on time, you cover boo's loss of income.'

It was an extraordinary demand that could quite easily run into tens of millions of dollars.

'This isn't just important for us,' Salty went on. 'It's vital for investors.'

'Are you prepared to give us a written guarantee that you will raise the $100 million that you're talking about?' Pietersma asked.

Salty was dismissive. 'Of course not. We're only the advisers.'

'So you want us to be flexible on payment terms *and* to agree to a penalty clause as well?' Pietersma said incredulously. 'What does Ericsson get out of this?'

Ericsson badly wanted the deal, but it was obvious that we were going to have to compromise a little. Finally we agreed on a maximum penalty fee of $4 million, which effectively represented the profit Ericsson would make if they delivered on time. At last the technology box was ticked. boo was on its way.

A week later, the first versions of our completed private placement memorandum rolled off the presses. Each was ring-bound and numbered for security reasons. If there were leaks, we'd be able to track down where they'd come from. It had been a huge collaborative effort. Everything Kajsa, Patrik and I had learned in the last few months had been relayed back to J.P. Morgan and weaved into the painstakingly researched memorandum. The result was a slick, well rounded description of the rationale behind our idea and how we planned to achieve it.

The fact that boo.com was not a discount site, the memorandum explained, was the key to our being able to maintain a successful relationship with the leading sports/fashion brands and made high margins possible. It then detailed the attractions that we could offer our customers. There was international access to an unparalleled choice of brands, so that Europeans could buy brands which, through traditional outlets, had only been available in the US, and vice versa. There was the convenience of the Internet – open 24 hours a day, and making it possible for even those people who did not live near cities to purchase fashion/sports brands. There was swift free delivery and free return – customers could send back items they did not like or wanted to exchange for another size. There was excellent customer service through both the site itself and 24-hour call centres. And, finally, there was the highly innovative website: boo.com's powerful brand appeal, the stylish presentation and additional 'entertainment' features, such as an online magazine, would make the site a cool place to be for its target audience – 18 to 40 years old, time-starved, fashion-conscious, urban and educated.

Through a global presence and heavy promotion of the brand, we expected to build up a large customer base with a rapidity never achieved by a new company before. Our business model depended upon a 'big bang' rate of growth that the worldwide reach of the internet had – for the first time in history – made possible. With a launch date in May 1999, we estimated that we would have a customer base of 500,000 by the end of the year. Once this initial momentum had been achieved, word of mouth would fuel the company's continuing growth. The successful implementation of boo.com's business model would demonstrate that, contrary to the famous old saying, with modern technology at your disposal you *could* build Rome in a day.

J.P. Morgan helped us to construct an advanced financial model into which we could feed assumptions concerning the business – the number of customers, the logistics and handling costs, marketing expenditure, and so on. With products sold at full price, we estimated that the average value of each customer's order would be $85. The chief costs of such an order would be $40 for obtaining the product from the supplier and $12 for logistics, leaving a very large gross margin per average order of over $30. Over time, as the customer base grew, we expected to get higher discounts from our suppliers and to achieve economies of scale, increasing the margin still further. This large gross margin contrasted very favourably with the near negative gross margins of other websites – the expectation was that with it we would quickly achieve profitability.

In making our projections for the customer base, as well as the logistics and marketing costs, we were able to draw on our past experience with bokus, which provided critical reassurance to investors that our estimates were realistic. In any case, we made the financial model available to them as an Excel wordsheet so that they could check the figures for themselves. What if the average order value was only $60? What if the marketing spend was doubled? They could vary the cost assumptions, according to their own expectations, and see the effect it would have on the business.

We thought we had made a highly persuasive case. Now we had to wait to see if investors agreed.

4

THOMAS PAULMICHL WAS TRYING to get serious without being uncool about it. 'C'mon guys,' he said with a half-smile. 'You really need to rehearse this.'

We couldn't help it. Every time one of us started talking, the other two would crack up. There was just something a bit ridiculous about pretending to give a presentation to an empty room. It didn't help that everything had been so carefully scripted. The success we were at last having with suppliers was largely due to the fact that we were able to be ourselves, to put across a vision in a spontaneous, passionate way that came naturally to us. We were meant to be entrepreneurs, not consultants.

But Paulmichl warned us that passion would not be enough to convince the investors. They would be very sceptical, and would go to great lengths to establish whether or not the concept was sound.

'When they ask you tough questions, you'd better know the answers,' he insisted. 'Believe me. You need the practice.'

So off we went one more time, Kajsa speaking first because of her glamorous ex-model's presence and more easily understandable accent. 'Hello. We are the founders of boo.com, the global online leisure and sportswear retailer . . .'

It was early November and the meetings with investors were to begin in a fortnight – two months later than J.P. Morgan's initial and clearly optimistic predictions. Just deciding who to approach had been a challenge for the bank. They were used to helping multinationals raise billions in debt, or to launch hostile takeover bids. But raising money for a start-up required access to the sort of investor that bankers like Paulmichl and Samer Salty didn't normally have much to do with. So they had to improvise, sifting through phone lists and badgering colleagues in foreign offices for promising contacts.

The plan was to find a credible lead investor that others would follow. A major fashion retailer, or large venture capital firm, would be perfect. A few days earlier, Paulmichl had sent out a tantalizingly brief 'teaser letter' to around forty potential investors. Our company name had been blotted out and replaced with 'X.com'. To find out more, they had to sign a strict confidentiality agreement. 'That should get them all fired up,' he said.

Since then, two VCs had already shown some interest. Even better, Salty had used his Middle East connections to arrange a meeting with SEDCO, a Saudi Arabian investment firm. But first we had to polish our sales pitch.

'You're mumbling,' Paulmichl told Kajsa, who was slouched in a chair and looking utterly uninspired. 'Don't be afraid to speak up. And try not to look down when you're talking.'

Once Kajsa had delivered some more well-worn phrases on marketing, branding and the website, she handed over to me to talk about technology, logistics and company vision.

'Delivery process to the customer is fast and cost effective,' I would say. 'Our technology is proven yet innovative . . .' It was hardly original stuff, but it made the point. My biggest problem was keeping quiet when the others were speaking. Every time Patrik or Kajsa was slow to answer a question, I jumped in to help, and, only made more flustered, they angrily told me to keep my mouth shut.

Patrik's role was clear-cut. He was the numbers guy. About the sexiest thing he got to talk about was the significant return that investors could expect on their investment. Most of his presentation was devoted to running through projections for bad debt, marketing expenses or the cost of returns. This wouldn't have bothered him a couple of months ago. But he felt that he'd evolved since then. 'Why can't I talk about the suppliers as well?' he asked.

Paulmichl weighed his words carefully. 'It's an important selling point that you each have different types of skills,' he said. 'It shows that the company has an efficient internal structure.' There was another reason, which he didn't mention. Patrik was a banker. He looked and acted like a banker. It was just easier and more believable to sell me and Kajsa as the entrepreneurs.

In any case, Patrik had quite enough to think about. While he was great at doing the crucial deals, his ability to explain the underlying logic behind our financial assumptions was shaky. Paulmichl made a point of grilling him on the sort of questions that the investors would ask.

'When will the company break even?'

Patrik looked down at his notes.

'What are your EBIT* margins?'

Patrik looked up, irritated.

I sensed a certain banker's rivalry. Patrik had always wanted to work for a Wall Street investment bank, while Paulmichl probably wished he was our partner instead of our adviser.

'How does your EBIT compare with the industry average?' Paulmichl went on.

'I'm not an accountant,' Patrik countered.

'That's why you have to remember this stuff.'

The training session ended with some general advice. 'Don't use words like "maybe" or "preliminary",' Paulmichl said. We didn't want to sound as if we were just getting started, even if we were. 'And keep mentioning bokus,' he stressed. 'That's the proof that you know how to build a business.'

Paulmichl had arranged a practice run for the following morning in front of people that he was dragging in from other parts of J.P. Morgan. 'Don't embarrass me,' he said.

'Don't worry,' I said, trying to sound reassuring. 'We'll practise this afternoon.' It never happened, of course. There were just too many other things to do.

The scene in the J.P. Morgan conference room the next morning felt a bit like a parole hearing. It was dim as usual, not helped by the gloomy winter weather outside. On the other side of a long, oval table sat seven bankers – five men and two women – who watched us come in with amused curiosity. The fact that they were here to

---

* Earnings before interest and tax

judge us, and were all roughly our own age, made me feel instantly self-conscious.

Paulmichl made quick introductions, then tried to psyche us up a little. These people weren't bankers, he said. They were investors. Important ones. Without their money, our company might not get off the ground.

I sensed that he was as uncomfortable as we were.

'Hello,' Kajsa began. 'We are the founders of boo.com . . .'

'Should we be standing up?' Patrik interrupted.

'I'm not getting up,' Kajsa said, almost challenging someone to make her.

'Let's just keep going,' said Paulmichl, a hint of anxiety creeping into his voice.

Kajsa continued in a wooden, lethargic tone, looking down at the table instead of up at the 'investors'. I took over and raced away until, halfway through, I noticed Paulmichl mouthing the words 'Slow down'. Patrik started well, but then mixed up some of the numbers and forgot where he was in the presentation. He scowled at me as I leaned over to help.

The question and answer session went a little more smoothly. Our responses were quicker and more enthusiastic. But we had trouble remembering which questions each of us was supposed to be answering and kept talking over each other.

When it was over and the bankers had left, Paulmichl sank heavily into one of the chairs with a defeated look.

'I guess we didn't get the money,' I said.

He shook his head. 'I'm afraid not.'

It's a basic rule of the prudent investor always to visit a company's office before giving them any money. By taking a tour, an investor can see staff at work and get a feel for the business and its management. It's like doing a survey on a house: it might look great from the outside but still have leaks in the roof. So J.P. Morgan stressed the importance of us finding premises, as well as staff, as quickly as possible to provide the necessary reassurance.

Patrik would have liked our office to be in Mayfair, with its gentlemen's clubs and luxury hotels. But Kajsa and I insisted on Soho – the media, advertising and creative heart of London. This wasn't just a style statement, but an important part of making boo.com an attractive company to work for. After all, we were expecting talented people to leave secure, well-paid jobs to work for three unknown Swedes on a start-up. Briefly we had moved into offices in Brewer Street early in September, only to have to move out again two weeks later when the building was flooded.

Our recruitment efforts had begun as far back as late July, just after J.P. Morgan had come on board. Kajsa, after doing a bit of research, had lined up a meeting with Heidrick & Struggles. This was the prestigious headhunting firm IBM had turned to in 1993 when it needed a new CEO to steer it out of multibillion-dollar losses. It was vital that we fill the key senior positions that would help us to build the company. Critical among these were a merchandise buyer and a chief technology officer.

Anthony Harling, a senior partner, was intrigued but cautious when we showed up at the firm's smart office on Piccadilly, and only agreed to work with us after questioning J.P. Morgan about our prospects. Heidrick & Struggles had worked with a few start-ups in Silicon Valley, but the internet hadn't taken hold in Europe yet and he warned us that finding top staff wouldn't be easy: 'You're asking people to bet their careers on something that's very uncertain.' Nor would it be cheap. The agency's fee was a third of each successful candidate's hefty salary plus expenses. As we were still drawing on our own private funds it was a daunting commitment, but, as with our website prototype, we knew that filling these two appointments would help to persuade investors that we were serious.

The three of us also began to think of ways of easing our own escalating workload. I'd read about 'executive assistants' in a magazine. 'Politicians use them,' I explained to the others. They weren't secretaries, but smart, energetic 20 – 35-year-olds who could write speeches, handle paperwork and go to important meetings on our behalf. A lot of CEOs started their careers as executive assistants.

Harling couldn't help us here. The fees weren't big enough. But he steered us towards Judith Osborne, a headhunter who specialized in 'bright young things'. For months she had been fielding calls at her small recruitment agency from young people wanting internet-related jobs. They could see what was happening in the US and couldn't understand why Europe was so far behind.

The candidates that Osborne sent to meet us were firmly in this camp. We interviewed them in late September in the bar of the Metropolitan Hotel on Park Lane, where Kajsa and Patrik were staying. The 'members only' Met Bar, with its reputation as a hang-out for celebrities, was so exclusive that people had been known to book a room just to be able to get inside. The candidates had been told only that we were founders of a global internet start-up, but this choice of venue must have made it clear that we weren't in the used car or office supplies business.

If Charlotte Neser was impressed by her surroundings, she was far too level-headed to show it. She was a 26-year-old graduate from Oxford University, with a degree in theology. She had chosen the subject because of its cultural importance and the wide range of disciplines on which it drew – from history and literature to anthropology. She was an all-rounder who seemed to thrive on new challenges. Her commercial acumen was also obvious. At Oxford, she had been business manager of *Isis*, the university magazine, and, elected by the Student Union in 1992 to organize the Freshers' Fair, had been the first undergraduate in nine hundred years to make a profit out of the event. The breadth of her subsequent work experience was impressive. For the past year and a half she had been a strategic planner for an advertising agency, Ammirati Puris Lintas, and before that she had worked for the management consultancy Kalchas. She had a certain English reserve, but was articulate and spoke with warmth and enthusiasm. Dressed, as Judith Osborne put it in her appraisal, 'in the obligatory black of anyone who works in the media in London's Soho', she was slim, blonde and very attractive.

For the position of my executive assistant, I had to choose between Charlotte and the next candidate, a tall and disarmingly earnest 24-year-old named Edward Griffith. A rampant over-achiever, Edward was a gifted public speaker, a nationally ranked bridge player and one-time captain of his college boat club. He had studied theoretical physics at Cambridge, before changing courses in his third year to take a first-class degree in management studies. After completing a thesis that examined how the internet would affect the democratic process, he had worked for six months at the Xerox Research Plant in Cambridge co-ordinating an international research project on the application of new internet technologies. When we met him, he was a rising star in the technology practice of Boston Consulting Group, who were so eager to keep him that they offered to finance his MBA in either New York or San Francisco. His irrepressible manner and fierce intelligence could make him seem a little arrogant. As he bombarded me with questions about X.com and the role I envisaged for him, I couldn't help feeling that it was he who was interviewing me. He was something of a wild horse, although I had no doubt that he could be broken in.

On paper there was very little between the two candidates and at first I decided in favour of Charlotte. Judith Osborne, who had recommended her as more suitable, thought that with her quiet, firm manner she would complement my personality extremely well, but I couldn't deny that my choice was also influenced by the way she looked. I changed my mind only after talking the appointment through with Kajsa. There was no knowing where it could lead, she warned, and as CEO it was vital for me to keep a cool head. 'You've got to be professional about this.' So finally I chose Edward.

Even so, Charlotte was far too impressive a candidate to turn down, and I persuaded Patrik to hire her instead. I felt a little sorry for her as Patrik quizzed her on financial models and spreadsheets, but she had set her heart on joining the company and was prepared to pay the price.

In some ways, Martin Bartle, who would become Kajsa's executive assistant, was the odd one out. At 29 he was older than the others, with a psychology degree from the less prestigious London Guildhall University. But he'd been loosely involved with the internet for a few years by this point, working as marketing director for Delve, a small London-based website design agency. These were skills that Kajsa thought would come in handy.

The three started work in mid-November on generous, but not excessive, salaries of £40,000. We were shocked by how high the salaries of young graduates were in England. Judith Osborne was pushing us to give them far more, but we insisted that they had to take it or leave it. This would be an experience of a lifetime for them, I thought – ten times more useful than an MBA. Maybe they ought to be paying us.

The issue of share options was a bit more complicated. It was a Silicon Valley concept that we weren't too enthusiastic about, but the rapid growth of the internet meant that we had to offer such options if we were to be competitive. In the end, we set aside only 4.2 per cent of the company to parcel out among key staff over the next year. Our three new hires got 0.1 per cent each. 'This company is going to be worth a billion dollars by the time we do the IPO,' Patrik observed. 'They'll still be rich.'

For the first two weeks our new recruits had no office to go to, although they would hardly have had a chance to settle into one even if they had. Right from the start, they were all making constant trips abroad. Edward and Martin spent their first weekend in Stockholm, giving a presentation to fifty Ericsson staff, while Charlotte flew to Boston to lead a gruelling series of meetings with suppliers that had their headquarters in the area.

'Do you work hard?' I had asked Edward in his interview. 'Of course,' he scoffed. No one worked harder than a BCG consultant. But on a flight with me a few weeks later he admitted that boo.com was far tougher than he had expected. 'It's like basic training in the army,' he joked. He was astonished by how my pursuit of a vision could totally dispel any conventional notion of 'time off', and doubted whether he himself could sustain such a pace for more than a year or so without some sort of a break or significant time with family and friends. Being an entrepreneur, he began to realize, was a way of life that had to be lived and breathed around the clock.

When we were in London, we would meet for breakfast at the Meridien Hotel and then disperse to J.P. Morgan or various cafés across Soho, keeping in touch with our identical hands-free, Nokia mobile phones. Dress code was casual but chic, as Edward discovered when he turned up for his first day in a Marks & Spencer suit and a typical consultant's tie. We ribbed him mercilessly and the tie quickly disappeared into a pocket. When he turned up the next morning in a check shirt and a pair of chinos looking as if he had woken up in a bin, I knew I had to have a serious word with him about fashion. 'If in doubt,' I told him, 'dress in black.'

At last in early December we found another Soho office, this time on the legendary but now slightly faded Carnaby Street. The fashion boutiques had been overrun by souvenir shops and tourists with Union Jack T-shirts, but this British icon had never quite lost touch with its swinging past. We moved in with a few flat-packed Ikea desks and four Toshiba laptops that Ericsson had sold us. The six of us managed to occupy only a tiny corner of the 2,500 square-foot open-plan floor. But I knew it wouldn't take long to fill it up once the money started coming in.

Kajsa was a dangerous woman. At least, that's what the Saudi Arabian consulate seemed to be saying.

'They just aren't going to give a visa to a single woman,' Salty said.

'Isn't there anything we can do?' I asked.

'They'll only let her in if she travels with her father or brother.'

'I don't think we're going to be able to arrange that any time soon.'

Salty shrugged. 'Well, she can't go, then.'

It was mid-November and in just a few days we were supposed to be travelling to Saudi Arabia to meet SEDCO, the investment firm. This would be our first encounter with investors and Kajsa had been keen to go along. If nothing else, she was looking forward to the adventure. The sudden twist of events had thrown us all off balance. Of course, we knew that Saudi Arabia wasn't exactly a haven for feminists. Women couldn't even drive there. But this was a business trip – a quick one at that – and it was hard to believe there was nothing we could do.

'We've got some contacts at the embassy,' Salty told us. 'But they can't bend the rules on something like this.' Patrik and I had to decide whether we should still go.

Salty pleaded. 'It means a lot to these people that you make the effort to visit them,' he said. 'It'll be worth it.'

In the end, we relented. 'We'll tell you all about it,' I promised Kajsa.

SEDCO, one of the biggest investment companies in Saudi Arabia, was owned by members of the hugely wealthy and well-connected bin Mahfouz family. The family's interests ranged from banking to construction and oil exploration. A few months earlier, SEDCO had created a new fund to make direct investments in technology companies. It had asked J.P. Morgan for advice at almost the exact moment that the bank took us on as clients. 'This is a really exciting project,' Salty had told them. 'I can get you in on the ground floor.' The Saudis were so eager, Salty told us, that at one point they wanted to give us the entire $15 million for the first round.

We landed in Jedda around 9 p.m. after a zigzag journey that took us from London to Frankfurt, where we stopped off to hammer out final terms with Deutsche Post on our logistics, and then on to Cairo, where we changed planes for the final leg. No alcohol was served on this flight, I noticed.

Jedda, on the Red Sea coast, was a world away from the bustling chaos of Cairo. Everything was white. The streets were clean and quiet, and the air was filled with unfamiliar musky smells. Salty who had come on an earlier flight, was already asleep when we arrived at the Intercontinental Hotel. Patrik and I, although tired as well, sat down for a late dinner and chatted with the hotel porter, who, bizarrely, spoke fluent Swedish. He had studied technology at university in Stockholm.

It was shimmeringly bright and desert-hot when the three of us emerged the next morning and went looking for a cab. Not bad for November, I thought, as I glanced across at Patrik dressed for an English winter in a dark wool suit. As we drove to SEDCO headquarters, Salty gave us a quick rundown on the people we were about to meet. 'Their clothes might be a bit unusual but these are all very bright guys,' he stressed. Our chief contact was Dr Adnan Soufi, who, like a lot of Arab businessmen, was foreign-educated, with a Ph.D. from Georgetown University in Washington.

There were almost a dozen people in the small, featureless room. It felt like half the company had showed up for the occasion. All wore traditional white Saudi *robes* and, on their heads, red-and-white checked *gutras*. On the table in front of us sat a lot of tiny cups and an ornately decorated Arabian teapot.

In respectful silence the SEDCO group listened as Patrik and I went through the presentation. Every thirty seconds or so we broke off to take little sips of tea to ease our dehydration. Our performance was stilted if word perfect; everyone seemed impressed.

'I think a website like this would be very successful in Saudi,' one said. 'People here are very fashion-conscious.'

I was surprised, as all I had seen so far were lots of robes. It wasn't until later that Salty filled me in. 'They can wear anything they want inside their own homes,' he said. 'It's like a secret world.'

Our most unexpected supporter turned out to be SEDCO's religious expert. It was his job to screen all new investments in accordance with Islamic law. We sailed through on most counts. boo wouldn't be selling 'sin' products like alcohol or tobacco, and, being a start-up, didn't have any debt. Islamic law forbids investing in companies with loans amounting to more than a third of their assets. He had only one concern.

'How are women going to be presented on the website?' he asked. 'We can't invest in a company that encourages promiscuity.'

Salty nodded gravely. 'Of course not,' he said. 'I'm sure we can agree to a few guidelines.'

After the meeting, Dr Soufi offered to take us out for dinner that night. In the meantime, I went with Patrik and Salty to the huge Souk Al-Alawi. Salty bought a robe each for Patrik and me and a heavy black cloak for Kajsa. 'She'll love this,' he said, with a dry smile.

Back in the hotel, recovering slightly from the heat, I gave Kajsa a call. She had just come out of a meeting with Jerry Fielder at Leagas Delaney and was in a sour mood. They had been having creative differences about the look of our prototype. 'They've got some really old-fashioned ideas,' she said. I tried to sympathize, but wasn't really listening. 'I wish you'd been here,' I told her. 'It was just like the *Arabian Nights*.'

No business was discussed in the restaurant that night, but it was a memorable experience all the same. As we sat on a vast terrace that overlooked the Red Sea, Soufi talked freely about life in Jedda. It was more cosmopolitan than other Saudi cities, he explained. Tourism may have been forbidden, but each year millions of pilgrims poured through on their way to the holy cities of Mecca and Medina.

As the evening wore on, I turned to more worldly matters. On the table were bottles of water and various fruit drinks, but not a drop of alcohol in sight. 'What do people drink when they want to cele-brate?' I asked.

Dr Soufi smiled conspiratorially, took my glass and carefully filled it with equal measures of Perrier and apple juice. 'Saudi champagne,' he said.

If the bankers had been excited when they first began to work with us, they were now practically bouncing off the walls. It was late November and internet shares were taking off. Amazon.com had just soared 72 per cent in one week and analysts were advising all their clients to buy. Henry Blodget, an analyst at CIBC Oppenheimer in the US, captured the mood in an article in the *Seattle Times*. 'It's going nuts,' he said, referring to Amazon. 'It's hard to say where or when it will stop.' Salty, who had set up a chart on his computer to track the gains, kept a running commentary going for the other bankers. 'It's up another 5 per cent!' he'd yell. Teaming up with boo was beginning to look like a master stroke. No other investment bank in Europe had anything to match it.

SEDCO, brimming with enthusiasm after our visit, quickly sent us a 'due diligence' list of questions to be answered. 'Please provide details and an assessment of Ericsson's current progress to date,' they asked. We did better than that. We set up a video conference call with Ericsson, who showed off their technical wizardry by patching in staff from around the world. But SEDCO were under no illusions about their knowledge of the internet sector. They wanted us to find a lead investor – someone they could follow – before handing over any money.

So in the weeks leading up to Christmas Salty lined up a back-breaking tour of investment companies, which included a wide range of VCs as well as more strategic investors who could help us with their retail and brand experience. Top of our list was Louis Vuitton Moët Hennessy, the French fashion and luxury goods giant, whose collection of prestige brands ranged from Christian Dior, Givenchy and Guérlain to Krug and Veuve Clicquot. With LVMH behind us, we'd have easy access to hot young designers like John Galliano, Alexander McQueen and Marc Jacobs.

In normal circumstances it might have been difficult for us to get the attention of a company like LVMH, but its controlling shareholder, the billionaire Bernard Arnault, was passionate about the internet. On his frequent trips to the US, he had seen at first hand the impact this new medium was having on traditional retailers. Like us, he knew it was only a matter of time before the e-tailing craze hit Europe. For almost a year now he had been making small, but lucrative investments in US dot.coms like eBay and Webvan. Helping him scout for deals was Jean-Bernard Tellio, a suave, fast-talking, former curator of the famed Centre Pompidou in Paris. We met him at LVMH headquarters near the Arc de Triomphe shortly after our return from Jedda. The dozen or so investments he had already made on Arnault's behalf, he told us, made him just about the most experienced internet investor in Europe. During our presentation he chain-smoked Marlboro Lights and often had to break off to attend to one urgent matter or another, but he was clearly interested in what we showed him. 'If internet companies are going to work in Europe they're going to have to connect with the local culture,' he said. 'You've obviously thought that through.' With an anxious look at his watch, he then brought our brief meeting to a close. 'I'll get back to you.'

As our tour continued, we began to see a lot of VCs. Our attitude to these sorts of investor had been shaped by lessons learned from bokus. With their practical knowledge of working with new companies, we knew that a good one that had internet experience, could really help us to build the business. But we didn't trust them not to try to run the company. So in the expectation that VCs would be clamouring to invest we had asked Skadden Arps to draw up a shareholder agreement that would protect our control of the board. But we had been over-optimistic. European VCs, unlike their American counterparts, were still uncomfortable about investing in companies that didn't present an immediate prospect of making money. The idea of investing now in the hope of profits later meant overhauling age-old guidelines, and they weren't prepared to make that leap of faith. Some of the companies Salty contacted, like 3i, the biggest of all British VCs, didn't even want to meet us. 'We're not sure about e-commerce,' one of its partners explained. 'It just isn't the right time.'

The few VCs we did meet seemed wary and unenthusiastic. Their attitude was understandable but deeply irritating, and matters finally came to a head in late November, at a meeting with a British VC firm backed by Austrian money. Kajsa and Patrik were busy, so Salty and I attended the meeting at J.P. Morgan's offices with Charlotte Neser. It went badly from the start. A sharp-tongued Austrian woman went through a list of conditions that seemed to go on for ever. She had an opinion about everything. No aspect of our business escaped her carping words. I felt the blood rush to my head. She reminded me of one of my old spinsterly schoolteachers. These were the sorts of people, I knew, who would ruin our company if we let them.

'Samer, I need to speak to you outside,' I said.

In the hallway, I let fly. 'What a bitch. Just get rid of them.'

Salty's expression was a mix of shock and amusement. 'Aren't you coming back in?' he said, breaking into one of his huge grins.

'No. I can't work with these people. Tell them we aren't interested.'

Some promising news soon made up for the lack of progress with the VCs. 'I think Benetton is interested,' Paulmichl told us with unconcealed awe.

J.P. Morgan's Milan office had close ties to the Benetton family. A few weeks earlier, the bank had tried to orchestrate a joint venture between 21Investimenti, an investment firm majority-owned by the Benettons, and MTV in Italy. Alessandro Benetton, the young chairman of 21Investimenti, had dismissed the plan, but encouraged the bankers to keep the ideas flowing. When they mentioned boo, the reaction was extremely positive. The Benetton Group, in which most of the family's fashion interests were contained, was feeling the same pressure as other 'bricks and mortar' businesses to come up with an e-commerce strategy. So far, all it had done was to hold a few internet workshops with American universities. But now boo seemed to offer the prospect of an invaluable learning experience.

The attractions of a Benetton partnership for us were huge. It had global retailing experience, knew the fashion industry and had a flair for promotion that we hugely admired. 'Imagine if we could get Toscani to help with the marketing?' Kajsa said, hardly daring to pursue this wonderful dream. Oliviero Toscani was a photographic legend. His images – the dying AIDS victim; the black woman breastfeeding a white baby – had turned Benetton into one of the world's best-known brands.

But before we could have an audience with the Benettons or Toscani, Paumichl told us, we would have to pitch to Vito Gamberale, a board director of 21Investimenti – himself a powerful Italian business figure whose previous job had been running Telecom Italia Mobile, Italy's biggest mobile-phone network.

We met him at J.P. Morgan's Milan office in early December. Accompanying us were Paulmichl – who, as an Italian, seemed acutely conscious of the significance of this meeting – Samer Salty and two elegantly dressed bankers from the Milan office.

Gamberale, stocky, with grey hair and thick glasses, was casually charming in a way that suggested he was comfortable with his own authority. As we began our presentation, an aide loudly translated everything for him into Italian, and every now and then he interrupted our scripted performance with questions delivered in slow, gravel-voiced Italian. But he obviously liked what he heard. When we mentioned Ericsson, his eyes lit up.

'Mr Gamberale has done a lot of work with Ericsson,' the aide explained.

Our marketing strategy also found favour with him. 'Bene, bene,' he mumbled, as Kajsa ran through our plans for a $30 million global advertising spend.

The formalities over, we all sat down for a buffet dinner. Then Gamberale and the bankers retired into a side room to talk business while the three of us lingered awkwardly in the dining room. I felt a bit like a sports star waiting for my agent to negotiate a million-dollar contract.

'What do you think of this Gamberale guy?' Kajsa whispered, pouring herself a glass of wine.

'He looks like Don Corleone,' I replied.

Paulmichl joined us in the room half an hour later, looking immensely pleased with himself. 'He's going to speak to the

Benettons,' he said. 'He's actually talking about doing something more ambitious. Some kind of co-operation.'

'What does that mean?' I asked.

'I don't know exactly. But he obviously likes you.'

'So what next?'

'He's going to get back to us in a few days. We can't rush him. This is Italy.'

It was still early and the good news had put me in the mood for a drink. 'Who wants to go out?' I asked, only dimly aware that we were supposed to meet some German VCs in Munich the next day. Most of the bankers declined, making vague excuses about families and early starts. But Leopoldo Zambeletti, impossibly cool in his tailor-made black suit and tortoiseshell glasses, agreed to join us. Of all the bankers, he had the most obvious sense of style and was one of the few people we'd met who really appreciated what we were trying to do from a fashion perspective. As we drank vodka-tonics in the poky Café Vittoria, he promised to help as much as he could. 'I know the CEO of Prada. I can introduce you to him if you want.' Like the other bankers, he also seemed eager to learn. 'I am thinking about starting an internet company,' he admitted shyly.

At around three in the morning, when the bar closed, the four of us moved on to Plastic, a smoky transvestite club. It was almost dawn when we stumbled back to the hotel. Even in my drunken haze I sensed that the coming day would not be easy.

Our flight to Munich was at about 11 a.m. Dazed after the night before, Kajsa and I met in the hotel lobby with only an hour to spare. We jumped into a cab and raced off to the airport, assuming that Patrik was already on his way. But there was no sign of him.

The call came to board the plane. We decided to wait by the exit as long as we could, but soon after the last few people had straggled by we finally had to board. Flight control delays meant that we had to wait in the plane for another half an hour or so before taxiing out to the runway. Then just as the pilot was given the all-clear, there was one more delay – this time for Patrik.

Bleary-eyed and dishevelled, he came marching up the aisle, laden with luggage that there wasn't time to put in the hold. Out of breath, he sat down heavily in the seat next to us. 'Thanks for waiting for me,' he said sarcastically. 'You're really great partners.'

Our meeting with the executives of the German VC firm TVM did not go well. We met Thomas Paulmichl and Felix von Schubert outside TVM's offices. Von Schubert, who had flown in from London to act as our cultural go-between, might as well not have bothered. Battling with our headaches, we struggled to appear alert. Patrik, pale and unshaven, mumbled his way through the presentation and, still smelling slightly of alcohol, looked as if he might fall asleep at any moment. Friedrich von Freyberg, a former Siemens executive, watched our performance with clinical detachment and then, on behalf of his colleagues, thanked us for our time and showed us the door.

The J.P. Morgan bankers made no attempt to hide their anger. 'You can't behave like this in Germany,' von Schubert said. It wasn't until much later in the afternoon that they could bring themselves to speak to us again.

Paulmichl had got a call from the Milan office. 'The Benettons want to meet you in early January,' he said. 'It's amazing. Everyone's going to be there.' We were to meet Luciano Benetton, the family patriarch, his son Alessandro, and even the great Toscani. 'It's really unusual to get them all together like this,' Paulmichl stressed. But this time, he warned us, we'd have to act like professionals. 'You'll fly to Venice the night before. You'll have a quiet dinner. And then you'll go to bed.'

In December, after a long search, we hired a chief technology officer, although he couldn't start working for us until after Christmas. 'Don't worry,' Anthony Harling of Heidrick & Struggles had told us. 'Sometimes you've got to kiss a lot of frogs to get the prince.' In the end, we found our own 'prince'.

Steve Bennett was the European head of e-business research and development at Hewlett Packard. We'd first met him when HP pitched to build our website in late September. Bennett had promised to deliver a fully functional version within three to four months, faster than anyone else. By this time we were already leaning towards

Ericsson, but we had been impressed by Bennett, who had the sort of hands-on experience of the internet that was then hard to find in Europe. Earlier in the year, he had built the France 98 World Cup site. He had overall responsibility for designing, building and operating the site in three months. A team of forty people, based in four countries, reported to him. The site had held up under a massive volume of hits from fans around the world, and also incorporated a retailing operation that allowed visitors to buy official merchandise online.

He seemed the perfect CTO candidate. With his experience and Ericsson's clout, we'd have a formidable combination. As a precaution, I asked Harling to meet Bennett as well. His verdict was a resounding thumbs-up. 'He seems to have everything.'

Bennett, who was in his early forties and had long fair hair, did not look like a typical chief technology officer. Modest and unassuming, he lived with his wife and two children on a farm in Wales, together with 120 sheep, two horses and a dog. Patrik, Edward and I took him out to lunch at the Circus restaurant, near our office in Soho, to make our offer.

'It sounds really exciting,' he said, 'but I'll have to talk to my wife.' Over the next few days it became clear that his wife wasn't overjoyed about moving to the big city. A deal was eventually struck, but only after much haggling. We would allow Bennett to spend at least a couple of days a week on his farm. On top of his £100,000 annual salary, we would cover the cost of a flat in central London and equip him with a new Land Rover Discovery. It was an expensive exercise, especially since Kajsa, Patrik and I were still paying for everything out of our own pockets.

Although Bennett couldn't officially start work for us until the New Year, he agreed to look at the details of Ericsson's feasibility study, which was now nearing completion. I was especially interested in his opinion, because I was beginning to have doubts about Ericsson.

The relationship had started off well. Amost immediately after agreeing payment terms, Ericsson had pulled together forty people from different parts of the company and divided them into seven separate teams to focus on the key elements of our platform. The aim of the study was partly to identify which technology suppliers we should hire. As one team met with experts in website design, others were talking to suppliers of e-commerce engines, logistic systems and specialists in 3D imaging. Mostly, we left them to it, but as time went by, a few worrying reports had started to come in. In mid-November, Edward and Tony Barsham had returned from a meeting with Ericsson staff looking uneasy.

'They seem really unorganized,' Edward said. When he'd asked a project leader about ERP systems – crucial adminstrative software for managing finances, inventory and logistics – the man had been unable to answer his question and instead simply handed over a pile of glossy marketing pamphlets from ERP suppliers.

At my request, Steve Bennett agreed to join me, Kajsa and Patrik for two days of technical workshops at the Ericsson complex in Stockholm although he wasn't formally due to start work for us yet. In addition to Ericsson's own staff, there were representatives from each of the tech companies whose equipment Ericsson was planning to use. We found the sheer number of people disconcerting. While some were clearly top notch, others looked like they'd just come out of school.

Bennett was unimpressed. 'They're using way too many people,' he said, 'and not all of them know what they're doing.'

When we got back to London, I raised these concerns with Ann-Catrine Appelquist, Ericsson's project leader. 'Some of these people seem really junior,' I said.

'This is a complicated project,' she replied. 'If we don't have lots of people, we won't finish in time.' But she also admitted that our project was an opportunity to educate junior staff. 'Don't worry,' she said. 'We won't charge you for all of them.'

It was Christmas and, from our office window, I could see the glow from the lights on Regent Street. Soho had been in a permanent state of drunkenness for the past two weeks. By lunchtime each day, the pubs were bursting with advertising and media people, most of whom were still there when we finished work late in the evenings.

As a reward for all their hard work and loyalty, we bought each of our executive assistants membership to Home House, a private club and bar that had opened a couple of months ago in Portman Square, near Hyde Park Corner.

By now, Leagas Delaney's technical division, Media Direction, had managed to produce a prototype of our website, a vital tool with which to attract both suppliers and investors. It had been a difficult and often painful process. Their first attempt had been awful. When the demonstration began, on a laptop in Fielder's office, our faces dropped. The design looked cheap and had a futuristic, digital feel, although we'd asked for a retro style.

Kajsa was so upset that she had wanted to fire Leagas Delaney on the spot. A heated argument with Jerry Fielder followed. 'Forget it,' Fielder snapped. 'We won't be fired by you. If anyone does any firing around here it'll be us.' And when everyone had calmed down, we agreed to give them another chance. This time the results were stunning.

The homepage featured a series of white concentric oval rings against a black background in a Sixties style. In the very centre was our name, boo.com. The dot blinked slowly on and off, as if everything else on the screen radiated from it. Another dot orbited continuously around the outermost oval. These two tiny bits of animation had a mesmerizing effect, somehow drawing you in to explore further.

Once inside, our virtual salesperson, the glamorous Miss Boo, was on hand to lend assistance. Wearing the headphones of a call centre assistant, she waited discreetly in a corner of the screen until a click caused her to pop up in a help box. 'I'd love to help you choose a good outfit . . .' she said in a seductive voice that sounded like Liz Hurley.

Choosing an item was not only easy but incredibly satisfying. With a click you could instantly change the colour of a shoe, or zoom in close enough to inspect its stitching. But the *pièce de résistance* was the 3D click that caused the shoe to spin right round. On another screen, you could try out your clothes on a mannequin. By clicking a male or a female symbol, you could switch between a perfectly proportioned figure that resembled Michelangelo's David and another that seemed to have been inspired by Lara Croft. To dress them, you just dragged your chosen items of clothing across. Other features included 'micro sites' that showcased individual suppliers' brands and 'boo.world', our online magazine. The overall impression was of a deliciously cool, carefully thought-out site. It was irresistible.

On Boxing Day, Charlotte Neser and I flew out to Los Angeles with our secret weapon. Our first meeting was with Gary Schoenfeld, the CEO of the sports-shoe company Vans. Charlotte had been trying to arrange a visit for weeks, but Schoenfeld was always so busy that his PA had to keep rescheduling. In the end Charlotte said that we would be in town for only three days and had to squeeze all our meetings into that period. This was much more difficult to turn down. When we arrived at Schoenfeld's office, his secretary warned us that he had another meeting in half an hour, but the feeling we had when we met him was that if we didn't catch his attention in ten seconds we might as well forget it.

It turned out to be more than enough time. From the moment he saw the homepage, he was hooked. He watched with rapt astonishment as Charlotte spun products, put them on mannequins and got Miss Boo to talk. 'Hold on a moment,' he said as he got up and opened his office door. 'Guys!' he called. 'You've got to come in and see this!' Soon there was a huddle of five or six people around his desk, all equally amazed as Charlotte showed off a few more tricks. When it was over, Schoenfeld shook his head and smiled. 'Wow,' he said. 'You could sell Florida with a demo like that.' We sold the concept to Vans on the spot. It had never been so easy.

'You sound like you're in an airport,' said Jean-Bernard Tellio of LVMH, as Charlotte and I drove to another meeting. 'No, it's just a convertible,' I shouted, cupping my hand over the receiver. Tellio wanted to meet us again. As we sped down the freeway, the wind whipping through our hair, I felt a surge of almost irrational confidence. We had momentum now and a killer application.

I got my first sight of Venice from the deck of a slow-moving taxi boat from the airport. It was early evening and the canals were lit with the amber glow of street lamps. Patrik and the bankers were arriving the next morning, but Kajsa was already waiting for me in the foyer of our hotel – the magical Gritti Palace. It was the night before our meeting with Benetton and we'd promised the bankers we wouldn't drink. But we didn't feel like sitting in the hotel all night either, so we headed out to a jazz café to talk things over. The bankers had produced a special, expanded version of our presentation, which we still weren't completely comfortable with. So, over a couple of coffees, we rehearsed it carefully and, leaving the bar well before midnight, decided to get up early in the morning to have one final run-through.

Benetton's headquarters weren't actually in Venice, but a forty-minute drive to the north in the tiny town of Ponzano. It was here that Luciano Benetton had grown up in the tough, post-war years with barely enough money for food. It was also here, in 1955, that he had sold his accordion and bought the family's first knitting machine. Almost half a century later, the Benetton family controlled a multibillion-dollar fashion and industrial empire. These were people, I felt sure, who would understand what we were trying to do.

Kajsa and I caught a taxi to Treviso airport, where we collected Patrik, Paulmichl and Salty. At a nearby café, we met Leopoldo Zambeletti and Francesco Silva, another banker from the Milan office. They made it clear that they were coming along mainly as observers.

'We're just going to introduce you,' Zambeletti said. 'It's your job to sell the story.'

After a short drive through beautiful, strikingly flat countryside, our car drew up outside a pair of gates. Looking around, all we could see were isolated farms, but we had reached the nerve centre of the Benetton empire. The centrepiece was the Villa Minelli, a gleaming white sixteenth-century mansion that had been built as a holiday home for a wealthy Venetian silk merchant. When the Benettons had bought the villa in 1969, it was on the verge of collapse. The roof had caved in and chickens wandered through its damp hallways. Now, set in lush gardens and covered with bright frescos, it was a stunning sight.

An aide ushered us in and led us up a grand staircase and into an empty meeting room. Within minutes, people started filing in. First came Carlo Gilardi, the stern-looking chief executive of Benetton

Group, then Vito Gamberale along with various advertising, marketing and communications executives. The really big guns followed: Alessandro Benetton, Oliviero Toscani, grizzled and mischievous-looking, and, last of all, Luciano Benetton himself, his round glasses and white, shoulder-length hair giving him a professorial air.

There was a fairground atmosphere in the room. The entire management team had turned out for the show. The young internet 'visionaries' they had heard so much about were here at last. We in turn were very conscious of their reputation: with an unrivalled mystique and provocative style, they had established one of the most powerful brands in the world.

More than usually nervous, we felt like pretenders at the court of the great king. But as the presentation progressed, we quickly gained confidence from the sense that they understood and appreciated our vision. Several people asked questions. Only Luciano Benetton, sitting at the head of the long wooden table, remained silent, simply looking on with an enigmatic half-smile. 'Luciano isn't the kind of guy who thumps the table,' Zambeletti had warned me beforehand. 'He lets others do the talking for him. But he's always listening.'

Most of the questions were broad and conceptual, so Patrik's memory for numbers was never really tested. The presentation ended when Kajsa picked up her laptop and put it down in front of a surprised Luciano to demonstrate the prototype. As she skipped through the homepage and began spinning clothes around, Luciano beckoned to Toscani to come and have a look. The rest of the room soon followed, gathering around Luciano's end of the table to watch this amazing display. They took turns to spin the shoe or dress the mannequin, while speaking to each other in rapid-fire Italian. When Kajsa introduced Miss Boo, they erupted in laughter.

A free-flowing discussion followed. I told Toscani about our plan for a 'cool hunter', whose job would be to seek out the latest underground trends from around the world. His eyebrows shot up. 'This is the kind of thing that young people are going to love,' he announced to the table. There was a sudden hush. God had spoken.

The only awkward moment came when we ran through the names of suppliers who had signed up. 'You have Fila?' Carlo Gilardi asked, a dark shadow crossing his face. 'We can't support a company that works with our competitors.' But the discussion quickly moved on to safer issues, such as logistics and strategies to avoid alienating retailers. They loved the prototype, but were just as impressed by the thought we had given to such behind-the-scenes details.

There was an exhilarating sense of like minds having discovered one another. After the meeting we all went to lunch, chatting together as we ambled through the grounds to a small farmhouse, where we took our places at a large oak table before an open fire. I found myself sitting between Toscani and Laura Pollini, Benetton's director of communications. Toscani, it turned out, had a Norwegian wife and knew Sweden very well. At one point I was the subject of a small mystery. 'So what do you think?' Toscani asked Pollini in Italian. 'Is he a dropout? Or was he top of the class?' 'Let's ask him,' said Pollini.

Toscani was also curious about Kajsa. 'Haven't I seen you before?' he asked. 'Were you ever a Benetton model?' Kajsa looked embarrassed. 'Uhh . . . Yes. But that was a long time ago.'

After lunch, the Benettons shook hands with us and excused themselves while Thomas Paulmichl and the Italian bankers sat down to talk business with Gamberale and Luciano Favero, another executive from 21Investimenti. Samer Salty, who couldn't speak Italian, stayed with us.

'You don't need to be involved,' said Paulmichl, flashing a triumphant little smile at Salty, who in his role as senior banker was being briefly upstaged. 'Why don't you go for a walk in the grounds?'

It was cool outside, it looked as if it might start raining soon, but the three of us didn't care. These people knew what we were trying to do and they really liked us. I was sure that something was going to come of this. The trouble was, it turned out later, they liked us too much.

Paulmichl caught up with us about an hour later. He wore a worried expression. 'OK,' he said, taking a deep breath. 'They're very interested, but they have just a few conditions.' He glanced at Salty, who gave him a cold look. 'They want to link some kind of commercial agreement to the investment. Basically, they want a guarantee that boo will sell at least some of their products.'

'We can't do that,' I said at once. A lot of suppliers had only signed up with us because we were totally independent. It was a key plank in our strategy. 'If we sell Benetton clothes, it has to be something we decide for ourselves.'

Salty agreed. 'You're right not to let them get too close,' he said. He then turned to Paulmichl. 'I hope you made this clear.'

'This is Benetton we're talking about here,' Paulmichl said, beginning to flush. 'If you want to work with a brand like that, you have to make sacrifices.'

'You're not acting for Benetton,' Salty fired back. 'The client says they don't want to do it this way and I agree.'

'Well, I don't.'

'It's not your decision, Thomas,' Salty said flatly. 'I'm more senior than you, so let's just drop it.'

There was some history to this outburst. boo was supposed to be Paulmichl's project, and he wanted to make sure it stayed that way. To make things worse, the bankers had different ideas about what J.P. Morgan's role should be. Salty's attitude was that boo had hired J.P. Morgan as a conventional adviser. It was his job to do what the client asked. Paulmichl, on the other hand, wanted to guide us in what he believed was the right direction.

Both were now fuming. I wondered if they would start throwing punches. Patrik, who had been eyeing the scene with concern, now spoke up. 'Just remember,' he said. 'We make the decisions. Not you.'

I was more amused than worried, reassuring myself with something Zambeletti had told us on our bar crawl a month ago. 'Don't expect things to go smoothly,' he'd warned. 'Doing business in Italy is always complicated.'

As we waited in awkward silence by the front gates for a cab to take us to the airport, I heard a car horn beeping and turned to look. It was Toscani, a red shawl draped elegantly across his shoulders, racing past in his white MK2 Jaguar.

Jean–Bernard Tellio looked around in astonishment. 'Do you always bring people in here?' We were in the great hall at J.P. Morgan. It was vast, capable of seating 500 people with room to spare. It echoed when we spoke.

Salty looked pleased with himself. 'All the other meeting rooms were booked,' he said. 'What can I do?'

Tellio had been almost impossible to pin down. The two meetings we'd had with him so far had been hurried, breathless occasions. He was always rushing to get somewhere. Now at last he had managed to set aside a couple of hours for a due diligence session that would determine whether LVMH would invest.

We wanted this badly. Getting LVMH would be a huge boost to our credibility and a spur for other investors, including our Arab friends at SEDCO, to pile in behind. To bolster our pitch, we had brought along Tony Barsham, who gave a detailed rundown of the progress we had made with suppliers, and Jerry Fielder who explained our branding and marketing strategy.

Tellio continued to take calls on his mobile, which rang every few minutes, but, in between snatched conversations, he took in what we said with a ferret-like intensity, especially when the subject turned to money. We wanted to raise $15 million at a pre-money valuation of $35 million – the value that we put on our company before any money had been raised. By contrast, the post-money valuation, would combine that $35 million with any money we actually did raise. If we were successful in raising $15 million, for example, boo's post-money valuation would be $50 million.

When we'd finished, Tellio grilled us with incisive questions about everything from logistics to management structure. 'If this company does really well and grows into something big,' he said, 'you'll probably have to bring in a stronger management team. Maybe even a CEO.'

'Sure,' I replied, figuring that if we got someone to manage the day-to-day affairs, I could focus on more important stuff.

Tellio seemed satisfied with the way the meeting had gone, but as usual didn't have the time to hang around. 'I'll call you,' he said, getting up to leave.

'How long do you think it will take?' Kajsa asked.

Tellio gave a little Gallic shrug. 'You have to understand that I don't make the decisions.' Each month, he explained, he simply presented a list of possible investments to his billionaire boss. 'Arnault is very hands on. It's his call.'

'Sure. But what do *you* think?' Patrik asked.

'I think the valuation is very high,' Tellio said bluntly. 'But that's just my opinion.'

His opinion turned out to be the key factor in our negotiations over the next week and a half. At first, it looked as if everything was going to work out. 'We're interested,' Tellio told Salty a couple of days after the meeting. But just as we were starting to celebrate, Salty got an email that turned everything upside down again. 'I'm sorry,' Tellio wote. 'I've spoken to Arnault. He thinks it's too expensive.'

We weren't sure if this was for real or just a shrewd negotiating tactic. If it was, it worked.

'We have to see him in Paris,' I said to Salty. 'We have to solve this somehow.' But Tellio had disappeared again. His phone was turned off and he didn't return calls. Two days later he rang back and reluctantly agreed to see us. We found him in a bar near the LVMH office, drinking Perrier and looking slightly uncomfortable at the prospect of a confrontation. I needed something stronger than mineral water, so I ordered a vodka and grapefruit juice as Kajsa laid out for him one more time the progress we had made so far. 'We're this close,' she said, pinching her fingers together. Tellio was apologetic. 'I just don't think we're ready to do this yet,' he said.

'We're willing to negotiate,' Salty said.

Tellio sighed. 'This isn't a democracy,' he replied. 'I can't tell Arnault what to do.' He left this hanging in the air for a second. Then his expression softened a little. 'Let's talk tomorrow. I'll see what I can do.'

We returned to London and waited anxiously for news. It was late in the following afternoon when Salty called the three of us to his office. He looked tired. 'OK. This is the deal. He wants a discount for being the lead investor.' This seemed fair enough. LVMH was a prestigious name whose support would guarantee our reputation in the market. Tellio wanted a 10 per cent stake for $3.8 million, instead of the $5 million we were asking. More importantly, he wanted a 25 per cent discount for investing in the next funding round. This meant that if boo's pre-money valuation was $100 million, LVMH could buy shares at a level of $75 million. Tellio had us. He knew that Benetton wasn't ready to sign yet. And he knew we were running out of time.

'OK. Let's do it then,' I said, feeling a huge surge of relief. Kajsa and Patrik agreed, although he was a bit disappointed at the slight cut in our valuation. 'Maybe we can make some of the other investors pay more,' he said.

Paulmichl, having joined us in the room, had a suggestion. 'Why don't you get SEDCO to pay extra?' he asked Salty.

'That's not exactly fair,' Salty said. 'They were in at the start.'

'Yeah. But they don't bring anything to the table apart from money.'

Paulmichl had a point. We also knew that the Saudis were hungry to get in, and LVMH was just the sort of lead investor they had been looking for. They would probably be happy to put up a little bit more.

'All right,' Salty said, bowing to the pressure. 'I'll give it a try.'

The slight unease we'd felt about Benetton was growing. After our meeting at Villa Minelli, Vito Gamberale had put in a call to Ann-Catrine Appelquist at Ericsson, asking what she thought of us. This was dangerous territory. Because of our slow progress in raising money, we still hadn't paid Ericsson a penny and they were starting to get annoyed.

Appelquist, to her credit, had stood up for us. 'I believe in these young people,' she told Gamberale. But when he called again a few days later to request a formal meeting, she decided to ring me first. 'What do you want me to do?' she asked. I was shocked. Both Benetton and Ericsson were bound by confidentiality agreements. They weren't supposed to be talking at all. Paulmichl immediately rang Benetton to complain, but all he got was a flat denial. 'You better be very careful about making accusations . . .'

We tried to brush it off. But there was something claustrophobic about Benetton's attentions. In mid-January, a couple of days after reaching an informal agreement with LVMH, two representatives from Benetton's internal advertising agency, United Colors Communications, flew in to meet with us at J.P. Morgan. There had been some vague suggestion that Benetton could help somehow with our marketing. But it seemed they now had bigger plans. They wanted to do all our media buying and produce our ads. The pitch they gave us included examples of previous Benetton and Telecom Italia Mobile campaigns, including one that featured a semi-naked woman. 'SEDCO won't like that,' Salty observed. But there were more important reasons why we couldn't let Benetton do our ads. We already had an ad agency, Leagas Delaney, and in any case Kajsa was uncomfortable about one of our investors handling our ad campaign.

'I think this is a really bad idea,' she said, after the meeting was over.

'It would be much better if we could just have Toscani on the board as a consultant.' We welcomed Benetton's advice and support, but we didn't want them running our company.

Paulmichl seemed disappointed. He was still convinced that we should go along with almost anything Benetton asked. But he agreed to speak with them and explain our concerns. It didn't go down well.

'I think they're taking it as a brush-off,' he said, after speaking with Luciano Favero at 21 Investimenti.

'So what do we do now?' I asked. 'Maybe we should see them again.' If it had worked with LVMH, maybe it would work with Benetton as well.

Paulmichl seemed dubious. 'No. Let's save that until we really have to.'

His idea was to write a 'side letter' – a non-legally-binding statement of goodwill. Side letters, he told us, were a way to smooth over potentially deal-breaking problems without actually committing yourself to anything. The letter we sent explained that we wanted Benetton as an investor, but decisions about any relationship beyond that – whether in advertising or selling Benetton products through our website – could only be made on commercial grounds. At the same time, it stressed the importance of the relationship to us and our desire for a close partnership, within reason.

'I hope this doesn't make things worse,' Paulmichl said, as he slipped the letter into the fax machine.

It was 5.20 a.m and the phone was ringing beside my bed in the SoHo Grand in New York. 'Hello,' I croaked, my throat dry from having left the air conditioning on all night. It was Kajsa, calling from London. She was speaking so quickly it took a few seconds for her words to register. 'I said LVMH is out,' she repeated.

'What do you mean?'

'They've changed their mind.'

'What does he want this time?' I asked, sitting up in bed. Maybe this was just another of Tellio's negotiating tactics

Kajsa's voice was flat. 'No, Ernst. They're out for real. He said we were too slow.'

'Too slow?' I couldn't believe it. This was a disaster. If LVMH pulled out, everything could fall apart. SEDCO, which had said it would invest only after LVMH was on board, would probably back out. Benetton, already looking shaky, might have second thoughts as well. At the very least, we'd have to back down on terms, and then we'd still need to find new investors to raise the full $15 million. That could take a long time, and time was something we didn't have right now. Between the three of us, we had already spent close to $1 million and the bills were mounting up. We had salaries to pay, not to mention outstanding fees to companies like Leagas Delaney, KSA and, of course, Ericsson. They were all getting impatient. It was simply too late to start looking for new investors.

'I'm coming back,' I said. 'We've got to speak to Arnault.'

Salty was flustered. 'My God, it's like trying to get through to the Queen. Who are you? What do you want? Where do you come from? That's not even talking to his secretary. That's the secretary's secretary.'

We were all sitting in one of J.P. Morgan's dingy conference rooms, trying to line up a meeting with Arnault. I had just arrived back from New York that morning and was feeling a bit dazed. LVMH's reasons for pulling out were vague. They were apparently annoyed because, although we had lawyers in New York and Holland, we didn't have any that could sit down with LVMH's lawyers in London and hammer out final terms.

I could picture the scene. Bernard Arnault, busy running his empire, is handed a list with internet deals that have yet to be closed. At the top is boo. 'Why isn't this done yet?'

'Lawyers,' replies Tellio.

'Fine. Drop it.'

The first thing we'd done this morning was to call Tellio. But he'd refused to intervene this time. 'Call him yourself if you want.' So that's what we did. But getting a billionaire to pick up his phone wasn't easy. Now, frustrated and angry, we tried to think of something else.

'I think we should write him a letter,' Salty said.

It turned into something of a cathartic exercise: 'We heard yesterday from Mr Tellio that you have decided to pull out from this deal for documentation purposes,' we wrote. 'Quite frankly we were shocked and highly disappointed by this decision.' We went on to point out that boo had 'closed the door to new investors based on LVMH's offer to invest' and that LVMH was actually getting a better deal than anyone else. What we were trying to say – without actually saying it – was that Arnault was being arrogant and unprofessional. We ended the letter by asking Arnault at least to allow us to present our case to him in person.

Salty passed the letter to other bankers in the office for comment. The consensus view was that we had gone collectively insane. 'You don't talk like that to the richest man in France,' one pointed out. 'He probably doesn't even know you exist.'

Salty faxed it, anyway. If we could just get into Arnault's office and make our presentation, we knew he'd change his mind. For the next hour, we sat around nervously drinking coffee. After another hour went by, Kajsa began to leave messages. It was late in the afternoon when the call came in from Arnault's secretary. Her tone was clipped. 'Mr Arnault will see you at 11 a.m. tomorrow.'

It was 10.45 a.m. and we were standing outside LVMH headquarters on the Avenue Hoche. 'You're wearing a Cartier watch, Hermès scarf and – are those Gucci shoes?' asked Georges van Erck, a senior banker from J.P. Morgan's Paris office.

Kajsa laughed. 'How do you do that?'

Van Erck was a fashion junkie. His ability to catalogue people at a glance was extraordinary. I felt relieved that he was joining us. He was older and more experienced than our London team, had done a lot of work for LVMH over the years and knew Arnault personally.

Arnault's office on the top floor was accessible only by a special elevator, for which we needed a special pass. When the doors opened, the five of us, including Salty, emerged into a futuristic glass cocoon. 'It's bulletproof,' van Erck whispered, as two burly security guards examined us closely from the other side. I wondered if we were being X-rayed.

The office was spacious and had a commanding view of the Paris skyline, but didn't scream out 'billionaire'. I had heard a lot about Bernard Arnault. He was warm to those he liked, but had little patience for sycophants. Right now, he was in the press almost daily because of his creeping purchases of shares in the Italian fashion house Gucci. He denied that he was planning a hostile bid, but nobody believed him; the media had started calling him the 'purse snatcher'.

Arnault was elegant, with a charismatic presence, and impeccably dressed in a classically cut suit and silk tie.

As he walked over to greet us, his eyebrows rose slightly when he saw van Erck. 'This must be important if you're here,' he said.

Also in the room was Myron Ullman, Arnault's second in command, and another close associate, the Iranian-born Chahram Becharat.

Feeling tense, we got in each other's way while trying to take our seats. After we had exchanged some awkward smalltalk, in which no mention was made of our earlier problems, Kajsa launched straight into the presentation. We knew that the next half an hour would decide everything and this realization spurred us into giving one of our best performances.

When the prototype came out, Arnault leaned forward slightly in his chair and for a second looked set to say something, but the moment passed and he sat back again. There was an almost uncomfortable hush in the room as we waited for the verdict. No one seemed sure what to say.

Finally Kajsa spoke up. 'So what do you think?' she asked.

Her simple candour seemed to catch Arnault by surprise.

'I like it,' he said, with a faint smile.

The tension was broken and everyone began talking at once. Ullman wanted to know if we had appointed a merchandise buyer yet. We hadn't, I explained, but were close to hiring someone from Barneys, the upmarket US department store. Ullman looked thoughtful. 'We almost bought Barneys a little while ago,' he said, almost to himself.

At last, Arnault looked at his watch and stood up, signalling that the meeting was over. 'Take care of this,' he said, turning to Becharat.

A secretary ushered us out. It wasn't until we were going down in the elevator that I started to wonder what had actually happened. Kajsa was equally perplexed.

'What did he mean by that?' she asked, referring to Arnault's final remark.

'That means yes,' said van Erck.

'Oh,' she said.

Van Erck dropped us off outside the famous Café de la Paix on the Boulevard des Capucines, where we sat down for a celebratory coffee.

Salty thought Kajsa's question to Arnault was hilarious. 'You really put him on the spot.'

We were talking so loud that people started to glance at us irritably. I didn't care. Even my stale ham baguette tasted fantastic.

We were almost there. We'd stood on the brink of disaster and somehow pulled through. LVMH was in. As Salty had predicted, SEDCO wasn't exactly overjoyed about being asked to pay more. But in the end, a compromise was reached: in exchange, SEDCO would also get a discount on the next round of funding, which was scheduled for April.

Only the Benettons were still causing us problems. Their reaction to our side letter was one of near disbelief. They'd taken their anger out on Paulmichl. They simply couldn't understand why J.P. Morgan couldn't force us to accept their terms.

Vito Gamberale had stopped dealing with Paulmichl altogether and made a complaint to the Milan office. The Italian bankers had thrown up their hands. This wasn't their deal.

Gamberale had then called Salty: 'It's important to us that we have a good relationship with J.P. Morgan,' he told him, insinuating that things might not stay that way for much longer.

We were a bit annoyed with Paulmichl as well. 'I don't think he's experienced enough to handle this,' said Patrik. The tension was beginning to build between Patrik and Paulmichl.

Our dealings with Benetton became increasingly bizarre. At one point, they wanted the three of us to sign a letter promising them the opportunity to invest in any future businesses. It was flattering, but weird. Then their lawyers insisted on having tag-along rights that allowed them to sell some of their shares whenever we did. We refused. A further complication was that we were never quite sure who we were dealing with. Was Benetton Group going to invest? Or was it just 21Investimenti, the merchant bank? If so, why was it trying to push Benetton products on to us?

By the end of January, we had had enough.

'Just tell them to forget it,' Patrik said.

Paulmichl was anxious. 'They're going to kill me.' But he made the call, and survived. We closed the first round with $8.8 million in the bank – just over half what we'd been hoping for.

5

A S I WALKED AROUND our new Carnaby Street office, I had
to step over cables and squeeze past crates and boxes that
seemed to arrive by the hour. Amundsen's house must have looked
like this, I thought, just before he set off for the Pole. The constant
ring of telephones was drowned by the deafening sound of
hammering and drilling. We were in a state of purposeful, yet chaotic
activity. The small nucleus of Ikea desks with which we had begun
our occupation just a few weeks ago had multiplied. About fifteen
people were working in the London office now. Many more were
working for us elsewhere, at Ericsson, Leagas Delaney and KSA. In
Stockholm, Munich and New York we now had managers in place
to start building our global infrastructure. I couldn't help thinking
back to the meetings Kajsa and I used to have in the Saturnus Café,
where the dream that would become boo.com first took shape. In
less than a year, we had come a very long way.

Now, with the crucial funding in place, we were ready to go into
overdrive. It was early February and our website was due to go live
in three months' time. It meant that we had to move incredibly fast.
The Herculean effort that had brought us this far, I knew, would
seem insignificant compared to all that still lay ahead.

To get some handle on the dizzying workload, we drew up a list
of all the things that needed immediate attention. Hundreds of
individual tasks were divided into twenty-seven broad areas of
responsibility – office infrastructure, logistics, product information,
pricing, front-end applications, call centres, packaging, suppliers,
designing logos, advertising/PR, legal issues, recruitment . . . and so
on. Any one of these areas generated enough work to keep dozens
of people occupied for months to come. Call centres, for example –

they had to be designed and built; appropriate IT systems had to be chosen and put in place; procedures had to be devised for their effective operation; staff had to be trained; the centres had to be tested . . .

Next to each task was listed the individual responsible for ensuring its completion – at this early stage just a handful of names. If consulting the list served to focus us on the essential things to be done, the sheer scale of those things could as easily induce a nervous breakdown. For example, I had to organize the packaging; oversee the establishment of our various offices; sort out our distribution arrangements; work out agreements with the clearing banks; research new markets; devise operational roles and responsibilities – and do a hundred and one other things besides. Distilled into those few sheets of closely typed paper were all the things necessary to build a global company. In just a few months we were attempting to achieve something that usually took years, if not decades.

No wonder our executive assistants looked worried. Their roles had already been expanded. Charlotte was managing our relationships with clothing suppliers; Edward was spending more and more of his time setting up and negotiating the European and US logistics and making arrangements with the clearing banks, but also helping our CTO Steve Bennett to recruit staff; and Martin Bartle was working side by side with Leagas Delaney on marketing issues. Their dedication and enthusiasm was beyond question. But now we needed more help – and lots of it.

At first Boston Consulting Group had been our happy hunting ground. Edward, my executive assistant, had joined from BCG and knew plenty of others who would do the same, given half a chance. Alongside McKinsey and Bain, it was one of the three big management consultancies and was known for its detailed strategy work and high-powered intellectual approach. But the people who worked there prided themselves on their independent mind and entrepreneurial spirit.

The first person Edward led us to was Jay Herratti, a consultant in the firm's retail and consumer division in New York. The slightly-built Israeli had a laid-back, breezy attitude to life. Ultra smart, with a warm sense of humour, it was hard not to like him. He was fiercely ambitious but disarmed people with his easy manner. 'My aim isn't to be the top guy,' he told me once, 'but second in command, close to the people with all the glamour and publicity, but without the stress.'

We had actually met Jay for the first time in November when he was in London helping Universal Music Group with its recent acquisition of Polygram. We were instantly impressed, by his attitude, but also by his credentials. At only 22, he and his brother had started White By Herratti – a concept store, in Miami, that sold only white clothes for women. After this, Jay had a three-year stint at GE Capital and completed an MBA at the prestigious INSEAD in France. Within two minutes of having heard the concept, Jay, now 32, knew that he wanted to work for us. It was an opportunity to return to the world of retail, fashion and style, yet to be part of a pioneering venture. 'Apparel is going to be the next big thing on the internet,' he said, 'and you guys are the first to see its global potential.' At the same time, it was a great opportunity for him to build something out of nothing. He would set up, then run our New York office, with specific responsibility for marketing boo in the US. It was a tough but vital market for us. Jay's role in developing our US business was so important that he was the only country manager to become part of the senior management team. He insisted that his title should reflect his level of responsibility and communicate the right message to people both inside and outside the company. He was pretty pleased with what we came up with. President North America. 'President, boo.com North America,' he said, when he began at the end of January. 'I like the way that sounds.'

We weren't exactly short of BCG consultants by now, but Jay quickly introduced us to another one – a brilliant young Englishman named Luke Alvarez, who was doing internet strategy work at BCG's London office. Jay thought he would be perfect as our head of business development. Alvarez had graduated with the top philosophy first in his year at Cambridge, then won a Fulbright scholarship to Berkeley in the US. After that he'd gone into the software business and invested in a fashion label.

It bothered me that so many of our senior staff had the same consultancy background, but Alvarez was too good to turn away. Any remaining reservations evaporated when I discovered that his father was Al Alvarez, who was one of LeanderMalmsten's authors and had also read at the New York poetry festival. In addition to heading business development, Luke would have responsibility for building our call centres and supervising the website interface to ensure that consumers would find it easy to use.

Fiercely competitive, Luke lost no time in dictating terms. He would accept the job, he said, only if he could hire an assistant. Jay warned him not to test our patience, but finally we agreed that he could bring along Karl O'Hanlon, with whom he had worked at BCG. A straight-talking Irishman, O'Hanlon had a 'sergeant-major' personality that made him notably untypical of the BCG breed, but I could see that his willingness to dirty his hands if necessary, and to get things done, might prove an invaluable quality.

At about this time we also hired James Cronin to oversee technology operations. We had met him for the first time back in November when Anthony Harling was helping us to find a chief technology officer. Very bright and in his early twenties, he was then working for virgin.net. 'He's too young for the job of CTO,' Harling told us, 'but he's a guy you really ought to have around.' So we encouraged Steve Bennett to take him on, and, with his dedication and ingenuity, Cronin quickly became the single most indispensable member of the technology team.

Of all the positions we had to fill, though, none was more important than that of merchandise buyer. A retail company without a good buyer is like a restaurant without a chef. We needed someone who knew how to draw from the offerings of our various suppliers to create a fantastic collection that would epitomize the identity of boo.com. The job required not only a strong eye for fashion, but also practical judgement. The successful candidate had to know what sorts of brands to stock, as well as the specific products, sizes, colours and quantities of each that we should be buying. One bad decision and we'd be left with crates of stock at the end of the season.

Most of the suppliers we had met so far had harangued us for not having a buyer. It was hard for them to take us seriously until we did.

Others, like New Balance, just wanted us to hurry up and start placing orders, but with three months to go until our launch we still hadn't bought a single pair of trainers, or anything else for that matter.

With the help of Anthony Harling's colleague Milena Djurdevic, from the New York office of Heidrick & Struggles, we had been interviewing candidates since November. The problem was that most of the people we liked – buyers from department stores like Bloomingdales in New York and Harvey Nichols in London – had wanted nothing to do with us. I had always thought fashion was a young person's game, but it turned out to be the opposite. It took decades to make a name in the industry and the ones who had weren't about to risk it all for a start-up on the internet. Indeed, according to the headhunter's progress report, several of the prospective candidates barely knew what the internet was, and those who did usually considered it to be 'too futuristic' or 'way out' to contemplate.

The one exception was Michael Skidmore, a garrulous 52-year-old who was senior menswear buyer at Barneys, the upmarket New York department store.

If his bushy mane of silvery-brown hair made him look rather like Rod Stewart, he sounded more like Robert De Niro. He was a lifelong New Yorker who had started his career as a ski photographer, before realizing there wasn't any money in it. He had then worked as a sales manager for a casual menswear firm called UFO, before moving on to Barneys in 1975. He arrived just as the store was establishing a reputation for supporting talented young designers like Giorgio Armani and Gianni Versace. Over the years, Skidmore had personally brought in labels such as Gucci and Dries Van Noten for men, and Issey Miyake and Kenzo for women.

Along with a discerning eye for fine clothes, Skidmore was known as a bit of a wild man. He had been a regular at the legendary Studio 54 nightclub in the Seventies, often showing up with Gene Pressman, whose family owned Barneys. 'He has enormous pace and energy,' the headhunter noted in the appraisal prepared for us. 'His enthusiasm is such that he tends to go off at 120 miles per hour.' What drew him to the fashion world was the excitement and new thinking that it generated. But now he felt that he had reached the stage where he had to move on to continue to find that excitement.

By his own admission, Skidmore was going through a mid-life crisis when I first met him in New York in December. He had just separated from his wife and was thinking about moving to Paris or starting his own store. He didn't know much about the internet. But he liked what it represented – youth, glamour and the opportunity to be part of something revolutionary.

When I was back in New York a month later, I booked a table for us at my favourite East Village restaurant, Indochine, only to discover that he had done the same. We were obviously going to get along. None the less, it took weeks of haggling before he agreed to come on board. Like all good buyers, he was a tough negotiator. We ended up agreeing to a base salary of $300,000, with a bonus of another $100,000 after the first year. This was more than three times what Kajsa, Patrik and I were paying ourselves. He also insisted on a three-year contract and a clause that meant we could only fire him if he did something illegal.

If there was a catchphrase that summed up the weeks that followed the first round of funding it was 'Hire now, ask questions later'. How many people did we actually need? More than 100 in London alone. Then there were our new offices in New York, Stockholm, Munich and Paris. It was a build-up that headhunters are probably still talking about in wistful tones.

For almost a year, Kajsa, Patrik and I had done everything together. Now, with our workload spiralling out of control, it was time to start dividing up responsibilities.

As usual, Patrik was put in charge of all the money-related issues. A key task was to build a department capable of managing the finances of a fast-growing global business. More immediate duties included designing a day-to-day financial structure, handling the payroll, keeping a tight grip on expenses, managing our contracts with outside suppliers and negotiating good payment terms.

But this was pretty dreary stuff. What really invigorated Patrik was racing between meetings with bankers, lawyers, tax advisers and

investors. This appetite for deal-making could often cause difficulties. In the days after we closed the first round, for example, he
focused his attention on Benetton. Exasperated by J.P. Morgan's
inability to complete an agreement, he began negotiating directly
with Alessandro Benetton. But Paulmichl, who had advised us
against any direct contact, somehow found out and was far from
pleased with Patrik's interference.

Kajsa took charge of our branding and marketing strategy, a job
that was complicated by her steadily worsening relationship with
Leagas Delaney. While they had in the end done a fantastic job for
us on the prototype, and their grasp of strategic issues was superb,
Kajsa found herself increasingly frustrated by the length of time they
took to develop their creative ideas. She was even more upset when
she finally saw them. While our aim had been to sell leisure and
sportswear to the fashion-conscious, their ads were pitched at the
sports-conscious. Somebody would be snowboarding in the desert;
or a golfer would be teeing off on a snow-covered mountain in the
Himalayas. These were images that spoke to would-be athletes, not
to the average guy who wanted to buy a cool pair of trainers. To
Kajsa they were unimaginative and predictable.

When she tackled the creative director, Tim Delaney, who was
also one of the founders of the agency, he stoutly defended his team's
work. 'Look, this is really good advertising,' he insisted. 'You've got
to try to understand what we're doing.' When she still wasn't happy,
they asked her to sit down with them and look through some fashion
magazines so that they could get an idea of what she did like. She
thought this ridiculous and didn't hesitate to say so. They were being
paid a lot of money to come up with the ideas, not her. As the
relationship worsened, she began to make discreet inquiries with
other agencies.

The sort of difficulties we were having with Leagas Delaney were
always a possibility because of our total devotion to the brand we had
created. We were determined that every aspect of our business, from
the look of our website to the design of our business cards, should
send out a clear message about who we were and what we stood for.
Our company logo was perhaps the most critical example of this: it
would appear on everything we did. Both Me Company and Leagas

Delaney had made unsuccessful attempts to produce one. Finally I suggested that we hire our own in-house designer to work on it. Not only would it be a lot cheaper, but we were likely to be much happier with the result.

Kajsa turned to Niclas Sellebråten, a thoughtful 28-year-old Swede, who had designed some of our book covers a few years earlier. When she first called him, he was working for the prestigious Stockholm Design Lab and had just finished a huge project for Scandinavian Airlines, which involved redesigning everything from its airline lounge to the hairbands worn by stewardesses. At a time when boo was still being referred to in hushed whispers as X.com, Kajsa was so anxious about secrecy that on the phone she didn't even tell Niclas what the job was that she wanted him to do. Instead, she had him flown over to London and offered it to him in person. It was agreed that he would not only work on our logo, but also lead an in-house design team.

Niclas's very first challenge, when he began to work for us in mid-January, was to figure out what Kajsa and I actually wanted. This wasn't easy. 'I don't understand your positioning,' he said, when the three of us got together around Kajsa's desk one morning. 'Is this going to be more of a fashion company or a sports company?' If it was a sports company, Niclas said, he could design a logo that suggested movement; like the famous Nike swoosh, which was derived from a classic 1960s photograph of an Olympic long jumper. A fashion company, on the other hand, would need something more stylish. As his comments reminded us of conversations that we had been having with Leagas Delaney for months now over exactly the same issue, we weren't exactly surprised that he was having problems. But there wasn't a lot we could do to help.

'Try and do something that has a bit of both,' I suggested, a little half-heartedly.

'Look at the prototype,' Kajsa added. 'Think contemporary and simple.'

'Contemporary and simple,' Niclas muttered, running his hand through his cropped blond hair. 'That narrows it down.'

As CEO, my role was to supervise every aspect of the business, but, above all, to provide leadership – to inspire everyone to embrace our vision and to aim for a common goal. I hoped that at boo we would create a climate in which people would be able to develop their strengths, but I was equally determined that they should put aside their weaknesses. So I was encouraging, but also extremely demanding. boo meant everything to me and I believed that it should mean as much to everyone else. Working for boo, I felt, was not a job but a cause to which you had to be prepared to devote yourself twenty-four hours a day. On a more practical level, my most immediate concern, in these weeks before the launch, was building our technology platform. This was a job that seemed to be getting more complicated by the day.

A lot had happened on the technology front over the past few weeks. For a start, Ericsson was no longer in charge of building our platform. The breaking point had come in early January, when its 30-page feasibility study landed on my desk. The first thing that struck me was how flimsy it seemed. Then I got the bill. At $500,000, it was roughly five times more than I'd expected. It was like sending your car to a mechanic for an oil change and getting billed for a new engine. As we had been having considerable doubts about working with Ericsson, I saw no reason why I should accept it.

'This is way too much,' I told them. 'We need to negotiate.' As the matter was handed over to the lawyers, Patrik had some fun devising a scheme to ring-fence the agreement in case no acceptable compromise could be found. Under our company structure, boo.com's technology platform and intellectual property were owned by a company in Ireland. Patrik now created a second Irish company especially for the purpose. It was a neat idea, but eventually we agreed to pay half Ericsson's fee.

I was confident that we were right not to continue working with Ericsson, but it left us in a tight spot. Time was running out and we were right back where we started. My only comfort was that Steve Bennett, our brilliant new CTO, seemed to be taking our predicament in his stride. Ericsson's feasibility study may have been skimpy, but it had at least identified the technology vendors that should supply each part of our platform. Bennett now proposed that we should finalize their contracts so they could start work immediately. 'It will give us some breathing space,' he said.

These companies weren't multinationals like Ericsson or IBM. Most were start-ups like us. They were the pioneers of a new industry that had sprung up to meet the every need of budding e-commerce companies. The job of designing the front end, or 'look and feel', of our website was in the hands of Organic, which had offices in San Francisco and New York. Its job was to bring our visual ideas to life – the online mannequin, 3D images, zooming and spinning and, of course, Miss Boo. Our e-commerce engine, the heart of any online retailer, was being supplied by Interworld, also based in New York. Despite conjuring mental images of heavy machinery, the e-commerce engine was actually a piece of software. Its role was to process all interactive requests on our website – from product searches to actual purchases. Finally there was the back end, which was being handled by IFS, a Swedish company whose clients included the likes of Volvo. This was a complex administrative system that handled multiple tasks from managing our product inventory to shipping goods to customers.

By February, all three companies were working full steam ahead and promising to deliver their respective parts of the platform in time for a May launch. But we still had to find a company to take Ericsson's place in co-ordinating and integrating their work. The most promising of those we approached was Cambridge Technology Partners, but we were unable to agree terms. It was on our way back from one more fruitless meeting with CTP's chief executive that Bennett came up with a new suggestion. He'd been critical of all the companies we'd met so far. He couldn't see how any of them were an improvement on Ericsson: they all wanted to use too many people and charged too much. So why not bypass them altogether? 'I don't think we need them,' he said. 'We can do this ourselves.'

I gave the go-ahead, although I was very hesitant at first. This was the exact opposite of what we'd always planned – we were a retailer, not a software company. But when Bennett explained things further, I began to see his logic. If we could get the small technology suppliers to work closely together, he pointed out, it would limit the amount of integration we needed to do. At the same time, he could build a small in-house technology team to take responsibility for the small amount of co-ordination that would be needed.

He had already brought in Richard Sewell, Iain Barclay and Kevin Vernon, contractors from Wales who had worked with him in the past. They turned up at the office one day wearing red, yellow and blue T-shirts, so we nicknamed them the 'Primary Colours' team. They were going to work closely with IFS, Organic and Interworld. Now he brought in Richard Sharp and his son Chris, who ran a family firm that we called the Gigastream team. Their job was to build the internal infrastructure for London and boo.com's offices abroad. But it soon became obvious that we had taken on a much bigger job than the Primary Colours and Gigastream teams could handle alone.

Bennett looked a little uncertain when he became aware that he would have to hire a lot more people. So I asked Edward Griffith to help him out, and was relieved when shortly afterwards Bennett found an executive assistant of his own, Alison Conway. At last our technology troubles are over, I thought, little realizing that they were just about to begin.

The 'Super Show', at the Georgia World Congress Center in Atlanta, is the world's largest sporting goods trade fair. Each year, around 100,000 wholesalers, retailers and industry reps converge on the main hall to schmooze and show off their latest products. The organizers, in a typically American piece of trivia, boast that it would take one person seven and a half years to set up all the displays.

It was a fantastic opportunity for us to see and be seen – to prove that we were now part of the industry. So we showed up in force. Our new merchandise buyer Michael Skidmore led a contingent that included myself, Patrik, Charlotte and our New York boss Jay Herratti. Kajsa, who was looking for an apartment in London, had stayed behind. She was cutting back on travel anyway to spend more time with her daughter.

We flew in on the evening of 11 February, the night before the show was due to kick off. As our plane touched down, the thought occurred to me that this was the third time I had seen this town in six months – both our retail consultants KSA and our logistics partner UPS had their head offices there. It was beginning to feel like home.

We had hoped to make an early start, but things were already well under way by the time we had eaten breakfast and walked the short distance from our hotel. The main hall looked like a converted aeroplane hangar, with swarms of people moving slowly among the endless rows of stands, some of which looked like ornately decorated houses.

'Just keep walking,' said Skidmore, shaking his head with a cynical smile. 'The bigger the stand, the smaller the brand.'

If most of the suppliers already seemed to know who we were, this was above all due to Charlotte. Although she had formally been Patrik's executive assistant, Patrik, who was not a natural delegator, had left her very much to her own devices. Quickly she realized that dealing with the suppliers provided her with an opportunity to carve out a role of her own. Since they found it much easier to talk to her than Patrik, whose accent they often didn't understand, she became our key contact. Persistent, friendly and highly disciplined, she had in the last few months travelled the world with the prototype in a massive effort to sign up new suppliers. Together, as we would discover in Atlanta, they were an irresistible combination.

The first of a series of meetings that Charlotte had lined up for us was with Everlast, best known for its boxing equipment but also an established name in women's athletic clothing. It took us a long time to find their stand, but it was worth the effort.

'Hey. It's the boo folks!'

George Horowitz, CEO of Active Apparel, the company that owned the Everlast brand, practically hugged me. Charlotte and I had met him during our fruitful trip to meet suppliers at Christmas. At that time, Active Apparel had just unveiled its own e-commerce site – a move that had sent its shares soaring more than 1000 per cent in two days. As far as Horowitz was concerned, the internet was O.K. 'Do you like the stand?' he asked.

'Yeah,' I said in a tone of genuine admiration.

Next to a full-size boxing ring stood a group of cheerleaders, pom-poms dangling at their sides.

'They're the Atlanta Hawks girls,' Horowitz said proudly.

Inside the ring, two women fighters were exchanging blows for the entertainment of mostly male spectators. 'That's Kathy "the Wildcat" Collins,' Horowitz whispered. 'She's the world champion right now.'

Horowitz and Skidmore seemed to hit it off straight away. For a good ten minutes, we listened while the two of them swapped tips on coming trends. Then Horowitz handed us over to one of his salesmen so we could place an order.

'You need to look at these,' the salesman said, as we sat around a small table beside the boxing ring. He pulled out a rack of women's tops. 'I just love them.'

'Aren't those last season?' Skidmore asked drily.

The salesman froze for a second, then recovered. 'Well, yes. But they aren't really season–sensitive.'

'Uh–huh,' replied Skidmore. 'Well, maybe you can show me something new instead.' His tone was light, almost playful. But the message was clear and the salesman looked uncomfortable.

The next rack was better, but Skidmore didn't like the colours. 'Have you got those in blue?'

'I think so.'

'Good,' he said, turning to a leggy assistant who was standing by the wall. 'Could you try this on for me, please?'

After putting the top on, she turned around a few times so Skidmore could check her out from every angle.

'OK,' he said finally. 'We'll take fifty. Blue, red and green. Split them evenly – small, medium, large.'

As he spoke, the salesman jotted furiously on a pad.

'Do you always get someone to try things on before you buy them?' I asked once we'd left.

'Of course. It can be great on the rack but still look like shit when you put it on.'

As we strolled on down the aisles to our next meeting, Skidmore gave rapid-fire opinions on every brand we passed. 'Crap . . . Crap . . . Pretty cool . . .'

There was no doubt about it, I thought. We definitely had our man.

We came to the stand of Fubu, the streetwear brand that had grown into a $350 million business in a few years by catering to the hip-hop crowd. Pounding rap music blared from giant speakers, while a group of huge Ice Cube lookalikes, with dark glasses thrust their arms into the air. It was pointless making conversation. No one could hear a word.

'You should see their office,' said Charlotte, who two weeks previously had visited them at their New York headquarters in the Empire State Building. There the same loud rap music played constantly and everyone observed extreme informality. When Charlotte arrived to meet the senior executive, Norman Weisfeld, he turned out to be in a meeting. The secretary didn't bother to knock, but just marched straight in. This was the Fubu way.

'Where's Norman?' Charlotte shouted to one of the Ice Cubes, who, keeping in time with the rap, flung an arm in the direction of a small office at the back of the stand.

'Follow me,' said Charlotte. Without a moment's hesitation, she flung open the office door.

'Hey, Charlotte, great to see you!' said Weisfeld.

'Norman, I'd like to introduce Ernst Malmsten . . . '

After the din and controlled chaos of Fubu it was a relief to spend some time at the Converse stand. After a long wait, they gave us a sneak preview of their new 'helium shoe', their secret weapon against flagging sales – so secret, in fact, that a security guard held the box while we peered inside.

'It weighs only 12 ounces,' whispered the marketing manager. 'That's 3 ounces less than your average basketball boot. We call it, "Lighter than air."'

Perhaps Charlotte's biggest coup had been to secure a meeting with Roger Wood, the new head of e-commerce at Reebok. As we sat down with him to explain our concept, Michael Skidmore kicked Jay under the table: 'Just let Charlotte do the talking.'

Our last stop was with Gary Schoenfeld, the CEO of Vans who had been so impressed by our prototype when we visited him in LA over Christmas. He was as enthusiastic as ever and by the time we left had asked us to sponsor Vans's European 'Warped' Tour – a rock festival mixed with skateboarding events. It was a fantastic opportunity for us to raise an awareness of the as-yet-unknown boo name among our core audience of 18–24-year-olds.

It had been a long, but incredibly satisfying day and we were all in the mood to go out that night. Our first stop was a party being thrown by New Balance in an office they had bought during the Atlanta Olympics a few years earlier. Russ Lucas, the first person to support us, wandered over. Although it had been only six months before, the visit to his office in Warrington now seemed an age ago. It was great to see him again.

'You've really come a long way,' he said warmly, clutching a glass of champagne.

Suddenly Charlotte grabbed my arm. 'Listen,' she whispered. 'Over there.' She nodded to a group of about five retailers standing a few feet away. 'They're talking about boo!'

'Are they proper sports or not?' one was asking.

'It's more of an urban site,' another replied. The tone was a mixture of curiosity, intrigue and envy. We didn't catch the rest, but it was a thrilling moment, much as a writer must feel when he sees people on the subway reading one of his books.

'Let's get out of here,' said Skidmore, who wanted to find somewhere more exciting. The only question was where.

'Can you take us to a place with a velvet rope?' I asked the cab driver.

'Forget it,' he replied, eyeing me curiously in his rearview mirror. 'You're in Atlanta, not LA.'

'Just take us to the Gold Club,' said Skidmore.

'What's that?' I asked.

'Don't worry. You'll like it.'

The Gold Club turned out to be the biggest strip joint in America whose visitors often included members of some notorious mafia families. A sign at the entrance promised us 'the best hospitality, classiest girls and private VIP rooms rented by the hour'.

Inside it was the size of a football pitch. Everywhere we looked there were bald men and gyrating girls. No wonder the trade shows in Atlanta were so popular. We didn't get a VIP room, but slumped into the soft lounge chairs and ordered round after round of extortionately priced drinks as a procession of naked women danced before us on a mirrored stage.

It was a few hours later, at around 4 a.m., that I noticed Skidmore slip quietly away. A few minutes later he returned with a blonde, sequined stripper. 'Here's a little present,' he said, slipping $20 bills into her belt and standing back as she took turns lap-dancing on each of us, Charlotte included.

Patrik was so drunk I thought he was going to fall out of his chair. 'Don't tell my wife about this,' he slurred between puffs on an enormous cigar.

Glancing across at Skidmore, I noticed he had a huge smile on his face. I'm going to enjoy working with this guy, I thought.

'Ernst. We've got to sort this out.' Jerry Fielder's voice sounded uncharacteristically heavy. 'We need you to sign the contract now. Otherwise we can't do any more work.'

It was a couple of days after our return from Atlanta. I was standing by the doorway of our office, watching as a group of workmen lugged in our latest batch of Ikea desks. The contract that Leagas Delaney wanted us to sign was supposed to cement a more permanent partnership. Only with the guarantee of millions in fees that our signatures would give could Leagas start moving ahead on our ad campaign. Fielder had been badgering us about this for weeks. But we'd kept stalling, blaming our lack of money. Now that we had the money, our excuses were starting to sound forced.

'We're still looking through it,' I said, already knowing Fielder wouldn't believe me.

'It's Kajsa, isn't it?' he asked.

I hesitated.

'Look. It's obvious she doesn't like our creative work,' Fielder went on. 'But we can't make her happy if she doesn't even speak to us. This is a two-way street, you know.'

'I know,' I said, taking a deep breath.

'So what happens next?'

'It's complicated,' I said. 'I'll have to call you back.'

'Whatever you decide, just do it soon, OK? We're all a bit tired of this.'

The situation was complicated because Kajsa and I were still divided on whether to fire Leagas, as she wanted, or to try to sort things out, which I was pushing for. It was becoming a touchy subject between us.

It was of course obvious why she was so upset. Not only did the ads that Leagas had shown us lack flair, but they looked like they had been flung together in a hurry. Kajsa, who was passionate about getting even the smallest details right, saw this as further confirmation that we should have broken with them a long time ago. There was also Leagas's insistence on positioning boo as a pure sports brand. It was crucial, they argued, to send a simple, focused message to the market. This had been the strategy behind its successful campaign for Adidas. But we still felt strongly that we were as much a fashion brand as a sports brand, and were frustrated by their refusal to think along these times.

'I don't think they even understand fashion,' Kajsa complained.

None the less, Jerry Fielder had been a huge help to us and I did not want to treat him badly. I also knew that Kajsa could be very difficult to work with. She knew what she wanted and had strong creative ideas, but she sometimes had difficulty articulating her views to others.

After my conversation with Fielder, I headed over to Kajsa's desk. She was on her way out to get lunch, so the two of us wandered down Carnaby Street together, side-stepping puddles in the drizzle.

'Why can't we give them one last chance?' I said. It wasn't just our relationship with Fielder that was on the line, I explained. I had recently started talking to the people in Leagas's digital division about the possibility of them handling the 3D photography needed for our website. We had even discussed creating some kind of a joint venture company. It seemed a pity to jeopardize it.

'We've talked about this already,' Kajsa said, stopping to light a cigarette. I noticed her hand was shaking. 'If we start building our brand like this, we're going to fail. Their ads aren't going to make our brand famous. They're going to hurt us.'

'Let's ask them to make some different ads, then.'

'There's no point,' she said, glaring at me. 'They'll never understand what we want. We don't have $200 million to spend on advertising. We have to get this right.'

I could feel myself getting annoyed. 'Why don't you just take them out to dinner and talk about it?'

'You take them out. I don't want to work with them any more.'

'We can't keep firing people,' I shouted.

'Fine,' Kajsa said, throwing her cigarette on the ground. 'Then I quit. Go find someone else to do the marketing.' She began striding off through the puddles, but then turned back. 'This is the worst mistake you can make. You're going to regret this for ever.'

Of course I knew she wasn't serious about quitting. But I also realized that there was no point in pushing things further. Later that afternoon, when we had both cooled down a bit, I sat down on her desk and made a final suggestion. 'How about if we get someone else to do the creative work, and we just work with them on strategy and 3D imaging?'

Kajsa looked nonplussed. 'How?'

I shrugged. 'Maybe I can ask Tim Delaney to bring in a freelancer to do the ads.'

'I don't think that'll work.'

'If it doesn't work, we'll get another agency.'

'OK,' she said quietly.

No one gave much for my chances of getting Delaney to agree. Charlotte, in her previous job as an advertising planner, had heard a lot about him. 'He doesn't compromise,' she warned. Jerry Fielder was equally doubtful when I ran the idea past him. But he said he would set up a meeting all the same.

Delaney was busy all week, but agreed to see me on the morning of 20 February, a Saturday. Kajsa had refused to come along, so I showed up at Leagas's office alone. I had actually met Tim Delaney a couple of times before. In his late fifties, he was tall and balding, with a quick mind and sharp tongue. Despite his fearsome reputation, we'd always got along pretty well and he seemed cheerful enough when I walked in.

It was a short meeting. We both knew that one way or another this was going to be a decisive occasion so we kept the smalltalk to a minimum.

'We still want to work with you, but not on creative,' I said. It was like telling Microsoft that we wanted to have them as consultants but not to use their software.

'That's the most important part of the relationship for us,' Delaney replied calmly. 'You either take everything, or nothing.'

'Then I guess we can't work together any more.'

'I guess not,' said Delaney.

'I'm sorry it has to end this way,' I said, turning to leave.

'It's a shame,' said Delaney. 'I like you guys. And that means Kajsa too. I don't understand her, but I like her.'

Kajsa was right. My idea hadn't worked. But at least we had tried to talk about it.

Almost a month had passed since our initial funding had come in and our office, which had always felt spacious, now seemed almost cramped. For probably the first time, I had the feeling that boo was a real company. We didn't even have to travel as much as we used to. People were now coming to us. Several small, round tables, which had been placed in different parts of the room, were almost constantly in use for meetings with technology companies, logistics companies, call centre specialists, headhunters and bankers.

As CEO, I was at the centre of all this activity. My desk was piled high with faxes and progress reports. My mobile phone rang so often that I'd taken to switching it off and checking my messages every half-hour instead. I loved the drama of it all. I was at the middle of a spinning universe. But staying on top required struggling daily with hundreds of infuriating, often unpredictable, problems.

Few were more infuriating than those caused by our product database. It was essentially a catalogue of what we were selling. When a customer did a search on our website, the results would be pulled out of the database. With bokus, we had bought a ready-made database with around a million book titles already loaded into it. But with boo we had to build it up ourselves. It was an enormous job. Each product needed something like fifty pieces of descriptive information. There were such things as brand, colour and size, not to mention the prices in eighteen currencies, but there were also the different search categories to which the product belonged. You could, for example, browse by activity. So we had to know if a particular shoe was a hiking, running, tennis or basketball shoe.

The real complexities only started to become clear in late February, when Charlotte and a new recruit named Toby Merchant tried to persuade suppliers to provide us with the necessary information. 'They're not used to giving this level of detail,' said Charlotte. They couldn't understand why we needed to know all this. Ordinary retailers never asked such questions.

Then there was the question of how to handle the information when it came in. The descriptions had to be precise and consistent throughout the website. I had the idea of creating a 'boo language' – an irreverent prose style that would somehow capture who we were. Kajsa and I had already come up with a few ideas. Instead of saying 'Join Now,' we'd have 'Be boo'; and instead of 'Your Order' we'd have 'Your Stuff.'

When I explained this to Charlotte and Toby, they almost fainted. 'Who's going to do the writing for thousands of products?'

'You'll have to hire some writers,' I said. 'See if you can get people from magazines like *Arena* or *Face*.'

As they began hunting for staff, new, more complicated challenges emerged. All our product descriptions had to be translated into several languages. The person who felt the full brunt of this was Annica Mattsson, who was now in charge of setting up and managing boo's Stockholm office. Having got to know her well at LeanderMalmsten, I was keen to give her this opportunity and knew that she would be very good.

It was a big job for someone of her age, requiring her to handle, among other things, marketing, logistics and the setting up of a call centre. But I believed that people were at their best when they were given maximum latitude and responsibility. I also felt strongly that a modern, progressive company had a duty to develop the talents of its employees and to respect them as individuals. If we came to inspire an extraordinary degree of loyalty from our staff, I think it was chiefly because we gave them both the freedom and the encouragement to fulfil their potential. But often, as Annica discovered, it could require insane levels of work and it was the product database that almost tipped her over the edge.

As our Stockholm office served all of Scandinavia, Annica was responsible for ensuring all our product descriptions were translated into Swedish, Danish and Finnish. She soon realized that her office would have to do something like 500 translations a week to meet our May launch date. As the most one person could manage was eighty a week, Annica tried to hire some top-quality translators. The first, a Swede who had worked on books for our publishing company, started work in mid-February. It was soon afterwards that the first agitated calls started coming in.

'What do we do if a word doesn't exist in Swedish?' Annica asked. In English, she pointed out, there could sometimes be thirty different ways of describing a single garment. The Swedish language wasn't that rich. 'Do you want us to invent new words?'

I did my best to help. 'If you need to use two words instead of one, go ahead,' I said. 'Just try to get the tone right.'

But things kept getting more complicated. Annica's office still lacked even the most basic technical infrastructure and was using a Hotmail account to receive the product descriptions from London. But there were so many of them that her email inbox was constantly overloaded. Emails were getting lost.

'This is killing me,' Annica groaned, in one of our increasingly fraught conversations.

'I know it's complicated,' I said, trying to sound understanding. 'You're doing a fantastic job. This is all going to work out.'

It was a cool but cloudless Sunday in late February and I had just walked through Regent's Park, on my way to Kajsa's new apartment in Primrose Hill. From what I could see, it was a pretty nice area. Quieter than Notting Hill, where I was still living in my parents' house. The buildings here were mostly Victorian and they looked clean and well-kept. There also seemed to be some interesting shops. I spotted an Italian deli, a small designer clothes boutique and a cosy-looking pub with roast lunches. When Kajsa called in the morning to invite me over, I'd accepted quickly. It was a welcome interruption from the intense activity of the past few weeks. Almost every day we'd been starting work at 7 a.m. and often not leaving the office until midnight.

'Ernst?' Kajsa's voice sounded fuzzy over the intercom.

'Yeah.'

'It's the second floor,' she said, buzzing me in. 'Watch out for the fresh paint.'

Kajsa was looking casual, in a pair of drawstring trousers and a T-shirt. 'Let me give you the tour,' she said, after I had taken off my coat.

Kajsa had warned me that not everything was perfect with her flat. At first, though, it was hard to see what she meant. The place looked and smelled as if it had just been completely redecorated. The walls were dazzling white, the carpets new. There were three spacious bedrooms: one for Kajsa and Joel, her boyfriend; one for her daughter Alva; and the third for a live-in nanny that she'd brought over from Sweden. It was only when we got to the living room that I began to see why she wasn't completely happy. 'Have a look at this,' Kajsa said, lifting the curtains. Just 100 metres away was what looked like a major train junction, with spaghetti-like intertwining tracks.

'Didn't you know that was there?' I asked. Kajsa threw up her hands. 'The agent showed me around at night,' she said, hopelessly. 'I guess he didn't think it was important to mention that the flat shakes every fifteen minutes.'

Then there was the problem with her heating. For the first few days it hadn't worked at all. She had been boiling water to wash each morning. Now it worked, but hummed all night.

Kajsa grabbed a couple of cushions and we sat down on the floor, where we spent the next couple of hours chatting aimlessly. Kajsa had some leftover pasta, which we ate off plastic plates that she had bought for the occasion.

Later that afternoon, Joel came home and the three of us sat around talking. He had just come back from doing a photo-shoot for the retailer H&M in the Moroccan desert. 'There were no showers,' he said. 'Three days and no showers.'

Eventually, I decided it was getting late and ordered a cab. As we waited for it to arrive, Kajsa remembered something and dashed into her room. She came back with a single sheet of A3 paper on which was a sketch of our corporate logo.

For the past few weeks, Niclas Sellebråten had been producing dozens of variations of our logo. The company name didn't give him a lot of letters to play with, and his idea was somehow to exploit the similarity of shape between the b and the o's. But he soon discovered that although o was in theory the simplest letter in the alphabet, it was capable of endless variation. Some of his o's turned out to be too flat or too narrow or to have too much space in the middle, while others failed to harmonize with the b or to lend themselves to more general adaptation. Niclas's great mission became that of finding the perfect o, and each morning he would show Kajsa his latest attempts. But she was as exacting as ever, and for a few days a major part of her job seemed to be turning down Niclas's o's.

The sketch that she now handed to me was his latest effort. It was a simple, but striking shape, halfway between a square and a circle. The technical term was a super ellipsoid or, as we later came to call it, a squirl. The fact that the shape worked perfectly with the 4 letters of boo.com but didn't support a whole typeface gave our logo-type a unique quality. At the same time, it lent itself to being used as a graphic element in the design of promotional material and the website itself, to frame our products or make patterns.

'I think he's done it,' I said, smiling.

6

AS A LARGE COMPANY sprung up around us, it was time to focus once again on the big picture. boo.com aimed to harness the explosive growth in e-commerce to establish itself as the first global retailer of sportswear and fashion. Our strengths were a consumer-friendly, cutting-edge site and worldwide access to brands otherwise hard to find. But ultimately success depended on the rapid expansion of our customer base that would build boo.com itself into a powerful brand. If people were to visit our website in the large numbers we had forecast, then we had to get the world talking about us – our goal was to be as much on everyone's lips as other brands that had become an inseparable part of everyday life. If you want to quench your thirst, drink Coca-Cola; if you want a practical car, drive a Ford; if you want to be urban and cool, buy your gear from boo. The strength of our brand lay in the degree to which it could represent a set of values with which our target audience strongly identified.

The trick was to promote boo.com not simply as an online store, but as a lifestyle. In doing this, Kajsa and I felt we had a great advantage over a lot of the other brands, because we believed in everything we claimed for boo. We ourselves belonged to our target audience of the young, educated and fashion-aware. There was a continuum between the sophisticated, stylish attitude we wanted boo to suggest and our own lives. If there was one quality, besides a dogged persistence, that we prided ourselves on, it was a sense of style. We seemed to have a knack of making whatever we turned our hands to contemporary and eye-catching, whether it was a Nordic poetry festival in New York, a small Swedish publisher or an online bookstore. These ventures had been a perfect training-ground for learning how to build a brand, but they had also all stemmed from our personal concerns.

This authenticity of image received its purest incarnation in our plans for an online magazine. boo.world, or *Boom* as we eventually called it, was intended to declare who we were and what we believed. In short, it was the standard-bearer of the boo brand. We wanted it to contain articles that reflected the urban lifestyle – movies, music, fashion, sports – and to have a free editorial voice, without being overtly commercial in the rather crude way of many American online sites. There would be no articles urging you to buy things from boo; just the obvious but unspoken assumption that you were the kind of person who would.

In our quest to give the magazine editorial independence, we contacted the deputy editor of the *Times Literary Supplement*, Alan Jenkins, whom we had known since our LeanderMalmsten days. He agreed to work for us as a consultant. On his recommendation, we then hired yet another Alvarez – Luke's sister, Kate – to manage the magazine. The idea was that *Boom* would attract the top freelance writers, who, within the general remit that this was an urban lifestyle magazine, would be free to write as they chose. Jaron Lanier, for example, the 'father of virtual reality', was going to write on his project to build a virtual brain, and Will Self would review an exhibition of Jackson Pollock's paintings. The key thing was that the magazine should strengthen the integrity and appeal of our brand, cementing customer loyalty and attracting people to our website.

boo.com was accumulating formidable expertise in many areas, but Kajsa and I believed that our ability to create a powerful brand was perhaps the greatest asset of the company, and we were determined to exploit this to the maximum. It was so important to us that advertising and PR on a worldwide scale were at the heart of our business strategy. The fastest way to achieve brand recognition would have been to launch a massive advertising campaign, but our budget was small for our global ambitions. So we concentrated instead on forging a brand-focused strategy that integrated advertising into a creative campaign making the maximum use of PR. A double-spread advertisement in American *Vogue* costs around

$140,000. A full-page write-up is free. It also gives you more credibility than you could ever achieve through ads alone.

Our strategy meant working with PR agencies in every country where we planned to launch. By far the most important of those countries, with its huge market and internet awareness, and also the most competitive, was of course the United States. A successful presence there was the key to establishing the boo name worldwide. It meant that we would develop a particularly close relationship with the New-York-based PR agency, Hill & Knowlton. It had the vital expertise and contacts we needed in the US, but its international network – our first contact had been through its London office – also made it the ideal partner to help us plan a global PR strategy. 'The model is a honeycomb,' its publicity brochure boasted. 'Each office is put on its mettle, but ideas are shared.'

Founded in 1927, Hill & Knowlton was the grandfather of all PR firms. Its clients included a long list of respectable, old economy companies like Kellogg's, American Express and British Telecom. It even acted for governments. This was the firm that, in 1990, Kuwait's leaders hired to lobby for US military intervention in the Persian Gulf.

But while we valued their connections and prestige, we found that they took some time to adapt to our pace and style. Some of the ideas they had presented at our first proper strategy session, in mid-January, had been almost embarrassingly bad. It was difficult to know where to turn when they suggested that Miss Boo should appear on the *Muppet Show*, or that KC and the Sunshine Band should record a boo theme song, 'Shake Your boo-Day', to be launched in clubs with a 24-hour dance-a-thon. Then there was the Chinese takeaway promotion: 'Find Miss Boo in your fortune cookie and receive a lifetime supply of sneakers.' These sorts of ideas might be fine for Kellogg's Cornflakes, but were hardly going to help to establish boo.com as an icon of fashion.

A month later, we returned to New York determined to refocus them on what they really needed to do for us – use all the contacts they boasted about to get us access to the top editors and journalists.

If they could do that, we'd be able to handle the rest ourselves. But as our cab drew up outside their massive office building on Lexington Avenue, I had a feeling that this was going to be a tall order.

With Charlotte, Edward and Jay Herratti, Kajsa and I took the elevator up to Hill & Knowlton's floor and stepped into a windowless world. If only they could let a little real light into the place, I found myself thinking, maybe they'd have some better ideas.

Pam Fields, our senior relationship manager, introduced us to four of her colleagues and led us all into a meeting room dominated by a huge polished wooden table. A whiteboard stood in the corner, still covered with notes from an earlier session.

I got straight to the point. Our goal was a wave of publicity to coincide with our launch in May. 'We want to start with the top fashion magazines like *Vogue* and *Harper's Bazaar*.' Articles in these sorts of magazines usually had to be arranged at least three months in advance. 'Once we've done those,' I continued, 'maybe we can do *Time* and *Newsweek* and some of the other weekly magazines. Then, last of all, newspapers and TV.'

After an awkward silence Pam Fields was first to speak. A former management consultant in her early forties, she combined a motherly manner with the smart and tough persona of a typical American career woman. Usually she was self-possessed and calm, but now I detected a slight edge in her voice.

'Ernst,' she said, clasping her hands together. 'You have to remember that this is a country of 300 million people. The competition for media space here is probably the toughest in the world.'

'I know,' I said. 'But this is a great story. There's a fashion angle, an internet angle, a business angle . . .' I was ticking them off on my fingers.

At this point Janet Bartucci, one of the agency's senior executives, joined in. 'What you need is to build some credibility before you go out to these sorts of publications.'

'We have a track record,' Kajsa replied. 'We've already built and sold one internet company.'

'That was in Sweden, wasn't it?'

'So?' said Kajsa testily.

'All I'm saying is that people here often don't care what you've done unless you've done it in America.'

I was beginning to lose my patience. I thought of the poetry festival we had put on in this town, how we had been just two unknown Swedes then, yet had got everyone talking about us. If these guys wanted to work with us, I thought, they were doing a pretty lousy job of showing it.

'If you don't have the contacts,' I said in an abrupt tone, 'maybe we should go somewhere else.'

Pam Fields leaned back in her chair, a faint smile on her face. 'We have the contacts,' she said. 'And we'll do our best. We just don't want you to have unrealistic expectations.'

Having reached an understanding of sorts, Fields introduced us to the two more junior people in the room, John DeMaria, a fast-talking New Yorker who handled the PR agency's relations with the internet media, and Jessica Kogan, who had done PR work for the likes of New York fashion house DKNY and cosmetics giant Elizabeth Arden. The obvious hope was that these younger people would be more in tune with what we were trying to achieve.

'Jessica here will be making the calls to journalists,' said Fields. 'You'll be dealing with her more than me, but I'll keep a close eye on how things are going.'

While the other executives excused themselves, Kogan and DeMaria began to discuss with us the most promising pitches. There was the 'Europeans taking on the world' angle: we were the first major European start-up in a sector heavily dominated by Americans. Then there was the fact that we had LVMH, one of the biggest fashion names in the world, as an investor. Other angles included our state-of-the art technology, which would make fashion available to people wherever they were; and, perhaps most important of all, the personal side of our story. The partnership between Kajsa and me provided the sort of 'human interest' angle that the media loved. Kajsa was an ex-model and – as Jessica put it – a 'working mom', while I was a 'quirky' former poetry critic. Then there was the poetry festival itself. 'People here will remember us,' I said, leafing through my papers for the piece that had appeared in *Esquire*. The session lasted around four hours. We must have seemed rather intimidating, such was the confidence we had in our ability to promote ourselves. There may have been a lot ahead for us to learn about running a global business, but PR had been the centre of everything we had done since the festival. Kogan was young, energetic and enthusiastic. That was a good start. But we needed results as well. I tried to impress this on her before we left.

'We'll be back in New York in three weeks,' I said firmly. 'I want a full schedule of meetings lined up by then.'

In the evening, the boo group gathered in a bar for a post-mortem.

'It was like a bunker in there,' said Jay. 'Post-World War Three.'

He was right. In a place like that you could quickly forget that the outside world even existed.

'Maybe they *don't* have the contacts,' I mused. 'Maybe we should ring the editors ourselves. That's what we did with the poetry festival.'

Jay grimaced. 'If I have to hear about that poetry festival one more time . . .'

Back in London, we turned our attention to advertising. In the days after our falling-out with Leagas Delaney, I had tagged along with Kajsa to meet with several possible replacements. Top of Kajsa's wish list was Wieden & Kennedy. She was particularly impressed by the work they had done for Nike. It was a huge multinational corporation, yet its brand was still something that the ordinary guy could identify with: 'Nike reminds people that sport is for everyone, not just superstars.' It was a great angle – we could do with something like that ourselves. We were confident that Wieden & Kennedy would grasp our concept of promoting sports and fashion together. So it was a disappointment to discover that their contract with Nike prevented them from working with potential competitors.

Understanding the concept was an essential requirement of any agency we chose to work with. Visually stunning ideas were not enough in themselves. Trevor Beattie, the creative director of TBWA who pitched to us, had plenty of those – we especially liked his campaigns for French Connection, Apple and Wonderbra – but in the end we were sceptical about whether the creative work he showed us was putting across exactly the message we wanted. The one agency that seemed able to listen closely to our ideas and then translate them into powerful advertising was BMP. A division of DDB – the world's biggest ad agency, with offices in seventy countries – it had clients like Sony, Volkswagen and Budweiser. We gelled immediately with their creative team, whose work had the contemporary edge we were looking for. Their pitch played on the idea of being uncool in order to be cool – 'geek chic'. It was perfect. That was what we had been trying to say all along.

Now that we had found our ad agency at last, it was time to set out our overall marketing strategy and bring together the key members of the team. In early March, Kajsa arranged a global marketing meeting at BMP headquarters near London's Paddington station. It was quite a gathering. Richard Morris, our account manager at BMP, had set aside a huge meeting room, but, just before our scheduled start at 9 a.m., still had to rush off to get more chairs.

BMP made the most of the home advantage to turn out in force. Richard Morris was joined by two other account managers, two creative directors, a media planner, a media buyer and one of the firm's top advertising executives from New York – and those were just the people I happened to recognize. The boo delegation consisted of Kajsa and me, Jay Herratti from New York, Christoph Vilanek, the head of our German office, Therese Agerberth, marketing manager for Scandinavia, and Niclas Sellebråten, our head of design. Jessica Kogan and John DeMaria had come over on behalf of Hill & Knowlton, and also there was a young designer called Fanny Krivoy, representing Organic, the technology firm that was dealing with the 'front end' of our website.

The atmosphere was electrifying. It wasn't very often that companies built an international brand from scratch, let alone a fashion brand, let alone an *internet* fashion brand. We all sat down at an enormous round table with an inner ring that could be spun around to pass documents from one side of the table to another. Kajsa opened the proceedings with a quick introduction of everyone and an overview of why we were all there. 'The only way this is going to work is if we all act as a team,' she said, before handing the floor to BMP.

Jeremy Craigen and Jo Wenley, of the creative team, presented first. Both were easygoing and dressed in casual clothes.

'Geek chic,' declared Jeremy Craigen. 'It's about not taking yourself too seriously.' To explain what he meant, he switched on a giant TV and ran a video for the song 'Praise You' by Fatboy Slim. A group of nerds in a crowded shopping mall danced to a song blaring from a huge ghetto-blaster, uncoordinated and unaware of the amused stares of the passers-by. Instead of featuring top sports people, Craigen explained, boo's ads would show geeks trying to be sporty and failing. 'We're trying to say that boo.com is where sports meets the computer world. The geeks have found out about sports by buying their clothes from boo.'

Now Jo Wenley stood up. 'This is the sort of thing we have in mind.' She showed us a mock-up ad of a skinny guy with shorts and running shoes throwing up in a rubbish bin on a street corner; then a second ad of a nerd with blood on his knees and a skateboard under his arm.

'The TV commercial will pick up on the same theme,' said Craigen. 'We're going to let a bunch of geeks loose on the streets of LA, then film the reactions of genuine passers-by as our geeks fail at being sporty.' He then explained that the Fatboy Slim video had been made by Roman Coppola, son of the famous movie director, and they would try to get hold of him to shoot the commercial. 'He'll be perfect. He has a really spontaneous style.'

BMP's planner, Myriam Van Der Elst, spoke next. Her job was to decide how our advertising spend should be divided up. It called for some ingenuity, because our total marketing budget for that year of $25 million was tiny for the global print, television and cinema campaign we were planning. Just one 30-second television slot played during peak viewing time in the US could set us back up to $100,000.

The first ads would not appear until June, a month after our website had launched. That would give us enough time to sort out any technical glitches in our system before too much traffic visited the site. Even then, the ads would appear only in a few style magazines like *ID*, *The Face*, *Arena* and *Details*. 'It'll make you seem more exclusive.' Mainstream publications like *Vogue*, *GQ* and *Elle* would follow, and then a cinema and outdoor campaign – billboards and bus stops. As TV was so expensive, we would have to be very careful to choose slots in those programmes that were most popular with our target audience. 'We'll probably start with *Ally McBeal* and *Seinfeld*.'

It was Kajsa's turn to speak again. boo, she explained, had built up a sizeable marketing team of its own, which would back up the advertising and PR campaigns with 'grassroots', or 'guerrilla' activities. We now had people in place in all the boo offices to come up with ideas appropriate to the local markets. This third strand of marketing would help us to get as much for our money as possible. We planned to put up fly-posters and stickers on walls and lamp-posts, sponsor summer festivals and put on special events in beaches and bars. We were also making a massive effort to bolster our presence online, forging alliances with other sites and speaking to all the search engines. Then there was the boo shoe. We had asked one of our suppliers, New Balance, to make up 300 pairs of trainers, with our name boo.com on the side and in a special colour that wasn't on the market: we were going to send them to the movers and shakers in the fashion industry. To help us with our guerrilla campaign in the US, we were planning to hire the movie director Spike Lee, who had a company that specialized in this kind of work.

As the presentations continued, papers spun back and forth on the inner ring of the table like dishes at a Chinese restaurant. I had to look away every now and then to stop from getting dizzy. The only slight distraction, during the afternoon, was Jay Herratti's constant slipping in and out of the room to take calls from New York. He had just opened the boo office there, and recruiting was in full swing. Otherwise, there was an exhilarating sense of mental energy and intense concentration, as everyone took in the details of a complex and carefully planned campaign. We didn't break for lunch; instead, food and refreshments were shuttled in to us at regular intervals, as we brainstormed on through the day.

Niclas Sellebråten unveiled our brand-new super-ellipsoid logo and explained how its unique shape would be exploited throughout our website. Fanny Krivoy from Organic then talked about the work that had already begun on our website design.

The mood in the room was immensely positive and upbeat, although the proposed tagline for our ads was a cause of brief controversy. BMP's creative team had come up with 'boo.com – the sports shop on the net'. It seemed inoffensive enough, but opinions were strong.

'We're not just selling sportswear,' Kajsa stressed.

'What about "sports and fashion"?' suggested Christoph Vilanek, boo's German boss.

'No,' Kajsa retorted at once. 'A really fashionable fashion shop wouldn't use the word "fashion".'

Jay had a problem with the word 'shop'.

'That won't work in America,' he said.

'Why not?' Kajsa asked.

'It sounds too small. Like 'the shop around the corner'. We need something that suggests we carry a lot of brands and a lot of products.'

'What about "store"?' suggested John DeMaria.

'Too downmarket,' I said.

Ideas began flying around the room. 'Emporium', maybe – or what about 'bazaar'?

The climax came when Stuart Mattson, BMP's creative guru from New York, spoke up. Blond with glasses, he had been listening intently, his eyes half shut as if focused on some powerful abstract idea. 'boo,' he said, in a slow voice, 'is like the centre of a trade route. Like Casablanca, or . . .' He hesitated. 'Or like that town in *Star Wars* where Luke and Obi-Wan meet Han Solo for the first time.' Then, waving his hands in the air like the conductor of an orchestra reaching the finale, he declared, 'boo is like a souk. It's a global souk on the internet.'

But the idea didn't really catch on. The tagline we eventually agreed on was 'boo.com – sports and streetwear on the net'.

Jay thought it worked well, but pointed out that we would have to be very careful in the US about the juxtaposition of sports and fashion. 'The word "fashion" will really turn off the sports enthusiasts,' he warned. 'Americans take the athletic lifestyle very seriously and we need to take account of that.'

But with one or two similar reservations aside, the general mood as the meeting broke up late in the afternoon was one of jubilation.

We had worked out a brilliant campaign. I could already imagine boo's name appearing on lamp-posts, in magazines, at the movies. The thing that bothered me most now was the technology. If we were going to generate all this publicity, we really had to deliver.

There was one critical piece of technology that had yet to be finalized. For months we'd been hunting for a company that could handle the job of producing 3D photographs for our website. This was central to our entire business concept – it was what made us different from every other website in the world. For the first time, customers would be able to zoom in on items of clothing and manipulate them online. This was what had so excited the investors and the suppliers when we toured the world with our prototype. If we could turn the spinning shoe they had seen into online reality, we would have made a huge advance in bridging the gap between e-commerce and traditional retailing.

But being a pioneer had its drawbacks. Only a handful of companies around the world specialized in such cutting-edge technology, and all were tiny. The main users of 3D photography were the car companies, but they rarely placed orders for more than 100 or so photographs at a time. What we were talking about was in a different league: 3D images for an entire product catalogue of around 5,000 items to be delivered within weeks. Most of the companies we contacted told us it was impossible. Only a small Los Angeles-based firm named eVox was prepared to take on the challenge.

I had visited eVox's CEO, David Falstrup, during the Christmas trip Charlotte and I made to Los Angeles. He hadn't been easy to find. eVox's office was in an industrial zone on the edge of the city. Angry dogs jumped at the car as we pulled up outside. At the entrance to the building we had to answer detailed questions about who we were and sign a non-disclosure agreement before we were allowed to enter. Security cameras were trained on us as we went inside.

'Maybe they've got a Stealth bomber in here,' I joked, as a guard led us into the inner sanctum.

'And I thought you guys were secretive!' said Charlotte.

Falstrup turned out to be an almost religious believer in the future of 3D technology. 'I knew this day would come,' he said, making no attempt to hide his rapture as I explained our plans.

Eventually I handed over responsibility for dealing with eVox to Luke Alvarez, our new head of business development. Now, a couple of days after our marketing summit, Luke asked me if I would come along to a breakfast meeting at the Metropolitan Hotel with the co-founder of eVox, Kelley Peters. Luke had been working closely with eVox over the past couple of weeks on the project plans for the job ahead, and now was the time to decide if we were ready to finalize a deal.

It was London Fashion Week and the hotel's breakfast room was packed with small clusters of middle-aged women chatting loudly about the latest collections. Luke and I spotted Peters in a corner, looking slightly uncomfortable in a suit and tie. After we'd all ordered breakfast, Peters opened a glossy booklet and began talking me through the plan. It was a lot more complicated than I had realized.

'We're going to need four teams working simultaneously to photograph all the clothes,' Peters said.

'How many people is that?' I asked.

'At least sixty,' he replied, flicking to another page in the booklet. 'We'll need twenty-eight people to do the manual work; another eighteen to take the photos and cut out the backgrounds so all you see are the clothes. The rest will be stylists.' He noticed my confused expression. 'They'll dress the mannequins,' he explained. 'We'll also need a couple of extra people to tag and identify all the boxes that come in.'

I was stunned. 'Do we really need all of that?' That was more people than we then had on our entire payroll.

'Do you want it done by May?' he asked.

'That's when we launch.'

'Then we need all these people.'

There were further complexities, Peters explained. Like the mannequins. We needed two male and two female mannequins that had to be identical in shape and pose to the virtual mannequin on our website. If there was even the tiniest difference, the clothes we photographed on the real mannequins wouldn't fit on to the virtual one.

'You'll also have to decide what they look like,' he added. A white Anglo-Saxon-looking mannequin would not be appropriate for a global online retailer. We'd have to work out some kind of racial hybrid. 'Maybe we can paint them grey or something,' Peters mused.

I was impressed by the thought that eVox had given to everything. This was a make or break project for them and they were obviously taking it very seriously. We ended the meeting with an agreement in principle. All that remained was to iron out the terms, which Luke would handle. The key factor, as always, was speed. If eVox didn't get started soon, it would never be able to deliver enough 3D images in time for our launch. Alvarez and Peters spent the next couple of days cooped up with lawyers, trying to reach some common ground.

Late in the first afternoon, Alvarez came over to my desk. 'They want $1.5 million,' he said, 'but $500,000 up front.'

'Can't you get them down a bit?' I asked.

'I tried,' he said. 'But they can't afford to buy all the equipment.'

I found this news worrying. I knew eVox was a small company and I wondered how safe it was to hand over a large amount of money to people we knew almost nothing about. For a second, it crossed my mind that they might run off with it.

'Ask if we can look at their balance sheet,' I said. 'I think we need to know more about them.'

eVox agreed, reluctantly, to supply some basic financial accounts for us to glance through. The company's revenues in the previous year had been only a few hundred thousand dollars. So they were a real company after all, if a small one.

I told Alvarez to do the deal. In just a few days, I was due to head back to New York with Kajsa and Patrik to start meeting journalists. I wanted everything signed and sealed before we left. Even so, I insisted on a few clauses in the agreement first. These included a guarantee from eVox that it wouldn't work with certain competitors. If we were going to spend millions helping eVox create an industrial-sized 3D imaging operation, we didn't want them selling their services to our rivals. The list we gave them contained around fifty names, including internet companies like Amazon.com and retailers like Foot Locker. If anyone wanted to copy what we were doing, they'd have to start from scratch, with a different company. As far as I could see, we had effectively cornered the world market in 3D imaging – for a while at least.

We arrived back in New York late on the evening of 8 March for what was scheduled to be a hectic week-long visit. Apart from launching our PR offensive, we had promised to help Jay with setting up his office and hiring senior staff. Then, between whatever interviews Hill & Knowlton had managed to line up, there would also be meetings with Organic and several potential new suppliers.

We were tired and irritable as our plane touched down, two hours late, at JFK airport, but excited at the prospect of finally telling our story to the world. Since our last visit three weeks ago, we had remained in regular contact with Jessica Kogan, who had produced a series of press releases, each angled at a different kind of publication.

For women's magazines, boo.com was a new age shopping experience: 'From this summer on, there will be a way to purchase sports and gymwear whilst avoiding the imposing masculinity of the high street sports store.' For financial publications, it was all about money: 'boo.com has successfully raised finance through J.P. Morgan and achieved the highest ever valuation for an internet start-up.' For the technical magazines, the pitch was that at last a website had arrived which used technology with style: 'boo.com will deliver a unique combination of the e-commerce expertise usually associated with US sites, and the innovative visual design for which Europe is renowned.'

Results were already starting to come in, Kogan had told us just before we left London, but she had been vague about details. 'I'll tell you everything when you get here.'

Our usual hotel – the SoHo Grand – was full, so we had booked rooms at the Royalton in mid-town. We arrived to find a faxed schedule of magazine interviews from Kogan already waiting for us. There were just three names.

What is this? I thought. Some kind of a joke? I went to bed tired and angry.

We met Kogan in the hotel's lounge bar at nine the following morning. She seemed edgy.

'How was your flight?' she asked.

'Late,' I replied. I'd been awake since 5 a.m. and had a dull ache in the back of my head. It was difficult to appear cheerful. Kajsa and Patrik, who were sitting in a deep sofa, looked equally tired.

'Things are going pretty well,' Kogan said, reaching into her bag and handing each of us a sheet of paper. On it was a list of all the meetings that had been lined up so far.

'Yes. We've seen this. *Vibe . . . Allure . . . Women's Sports & Fitness . . .* Where are the rest?' I asked, turning the page over in case I'd missed something. They weren't exactly A-list magazines. I could probably have arranged most of these meetings myself. 'Have you spoken to *Vogue* yet?'

'That's all we have right now,' Kogan said, in a slightly forced, light tone.

'You need to try harder,' I said, bluntly. 'This is really important.'

'I am trying. I'm really doing my best, but it's harder than you think. Some of these magazines take a while to respond.'

As if remembering something, Kogan reached into her bag and pulled out a piece of paper. 'This is a teaser letter,' she said. 'I've started sending it out to some of the editors. It should help.'

I glanced over it. 'The first truly fashionable experience on the web is on its way,' ran the heading. Underneath were a few points on the 'Concept'. A new global sports fashion boutique was about to offer 'an edgy shopping experience, but the most exciting part is' – and it went on in big letters – 'we can't wait to tell you all about it!!' The notes that followed on 'People', with the key words highlighted in bold, were even more irritating:

> **young**, trend setting entrepreneurs
> have graced **european** best dressed lists and walked down more than a few catwalks
> proven e-commerce/**fashion** track record
> if you want to meet the next e-commerce **superstars** . . .
> **we can't wait to introduce you!!**

'This is really tacky,' I said, handing it to Kajsa, who pursed her lips.

'This isn't the kind of message we want to send out,' she observed. 'It's really self-promotional.'

'I know what you mean,' Kogan said, 'and if we were in Europe I'd never send out something like this. But Americans respond to hype. We've got to do everything we can to sell this story.'

I disagreed. As far as I was concerned, the story didn't need to be 'sold'. It was good enough to sell itself. By now, though, I was feeling a little sorry for Kogan. We were very demanding and probably totally different from her usual clients. She just had to get to know us better.

We spent the next half-hour preparing for our first scheduled meeting, with *Vibe* magazine, later that morning.

Vibe was a hip music and lifestyle magazine. 'I know the editor,' Kogan said. 'He's a really nice guy. I think this will be a really good place to start.' As she spoke, the three of us listened quietly, trying to stay positive. However cool it was, *Vibe* was hardly going to help us to take America by storm. It would have been nice if Jessica had managed to fix up more than just three interviews. Whenever we were in New York, we tried to pack our schedule as fully as we could. It was too expensive and time-consuming a trip for us to take kindly to just kicking our heels.

Patrik, luckily, had already worked out a full schedule of his own. He had a meeting lined up with David Bolotsky, the Goldman Sachs retail analyst that we'd met almost a year earlier. He was also making serious headway in his financial negotiations with Alessandro Benetton. Things were going so well, in fact, that he was to attend an urgent meeting with lawyers from Skadden Arps to help draw up a shareholder's agreement.

Kajsa and I turned up at *Vibe*'s offices with Michael Skidmore. He was a big name in New York fashion and I wanted to show him off as much as possible. Kogan had gone back to her office to pick some things up, but was waiting in reception for us when we arrived. As we were a little early, she gave us a few final tips for the interview. A quarter of an hour later, we were still waiting. Eventually, Kogan got up. 'I'll just go see what's happening,' she said, walking past the receptionist and into the office. She was back a few minutes later, looking flushed. 'I'm really sorry about this, guys. He forgot.'

'So let's go in now, then,' Skidmore said.

'He can't do it now. He's busy with something else. But he can probably see us tomorrow.'

'I don't believe this!' said Skidmore, glaring at Jessica. 'We're professional people. We arrive on time, and we expect people to be ready to see us.'

I agreed. 'You can't waste our time like this.' I knew it wasn't all her fault. But she couldn't be selling our story very well if people forgot about us that easily. Kajsa, Skidmore and I picked up our things and marched out, while Jessica, almost on the point of tears, sheepishly headed back to her office.

As we walked down the street, Kajsa rang Pam Fields. 'Maybe Jessica's not the right person to handle us. Can you give us someone else?'

Fields, with her motherly manner, tried to calm things down. 'Jessica is good at her job,' she said. 'Just give her another chance.'

After our abortive meeting with *Vibe* we had some time to kill, and I decided to go on a quick shopping expedition. This wasn't just for pleasure. It was a necessity. Kajsa had lined up a photo-shoot for the following day at a Manhattan studio called The Space. We needed some glossy pictures to complete our press kit. Good photographs always help when it comes to getting media attention. If an editor has to choose between an article with a great picture and one without, he'll usually choose the first.

But we weren't going to have any great pictures unless I made some effort to look the part, as Kajsa was quick to point out. 'That's a winter suit,' she said, fingering the thick fabric of my jacket. 'By the time the articles come out it will be summer.' It wouldn't do, I agreed, for the CEO of a fashion company to be wearing last season's styles.

For tips on where to go, I turned to Michael Skidmore. 'I don't want to waste too much time,' I said.

'No problem,' he said. 'Just head over to Barneys. I'll get them to fix you up with a personal shopper.'

I invited Jay and Edward to tag along. Jay, who would be getting his photo taken as well, was looking for a new suit, anyway.

The idea of having my own personal shopper wasn't something I had really considered before. I didn't even know what it involved. When we arrived at Barneys, I asked our shopper, a groomed, obliging fellow named Brad, to fill us in.

'Is this just for rich people?' I asked.

'Oh, no. It's all sorts now.' He waved his arm at the crowds of people picking through the clothes racks. 'People don't have as much time as they used to.'

Brad led us into an empty room just behind the fitting rooms. 'What sort of suits are you looking for?' he asked as we sat down on some comfortable chairs.

Jay and Edward looked to me as CEO to lead the way.

'This season, please,' I said. 'Something contemporary.'

'What sort of brands do you like?'

'Prada, Gucci and Paul Smith.'

'Do you want something casual or tailored? . . . What kind of colours are you after?' As I answered his questions, he took notes on a small pad.

A light lunch was brought to us while Brad went off to fetch some suits. A few minutes later he returned with five or six, which he hung up on a wall.

In between mouthfuls of a pastrami club sandwich, I pointed to the ones I liked. What a wonderful way to shop, I thought. This was obviously the way that department stores would have to go in the future to compete with the online experience.

As I hardly ever had time to buy clothes, I decided to make the most of the opportunity, choosing two Prada suits – one navy, the other light bice – and a very classic linen suit by Hermès.

'I'd like something suitable for work and receptions,' said Jay when it came to his turn. 'Black, please. And could I try something Hermès too?'

Edward looked at suits and overcoats. Since that first day when he turned up in a Marks & Spencer suit, he had been working hard to develop a fashion sense. Indeed, one of the small triumphs of boo.com was that he now realized the importance of boo.com's global fashion brand.

Once we had tried everything on and made our final choices, Brad led us off to see a tailor to have our suits adjusted. I explained that they were needed urgently and it was arranged that they would be delivered to the photo-shoot studio the next day.

This sort of shopping expedition could hardly be charged as a company expense, so we gave Brad our personal credit cards, which he took out to a sales till on the shop floor. The total bill came to something like $10,000.

He returned again a few minutes later, looking embarrassed. 'They've been rejected,' he said.

'Which one?' Edward asked.

'All of them.'

Our cards had been maxed out from all the travelling we had been doing. But Brad kindly allowed us to open an account instead, using Jay's driver's licence as proof of ID.

'I'll bet you his customers haven't done that to him too many times,' Edward said as we left the store.

In the afternoon, we headed over to have a look around the new boo office, near the piers on Hudson Street. 'It's just a temporary space,' Jay explained. 'We're going to move upstairs in a couple of weeks.' There were boxes everywhere and just a few lonely-looking pieces of furniture.

He led us upstairs to inspect boo's new premises. Previously a printer's workshop, the place had an industrial feel to it, but with its huge open-plan layout had a lot of potential. Jay was clearly relieved to have found somewhere at last, after having worked out of his living room for more than two months. It meant he could start recruiting. Although Skidmore was based at the New York office, Jay had only two staff of his own – an assistant and an office manager. Over the next month, he planned to add forty more.

We joined Kajsa and Skidmore who were sitting at a small table by the window, talking about furniture. Kajsa wanted to hire a Swedish architect to design all our offices. As we discussed furniture and colour schemes, my phone rang. It was Jessica Kogan.

'I've got some great news,' she said. 'I just got off the phone with one of the editors at *Women's Wear Daily*. They're really interested in the story.'

This information had no effect on me at first.

'I've lined up an interview tomorrow with one of their reporters,' Jessica continued.

Then it hit home.

'What are you talking about?!' I said.

Women's Wear Daily was a daily publication. But we had made it clear that we wouldn't talk to dailies or weeklies until we were ready to launch. This had been a cardinal rule of our entire PR strategy.

Jessica, who hadn't noticed my tone, said, 'I think they want to do a cover piece for later this week.'

Now I was really upset. 'This is a disaster,' I said, my voice rising sharply. 'How could you do this? You're going to destroy everything.'

There was silence on the end of the line.

'Did you call them?' I said.

'No . . .' Jessica's tone was hesitant. 'They just found out. Maybe someone at *Vogue* told them.'

I didn't believe her. 'We can't let this happen. We have to stop it. If this comes out, all the newspapers are going to see it.'

'I really don't think other papers will pick this up,' Jessica said, almost whispering now.

'Look, I can't speak to you any more. We need to speak to Pam immediately.'

'She's not here at the moment.'

'Well, tell her to call us.'

The others in the room had been listening and looked worried. When I explained the situation, the reactions were mixed. Kajsa agreed with me. 'The internet is so hot,' she said. 'Everyone is going to write about this.'

Jay tried to calm us down. Both he and Skidmore thought we were overestimating the media's interest in our story anyway.

'It's really not that terrible,' Michael Skidmore said. '*Women's Wear Daily* is a respected trade magazine.'

'It's two months too early,' I said. 'This blows our secrecy completely.'

When Pam Fields finally called two hours later, we put her on the speakerphone. She listened sympathetically as we explained our concerns.

'What you have to realize,' she said, finally, 'is that *Women's Wear Daily* is the fashion bible. Everyone in the fashion world reads it. This could really help you a lot.'

'That's great. But why now?' Kajsa said. 'Can't you stop the story somehow?'

'Try to think about it rationally,' Fields said. 'You don't want to upset a trade magazine. They can make life really difficult for you.'

Remembering the trouble that LeanderMalmsten had once had with the *Svensk Bokhandel*, I had to concede that she might have a point.

She proceeded to reel off some examples of people who had offended *Women's Wear Daily* and paid the consequences. Like Geoffrey Beene, a designer who had been blacklisted from its pages since allowing a rival publication to photograph his country home more than a decade ago. Even the great Giorgio Armani had been banished for a year when he got too friendly with *Time* magazine. 'They can crush you,' Fields said. 'You have to do this interview.' Her manner was calm and authoritative. 'As for keeping it a secret,' she added, 'you can't keep a secret for more than five minutes in the garment district.'

'What happens if the *Financial Times* sees it?' I asked.

'If this is picked up by the dailies,' she said, 'you can fire us.'

I was so upset that I was half sorry we hadn't done so already, but I knew we had to make the best out of the situation. 'We'll just have to hope everything works out,' I said icily.

There were a few immediate issues to deal with. Some of our suppliers, like North Face, had made it clear they didn't want any press coverage about their involvement with us until they had informed their retailers. Charlotte had to call around urgently to warn them all. This meant getting up at 3 a.m. so that the European suppliers could be told as they arrived at their offices in the morning. Patrik got little more sleep that night. He had to call the investors. His first concern was Benetton. They were now on the verge of signing and he didn't want anything to jeopardize the deal.

The following morning, Kajsa and I headed over to Hill &

Knowlton's office with Michael Skidmore to meet the journalist from *Women's Wear Daily*. We were very nervous. Dealing with the media was something Kajsa and I had never much liked in the first place, and the circumstances made the occasion even more stressful than usual. The three of us agreed to say as little as possible. 'The less we say, the less he can write,' I pointed out.

Pam Fields was waiting for us when we arrived, but Kogan was nowhere to be seen. That was fine with me. She'd done enough harm already.

Fields ushered us into a meeting room. 'He'll be here in twenty minutes,' she said. 'We should go over a few things first.' But we hardly needed any encouragement from her to avoid questions about our finances and our suppliers.

'Stick to your roles,' she said finally, with a pointed look at Skidmore. 'You should probably only answer questions about fashion.'

I agreed. Skidmore was a great talker, but I didn't want him jabbering on about company-related issues.

The journalist, Miles Socha, arrived soon afterwards. He seemed laid-back and friendly, but I sensed a slight wariness in his tone. Maybe Kogan had warned him about us, I thought to myself. I hoped it was just my paranoia.

'This is the first feature we've ever done on the internet,' Socha said. 'We're especially interested in the LVMH angle.' After weeks of circling, he explained, LVMH was about to launch a hostile takeover bid for Gucci. 'Everyone's interested in LVMH right now.'

At first the interview was a cat-and-mouse affair. Socha would ask questions and we would give short, tight-lipped answers, which only provoked his curiosity even further. As he pressed harder, we went a little further than giving name, rank and serial number, but not much.

'Tell me about your suppliers,' he asked. 'How many have you got now? How are they dealing with their existing retailers?'

We froze.

'What do we say?' Kajsa asked me in Swedish.

I wasn't sure. 'Excuse us a moment,' I said, as Kajsa and I dragged Pam Fields out into the hallway to ask her advice.

'How much have you told him already?' I asked.

144

'Hardly anything,' she replied. 'You've got to relax a bit. You're making him suspicious.'

Kajsa took control once we got back inside. 'We've got some great suppliers on board – New Balance, Converse, Puma, Vans . . .' And she pointed out that we posed no serious threat to the retailers because we were not discounters.

The mood lightened as Socha's photographer came in to take a few pictures. We chatted away in a more relaxed manner and, at last, an hour and a half after it had begun, the interview was over.

We thought that the interview had gone about as well as we could have hoped for, but there was no time to dwell on it because we had to dash off at once to our photo shoot on the other side of town. The studio was in an enormous warehouse on West 15th Street, with wooden floors, exposed brick and open-beamed ceilings. The atmosphere, when we arrived about twenty minutes late, was chaotic. Everywhere people were arranging lighting, preparing different coloured backdrops and just hanging around smoking cigarettes.

Jay was already there, standing against a dark backdrop: the sober smile of President, boo.com North America was frozen in the bright studio lights. When he had finished posing for his portraits, he joined us with an incredulous smile.

'Are you guys out of your mind? This is like a movie set. How much is all this costing?'

Both amused and puzzled, Jay had never understood the need for this fashion shoot. But it wasn't vanity. The photographer's assistants and stylists were certainly very expensive, but if the pictures persuaded papers to write about us – maybe drawing us to the attention of important potential investors or business partners – they would have paid for themselves many times over.

'And what's with the big fan here?' Jay continued. 'Is this a business portrait or a hair commercial?'

I laughed. It was pointless to try to explain that it was a bit of both.

'Enjoy yourselves,' Jay said, as he headed for the exit. 'I've got some *real* work to do. Ten more candidates to interview today.'

Kajsa began to look through two huge racks of designer outfits. The brands, hungry for the opportunity to show off their clothes, gave them to studio fashion stylists for free. It was difficult to choose, but with Charlotte's help she finally settled on a dark Marc Jacobs jacket which she handed over to the stylist to iron. She then went off to be made up and to have her hair done.

The photographer, a Swede named John Scarisbrick, had taken the picture of Kajsa and me for *Esquire* magazine in 1993. Back then, he was just starting out. Now he was one of New York's better-known fashion photographers, and had also done portraits of people like Hillary Clinton, David Bowie and the Red Hot Chili Peppers. While we waited for Kajsa, we kept ourselves busy in different ways. Charlotte and Edward plugged in their laptops and tapped away; I had a bite to eat and then helped Michael Skidmore to interview a bewildered-looking candidate for the position of junior buyer – the boo mobile office in action.

All the while there was soft music playing. It was an important element of any fashion shoot – there to encourage the photographer's subjects to relax. When Kajsa returned, I changed into my new Prada suit and Doc Marten shoes and we were ready to begin. 'Try to breathe in deeply,' said John Scarisbrick, 'and make yourself as comfortable as possible.'

He began with various group shots, placing the industrial-strength fan that Jay had found so amusing just behind us to make Kajsa's long blonde hair fly up like something out of a Bee Gees music video. The lights were so bright that I kept blinking.

'Oh, I remember that,' said Scarisbrick. 'Last time you did that, we had to destroy all the photographs.'

One of the stylists remarked on the awkward way in which Patrik in his banker's pinstripe suit contrasted with Kajsa and me in our brand-new designer clothes. 'It doesn't quite work,' she kept saying. It was a difficulty that Kajsa and I had long been aware of, although we could hardly do anything about it now. But when the shoot was over, Kajsa asked if she and I could have some photos done together, without Patrik. 'It could come in useful for the publishing company,' she said. Our quiet hope was that we'd convince Patrik at some point to take more of a back-seat role when it came to PR.

★

Next morning we had a copy of *Women's Wear Daily* delivered to the Soho Grand. Jay had joined us at breakfast for the occasion. We stared at the crisp new edition, hardly daring to open it. The big story that day was the appearance of the 'Mistress of Wales', Camilla Parker-Bowles, at a Chloé fashion show in Paris. But across one corner of the cover picture of a model dressed in an Emanuel Ungaro 'Haute Hippie' cardigan was a thin red banner with the words: 'LVMH's New Online Investment.'

With a strange mix of excitement and fear, I finally opened the paper to find inside an entire page devoted to our story, with a photograph of Kajsa, Skidmore and me:

> Bernard Arnault has been described by colleagues as an avid Internaute – the French term for Internet user. Avid indeed. *WWD* has learned that LVMH Moët Hennessy Louis Vuitton is a key investor in a new international online superstore devoted to active sportswear — at least initially. Called boo.com, it is slated to become active in early May, selling apparel and footwear from the likes of New Balance, Puma, Converse, The North Face and Vans.

The article went on to note that investors were pumping 'tens of millions of dollars in the startup, which involves establishing offices and distribution centers in New York, Stockholm, Munich and London'.

Socha had also been in touch with some of the suppliers that we had done deals with in Atlanta a few weeks earlier. 'The initial order placed for Vans was just under $500,000 worth of product,' he pointed out. I was delighted to see that the suppliers had only good things things to say about us. Like the comments made by Jim Gorman, president of Puma North America: '"The Internet poses a new opportunity," Gorman said. "This is a fact of retail. This is the way we would prefer to go, as opposed to selling directly online ourselves."'

Then there was Jennifer Murray, vice president of marketing and communications at Converse: '"We're certainly sensitive to our accounts. We look at boo.com as another retail partner."' Converse was impressed with the company's merchandising skills and the success of bokus.com, she added.

Overall, it was an enormously positive article. Despite my misgivings, I couldn't help feeling a thrill at seeing the boo name in print for the first time. I looked up at the anxious faces of Kajsa, Patrik, Charlotte, Edward and Jay. For a while I had forgotten that they were there.

'It's OK,' I said. 'Everyone can have another piece of toast.' The first reactions soon arrived. At around 10 a.m., I got a call from Jean-Bernard Tellio of LVMH. He was in New York and wanted to meet for lunch.

Kajsa and I found him in the downstairs restaurant at Barneys.

'Did you see the article?' I asked.

He nodded cautiously. 'Yes. There's a bit of a problem.'

'What kind of problem?'

'Our PR people don't like the headline,' he said. He paused for a moment before continuing. 'What I should probably have made clear to you is that LVMH isn't technically an investor in boo.'

I grinned, assuming this was a joke. But his expression didn't change.

'The investment in boo was made with Bernard Arnault's personal money,' he went on. 'It was his private company – Markas Holdings.'

This was news to us. We thought we had been dealing with LVMH from the start. Even Tellio's business card had LVMH written on it.

'It's not that we don't like the article,' Tellio went on. 'It's great. But just try to play down the LVMH bit next time.'

There was some even more surprising news waiting for us when we got back to the office. Patrik, red-eyed from being up most of the night, had just spoken to Alessandro Benetton. 'They've decided to invest,' he said.

The Benettons had seen the article and loved it. Already close to signing, it was the final little push they needed. Patrik handed me a fax that had just come in from Luciano Favero of 21Investimenti. His English wasn't great, but the message was clear enough:

In our view, the first reason to invest lies in the trust the Benetton Group put in the founders and their business idea, so we like to stay with them, i.e. following them all the way through the initiative and in the exit process like real entrepreneurs used to do when they join together in a new venture.

The deal that Patrik had struck involved reopening our first round of funding, allowing 21Investimenti to take a 5 per cent stake in boo for $2.2 million. In exchange, the Benettons would get a board seat, but no other special favours. It was what we had wanted from the start.

We spent the rest of that day and the following day scanning the news wires and newspapers like the *Wall Street Journal* and the *Financial Times* for any mentions of boo. There was nothing. I wasn't sure whether to be pleased or disappointed. If people had seen the article, why were they ignoring it?

Kajsa and I started to feel a little guilty about how we had treated Jessica Kogan. By now, we knew for certain that she had leaked the story to *Women's Wear Daily* – it had been a ploy to get the attention of other fashion publications. But we had to admit that the gamble seemed to have paid off. We sent her a huge bouquet of flowers.

That same afternoon, she rang me on my mobile. She started by thanking me for the flowers. 'That was really nice of you,' she said. But she also had some news. 'Things are going amazingly well. Everyone saw the article. You're meeting *Vogue*, *Harper's Bazaar* and *Details* next week.' There were several other interviews besides. The meetings were due to start in a few days.

This was fantastic news. It was exactly what we'd been pushing for. At last, everything was on track. But it meant we'd have to stay in New York for at least an extra week, which raised certain logistical problems. Kajsa, who didn't like being away from her daughter for too long, decided to head back to London for three days, before joining us again when the meetings started.

For me, Michael Skidmore, Jay, Charlotte and Edward, the next few days passed in a blur of activity. We were up most mornings at 5 a.m. to get progress reports from the London office. Then we spent our days dashing from meeting to meeting. Among these was an intense day-long session with the web-design team at Organic. They had produced a creative brief that outlined what we were trying to achieve with the website. 'The design should be sporty and edgy "with a smile on the face,"' it read. 'The customer should come to the site not only to purchase clothes, but because the site is stylish and cool.' They had also produced templates illustrating the basic layout of each web page.

We were all absurdly busy, but none of us more so than Charlotte, who in effect was required to do the jobs of three different people. She had to get Michael Skidmore up to speed, helping him to recruit, and introducing him to suppliers; she had to sort out some business for Patrik, to whom she was still formally an executive assistant; and finally, she had to continue to build up her own contacts with suppliers around the world. It was hardly surprising when one night, still up at about 2 a.m. finishing some urgent task, she broke down in tears, caused by the sheer amount of work she was faced with. Of all the meetings Charlotte arranged with the suppliers, the most impor- tant by far was the one with Donna Karan – important because, although we had signed up more than a dozen sports-related brands so far, we still didn't have any big designer fashion labels on board. We hit it off immediately with the CEO John Idol, who had read the article in *Women's Wear Daily*. He watched intently as Charlotte took him through the prototype. Afterwards, he sat up straight in his chair.

'I get schmucks coming into my office every week,' he announced. 'But you guys are the only ones so far that have made any sense.' DKNY signed on the spot.

When we weren't racing around, we tried to make the most of the New York nightlife. Skidmore was often our guide on these outings. One evening, he took us out to a basketball game at Madison Square Garden, where we sat in the tiny VIP lounge with Woody Allen, actor Edward Norton and Scottish rock band Garbage.

When Kajsa got back, things became even more hectic. Kogan had lined up yet more interviews for us. In the week that followed, we were doing three or four a day. The high point was our brief but encouraging encounter with Kate Betts, the fashion news director of *Vogue*. Heavily pregnant, Betts showed us into her office, which was crammed with an odd assortment of clothes and other gifts from fashion suppliers clamouring for *Vogue*'s attention. I almost fell over a pair of Prada skis, lying on the floor.

'It's incredible the stuff we get sent in the mail,' Betts said casually.

Like everyone else, she had read the *Women's Wear Daily* piece. We showed her the prototype, which she loved. No promises were made, but we left feeling confident that a write-up in *Vogue* would probably follow.

That night I went out with Charlotte and Edward to celebrate. We didn't get back to the Soho Grand until about 1 a.m.

'Let's have a nightcap,' I said, heading for the bar.

They both said no, Charlotte pointing out that she'd have to be up again by 5 a.m. to begin her round of telephone calls to Europe.

'Only one,' I said. 'Don't be so boring.'

With weary shrugs of resignation, they followed me into the bar.

I ordered three vodka and grapefruits, with the grapefruit in a jug.

I put them down on the table to find Edward in one of his questioning moods.

'Why the jug?'

'The jug?'

'Why do you always ask for the grapefruit in a separate jug?'

'Because I don't like to have too much grapefruit juice,' I explained. 'This way you can control the concentration. If you want to drink a bottle of Absolut, you don't also want to drink ten litres of grapefruit juice.'

He looked at me quizzically. It was the start of a long interrogation that left me feeling a little like an illegal alien picked up on the beach without any papers.

'So how did this all begin?'

'How did what begin?'

'boo.com. How does a literary reviewer get to dream up the world's first global internet retailer? What's the secret?'

'How far back do you want me to go?'

'We've got all night.'

So I told them about my grandmother. When I was small, I spent a lot of time with her, as my parents were both professional people who worked very hard. One day she asked me, 'Can you play the violin?' As I was only five at the time and didn't even know what a violin looked like, it seemed a very silly question and I answered no. 'How do you know?' she then said. 'You've never tried.' It was her gentle way of instilling within me the Malmsten attitude. As an only child, I was probably slightly spoilt, but we were a very close family and I was encouraged to feel that I could achieve anything.

I could see that Edward, who was listening with a cynical expression, wanted to shove a violin in my hands there and then. But the point I was trying to make was that being an entrepreneur was not about making money; it was about making dreams come true.

Although I also had a knack of making money – from quite an early age. I told them about the stamp exhibition I held in our flat when I was about eight. I stuck homemade flyers up all around Lund to advertise the event and charged an admission fee to the visitors who turned up. I displayed my most valuable stamp, which was worth about £2, under a cheese dome, and set up a little museum shop in the hallway, where I sold stamps on cards. Two years later I organized a bottle-collecting club. The members would go around the Lund university campus asking the students for their old bottles and then collect the deposits. We made far more money than we knew what to do with. So we put on a big party with hamburgers and Coke and hired the film store's complete stock of old Super-8 comedies.

'You see, everyone has fun with me,' I said.

But Charlotte didn't look convinced.

'Why do you never sleep?' she asked in a half-reproachful tone. 'Why do you never take a holiday?'

She needed *her* sleep and, after months of deprivation, the story from my childhood that struck the biggest chord with her was the one about the sandpit.

'I was a terror,' I admitted.

'Those poor children,' she said. 'No wonder you're such a dictator.'

'Your grandmother has a lot to answer for,' added Edward.

'Don't worry,' I said to both of them. 'It's fantastic what we've achieved here, and everything will be much easier once we get back to London.'

But we all knew it was only wishful thinking.

7

'IT LOOKS LIKE A TOY,' Kajsa said, as we drove through the steel-fenced entrance of a small airfield just outside Hamburg. The place was almost deserted, apart from a few lonely-looking ground crew and a tiny plane that was quivering in the strong afternoon breeze.

Kajsa hated planes, especially little ones. I didn't like them much, either. But this wasn't some propeller-driven death trap, as we realized when our driver pulled up alongside. It was a jet. Tiny, yes. But still a jet.

A middle-aged official in uniform was standing on the tarmac, waiting to greet us. He was the representative, I assumed, of Metro Business Aviation of London, whose jet we were renting. 'Ernst Mulms . . . Mell . . .' He was squinting at the piece of paper that was fluttering in his hand.

'Malmsten,' I said.

'Right, right.' He smiled, stepping forward quickly to take Kajsa's bag. But she had another idea. 'Just a second,' she said, rummaging inside and pulling out a Polaroid camera. She then handed it to the man, telling him which button to press.

'Smile, Ernst,' she said, grabbing my arm. 'This is our first private jet.'

It was 13 April 1999 and the two of us had just spent a day with Christoph Vilanek, head of our German office, meeting magazine editors in Hamburg. We'd arranged the trip weeks earlier and couldn't cancel, even though more pressing commitments had since emerged. Germans tend to attach great importance to meeting times and do not like to see them altered. As we were anxious to create a good impression in a country with a huge market of 80 million people, we had to think of some other way of solving our time-keeping problems.

It was now 4 p.m, and that evening we had to be in Chicago for the beginning of a three-day fund-raising tour of the US. But as there were no direct flights from Hamburg, the only way we could make the schedule was to get back to London in time to catch Concorde to New York, where we could pick up a flight to Chicago. Hence, the private jet.

In a little under three months we had managed to spend something like $4 million, and, as we strove to build the business as rapidly as possible, costs were continuing to rise by the day. Our staff costs were a large part of this – by the end of March, we had spent $436,000 on salaries and another $586,000 on headhunters' fees (for the staff we had then and for new staff who had been recruited but had yet to start work at boo). The time had come to think about the next funding round. To take us through to our launch, we estimated that we would need another $12 million. But it could be no more than an estimate, because the costs of building such a complex business defied precise analysis, particularly in this period of hypergrowth.

Patrik had overall responsibility for finance issues, but at the moment he was having trouble keeping up. He had managed to create a small in-house team of finance staff, but they were hugely overworked and hampered by accounting software that hadn't been fully installed and was extremely complicated to use. Kajsa and I suspected that the problem was partly Patrik himself. He wanted to do deals more than to handle our expenses. It was becoming a touchy subject between the three of us, which would have to be resolved sooner or later.

After stowing our bags in the back of the plane, Kajsa and I climbed the narrow steps and took our seats. It was a little cramped inside. The décor was comfortable rather than flashy, with a dark blue carpet and matching soft leather seats. There were a few extras too, I noticed, after we'd fastened our seatbelts. Just in front of us was a 'catering console' – or bar – containing a full selection of drinks, as well as a punnet of strawberries and freshly whipped cream. I pointed this out to Kajsa, but she had other things on her mind, like surviving take-off. As the plane taxied down the short runway, she tightened her grip on the armrest. It wasn't until we had levelled out that she began to relax a little.

'How long is the flight?' she asked.

'Just over an hour,' I replied, flicking open the schedule that Tanya Tracey, the formidably well organized roadshow co-ordinator at J.P. Morgan, had prepared for us. It was incredibly precise, with almost every minute of the day carefully accounted for. We had meetings lined up in Chicago, Minneapolis and San Francisco, followed by several more when we got back to London. Black town cars would pick us up from the airports and whisk us away to each meeting. Tanya had even listed the names and mobile numbers of our drivers. I was still marvelling at the attention to detail and considering whether to offer her a job, when one of the pilots emerged from the cockpit. He was tall and stooped, with a weathered face and a cap that looked too big for him.

'You all right back here?' he asked.

'Not bad,' said Kajsa, still looking a little uncomfortable. 'I could do with a cigarette, though.'

'Don't let me stop you,' said the pilot with a grin. 'In fact,' he added thoughtfully, 'I wouldn't mind a smoke myself.'

As the two of them puffed away, I poured myself a drink. The bar had vodka but no grapefruit, so I settled for orange.

The pilot liked to talk, especially about his plane. 'This one's a Learjet 35,' he said. 'We're cruising at 35,000 feet and travelling at about 500 miles an hour. It can go faster, of course, but it's a bit gusty out there today.'

It wasn't until a good half-hour later, as we began to fly over the patchwork farmland of southern England, that our friend slipped back into the cockpit. The plane began to lose height and judder in the wind. Kajsa's grip on her armrest tightened again, as I helped myself to one last drink from the bar. Opening a small bottle of champagne, I poured a couple of glasses.

'To a successful roadshow.'

After the pampered comfort of a Learjet 35, Concorde was a bit cramped. But it was fast, and I found myself childishly impressed by our easy-to-remember flight number, BA3. So there were only two planes better than this one.

As we made our way to our seats, having joined up with Patrik in the Concorde lounge, I squeezed past the actor Hugh Grant and thought I recognized an African dictator. Celebrity-spotting was an obvious way of whiling away the boredom of our three-hour flight, but Kajsa, Patrik and I had too many things to get off our chests. Shortly after the plane took off a massive argument broke out in which all our long-buried resentments rose to the surface.

It started with finances. Patrik must make more of an effort to keep on top of them, Kajsa said. Whenever he was asked to explain the financial model, he was not sufficiently forthcoming with the figures. It was beginning to get embarrassing. Patrik retorted that it would be a lot easier for him to get round to this sort of detail if Kajsa didn't expect him to do all her negotiations on advertising all the time. It was too much work for him. The bickering took a personal turn. Patrik would be able to work a lot harder, Kajsa said, if he made the effort to move over properly to London as she had done. It was ridiculous that he was still commuting back to Stockholm every weekend. Patrik answered back that during the week he stayed in the office working every night until ten or eleven, long after Kajsa had gone home. A stewardess asked us to keep our voices down: some passengers were beginning to complain. I tried to play the peace-maker, but it only made things worse. My problem, it seemed, was that I kept on interfering in things that were none of my business. 'Everything's my business,' I retorted, exasperated that we should be arguing about finances in Concorde of all places.

By the time we touched down at JFK airport at 5.50 p.m., a whole hour before we had left London, the air had been cleared but the underlying problems were still unresolved.

After we had cleared customs, a black town car whisked us off to JFK's general aviation terminal to board the company jet that for the next 24 hours would ferry us back and forth across America. Chartered by J.P. Morgan from the aptly named 'Million Air', it was a ten-seater or − as the company's promotional material put it − our 'home from home', where we could relax or plug in our laptops at fully equipped work consoles. It was the perfect way to do business.

No queues, no waiting for luggage, no flight times to worry about – you just took off whenever you were ready to go. We could never have met so many investors in different cities in such a short space of time without it. It might have seemed a luxury, but in reality it was a powerful money-raising machine. I was tempted to get one for boo.

By 9 p.m we had arrived at the Four Seasons Hotel, Chicago. The next morning we met Thomas Paulmichl and Tanya Tracey at breakfast and discussed the strategy for the next three days. Unlike our first funding round, there would be no opportunity for detailed due diligence. Investors would be asked to state how much they wanted to invest purely on the basis of our business plan and the impressive names that were already backing us. The underlying assumption – important to encourage – was that this round would be oversubscribed, and that investors would receive their reduced allocations according to the size of their bids. The incentive, therefore, was to bid high.

In this round we would be meeting a completely different kind of investor. Instead of organizing another tour of VCs, which had proved so unsatisfactory before, Patrik had persuaded J.P. Morgan to put us before the pension funds and other large institutional investors. These were the market heavyweights. They had billions to play with.

A year ago it would have been unheard of to approach this sort of investor at such an early stage. They were, by nature, a cautious bunch who preferred steady returns over unnecessary risk. But these were unusual times. The Nasdaq index had hit another record high on 12 April, the day before we set off on our American tour, of 2598.81. It was now up 20 per cent since Christmas and showed no sign of slowing down. There was a growing feeling in the market that it was impossible to lose money on internet IPOs. Just a few weeks earlier, shares in Priceline.com, an online reseller of discounted airline tickets, had soared 330 per cent on their first day of trading. Internet companies were now the top fifteen most successful IPOs ever. For this reason, some institutional investors were considering the idea of getting in a little earlier. Admittedly, it was unusual for them to invest quite as early as this, but our bankers agreed it was worth a try.

We had high expectations as we climbed back into our jet the next morning to begin our American tour, but quickly discovered that raising money here was going to be much more difficult than we had imagined. To these ultra-conservative investors, the fact that we had a unique new concept was almost as unsettling as the fact that we came from Europe, a place they had heard of but didn't entirely trust.

Our first stop, just an hour's flight from Chicago, was Minneapolis, where we met Lou Giglio of the giant fund manager American Express Financial Corp. Giglio, one of the company's star technology investors, liked what we showed him, especially our shapely male mannequin. 'I'll give you $10 million right now if you can make me look as thin as him,' he joked. But when it came down to it, he wasn't ready to commit. 'It's pretty rare for us to invest before an IPO date has been set,' he said. 'Why don't you come back to us in a few months?'

Half an hour later we were airborne again, heading back to Chicago. Here two meetings were abruptly called off when the fund managers explained that they only invested in American companies. J.P. Morgan ought to have known this, Patrik pointed out crossly to an embarrassed Paulmichl.

A lunchtime meeting with Alex Paul of Lincoln Capital Management was not much more successful. The mouse of Kajsa's laptop computer broke while she was demonstrating the prototype and she was unable to continue until it was fixed. Paul looked on with good humour, but the mishap seemed to shake his faith in us. At the end of an hour, he sent us off with what would become the familiar refrain of our trip: sorry, but it's too early to make any commitment.

There was a strange disparity between the ease with which the black town cars deposited us in front of our jet which then instantly flew us off to our meetings and the results of those meetings when they actually took place.

Our next stop was San Francisco, where we had a dinnertime meeting with Larry Lenihan of Pequot Capital. It was our third flight that day and we were running low on fuel. About an hour or two after we left Chicago's Midway airport, the pilot put down at an airfield somewhere in Nebraska.

'It'll take a little while to fill her up, guys. Why don't you stretch your legs?'

Outside there was nothing except endless prairie, an empty hangar and a shack. We were in Marlboro country. As a small tanker drew up alongside the plane and Patrik strode up and down in his pinstripe suit tapping numbers into his mobile, it occurred to me that this was the sort of advertising image that Leagas Delaney might have dreamed up.

Patrik was trying to fix up a meeting with Genni Combes, the retail analyst we had met the last time we were in San Francisco. The only problem was that out here he couldn't get a signal on his mobile. But then he saw a phone booth by the shack gleaming in the hot afternoon sun. Like a thirsty man finding an oasis in the desert he trotted off in its direction. But soon he was back again.

'Anyone got any quarters?'

As we went through our pockets I found myself thinking of Tanya Tracey's neat schedules. Somehow they never quite worked out on the ground.

We were twenty minutes late arriving at our meeting with Lenihan. Pequot Capital, in which he was a partner, was famous for having made a fortune from early investments in AOL and Yahoo. We met in a Hyatt hotel close to the airport. He was catching a flight out to New York that evening and was edgy and irritable, as we sat down amidst the sterile Seventies décor of the hotel restaurant.

'If you call a meeting, you should try to be on time,' he said crisply.

'Our flight was delayed,' I explained, but he was in no mood for excuses.

'So what do you have to show me?' he said. 'You'd better be quick, because I can't stay long.'

We began by giving him a quick overview of the business plan. He was impressed that our investors included names like Bernard Arnault and the Benettons.

'But why are you trying to launch in eighteen countries?' he asked. 'Most people can't even figure out how to do it in one.'

It was an absurd question. Obviously he couldn't have been doing any travelling in Europe lately. It also turned out that while Pequot Capital had invested in infrastructure businesses, it had little experience of e-commerce and none whatsoever of retailing or fashion. Its only private investment in an e-commerce business up to that point was Garden.com. It was hardly a recipe for a meeting of minds. So why were we meeting this guy?

He listened sceptically as we explained our global concept and the importance of maximizing our first mover advantage. 'Got a pen?' I gave him one. 'OK. What are your revenue predictions?' He jotted them down on a sheet of hotel paper as Patrik reeled the figures off from memory.

Shaking his head with a look of disbelief, he said, 'You must be making some extremely aggressive assumptions about the number of visitors to the site. There's no way you're going to do it. And even if you do, you're going to blow way too much money getting there.'

'You obviously don't understand our business,' said Patrik.

'Well, maybe you're right,' replied Lenihan. 'Let's put some numbers to it. How many visitors are you going to get to the site? What kind of conversion rate are you aiming for? How much does each customer have to spend? What's your customer acquisition rate? And what's your payback time on the customer acquisition cost?'

Lenihan waited with pen poised.

Patrik froze. Rather than answering these questions, he started talking about the assumptions behind our revenue forecasts instead. Lenihan looked at him as if he were crazy. I then made things worse by breaking into Swedish.

'Just tell him we don't have the numbers with us,' I said to Patrik. 'That we'll call him back later.'

Now Lenihan looked really fed-up. We had arrived late, we didn't have a clue about our finances, and, to top it all, we weren't even speaking in English.

To Patrik's embarrassment, Paulmichl, who had the numbers to hand, stepped in with the answers to Lenihan's questions.

Lenihan scribbled the figures down and then looked up at Patrik. 'Don't you think some of these numbers are a bit far-fetched?'

'No . . .'

'Well, I think you should scale them down.'

We sat quietly as Lenihan did more calculations on another sheet of paper, but he had ceased to take us seriously, if he ever had in the first place. I felt annoyed and frustrated – with Lenihan for not even trying to understand our business concept; with Patrik for not having our finances at his fingertips; and with J.P. Morgan, for not planning the meetings better. Why had they thought that someone like Lenihan would be a good person to talk to? Why had they put us in front of people who didn't even invest in European companies? Why, for that matter, had we been seeing investors in Minneapolis and Chicago instead of New York, where a global internet idea like ours would be welcomed more readily?

Eventually, Lenihan got up, handed my pen back to me and put on his coat. 'I apologize for my bluntness,' he said, 'but I think you're going to be out of business by Christmas. Thanks, but I'm not interested.'

After one more day of useless meetings, we flew back from San Francisco to London. But even in the air there was no respite, as I had to work my way through a long fax from Edward Griffith detailing various matters that would need attention on my return. Going through such faxes, and keeping in regular touch with the office by phone, were a wearying but unavoidable feature of my trips abroad as I switched to running the business by remote control. We arrived at Heathrow at 6.30 a.m. on a Friday morning. Ahead of us that day were six more meetings with investors, but at that precise moment, as I climbed into the car that was waiting to pick me up, there didn't seem much point. Exhausted after the long flight and depressed by our totally unproductive trip, I felt as though we had already crashed into the buffers. For perhaps the first time, I had a sense of our vulnerability. We existed only so long as investors continued to have faith in us; once they stopped, we were dead.

It was probably as well that there was no time to dwell on such thoughts. Our first presentation was at 10 a.m. The meetings that J.P. Morgan had lined up for us in London were mostly with hedge funds, which were more aggressive, risk-taking versions of the large investment funds we'd met in the US. Paulmichl did his best to put a positive spin on things. 'It's going to be easier here,' he said. 'They understand the story better.' But these people were not the sort to get easily excited. They threw millions of dollars around on a daily basis. boo was just another money-making opportunity that they would consider and make an impassive decision about.

Our first stop was at Perry Capital, where we met Chris Hohn. Businesslike and impersonal, he lost no time in making it clear that he wasn't interested, and within half an hour we were back in the car that J.P. Morgan had hired for the day. A similarly stiff and unsuccessful encounter followed with John Armitage, one of the founders of Egerton Capital, a small British fund manager. We had a more positive lunchtime meeting at J.P. Morgan's offices with Casper Lund, a young money manager from Goldman Sachs Asset Management, but he lacked the authority to make investment decisions on his own. 'I'll have to pass this upstairs.'

And so it went on. Tom Bannatyne of Tudor was not interested and at Meditor we saw Kjell Bengtsson, a middle-aged Swede who was excited to have an opportunity to speak in his own language for once, but felt that our valuation was too high.

Our final stop for the day was at Eden Capital, a small British investment firm with close ties to a giant US hedge fund called Moore Capital. Their office was on Upper Brook Street, just off Park Lane, but for some reason our car dropped us on the wrong corner. The heavens opened and rain pelted down as we dashed from doorway to doorway. When we finally made it up to Eden's second-floor office, we were drenched. It was so ridiculous that we were all laughing when Tom Henderson, the senior fund manager at Eden, came out to meet us.

Henderson – a tall, upper-class Englishman in his mid-thirties – luckily was quick to see the humour of the situation. 'I don't have any towels,' he said, smiling, 'but let me at least get you a coffee.'

The conversation that followed was light and spontaneous. 'This is our last meeting,' Kajsa explained. 'We're so tired. We've been on tour now for five days.'

As we sipped our coffees, we talked casually about the business plan. We were too drained by the past few days to care much about what sort of impression we made. Henderson listened carefully to our ideas for a global rollout, admired the prototype and was quietly impressed when we told him about the sort of people who were working for us. But although the meeting seemed to go well, I had no clear sense of what direction Henderson's thoughts were taking, and certainly had no reason to suppose that he was any more interested in us than the other people had been.

It had been a dismal few days. Somehow, something just hadn't clicked. I couldn't understand it. Our story was much more convincing than when we'd first approached investors a few months ago. The internet was hotter than ever. Yet it seemed that nobody wanted to give us any money.

Patrik blamed J.P. Morgan. 'Those weren't meetings with the right people for us,' he said, as we left Eden Capital's offices. 'After this round, we need to change banks.'

That Friday night I slept heavily, my body and mind recovering from the days of constant activity. It would have been nice to lie in a little, but I had to drag myself out of bed at 6 a.m. to get ready for another full day. Samer Salty at J.P. Morgan had arranged for us to see some wealthy Middle Eastern investors that were thinking of investing up to $2 million. 'They're almost committed,' he told us. 'But these are the kinds of people you have to spend time with face to face.' The meeting was due to start at 10 a.m. Before that, though, at 7.30, Kajsa, Patrik and I had to sit down for an urgent management meeting with Charlotte, Edward, Luke and Steve Bennett. A lot of problems had been building up while we were away.

By now we knew we wouldn't meet our original launch date of 1 May. Everything had turned out to be more complicated than we'd expected. This was especially true of our technology platform. Steve Bennett, who was supposed to be pulling the different pieces together, looked as if he was struggling. He was immensely capable technically, but the task was overwhelming. But whatever troubles he was having, it was vital that he solved them in time for us to launch before the end of May. Otherwise our whole marketing strategy would fall apart.

To save time, we met at J.P. Morgan, next door to the room where we would make our presentation to the investors. Even though it was a Saturday, there was the usual coffee and plate of chocolate-chip cookies laid out on the table for us. God bless those waiters, I thought.

Pale and lethargic, Kajsa, Patrik and I were slumped deep in our chairs, stuggling to fight off fatigue, but Steve Bennett's haunted look almost made us feel fresh again. He had obviously been having a terrible time.

'So how's it going, Steve?'

He looked at me with a deer-in-the-headlights expression. 'The database is still a big problem.'

'What do you mean?'

'Some of the information we're feeding into it is disappearing,' he said. 'It's a spider's web in there.'

'Why hasn't this been fixed yet?'

Bennett shuffled in his chair. 'I've just hired someone to look at it.'

'Fine,' I said. 'Just get it done quickly.'

My other worry was our global infrastructure. The Gigastream team still hadn't wired up all our offices. We didn't even have an internal email system yet.

'And what about our network?' I asked. 'The foreign offices have been ringing me up. Annica tells me the servers in Stockholm still aren't talking to the servers in London.'

'Andrew Jeffreys of Gigastream is going to fix it.'

'When?'

'Well, he's a bit tied up . . .'

'Then you need to speak to Annica and tell her what's going on. I don't want the foreign offices calling me all the time to complain about these things. You're the CTO. You've got to sort this out.'

Bennett was silent, his shoulders hunched.

Now I had started, I found it hard to stop. 'You should never have hired Gigastream,' I said. 'They're too small for this job. We needed an international company that had people in place. It's ridiculous that we should even be worrying about something like office infra-structure.'

An hour later, we filed into the room next door to meet the Middle Eastern investors. We gave the usual presentation, then asked Bennett to give a rundown of our technology. Perhaps he was still upset by my outburst earlier, for the presentation he gave felt hesitant and confusing to me. I was surprised because in previous presenta-tions he had spoken with enormous confidence and an impressive grasp of the technical issues. It was as if the sheer magnitude of all that he had taken on was finally beginning to weigh him down. Eventually, Luke stepped in to help out.

Afterwards we took the investors back to our office for a quick tour, before taking them to lunch at Home House, the private club near Hyde Park. Poor Steve Bennett, who wasn't able to join us, must have been more than usually glad that weekend to get back to his family and sheep in Wales.

As we waited to hear from investors, I began to worry more and more about Steve. Was he the right person to handle such a complicated technology project? I had already confided some of my fears to Kajsa and Patrik. Now, on Monday afternoon, I asked Edward to come for a walk with me. Over the past few months, Edward and I had become pretty close. He was my sounding board, my *consigliere*, on difficult issues.

As usual, we headed over to Golden Square, just behind Carnaby Street. This was the place that in *Nicholas Nickleby* Dickens described as 'not exactly in anybody's way to or from anywhere'. It was the perfect spot for a private chat.

'I think this job is too much for Steve,' I said, after we'd sat down on a bench.

Edward nodded. 'It's a shame, because he's such a nice guy. But you're right. He's really having a tough time.' He unwrapped a sandwich and took a bite. 'Did you see him in that meeting? That was really unimpressive. Luke did all the talking.'

I was pleased that Edward had noticed this as well. It meant I wasn't just imagining things.

'What worries me most,' I said, 'is his lack of leadership.' Each technology supplier was working independently on their piece of the platform without any clear idea of what the others were up to. They needed to be given a clear sense of direction, but weren't getting any from Steve. I knew it wasn't all his fault. I could be difficult to work for and often made unreasonable demands. But that was why we needed a strong CTO.

'So what are you going to do?' Edward asked.

'I guess we have to start looking for someone else,' I said, shooing away the scrawny pigeons that were loitering near our feet.

'And Steve? What are you going to tell him?'

'Nothing. Not yet. We'll have to find someone else first.' Regardless of how I felt about Bennett's performance, I definitely didn't want to be stuck without a CTO when the time came to launch.

'What if he finds out?' Edward asked, looking a little uncertain.

'He mustn't find out. We have to keep this really quiet. There's an investor angle. I don't want anyone knowing about this until we get a replacement.' I gave Edward a serious look. 'I'll tell Patrik and Kajsa when we get back. But no one else, OK?'

Back in the office, I got on the phone to Anthony Harling at Heidrick & Struggles. I wasn't too pleased with him. Heidrick & Struggles had given us the all-clear to hire Bennett and had pocketed something like £30,000 in fees as a result. I gave Harling a quick rundown of the situation and explained that we wanted a new CTO. 'But we want to be sure we've got the right person this time,' I said in a cool tone.

Harling sounded repentant. 'I'm sorry it isn't working out,' he said. 'Maybe I can cut the fee a bit for this one.'

'We also want you to move quickly,' I went on. 'The longer we wait, the harder it will be for someone new to come in. And it must be a complete secret.'

Harling sounded unconcerned. 'Leave it to me. We do this sort of thing all the time.' He promised to start looking immediately and would even bring in help from one of his colleagues in the San Francisco office. As for secrecy, he suggested that we open special Hotmail accounts under assumed names to communicate with each other. Worried that the tech team might possibly hack into our emails, I came up with a code name. In any future communications, our CTO search would be referred to as 'Project Diamond'.

Edward became the chief go-between, which wasn't easy because his desk was within earshot of Bennett's. In the weeks that followed, every time a call came through from Harling he would have to dash out of the room and call back from his mobile.

★

We were starting to get worried. Although nearly a week had gone by, we had still heard nothing from the investors. There was only enough money in the bank to last us another three weeks. It was like the first funding round all over again. Except that this time we had a hundred staff, offices around the world and million-dollar contracts signed with technology suppliers.

That morning, the three of us pulled up chairs around a small table in our office to talk things over. We had to talk loud to make ourselves heard above the din of workmen who were busy installing cables under the floor and building us a conference room.

'Maybe we should go back to the existing investors,' I said. 'They'll probably give us more.'

'Maybe. But how much?' Kajsa said, frowning. 'It will look really bad as well – like we can't find anyone else.'

But we can't, I thought.

Patrik didn't like the idea either, but for different reasons. 'It means we'll have to give them the 25 per cent discount,' he pointed out. This was the discount we had promised investors if they participated in our second funding round. 'Let's not go to them unless we have to.'

Patrik's idea was to try to approach some new investors. 'I'm going to get J.P. Morgan to call Bain,' he said. This was one of the most prestigious private investment firms in the US, with a fund worth $1.5 billion. The New York financier Jeffrey Leeds had recommended them to us over a year ago and, through him, we had then met Bob White, one of Bain's senior managers. But this was before we even had J.P. Morgan or any suppliers on board and although he had been positive, White suggested that we come back when things were a little more advanced. When we duly approached Bain once more during the first round, they said it was still too early. Since then we had sent them an updated information memorandum.

'Maybe they're ready now,' Patrik said.

That afternoon, J.P. Morgan arranged a conference call with Mark Nunnelly, a partner at Bain Capital. The conversation cheered us up. Nunnelly had looked through our memorandum and was impressed.

'I have to admit, we were all pretty sceptical that you'd get suppliers,' he said. 'You've done a hell of a job.'

The only awkward moment came when he asked what our attitude was to advertising on the internet. As we knew he was a board member of the internet advertising company, Doubleclick Inc, we felt uncomfortable having to tell him that we didn't believe in online advertising. But he laughed. We were probably right, he said. He agreed in principle to invest, promising to get back to us with a definite answer in the next couple of days. Things were beginning to turn our way again.

On Thursday evening, Tim Main, the senior J.P. Morgan banker who had been overseeing the fund-raising, linked Patrik, Kajsa and me on our mobiles. 'I just want to say congratulations,' he said. 'We've just received our first order.' To our surprise it wasn't Bain, but Tom Henderson on behalf of Eden Capital and Moore Capital. 'He wants to put in $8 million.'

We were speechless: this was the biggest sum a single investor had offered so far. Maybe we should turn up at meetings looking wet and exhausted more often, I thought. Suddenly, we were safe. More than safe. The sense of relief was enormous. We could concentrate on running a business again.

The good news didn't stop there. The next day, Nunnelly got back to us. 'We're interested,' he said. 'But we don't want to do this if we're only able to invest a couple of million dollars. How much do we have to bid to make sure we get at least $4–$5 million?'

It was perhaps the easiest question from an investor that Patrik had ever had to answer.

As a final sweetener, the Saudi Arabian investors soon made an offer as well. By the time the round closed, we had raised a total of $12 million. We expected this to carry us through to the next funding round, in three months' time.

With our money problems behind us, for now at least, we could spend more time on our PR campaign. Not that we had been slacking. Since our first PR trip to New York a month and a half ago, we had been back there at least once a week for meetings with journalists. After the *Women's Wear Daily* article, it seemed that everyone from the *New York Times* to *Playboy* wanted to meet us. We had now given interviews to nearly fifty publications. Of these, most were planning to write articles within the next couple of months. The reporter who had interviewed us for *Vogue*, Amely Greeven, loved the story so much that she even asked us for a job. We gave her one, as fashion editor of *Boom*, our online magazine. Fashion with a capital F had its place, she said, but *Boom* gave her the opportunity to write about street style too. Her true fashion heart beat in Brooklyn and Brixton. 'Plus I get to wear hooded sweatshirts to work now.'

The PR executives from Hill & Knowlton were astonished by the level of interest. According to their calculations, we had already lined up something like $15 million in free publicity. The combined circulation of the publications we had talked to so far was well over 50 million. Our progress, commented Jessica Kogan, had been 'better than excellent'. We were enormously impressed by the enthusiastic efforts that Jessica was making on our behalf, but we weren't so surprised by the positive response. We knew we had a good story.

At the end of April, the three of us headed back to New York for another round of interviews. We were also due to have our photos taken for the *Industry Standard*. Its reporter, James Ledbetter, had spent a whole day in our London office a week earlier and was planning to give us a big write-up – possibly even a cover feature. He had previously written for the *Village Voice* and it turned out that we had a friend in common. He already knew about us through Ann Kjellberg, a contributing editor at the *New York Review of Books* who back in 1993 had helped us to edit the accompanying anthology to our New York poetry festival. Ledbetter's piece would be an important break for us, because in the year since its launch the *Industry Standard* had quickly established itself as the Bible of the internet economy. Anyone who was anybody in the e-commerce world read it and took it very seriously.

On the surface, there was little about this latest New York trip to make it different from all the others. But it marked a turning point in the relationship between Kajsa and me, on the one side, and Patrik on the other. The fact was that despite our equal salaries and our equal shares in the company, Patrik had always been the outsider. Kajsa and I were just too close. Recently, the rift had been widening, especially between Kajsa and Patrik. She thought he was obsessed with money, while he thought her cold and distant. The growing concerns Kajsa and I had about his leadership of the finance team only made the situation worse.

In the aftermath of the US roadshow, J.P. Morgan received some negative feedback from investment managers over Patrik's performance. Larry Lenihan at Pequot Capital was the harshest critic: 'He couldn't even talk me through his own financial model. When a CFO doesn't even understand the numbers, I start to get very worried.' But it wasn't just his presentation of financial matters that concerned the investors; they also found it difficult to accept his role as a co-founder. They felt that boo.com was really Kajsa and I and that Patrik's presence clouded the issue. Now we were to receive exactly the same message on the PR front.

All of this came to a head the morning after our arrival in New York, when Jessica Kogan dropped into our office for a chat. Kajsa and Patrik weren't around, so Jay Herratti and I took her into a small meeting room overlooking the Hudson river.

'We have a problem with *Vogue*,' she said. 'They interviewed only you and Kajsa, but the pictures the photographer took are of all three of you.' Amely Greeven's piece had concentrated on presenting Kajsa and me as the stylish, creative brains behind boo. We were the 'duo'. It was the kind of story that *Vogue*'s contemporary, fashion-conscious readers loved. Now the editors at *Vogue* had been handed photographs that changed everything.

'They didn't expect three of you,' Jessica said. 'They're really upset.'

'Why?' I asked, still not seeing what the problem was.

'*Vogue* is a women's magazine,' she said. 'They don't like photos of men, especially not photos which show two men, as apparently these do, standing over a seated woman. It makes Kajsa look submissive.' The fact that Patrik had been wearing his pinstripe suit made it even worse. 'They really, really don't like photos of bankers. I had to beg them not to scrap the whole story.'

It was nobody's fault really, just a misunderstanding. But it highlighted the fact that when it came to PR, three was a crowd.

'We've been talking about this internally,' Jessica said. 'We all think that the story we should be focusing on is you and Kajsa and all the things you've done together in the past. Patrik just confuses the message.'

Patrik's presentation skills didn't help. A few weeks earlier, Hill & Knowlton had organized for us a day of media training sessions with a veteran broadcast journalist. Patrik's performance had been so poor that he was given an extra session of intensive training.

Jessica suggested that Kajsa and I should take him aside and explain the problem. 'He absolutely has to back off,' she said. 'This is really important.'

I knew that Jessica was right and something had to be done, but I didn't want Patrik to think that Kajsa and I were trying to squeeze him out of the company.

'I think it might be better coming from you,' I said to her.

She didn't look too happy, but agreed to speak to him. That afternoon Kajsa and I made ourselves scarce so that Jessica would have a chance to speak to Patrik alone. She rang me afterwards to tell me that it had not gone well. It was difficult to build a brand around three people, she had told him, and it made more PR sense to focus on me and Kajsa. But he had retorted angrily that he was part of the company from the beginning and was therefore just as much part of the story. Jessica then tried as tactfully as possible to broach the matter of his poor presentation skills, even suggesting that he risked harming the interests of his own company, but he wouldn't back down.

'He's going to speak to you and Kajsa,' Jessica warned me.

This was not a prospect I relished. After I had finished speaking to Jessica, I got straight on the phone to Jay. He was the one person, I thought, who might be able to get through to Patrik. He was easygoing, but also in his short time with boo had gained a reputation for speaking his mind. I hoped that Patrik would accept him as an impartial voice.

'Can you talk to Patrik?' I asked. 'At least try to calm him down a bit.'

'I'll do my best,' he said, cautiously.

Later that day, while Kajsa and I posed down by the Hudson river for the photographer from the *Industry Standard*, back in the office Jay took Patrik aside. 'In some companies,' he told him, 'the real power is behind the scenes.' He gave a few examples. 'Look at Versace,' he said. 'Gianni Versace was the designer and the face for the media. But it was his brother, Santo, that handled all the money.' Jay pointed out that Patrik still owned a third of the company. 'You're going to be rich no matter what happens,' he said. These words helped.

When I got back to the office an hour or so later, Patrik came over to me. 'I think it makes sense for me to be less involved in the media from now on,' he said.

I tried to sound surprised, but agreed with Patrik that it was probably for the best.

Back in London, the number of workmen had multiplied. I had asked them to install carpeting as a way of reducing noise, although in the short term this only added to the disruption. The good news was that we now had our conference room – a glass-encased cubicle which we called the goldfish bowl. But so many staff were crammed into the office that most had taken to using a nearby café on the corner of Carnaby Street to hold their meetings.

About this time, Kajsa went to Los Angeles to oversee the filming of our TV ads. It was a hilarious experience. She had spent the whole day wandering around tough parts of LA with Roman Coppola and a group of five 'geeks', each wearing brand new sports clothes. While Coppola filmed discreetly from a distance, the geeks walked on to basketball courts, challenging groups of bare-chested, tough-looking kids to games, which they then lost horribly. Caught on camera were genuine reactions of disbelief, amusement and, on one occasion, near violence.

My main preoccupation now was technology. As Steve Bennett continued to flounder, Luke Alvarez began to take on an increasingly active role. He was now managing our relationship with two of our technology vendors – Interworld and Organic – was overseeing our 3D photography and building our customer service department. Unlike Bennett, who looked more uptight every time I saw him, Luke relished the added responsibility. Over the past few weeks, he had been steadily growing his empire. While I had encouraged all of boo's managers to recruit, Luke had taken this to its extreme. He now had about thirty people reporting to him and was pressing me to give him a more lofty title, like 'President', to put him on an equal footing with Jay Herratti.

Like Jay, Luke had a clear philosophy about what he wanted from boo. 'There are three things this company can offer me,' he said to me over a drink one night. 'Power, fame and money. You have all three. That's OK because you're the boss. I only want power and money.'

This attitude didn't go down too well with the technology team, who didn't like the head of business development meddling in specific technology problems. But Luke was organized and structured in his thinking. He was also smart enough to spot problem areas, and could be brutally frank about them.

In early May, Luke and I got together in the goldfish bowl to talk through some of the key problems he had identified. 'We're way behind on the 3D imaging,' he said. 'There's no way we're going to get all of these products up on the website for at least a few more weeks.' The reasons, like almost everything else we were doing, were complicated. Before we could photograph a product, our suppliers had to send a sample to eVox in Los Angeles. All the samples had to be a specific size, so that they would fit on the mannequin. They also had to be exactly the same product and the same colour as what we would actually be selling on the website. But a lot of suppliers couldn't seem to grasp this. 'The shoes are the wrong size, the T-shirts are the wrong colour . . . It's a mess,' said Luke in exasperation. Some suppliers were even sending products to eVox with the word 'SAMPLE' spray-painted all over them. 'How is that going to look on the website?'

Luke was also critical of Interworld and Organic. Until recently, the companies had barely been talking to each other. This was a major problem given that Interworld's e-commerce engine and Organic's front end would soon have to be 'glued' together. It was already obvious that some of Organic's design ideas could not be integrated into the e-commerce engine and would have to be reworked.

Until all the pieces of our technology platform had been pulled together, we couldn't even start testing, which usually took at least a month to complete.

'When do you think we'll have a working version of the website?' I asked.

Luke shrugged hopelessly. 'It just depends on how quickly these companies can sort all their shit out.'

Next day, after a meeting with the UK head of Interworld, Bob Mann, Luke came over to my desk with his arms crossed. 'Everything is going mad at Interworld,' he said calmly.

The project manager for boo, he explained, had quit to start his own internet consulting firm and there was a great deal of concern that other Interworld staff would join him. Even worse, the person appointed in his place had now had second thoughts about the job and flown back to New York. 'He'd only been here three days,' Luke said. 'It's like he saw something that scared him.'

The reality of our situation dawned more slowly than it ought to have done. We simply weren't prepared to accept, without a struggle, that our launch would have to be delayed yet again. Luke and I flew to New York to meet with Alan Andreini, Interworld's chief executive, to try to get firm assurances on when the site would be delivered.

We sat down with Andreini on a sofa in his office. I got straight to the point. 'Your people keep saying that the website is almost ready. But we still don't have anything. We need you to put a lot more resources on this.'

Andreini, resting his feet on a small coffee table, seemed non-committal at first. 'We have a lot of important clients right now,' he said, citing Nike as an example. The last few months had seen a massive surge in the number of companies wanting to build e-commerce sites. 'Our resources are stretched very thin.'

But slowly he came around, especially when I told him about all the press coverage we were about to get.

'I'll look into it,' he said.

The meeting obviously helped. Within a day, Interworld had decided to put the management of our project in the hands of senior staff in New York.

A few days later we had a staff management meeting at Home

House, attended by one of Interworld's American project managers. He promised to deliver a fully functioning, English-language version of our website within two weeks. It was the most encouraging news so far, but it was now clear that we probably wouldn't be able to launch until mid to late June at the earliest.

Kajsa took the news badly. 'It's exactly what I was worried about,' she groaned, as we walked down Oxford Street after the meeting. For weeks, she had been pressing Steve Bennett and others in the technology team about our launch date. 'If we're going to be really late, I need to know.' Having been reassured that everything would be fine, she had started booking ads. Most of these – in US magazines, on TV and in cinemas – were due to come out in late August, but there was also a preliminary **round** of ads in some European magazines and an outdoor campaign in Sweden scheduled for mid-June. This would originally have been a month after our launch, but now we faced the prospect of having an ad campaign for a business that didn't yet exist.

'And what if it gets delayed again?' Kajsa asked.

'Maybe we can pull some of the ads or postpone them a bit,' I said.

She looked doubtful. With only a month and a half to go, that might not be so easy. That afternoon she phoned the media buyers at BMP, who promised to do what they could. The next day they got back to her with mixed news. They had managed to delay most of the ads until August; but the one thing it was too late to change was the Swedish outdoor campaign. Luckily, Kajsa had already thought up a face-saving solution. 'We'll say it's a test campaign,' she said. 'We just have to put "Coming Soon" on the bottom of the ads.'

The next question was what to do about the media. This was more straightforward. There was nothing we could do. As Hill & Knowlton had warned us months earlier, once we turned on the tap, we couldn't turn it off again.

'You've simply got to keep doing interviews,' Jessica advised.

The first articles would start coming out in less than a week. The last thing we wanted now was to send out signals that we were having problems. 'Be careful about making predictions for when the site will go live.'

'What if people ask?' I said.

'Say you're launching in the summer.'

8

IT WAS AN IRONY. In the trade everyone knew us. We had been familiar faces since the piece in *Women's Wear Daily*. Even in the editorial offices of the high-circulation magazines in New York and London we were on everyone's lips. After all, we had been giving interview after interview for the last two months now. But none of these pieces had yet come out. In the wider world, we were unheard of. Indeed, we had gone to great lengths to ensure that this should be so, and were still insisting that new employees should sign non-disclosure agreements – some people joined us without even knowing the name of the company they worked for. But all this changed on 10 May 1999. It was the day on which boo.com finally came out into the open.

I had been tipped off to buy the *Financial Times* that morning and turned up at the newsagent's just as the man was opening his shop. He hadn't even had time to open the bundles of papers. Hurriedly I riffled through the paper as I walked back home – and there it was. On the front of the Companies and Markets section, a slick colour photograph of me and Kajsa, her hair blowing in the wind. Our day at the photo-shoot had paid off, after all. The next thing I noticed was the headline, ONLINE FASHION RETAILER SETS EUROPEAN START-UP RECORD, and then the shout line beneath that: 'Arnault and Benetton back $125m launch of boo.com'.

$125 million? Where did they get that figure from? Our valuation had nearly doubled overnight. The correct figure was still only $75 million. But who cared? It would get people talking.

Quickly I read on:

A London-based company will open an online store, supplying

sports and streetwear, at the end of this month. boo.com raised launch capital valuing the company at an estimated $125m, a record for a European internet start–up.

The piece included a quote from Kajsa:

Sportswear is an international market and there are a lot of people in Europe who read about products in US magazines but can't go over to buy them. This is one of the few sectors of internet retailing that no one's done on a large scale and we want boo to be the number one brand.

It went on to give a simple but positive account of our plans. I was delighted. The *FT* was hugely influential in the European investment community. Everyone who mattered would see this piece. The secret was definitely out now.

I rang Kajsa with the news, then caught a cab to the office, where I began making calls. 'You're going to have a busy day today,' I told Christina Preisler, who handled PR in our Stockholm office.

'If you mean the *FT* piece, I already am,' she said, sounding harassed. 'The Swedish press are going crazy about this.' In Stockholm, an hour ahead of London, it had just gone nine o'clock. The day had barely started. I couldn't resist calling my parents and a couple of friends in Sweden. 'Buy the *Financial Times*,' I told them, enigmatically.

I cut out the article and put it on the wall in our reception, so that everyone could see it when they came into work. When Kajsa arrived, she sent out the office secretary to buy twenty-five copies. 'For the archive,' she said.

At some distant time in the future, I imagined, when a scholar sat down to write the distinguished history of boo.com, 10 May 1999 would be set down as one of its most memorable days. The office was buzzing with excitement that morning. Everyone was poring over the distinctively pink newspaper and chatting about what had been said. There was an enormous release of tension. At last they could talk after months of secrecy. They had been forbidden to send personal emails from the boo.com web address, or even to mention our name to their closest friends and family. All they had been allowed to say was that they were working for an internet company in Soho for a group of Swedish entrepreneurs. As Charlotte pointed out, for most people this could mean only one thing. 'My friends think I work for a porn site.'

Now at last everyone could redeem their reputations and even hold their heads up with pride. Suddenly, they felt noticed and important. The switchboard was jammed with calls from their friends who had read the piece and were phoning to chat and even to ask if there were any opportunities for work.

Edward probably summed it up best when we got together for our usual morning coffee: 'We've been bleeding for six months,' he said, 'and it's finally converting into some prime-time glam.'

The article in the *FT* hadn't been planned. It was just one of those wonderful pieces of good luck. Somehow the reporter had found out on her own and called for an interview. If she had done so two months earlier, we would have anxiously refused. But now we knew that the floodgates were about to open, anyway. In fact, we had been doing our best to push them open. That same day we were expecting the *Industry Standard* feature to come out.

Just after lunch, as the excitement of the *FT* piece was finally beginning to subside, Edward called me over to his desk. 'The *Industry Standard* have just put it up on their website,' he said.

There, on his screen, was a long feature. BOO.COM'S BOLD FASHION STATEMENT, ran the headline. Edward printed a copy out and I sat down on a corner of his desk to read it.

James Ledbetter had come up trumps. Adopting a rather more lyrical style than the *FT* piece, he began: 'It is that rarest of treasures – a warm, cloudless day in England and a bank holiday to boot. By all expectations, few Londoners should be at work. In the offices of boo.com, however, there's always work to be done.' The irresistible and consciously adopted theme was of Swinging London reborn: 'Mod and hippie styles drove the first incarnation of Carnaby Street,' wrote Ledbetter, 'but the internet is driving boo.com's attempted renaissance. It hardly matters that no one here is old enough to remember the '60s heyday of Carnaby Street. All they need is the *Austin Powers* send-up to know that boo.com had better be groovy, baby. And the goal appears to be just that – to make boo.com hipper and more exciting than the sporty clothes it peddles.'

But soon Ledbetter departed from the whimsical tone to give the most accurate and flattering write-up we could have hoped for: 'Make no mistake, however: this is a deadly serious e-commerce company. It has assembled an impressive group of financial backers led by J.P. Morgan, the venerated investment bank that had never put money into an e-commerce startup company until boo.com . . .'

He went on to cover everything from our concept to issues such as technology and logistics. There was a long almost philosophical commentary on Miss Boo, an account of our plans for *Boom* magazine, 'perhaps boo.com's pinnacle', and even an appreciation of our name: 'The word's vagueness is part of its appeal. "Boo," says one staffer with a Zen turn, "means nothing in 50 languages."' One thing was sure. We owed James Ledbetter at least fifty drinks.

Soon after I had finished reading the piece, Jay phoned from New York. 'This is a very big deal,' he said. 'Everyone reads the *Industry Standard* out here.' Jessica Kogan, who had worked so hard to set up the piece in the first place, also phoned, then Samer Salty from J.P. Morgan. As the congratulations poured in, we began to feel like opera stars at a first night.

There were calls from journalists, TV stations, job-hunters and headhunters, as well as companies looking to sell us their services. In the confusion, as newspapers raced to write matching stories, inevitably the story got a bit garbled. One of the wire services, took the *FT*'s $125 million estimate of boo's valuation and substituted a pound sign for the dollar sign. It then translated £125 million back into dollars. Suddenly, we were worth $200 million. Not bad for a day's work, I thought.

If we needed final proof of the impact of these articles, it came later that afternoon. Three weeks earlier, James Cronin in our tech team had put up a holding page. There was no information yet; it just said: 'boo.com. Please register.' Ever since, the number of hits had been creeping up slowly into the low thousands. Most of them, I figured, would have been people we had met some time in the trade. But now, in just a day, the number of hits was rocketing towards the tens of thousands.

I wasn't sure whether to be thrilled or terrified.

When would American-style internet euphoria finally hit Europe? People had been asking this question for months. For many, it had now been answered. In the days and weeks that followed our official coming-out, there was a noticeable increase in the number of articles talking about Europe's 'awakening'. Of course, boo.com wasn't the only internet start-up out there. Other high-profile companies, like Britain's lastminute.com, were beginning to emerge. But boo was the biggest and our concept – global, fashion, high-tech – seemed to capture people's imaginations. We provided journalists with the perfect story.

The most notable side-effect of this new found attention was the sudden flood of interest we received from potential new recruits at just the time when we were embarking on the second phase of our build-up. Through Heidrick & Struggles, we had just found a headhunter, Kate Griffith-Lambert, who joined us on a short-term contract to help recruit somewhere in the region of 200 people over the next two months. She had expected it to be a tall order, but, in the aftermath of the *FT* and *Industry Standard* articles, she could hardly move without tripping over yet someone else who wanted to join the internet revolution.

'This is getting ridiculous,' she said shortly after the media frenzy had begun. 'We're hearing from 700 people a day.'

They were sending in applications by email, snail mail, fax and phone. Soon they would be climbing through the office window. They came from every age, profession and social background you could imagine. Often they already had well-paid and responsible jobs, but were eager to do something more exciting with their lives.

The lengths some people went to make an impression were extraordinary. One programmer tried to hack into our network to show how good he was. Another guy sent us a baseball bat in the post with a CV and a short note: 'You can't help but strike lucky if you hire me.' Some people were ringing us four or five times a day. If proof was needed that the internet had arrived in Europe, this was it.

The response was such that Kate's first recruits were a human resources team. Her assistants made a point of sending a personalized reply to every applicant in the informal boo style: 'Great to hear from you. It's fantastic that you want to be part of our team . . .' Even when, as in the vast majority of cases, they were unable to offer a job, they were careful to leave open the possibility of employment on some future occasion rather than to reject anyone outright. It was not only kinder but also an opportunity to create goodwill for the boo brand, since every applicant was a potential boo customer.

Kate soon found herself interviewing non-stop. At one point the pressure was so intense that she would see people at her house in the morning, start talking to them over breakfast with her children and continue to interview them on the bus to work. When it came to taking on about fifty tech staff, a special fast-track, assembly-line method was devised. A boo interview team, including Edward Griffith, Steve Bennett and James Cronin, divided up into pairs and occupied four or five interview rooms, through which, one after the other, the candidates passed, answering a different set of questions in each. At the end of the day the interviewers then got together to compare notes over meals of pizza and Coke.

We almost always ended up with the brightest and best people in every sector. They literally came from around the world: Europe, Africa, Asia, Australia, America − a global workforce for a global company. It seemed like every day I had to welcome two, sometimes three, new recruits to the office. Soon, I thought, we'd have to start a boo town.

The avalanche of media attention had been wonderful, yet it was a great distraction when our thoughts were turning with increasing urgency to the launch of the website. The person who found the situation most difficult was Patrik: he had to watch quietly from the sidelines as the world fêted Leander and Malmsten. Yet he was a founder too who had played his full part in making boo what it was. Remaining discreetly in the shadows was not something that came naturally to Patrik, and it soon became clear that he was not going to tolerate it for much longer. I could hardly blame him. It was a bit like running a movie studio and being told you couldn't go to celebrity parties.

If he wasn't allowed to be a style icon, none the less he was determined to carve out for himself a meaningful role as one of the company's three founders, and to do what he could to raise his profile now that boo.com was in the open. So he hit on the idea of meeting research analysts at some of the banks. It would be an opportunity to talk up boo.com in the run-up to the IPO which we expected would follow soon after our launch.

The trouble was he had to be very careful about what he said. The day after the *FT* and *Industry Standard* pieces came out, we received a long memorandum from our American lawyer, Tom Kennedy, at Skadden Arps, warning us that we were forbidden by US law to undertake 'any form of general solicitation or general advertising' with reference to our IPO. In practice, this meant we could talk about the concept of boo.com and promote our commercial interests, but, Kennedy warned, could give no interviews that included 'predictions, projections, forecasts or opinions with respect to the value of the company or the potential or future offering of the company's securities under any circumstances'. This daunting list instantly knocked out Patrik's most natural topics of conversation.

Yet now that boo was so much in the limelight, he could hardly avoid meeting with the banks. Indeed, in the aftermath of the *FT* piece, the bankers came looking for him, inviting him out to expensive dinners and talking to him about possible co-operation in the future. Suddenly the financial community had woken up to the fact that Europe's internet industry was about to take off and that it would be wise to get involved as soon as possible. What better way than to handle boo's IPO?

In theory, boo already had a bank. But it was an open secret that Patrik had lost patience with J.P. Morgan. The dazzling list of admirers who would court Patrik within days of our springtime début included Hambrecht & Quist, BancBoston Robertson Stephens, Deutsche Bank and British corporate broker Cazenove. The attention was very flattering.

One evening around this time Patrik managed to make a space in his busy social diary for me. We had dinner at the Gallery Rendezvous on Beak Street, just around the corner from the office. As he ate his spring rolls, Patrik looked inspired by some new vision, as if he'd just come from a revivalist meeting. 'We need to start thinking seriously about changing banks,' he said firmly. 'You saw how much trouble we had raising money last time. We can't let that happen again.' He pointed out that we were rapidly moving past the start-up phase. Our funding requirements were becoming bigger by the day and we needed a bank that had connections with a better kind of investor. 'We've outgrown J.P. Morgan. There's no way I want them handling our IPO.'

I was uneasy. It wasn't that I was pleased with J.P. Morgan's performance, but I thought it was more constructive to put our energies into trying to make the relationship work. For all their failings, they had managed to secure the funding for us. A little pointedly, I reminded Patrik that we had some failings of our own. Whatever they might say to Patrik over the brandy and cigars, the other banks would quickly lose interest if our financial model was not up to date and in order, as it should be. Here was something that Patrik could usefully devote some of his time to. At this stage, getting our finances in shape was much more important than fretting about who might handle our IPO. Rather than fight J.P. Morgan all the time, he would do better to enlist their help. They knew our strengths and weaknesses better than anybody.

Patrik batted these concerns aside. He pointed out that he had just taken on a new finance director, Simon Jones, from Gap UK, who would sort out these trifling details in no time. It was the big picture that was important. With a tone of growing impatience he went on: 'It's not just me who wants to change banks. The investors think the same.' Jean-Bernard Tellio, he said, had encouraged him to speak to a banker at Crédit Suisse First Boston, whom he then met in New York on the day the *FT* piece had come out. The clear message he was getting from all the banks was that they badly wanted to work with us.

I continued to insist that he should try to mend fences with J.P. Morgan. Kajsa felt the importance of this even more strongly than I did. She was impressed by the amount of time J.P. Morgan had devoted to us and got on well with both Thomas Paulmichl and Felix von Schubert. But Patrik was not going to be deflected. So reluctantly I agreed to his proposal that he should meet more analysts and bankers. In the last resort, I knew that Kajsa and I would have to OK any decision to change banks anyway. 'Just make sure you only talk about the concept and not the finances,' I warned, repeating the message that Tom Kennedy had given us. 'We have to be very careful about what we tell them.'

Over the next few days, Patrik gave me regular updates on the various conversations he was having. One of these was with Margaret Mager, the Goldman Sachs analyst whom David Bolotsky had introduced us to during our trip to New York in mid-March. She was coming to Europe soon with fifteen of Goldman's most important institutional clients and wanted to introduce them to us. The more bankers Patrik met, the more I worried about what would happen when J.P. Morgan got wind of what he was up to. It wasn't too long before I found out.

In late May I got a call from Chris Bataillard, the Frenchman who ran J.P. Morgan's telecoms, media and technology (TMT) division in Europe. 'Can you guys come over here?' he asked. 'I think we all need to have a talk.'

Since our US fund-raising trip, Bataillard had become our main contact at the bank. This was partly because Patrik's relationship with Thomas Paulmichl was so bad, and partly because there was no one else left to do the job. Samer Salty had just quit to start his own VC firm and was about to be joined by Felix von Schubert.

It was raining, so Kajsa, Patrik and I jumped in a black cab for the short ride to J.P. Morgan's office.

Bataillard and Paulmichl were waiting for us in one of the bank's now familiar basement meeting rooms. We started by talking a little about the media coverage. Like us, J.P. Morgan had been inundated with calls. Its PR team was now co-ordinating with Hill & Knowlton to make sure a consistent message was sent out. But the two bankers had something else on their minds.

After a few minutes, Bataillard got to the point. 'I know things haven't been going perfectly between us,' he said. 'But this is a critical stage now for your company and it's really important that we work as a team.' He paused briefly. 'That means we need to trust each other.'

There was mumbled agreement from our side of the table.

Bataillard rubbed his forehead as if trying to decide how to continue. Then, directing his question at Patrik, he asked: 'Have you been talking to other banks?'

The suddenness of the question caught us all by surprise.

Patrik blanched. 'No,' he said.

There was a silence.

A faint smile crept across Bataillard's face. 'You have to realize,' he said at last, 'that we have contacts in this industry. Everyone talks. If you want to get another bank just tell us, because we're going to find out anyway.'

'We have talked to a few people,' I said quickly, trying to salvage the situation. 'But a lot of people have been calling us. It's not something we can control.'

Patrik nodded, as if suddenly remembering.

Bataillard didn't believe us, but was happy to leave it there. He had made his point. It was up to us what we did afterwards.

I later discovered that it was one of Paulmichl's friends at Crédit Suisse First Boston who had tipped them off.

In the grand scheme of things, Patrik's feud with J.P. Morgan was little more than a sideshow. What continued to trouble me as time went on was the extent to which his courting of other banks took time away from what I had always felt his main job should be – handling our daily finances and running the finance team.

Our vision had been to create a world-class finance department, which would instil a sense of financial responsibility in the company by making sure budgets were observed and expenses kept under control. The finance staff would also play a direct part in negotiating contracts with suppliers, ad agencies, consultants and so forth, driving costs down. This seemed to me more important than ever in the unpredictable circumstances of a hyper-growth environment. Its other vital role would be constantly to update our financial model, revising historical assumptions as we received more and more real information about the performance of the company.

But Patrik was too much of an individual to build such a

department around him. He showed little interest in its organization and the people he recruited were not strong enough personalities in themselves to make up for his lack of guidance. We had wanted a bean counter, but it had turned out that Patrik had no appetite for counting beans whatsoever. We probably should have realized this, and done something about it, a long time ago. But we hadn't. Our grand vision had failed to become reality.

By the middle of May, boo's finance team still consisted of only four full-time staff and a handful of contract workers, all of whom were swamped and demoralized. They were squashed into a tiny corner of the office. Whenever anyone spoke to them, it was usually to complain. Our accounts were more than a month late, and I had to keep calling the bank just to check how much money we had left. If there were any problems, we might not know about them until it was too late. This state of affairs was especially worrying given how quickly we were growing. We had to do something. If we didn't, we would be heavily criticized by investors and might have trouble raising more money.

boo's darker secrets were beginning to pile up. My *consigliere* Edward and I were spending more and more of our time conferring in Golden Square.

'Any progress on Project Diamond?' I asked him one afternoon, referring to our CTO search.

'Promising,' said Edward in a low voice. 'Harling hopes to see some people soon.'

'Good,' I replied. 'But hurry him up. We've got to get it sorted out quickly.'

We sat down on a bench.

'There's something else,' I said, looking at him darkly. 'It's Patrik.'

This was one of the trickier secrets to confide. Patrik was my co-founder. But, as I explained my concerns, I felt a load lifting. The problem was being addressed at last.

'This is going to hurt us a lot unless we do something quickly,' I said.

'Maybe you should hire someone senior to help him out,' Edward suggested.

'It won't work unless whoever it is has full control.'

We both knew now that Patrik would have to step down.

'He hates dealing with financial stuff anyway,' commented Edward.

'We'll have to think of something else for him to do.'

'Perhaps he could become chairman or something.'

'Listen, you must keep this to yourself for now.'

'Don't worry,' he said. 'I won't breathe a word.'

Back at my desk, I thought about the problem further. There was no doubt that Patrik would be hugely offended, even if I did offer him something else. Before I talked to him, I would have to be very sure of my ground. Nor could I afford to forget that he was a founder with a large shareholding. As this could tear the company apart, he would have to be handled very carefully indeed.

The one person who had already shown that he had the tact to deal with Patrik was Jay Herratti, and I rang him in New York. 'I need you to come over here and do an audit of the finance department,' I said. My propensity to hire ex-BCG consultants was now beginning to seem like wonderful foresight. Quite apart from the difficulties with Patrik, I felt that Jay possessed the analytical skills that would help us figure out how to build the kind of first-rate finance team we needed.

He didn't sound too thrilled. In New York, he was presiding over an office of seventy people. He had to supervise the installation of telecommunications equipment for a customer service centre and the recruitment of further staff. He had also taken over an extra floor, which was in the process of being refurbished. Then there were the endless PR meetings. In short, he had more than enough on his plate already without having to be away from the office for two weeks.

'Can't you get someone else?' he asked.

'No,' I said firmly. 'I need you for this.'

'Ernst,' he said. 'We know the answer to this problem already. We know what we're going to find out, and we know what I'll recommend.'

Now I had to square the visit with Patrik. I tried to play everything down. The finance department needed help getting on top of things. There was a problem and to fix it we had to find out what it was. Jay had kindly agreed to head an audit delegation. Their role was to help, I said. They should be thought of as friends . . .

'You're just wasting everyone's time,' Patrik replied. The department was shaping up and the only thing this 'audit delegation' would
achieve would be to scare everyone. But he could see that I wasn't
going to budge and reluctantly gave way.

Jay arrived in London on 18 May with his executive assistant, a
bright Asian-American named Soyoung Kang. Quickly they began
conducting rigorous interviews with each member of the finance
team.

Patrik was right about one thing. The audit delegation did scare
everybody. The finance director, Simon Jones, twice threatened to
resign and had repeatedly to be calmed down. The beleaguered staff
thought they were going to lose their jobs, although they seemed
grateful that someone was at last trying to sort out the mess.

Jay decided to work on the audit report in his suite at the
Meridien. The office was too crowded, he said, but the real reason
was that his presence made the finance team feel so uncomfortable.
It was just easier to write the report off-site. To help him and
Soyoung, he drafted in Dan Cotton, another ex-BCG consultant
who had recently joined the company.

About a week after his arrival, I had lunch with Jay at Cannellete,
a small sandwich shop near our office. By this time, he had boiled a
lot of the problems down to a single page with bullet points. It made
grim reading.

The department had been developed too late and was under-
staffed. The staff we did have suffered from poor morale, were
isolated from management and didn't understand the business. The
accounting software they were supposed to be using still hadn't been
properly installed. There was lack of cost control. The financial
model was out of date and based on assumptions that 'err on the
optimistic side'.

And then there was Patrik. 'CFO has busy schedule of external
matters,' Jay noted. It was a delicate consultant's way of saying he
wasn't managing his own department.

'What do you think we should do?' I asked.

'Isn't that obvious?' he said. 'Somebody has to start managing the
finance team.'

★

Before the full report had even been finished, Jay was interviewing candidates for an interim CFO at the Meridien. He received a lot of willing suggestions from J.P. Morgan, who had dreaded the prospect of having to work with Patrik on another round of fund-raising and had long been hoping that we would take this course of action. He also talked to Tim Gordon, our auditor at Ernst & Young.

But now I had to face Patrik. I had thought of another job he could do, but with the audit delegation still sniffing around I could hardly reveal the real agenda. Also, it had to be acknowledged that, whatever his failings as a CFO, Patrik had made a huge contribution to the business. He had handled a multitude of intricate legal issues; convinced the Benettons and Bain Capital to invest at a time when J.P. Morgan's efforts were getting us nowhere; and he had been a tough and extremely effective negotiator. When Kajsa had started booking ads, for example, she had been told that we would have to pay for everything in advance unless we found someone to give us credit insurance. This sort of insurance was unheard of for a company with no sales, let alone profits, but Patrik had somehow convinced a UK firm to insure us for $8 million.

It was late morning when I asked Patrik to join me for a coffee. Outside, it was another of those 'warm, cloudless days' that James Ledbetter had written about in the *Industry Standard*, and the two of us walked at a leisurely pace to the official boo café on Carnaby Street.

In another half-hour, the café would be packed with the lunchtime crowd. But when we sat down, there were only a handful of people. I noticed a couple of boo staff at a nearby table, but Patrik and I usually talked to each other in Swedish so I wasn't too concerned.

'I think we need to make some changes in the way we're handling the finances,' I said. I could feel my heart racing.

Patrik, who had been stirring his coffee, stopped and looked at me intently.

'I know. We've talked about that.'

'Yes, but the audit delegation . . .'

Patrik didn't want to hear about the audit delegation. 'So what do you want me to do?' he interrupted. 'I can start spending more time on this if you want.'

I took a deep breath and began speaking quickly. 'It's not that, Patrik. I just don't think you're the right person. I strongly believe that we need to have a new CFO in place.' I then tried to stress the importance of having a strong finance department if we were going to raise more money. This was something I knew would hit home if nothing else did. 'What I want to do,' I went on, 'is get an interim CFO while we look for someone more permanent.'

His reaction caught me by surprise. I had expected him to be defensive and even angry, but instead he just looked heart-broken. For a second, I thought he might even start crying. The cord for his hands-free mobile dangled listlessly by his neck. I had never seen Patrik like this before and it suddenly hit me just how difficult things must have been for him in the past few months. He had been under siege — squeezed out of PR, criticized for his presentations to investors, forced to accept the presence of the audit delegation, and now this. Kajsa and I couldn't have made life easy for him, either. We were a tight team. All the glowing magazine articles, which were now beginning to flood into print, were written as if we were the sole founders. He was the invisible man. No matter what he did, he would always be the outsider.

I was beginning to feel very sorry for him and a little guilty, but tried to concentrate on the positive. 'What I want to do,' I said, 'is make you executive chairman. That means you'll be in charge of the board. It's really important that the board works properly . . .' I tried to sound convincing, but Patrik just continued to sit there in dejected silence. This particular promotion wasn't going to cheer him up that easily. I pointed out that the CEO of a company — in this case me — had to report to the executive chairman.

'You don't even like doing that internal financial stuff,' I went on, taking a different tack. 'This will give you more time to do other things.'

Slowly — almost imperceptibly at first — Patrik's gloom seemed to lift.

'I always said I wasn't an accountant,' he mumbled.

'That's right.'

'It's hard for me to do all of these things at the same time.'

'I know. Of course it is.'

'I guess now I can spend more time on the fund-raising.'

'Hmm,' I said. Technically this was part of the CFO's job. When we found someone permanent to fill the role, Patrik would have to leave the investors alone. But I didn't want to mention this right now.

We talked a bit more about what Patrik's responsibilities would be and discussed what to do about the financial model. Jay had recommended that it should be taken away from Patrik and handed over to J.P. Morgan, which would be better placed to feed into it more impartial assumptions.

'I don't want them involved in this,' said Patrik. So we agreed that he should hire someone to work full time on the model instead.

The café was crowded when we walked out. All things considered, it had been a pretty successful meeting. But I knew that things had changed between us.

'Oh, you want a CFO as well!' said Anthony Harling, who was surprised but only too happy to take on the new assignment. Meanwhile, we had found an interim CFO, Rachel Yasue, a partner at KPMG in London. Yasue, in her mid-thirties with a dark bob, was the perfect accountant − tough and methodical, with an almost obsessive attention to detail. She began working in our office on a contract basis on 21 June. But this sort of firepower didn't come cheap. KPMG's fee for her services was £1,750 a day, plus VAT. In their letter confirming the arrangement, KPMG warned us not to get too attached to Yasue: 'You will not seek to recruit Rachel, but if you do, you will pay KPMG £300,000 plus VAT.'

So this was suppose to improve our finances? I couldn't help laughing at the irony of it all. But I knew it was an important step forward and was starting to feel positive about how things were shaping up in general. Although our technology was still a problem, everyone seemed confident that we would launch by late July. At our June board meeting the directors approved our latest financial forecast. With a July launch, we were predicting by the end of our financial year, on 31 January 2000, sales of $37.4 million and a total operating cost of $99 million. Of this latter figure, $26 million was allocated to technology, and $27 million to marketing, a surprisingly small amount for a company whose name would soon become one of the world's top 100 brands. The overall operating cost may have seemed high, but had to be viewed in the context of our ambition to establish with lightning speed the world's first truly global retailer.

The incredible success of our marketing strategy was beginning to cause us problems. The media pressure on Kajsa and me had become so heavy that we had to think about how we might lessen the load. In co-ordination with the PR agencies, Kajsa and I had been doing most of the interviews ourselves. Now we decided to hire some in-house PR people to help us. But in the interim I decided to delegate some of the work to one of our newest recruits, a 24-year-old Cambridge graduate named Paul Kanareck, who had joined a few weeks earlier as Edward's executive assistant and who would – with Edward promoted to chief of staff – soon become my executive assistant. He had previously worked for British merchant bank Rothschild, but wasn't typical banker material. Outgoing and funny, he had an almost chameleon-like ability to deal with different types of people and situations. Paul was genuinely passionate about his work, but liked to chat so much about football, movies or just life in general that he often found himself working late into the night to get things done.

Paul began to work closely with our PR agents at Hill & Knowlton, and with Modus, a London-based agency that was handling our British PR. The PR people would present a list of interview requests to Paul, who would then brief the journalists on the relevant company information, before passing them on, if necessary, to me or Kajsa for a few snappy quotes.

Paul, who quickly took to his new role, was amused by how receptive everyone was to our story. 'I never realized how easy it was to be a journalist,' he said, shaking his head. 'I'm literally dictating stories to these people and they're printing it, word for word.' These weren't small publications either, but major national newspapers and magazines. Just as amusing were the valuations that were being attached to the company. Since the *FT* article, some estimates had shot up as high as $250 million. The *Guardian* even reported that we had already spent £75 million, although, mindful of the warnings from Skadden Arps, we had been careful not to breathe a word about our finances to anyone. Our actual spend, up to the start of May, was a fraction of this – $15 million.

At my request, Paul began compiling a database of information about publications and journalists. As Sun Tzu once said, 'Know your enemy.' Paul sent out questionnaires to the heads of our foreign offices, which they had to fill in every time they did an interview. It meant that when Kajsa or I spoke to a journalist, we would know what they had written before, what kind of person they were and what sort of angle they were likely to take on the story.

So much had happened in such a short space of time that Kajsa and I felt the need to regroup, to take stock of what we had achieved, and to review our plans for the launch and beyond.

The boo Global PR Summit took place at Home House on 16 June. We booked one of the private club's upstairs suites, which included a balcony and large windows that seemed to magnify the bright midsummer sun. Those present that morning included Jessica Kogan from Hill & Knowlton, Julian Vogel from Modus, Paul Kanareck, Edward Griffith, and representatives from each of our foreign offices – the ever-cheerful Christina Preisler from Sweden, Christoph Vilanek from Germany, looking suave and slightly enigmatic as always, and Jenia Molnar, a former PR person for Calvin Klein who had just started working for us in New York.

Paul opened the meeting with a brief reminder of our objectives. 'We need to work together to build and maintain the image and mystique of the boo brand.' Everyone then took turns to summarize the media coverage in their respective countries.

In the case of the media avalanche in Britain and the US, this took some time. Jessica opened the account by passing around copies of the June issue of *American Vogue*, featuring the 'fearless and fabulous' Nicole Kidman on the cover. There, on page 106, was the photograph that had caused such a furore a month or so earlier. Patrik, although he was no older than we were, in his suit and tie looked like a benevolent uncle. After all the fuss the picture had caused, I was surprised that the photo editor hadn't attempted to airbrush him out or turn him digitally into a hatstand. *Dream team*, ran the caption, but in the article itself he was barely mentioned. 'Is this the future of retail?' Amely Greeven asked. Rather than reveal to readers that she was so convinced it was that she had quit her job to join us, she turned for a verdict to Erik Gordon, director of the Center for Retailing Research at the University of Florida. He thought it might be: 'Smart Web retailers will tap into the fact that what makes fashion "fashion" is having a story. And the Web, with its movement, music, and what we like to call high consumer involvement, is perfect for that.'

While the *FT* and *Industry Standard* pieces had spoken to the movers and shakers, there was a tantalizing sense in the articles that appeared now of getting closer to what boo.com was really about – no longer were we addressing investors or suppliers; at last we were reaching the people who would actually visit and buy from the site. It was hard not to feel a little big-headed. We had won virtually unanimous praise across the range of publications, from cool lifestyle magazines to the most august broadsheet newspapers. It was as if everyone had been waiting for us to come along. 'boo.com's dinky retro-graphics made us feel right at home,' commented *Wallpaper* magazine. 'With zippy five-day deliveries, 3D/360-degree product-viewing, styling advice from Miss Boo the virtual sales assistant/model, plus *boo.magazine* due to be launched online later in the year, we think we've seen the future of fashion.'

The *Daily Telegraph* agreed: 'If you are one of the many people who are sceptical about shopping on the Internet for anything other than books and flights, then boo.com, the first online urban fashion and sportswear "e-tailer" of its kind, is almost certain to change your mind.' Like the suppliers and the investors before them, the journalists found the technical features of the website irresistible. The spinning shoes, the dummies you could dress yourselves, Miss Boo – all these things, in the words of the *Telegraph*, made the site 'the best electronic playground on the Net'.

Everyone lost their hearts to our virtual sales assistant Miss Boo. Her picture was everywhere. It seemed only a matter of time before she would follow in the footsteps of Nicole Kidman and appear on the cover of *Vogue*. The consensus was that, like all the great screen goddesses, you had to be careful how you handled her. *The Times* warned that 'she bores easily if you do not browse briskly through the virtual shelves. But she will advise on all outfits, with the familiar sales assistant terms. "I like my fleece like my men, easy to remove when desired," she quips when you click onto one jacket.' Some commented that she bore a striking resemblance to Kajsa.

After Miss Boo, Kajsa and I were the obvious focus of attention. We were the 'over-achievers' described with the usual cheerful clichés – Kajsa the 'icy Nordic blonde', and me the 'archetypal Net-nerd' although, in fact, I had very little interest in computers at all. I was pleased too by how the atmosphere of the boo office also seemed to capture the imagination, in particular the 'boo crew' in training to operate our call centre. 'Fresh, funky, friendly individuals with vivid imaginations and good fashion knowledge, that's us,' one of them was quoted as saying.

While our fortunes in Britain and the US had been beyond our wildest expectations, news from the other countries was a bit more mixed. 'We're getting a lot of attention in Sweden,' Christina said, handing around an article that had recently appeared in *Dagens Industri*, Sweden's main business paper, 'and coverage in Scandinavia is generally on track'. But Denmark, she added, was a problem. 'It takes a lot to get the Danes interested in anything.' In Germany, things were also moving slowly. 'You and Kajsa really need to come over again,' said Christoph.

Having considered the press coverage so far, we moved on to more practical matters. Edward, who had been helping Luke Alvarez with some of our technology issues, gave an update on our most pressing concern – the date of the launch. Unless that was quickly sorted out, there was a great danger that all this media attention would be wasted. 'Right now,' he said, 'we're still on track to launch at the end of July. But I think we should prepare for the possibility that something will go wrong.'

We had all become cynical about the promises that kept being made, and broken, by our technology partners, and such difficulties had caused us to think about crisis management in general. How should we handle them from a PR perspective? We decided to try to think of all the possible things that could go wrong and to formulate a coherent response – systems collapse, suppliers leaving us, delivery delays, even tabloid scandal.

'Tabloid scandal?' I asked.

'Like if you're found naked with a prostitute in Hyde Park,' Paul offered.

'Of course. Yes, we'd better prepare for that.'

Our worst fear at the moment, though, was that the newspapers might start to get bored with us. With the continuing uncertainty about the launch date, we might end up *needing* a tabloid scandal. An important question was whether we should continue to push for media attention or back off a bit until after the launch. Julian Vogel advised the latter. 'There's a real risk of over-exposure.'

'Just because we stop talking to them doesn't mean they'll stop writing articles,' Kajsa said.

I agreed. 'If all the attention we're getting now is just because of a small window of opportunity, then we should take full advantage.'

So we decided to continue as energetically as ever in the UK where the media interest was most intense, but to ease off in the US and Europe, at least until we had launched.

It almost seemed tempting fate to discuss our PR policy after the launch, but we decided that Miss Boo, who had been such a hit, should become the focus. We would try to build her up into a media personality and put her at the forefront of our efforts to develop the boo brand. One day, we imagined, she might even be at the heart of a profitable merchandising operation – there would be Miss Boo dolls and Miss Boo board games.

But first we had to decide in what direction we wanted to take her personality. The newspapers had had plenty of their own ideas, several of them comparing her to Lara Croft, the big-breasted, gun-toting babe from *Tomb Raider*. Kajsa was appalled. Miss Boo was supposed to help customers, she pointed out, not shoot them or sleep with them.

'She should be someone you'd like to hang out with,' she said.

We left it there, but the debate over Miss Boo's personality, not to mention her hair and her accent, would continue for months to come.

As the meeting broke up in the afternoon there was a celebratory mood. We were sitting on top of what was the hottest new internet company in Europe, if not the world. We returned to Home House in the evening for dinner and drinks. The club had laid on several bottles of vodka and large jugs of grapefruit juice. It was one of those nights when everything seemed perfect. The skies were clear, the air was warm and we managed to commandeer a table in the club's back garden.

At one point, I sent a wobbly Paul Kanareck into the bar to try and find some more grapefruit juice. He came back a few minutes later, looking a bit damp. 'I just crashed into Pierce Brosnan,' he said.

Looking over his shoulder into the bar, I could see that he wasn't joking. Brosnan was standing among a group of friends, brushing himself down and looking a little put out. That night not even James Bond was a match for boo.

9

'WHY DON'T YOU TRY the shiromi usuzukuri? It's whitefish, with a little something extra.' Robin Leigh, manager of London's Nobu restaurant and partner at the fashionable new restaurant in New York called Bond St, was doing his best. But I wasn't the easiest customer he'd ever had.

'I don't like fish much,' I said. 'Do you have any meat?'

Robin thought for a second. 'Why don't you let me choose something . . . OK? . . . Great. I won't let you down.'

It was around 9.30 p.m. on a sultry evening in June and Nobu was buzzing with its usual mix of old money, celebrities and glamorous young things. I noticed Elle Macpherson sitting at one of the best tables by the window, studiously avoiding my gaze.

Michael Skidmore, an old friend of Robin, had used this connection to get our table. With us were Paul Kanareck and Lauren Goldstein, the fashion writer for *Fortune* magazine.

Looking around the restaurant with approval, she said, 'This is certainly a cool place. Ten out of ten.'

boo had been chosen for *Fortune*'s list of the 12 Cool Companies of 1999, and Lauren had come over to London to spend a day in the office and meet a few key staff. I'd been too busy to see her, but promised to sit down for a full interview the next day before she headed back home. I'd invited her to dinner this evening so that we could get to know each other on a more informal level.

So far, everyone seemed to be getting along really well. Skidmore told Lauren about our plans to sell fashion brands like Paul Smith, Prada Sport and Issey Miyake. The conversation then somehow turned to Royal Elastics and their amazing laceless sneaker, which

Skidmore was planning to order for boo after his success with it at Barneys.

'Who could have predicted that one of our bestselling shoes would be made by a small Australian start-up?' said Skidmore. 'I guess that's fashion.'

'So if you had to sum up boo's approach to fashion, what would you say?' asked Lauren.

'Well, Lauren, I'd say that we're attempting a symbiosis of designer and performance apparel. In the new millennium consumers are going to be looking for clothes that perform whether on the slopes or on the street.' Skidmore took his fashion very seriously.

Momentarily nonplussed, Lauren persevered. 'What about this geek chic image? Are you geeks?'

'Not entirely,' said Skidmore. 'We even have a boo skiing team.' And he told Lauren about an exciting trip we had made a few months ago with Charlotte and Edward to visit the suppliers, North Face. Their head office was near Aspen, Colorado, in the middle of the Rockies. So we flew in from New York a day early, to get some skiing on the slopes at Vail before our meeting. Lauren, it turned out, was a keen skier too.

'We work hard, but we play hard,' said Skidmore, topping up Lauren's glass with wine.

'boo's more than just a business,' I explained. 'It's a way of life too. People want to feel like they're helping to build something. They also get to do things they've never done before. It's a steep learning curve.'

'The start-up culture, huh?' Lauren said, a little dubiously. 'Do you have people sleeping in the office?'

'We prefer it if they go home,' I said, 'but yes, sometimes.'

Skidmore nodded. 'boo is like a cult. Just look at him,' he said, gesturing at Paul Kanareck. 'Two months ago, he was a banker. Now he's like Ernst's . . . secretary.'

'Executive assistant,' Paul pointed out. 'I wanted to be his secretary, but my legs weren't good enough.'

Lauren grinned. More than anything, she was amazed by the sheer number of people we managed to cram into our office, and the wide variety of nationalities working side by side.

'There must be a lot of arguments,' Lauren said.

'They're too busy for that,' I replied. 'When we're as big as Amazon, then people can start arguing.'

The food finally arrived, on Limoges china plates, with chopsticks. While the others shared an assortment of exotic-looking sashimi and sushi rolls, I got a shitake mushroom salad and beef 'toban' yaki.

'What do you think?' Robin asked, bringing a bottle of wine and joining us at the table.

'It's fantastic,' I mumbled with a full mouth.

Robin, an accomplished schmoozer, chatted with us for a while about the hard life of a restaurant manager.

'Oh, Gabby, Gabby,' he said, as a beautiful girl passed our table. 'Come and meet the boo people.' He introduced us to Gabby Harris, a hot new designer famous for her sweaters and crystal T-shirts.

By the end of the evening, we were all in the mood to go out.

'Where should we go?' I asked.

'Let's go to Momo,' said Robin's friend Martina, who worked in the Met Bar.

Momo, near Piccadilly, was a Moroccan restaurant with a basement bar that had become one of the most popular places in town after Madonna held a party there. The downstairs area, with its sofas and large cushions, was a great place to drink, dance or just take it easy.

'This is a boo night out,' I said, ordering several rounds of vodka and grapefruit juice. 'So we have to drink the boo cocktail.' We spent the next three hours dancing to Moroccan music and shouting to each other about fashion. When the bar closed, at around 3 a.m., we were all having trouble standing up.

I wasn't too surprised the next day when Paul came up to my desk and said that Lauren had rung to say that she had a massive headache and was feeling too ill to make the interview. I had only just managed to get to the office myself. But the main thing was that a cool company had given her a cool time.

The next week *Fortune* sent along a photographer who took pictures of Kajsa and me in Carnaby Street outside our office. We brought out a couple of our Arne Jacobsen chairs, and sat down on them in the middle of the street. I was wearing my favourite Paul

Smith check suit. Then the photographer asked us to sit in front of a blue wall he had noticed close by. 'No, wait a minute,' he said. 'Ernst, you stand up. On the chair.' Over the last few months I had become used to the whims of photographers, so I did what he asked and forgot all about it. But a few weeks later I picked up a copy of *Fortune* at a newsagent's in Piccadilly and nearly fell over. We had made our first cover. There we were against the blue wall. COOL COMPANIES '99 ran the headline. 'Twelve Startup Superstars: Will One Be The Next YAHOO?'

Inside, the very first paragraph established the tone of Lauren's article: 'It's worth noting that the investment banker at J.P. Morgan who decided to back boo.com's private equity offering is married to a woman who organizes circus competitions. Other bankers might have found boo's founders a bit, well, strange. Swedes Ernst Malmsten, a 28-year-old 6-foot-5 version of Elvis Costello, and Kajsa Leander, a 28-year-old blonde who used to model in New York, look more London night club than Wall Street boardroom.' It was a good piece, I thought, which made the point that our business sprang naturally out of our lifestyle. 'Malmsten and Leander expect to move their merchandise by riding a fashion trend,' Goldstein went on, and she ended with the comment that boo.com's challenge would be 'to stay as hip as its customers'.

As I sat on a bollard reading the article in the same Paul Smith suit I had worn on the day of the shoot, it was impossible not to succumb to momentary hubris. *Fortune*'s list of cool companies hadn't been presented in order of rank, but the fact that we were on the cover – didn't that mean that we were the coolest company of them all?

The temperature was rising in dot.com land. In the US, the media was awash with stories about record-breaking internet IPOs. In only the first six months of the year, internet companies had raised a total of $5.5 billion. Some of the bigger names to hit the market in recent weeks had included eToys, the online toys retailer, and TheStreet.com, an electronic business news site. Both had seen their shares soar by more than 200 per cent on their opening day of trading. Even some of the companies we were working with, including Interworld, the maker of our e-commerce engine, and Cybersource, an online payment clearing company, were planning to list on the stock market soon.

You could hardly pick up a magazine or turn on the TV without being swamped with stories about the internet and how it was changing the world. Terms like burn rate and day trader slipped into the vocabulary of ordinary people. On a trip to New York in June, I spent half an hour talking to a bus-boy at the SoHo Grand about his share portfolio. He'd already doubled his money but was too scared to sell. 'What if it keeps going up?'

The internet made business interesting. Not just a way of making money, but a lifestyle too. You could almost see the ad campaign. 'Tired of feeling undervalued and underpaid? Wish you could help create something new and exciting? It's time you joined a start-up.' And that's what an increasing number of people were doing. They were trading in their jobs as investment bankers, consultants, salesmen, journalists, you name it, in exchange for a few stock options and the thrill of calling themselves entrepreneurs.

Not surprisingly, perhaps, these developments weren't immediately welcomed in the oak-panelled boardrooms of corporate America, where the internet was decried as a fad, a bubble, a sort of hallucinogen for the masses. But at some point the old-school CEOs had no choice but to take it seriously. And when they did, it was a lot of fun to watch. Jack Welch, CEO of General Electric, the world's largest company, couldn't stop raving about it. 'I don't think there has been anything more important or widespread in all my years at GE,' he was quoted as saying in *Business Week* on 28 June. 'Where does the internet rank in priority? It's no. 1, 2, 3 and 4.' Media mogul Rupert Murdoch, who a few months earlier had scoffed at internet valuations, announced plans in early July to transform his News Corp. empire 'into an internet company'. 'The world is changing very fast,' he said. 'Big will not beat small anymore. It will be the fast beating the slow.' Merrill Lynch – the world's largest broker – had held out for months against the threat from internet-based rivals like Charles Schwab and E*Trade, but when it started losing business, it quickly unveiled plans for an online brokerage service by the end of the year.

What made all of these events especially interesting was that they provided a glimpse of what the future held for Europe. Not years in the future, either. Weeks, or months at the most. The signs were already there for anyone who cared to look.

This hadn't escaped the attention of American internet companies like Amazon, eBay and Charles Schwab. They were scrambling to draw up European expansion strategies and plant the flag before someone else got there first. At the same time, venture capital money was flooding into the region on an unprecedented scale. There are few better ways to stimulate entrepreneurial spirit than to start throwing money around. When Kajsa, Patrik and I had started approaching investors six months earlier, we'd had the field almost to ourselves. Not any more. As John Browning, European editor of *Wired* magazine, put it: 'Everyone between the ages of 25 and 40 seems to have a business plan in their pocket.' Samer Salty, one of our bankers at J.P. Morgan, was among them. He had just left the bank to set up a VC fund. Kajsa suggested its name: Zouk Ventures.

The trend could be clearly charted through the attendance levels at First Tuesday, a monthly cocktail party in London. Started in late 1998 by Julie Meyer, a Californian working for a British VC firm, First Tuesday was a way of getting friends together to talk about Europe's budding net economy. The handful of people who showed up at the initial event in Soho's Alphabet Bar were asked to leave donations in a bucket at the door to cover the cost of drinks. As word spread, so did the number of attendees. By the summer of 1999, interest was so overwhelming that the organizers began holding a lottery to choose the 250 people that could fit into the bar.

While the IPO frenzy hadn't yet taken off in the UK, the valuations now being talked about were as breathtaking as those on the other side of the Atlantic. British ISP Freeserve, for example, was being tipped to list on the UK stock market with a value of up to £2.5 billion. This was despite the fact that it had revenues of only £3 million a year.

Investors were now paying serious attention to Europe's fledgling internet companies. Unlike the US, where the market champions had already been identified, Europe was still wide open. Investors that got in fast had an opportunity to make staggering amounts of money.

It was a good time to start planning what would be our biggest funding round to date. The delays to our launch, coupled with our incredible growth rate, meant we needed another $20 million to get us through the next two months. For the first time, we weren't worried about whether we'd get the money. Ever since the media had pounced on our story a month earlier, Chris Bataillard of J.P. Morgan had been inundated with calls from potential investors. 'This is going to be very straightforward,' he told us.

One of the first things we had to decide was a new valuation for the company. As always, this was a bit of a guessing game. Since we were still a company without sales or profits, it came down to one question – what were people prepared to pay? Because of the buzz around us and the internet in general, we decided to double our pre-money valuation to $150 million and see what happened.

The response was instantaneous. Even before the round had opened, we had commitments totalling $15 million from our existing investors and Samer Salty's Zouk Ventures. J.P. Morgan also had an assortment of other clients that were pushing to invest, including a handful from Saudi Arabia, where boo was rapidly becoming a hit.

The issue was choosing which ones to invite in. This was something Patrik, in particular, had strong feelings about. Instead of just taking money from anyone, he wanted to try and broaden our shareholder base with some impressive new names. So while J.P. Morgan began collecting offers from potential investors, Patrik couldn't resist responding to persistent overtures from Goldman Sachs. Like a lot of the other banks that Patrik had been quietly meeting with in recent weeks, Goldman had already expressed interest in handling our IPO later in the year. But now it started dropping hints about making an investment as well. Patrik was delighted. Goldman was, alongside Morgan Stanley Dean Witter, the most respected of all Wall Street banks. 'It will look fantastic to have them as a shareholder,' he said.

Patrik had very little else to do except talk to banks now that Rachel Yasue, our new interim CFO, was looking after the day-to-day finances. It was an awkward situation. In his new role as executive chairman, Patrik regarded investment strategy as a key responsibility, which he pursued with renewed energy. I had hoped that he would take more of a back seat, but there was very little chance of this until we found a new permanent CFO. The potential for embarrassment very quickly became clear, when Patrik went to have dinner at Goldman Sachs's headquarters on Fleet Street to discuss a possible future relationship. I made sure that Edward Griffith went with him so that I was kept informed. On the way home, Patrik discovered that he had left his mobile phone in their office. But by then the damage had been done. The phone was handed in to reception, where the redial button was pressed in the hope of tracking down its owner. As it happened, the last person Patrik had called was Felix von Schubert at J.P. Morgan. Von Schubert saw to it that Goldman Sachs returned Patrik's mobile, but neither he nor his boss Chris Bataillard was amused. So Patrik was up to his old tricks again. Bataillard, having once worked for Goldman Sachs, probably felt the rivalry between the two banks all the more fiercely. But he reluctantly agreed to remain on the sidelines while Patrik continued direct negotiations, although it must have been obvious that Goldman was interested in not only making an investment but also possibly handling our IPO.

For Goldman, buying stakes in companies like boo wasn't just a great money-making opportunity; it was a way of infiltrating Europe's internet scene before things really took off. The extent of its interest was immediately obvious from the calibre of people it sent to meet us. First, Scott Kapnick, Goldman's head of European investment banking, showed up uninvited at our office with Lawrence Calcano, head of the bank's technology group in New York. About a week later, Mark Evans, the bank's head of Global Equity Research, paid us a visit. A few days later Kapnick was back again, this time with Adrian Jones, an Irishman from the bank's investment division.

It was at this meeting, in mid-June, that Goldman expressed its interest in making a 'sizeable investment'.

'We can do a lot for you,' Kapnick told us, before reeling off some of Goldman's achievements in the internet world. Their forceful attitude made me uneasy. These were people who were used to getting their own way and I had the feeling they wouldn't be easy to deal with.

It didn't take long for this fear to be confirmed. A couple of days after our meeting, Adrian Jones called Patrik with an offer. Goldman had decided to team up with one of its clients, Soros Private Equity, an investment vehicle controlled by billionaire financier George Soros, to invest a total of around $10 million. But there was a catch. Goldman wanted to make forty-two changes to our shareholder agreement before signing the deal. They were also talking to one of our other shareholders without telling us. It seemed pretty obvious that they wanted to loosen our control on the company, if they could.

Most of the things they wanted to change in the agreement were minor, but a couple stuck out. 'They want two board seats,' Patrik told me, after coming back from a tough session with the lawyers. Goldman and Soros thought that we should have more external directors, namely themselves, to offer impartial advice on how best to run the company. They were also asking for a special class of shares in boo, called preference shares, that would give them priority over our assets if the company ever went bankrupt.

'We can't do that,' I said, knowing that our other shareholders would never agree. 'It would be great to have Goldman, but not at any cost.'

'I already told them that,' Patrik said. 'But I don't think they understood.'

I was surprised that Goldman Sachs never expressed any interest to meet me to discuss their thoughts about the board or their proposed investment. I wondered whether they thought Patrik had more authority to make decisions than he really had.

Over the next week, Patrik managed to convince Goldman and Soros that he was serious about not accepting their terms. In response, their lawyers came back with a heavily reduced list of requirements. When Patrik turned these down as well, Soros backed out and everything went quiet for a while. But in early July, just as we were about to close the funding round, Patrik got a call from Adrian Jones. 'OK, we'll do it your way,' he told him: '$3 million. No conditions.'

By this time, though, demand from other investors had proved so strong that we had lifted our valuation slightly to $170 million. This meant that Goldman's proposed $3 million investment would now buy them fewer shares.

When Patrik explained this, Jones was exasperated. 'You can't do that. We've just made an investment decision in New York. I can't go back to them again.'

'Sorry,' Patrik replied.

Goldman, we thought, was too proud and powerful to tolerate being treated like this. We assumed that any hope of doing a deal was now gone and we closed the round soon afterwards, having raised $22 million. But two days later, Patrik got another call, this time from Scott Kapnick.

'Can you reopen the round for us?' he asked.

We agreed, and added Goldman Sachs to our rapidly growing list of blue-chip investors. But that of course wasn't the end of the matter. Very soon afterwards, Patrik told me that Goldman Sachs had expressed interest in doing our IPO. He pushed for us to negotiate with them. He said it wasn't just he who thought that Goldman Sachs was a leader in the field, but other investors too.

It was a needless distraction. We ought to have been concentrating on sorting out our technology problems, not worrying about switching banks. But Patrik was insistent. He was also a founder, and allowing him to talk to banks seemed a lesser danger than the conflict that might result from preventing him. In any case, Kajsa and I would have to approve before any decision could be made. But I insisted that if Patrik was going to talk to banks, he should do so in a controlled way by sending out formal pitch letters. Patrik happily agreed, and I hoped that that would be the last I would have to hear about banks for a little while.

Our office was bursting at the seams. We had spread through the building and now occupied three entire floors. Most recently, our finance department had relocated to temporary office space in Holborn. But it wasn't a solution, as anyone could see by taking a quick glance around the office. There were at least two and, in some cases three, people at every desk. It was a bit like working in a submarine, with people climbing over each other to get in and out of their chairs. And it was hot; unbearably hot. We were sucking up so much electricity in the office that there wasn't enough left to run the air conditioning. Instead, we opened all the windows and tried to ignore the chatter drifting up from Carnaby Street – now overrun by summer tourists.

It was the beginning of July. Our period of hyper-growth was reaching its peak. We had 200 employees who represented the cream in every sector, whether retail, technology, marketing, design or any of the other divisions we had created within boo – the payroll in July came to $1.4 million, and was now a substantial part of every month's outgoings. The atmosphere within the company as a whole was one of supreme self-confidence. Work in all departments pushed forward at an extraordinary pace. Whenever visitors dropped by the office – journalists, investors, friends – we felt we were showing off some brave new world.

The tour would begin on the third floor of the building. Here visitors would see ahead of them an open-plan area of about 15 by 15 metres, into which over 100 desks had been squeezed. At one end I sat with Edward Griffith and Paul Kanareck. Facing us, across a bank of Ikea desks, were Charlotte Neser, Megan Goodge – who was just about to take over responsibility for supplier relationships – and the PA Charlotte and Megan both shared, Felicity Tunbridge. I was CEO, but had no special privileges when it came to space. These five people were sitting so close to me that I could probably touch most of them without getting out of my chair.

At the other end of the third floor was to be found our fifty-strong tech team, whose responsibilities swung from the mundane – showing technologically illiterate staff how to use their email – to the complex job of testing every part of the site. With all the computers crammed side by side, the temperature in this part of the office became almost unbearable at times. Also on this floor was Luke's burgeoning business development team.

The floor above was divided in two. One half was made up of the overflow of tech and logistics staff. The other half, sealed off in a little world of its own, was the call centre, manned by our customer service team. These were probably the coolest, and most diverse, group of people in the company. They were handpicked. As the only people who had direct contact with the customer, they were the voice of boo.com and as central to our branding strategy as our marketing and PR.

Some people later questioned the logic of having a call centre located in London, where rents were so high. But this was where the best people were – and it would have badly dented the credibility of an online urban fashion and streetwear retailer to have its telephones answered by call centre assistants in some remote location in Scotland.

The head of the customer service team was Andrew Pines, an Englishman in his late thirties with spiky, silver hair. Pines had a naval fixation when it came to managing the office. Each of our call centres around the world had one 'admiral', or head of the office, and two or three 'captains', who were team leaders. Everyone else was part of the 'boo crew'. In London, we had around thirty call centre staff already on board. With no customers yet, they spent all of their time in training sessions. We had produced a whole book that outlined the philosophy of the company and all its inner workings and they had to learn this almost off by heart. They had to be able to answer questions about everything from how to use the website, to which brands we were recommending. And they had to answer with style.

The top floor was an attic space that had previously been occupied by the *Erotic Review* and had a slightly run-down feel to it. In contrast to the open-plan layout of the other two floors, it had been divided into separate offices. One provided a sanctum for Patrik and his staff – secretary Louisa Cunningham; executive assistant Sarah Arundel; and Heidi Fitzpatrick, a banker whom Patrik had recently hired to work on the financial model. When Patrik wasn't meeting bankers and investors, he could be seen through the glass of his office, leaning back in his chair talking loudly on his hands-free mobile phone. For some reason, he didn't trust ordinary phones.

But the top floor was mostly Kajsa's domain, housing our marketing and design teams, as well as journalists for *Boom*. This was the creative heart of our business. Here Niclas Sellebråten's design team was doing everything from designing stickers to producing a handbook with strict rules on how and where our logo could be used. Niclas was also starting to plan a redesign of the website, which was cluttered and difficult to use in its current form.

Like the techs, these people were working marathon hours to sort out all the fine details of our website design. On my way past the office after late night dinners in Soho, I would look up and almost always see the lights still burning on the top floor. I tried to make it up there at least a couple of times each day to see how things were going and keep people motivated. Invariably, we would end up talking about our new star Miss Boo, as we pored over sketches that had been produced for us by an American animation company called Mondo Media.

'She should be healthy,' Niclas commented during one of my visits.

'Yeah. But not too healthy,' replied Kajsa.

'Streetwise,' Niclas continued.

'Right,' said Kajsa. 'She should look like she's just come out of the Betty Ford clinic.'

'You mean she's a junkie?' I asked.

Kajsa shook her head impatiently. 'No. She's just a dabbler. She went off the rails a bit, but now she's fine.'

'Oh.'

The obsession with Miss Boo wasn't confined to the top floor, either. Someone in the tech team created a program that made her wink when you passed the cursor across her breast.

When Kajsa wasn't distracted by Miss Boo, she was busy managing the six people that now made up her marketing team. Working closely with our PR agencies, they screened the dozens of media interview requests that were flooding in every day. Each day they prepared packages of global press clippings about the company, arranged office tours for investors and journalists and produced boo merchandise, including hats, frisbees and T-shirts.

Perhaps because the division between our own working and private lives was so narrow, we strove hard to encourage a company culture. It was important to us that our staff should feel challenged but also cherished. The most noticeable outward manifestation of this to anyone visiting the office was the availability of free fruit, soft drinks and mineral water.

The boo summer party on 11 July was an opportunity to sample the company's *esprit de corps*. For me, the night began with a few drinks with Kajsa and Edward at Charlotte's apartment in Notting Hill. We then jumped into a cab and headed for the large hall in nearby Ladbroke Grove that had been booked for the occasion. It was an overcast but warm night and already dozens of people were streaming into the hall when we arrived. At the door, waiters walked around serving ice cold vodka and grapefruit – now the official boo drink – and a selection of oriental-looking canapés.

Among the early arrivals was Michael Skidmore, over from New York on a buying trip to London that uncannily coincided with the day of the party. Patrik drew surprised glances by turning up in a khaki trousers and a casual shirt. No one had ever seen him not wearing a pinstripe suit before.

Our founders' speeches were brief. Patrik and I both mumbled our gratitude to everyone for their hard work, but by far the loudest round of applause was reserved for Kajsa's two words: 'Let's party!'

We had hired a company named Urban Productions to organize the evening. Entertainment consisted of a DJ, a band and some floor shows, including trapeze artists and fire eaters. We also had a special display of our own. A week or so earlier, Kajsa had arranged for Jonathan Shrago of our business development team to tour the office with a video camera and interview every member of staff. These interviews were now being projected on the back wall against a soundtrack of thumping music. As the evening progressed, the drinks got stronger and stronger – an old party trick of mine.

Towards the end of June, I had begun to think more and more about what would happen after the launch. On one of our walks around Golden Square I outlined my thoughts to my new chief of staff, Edward Griffith. We had invested millions in building a global retailing platform, we had established a powerful brand name. So why stop at clothes? Why not use boo.com to sell other things as well? If we were quick, we could become the European market leader in a dozen different product areas before any real competitors got off the ground.

'We'll be the gatekeepers to Europe,' I said.

Edward was momentarily speechless. 'Wow,' he said finally. 'What an amazing idea! We mustn't lose this opportunity.'

It was obvious really. We had built up a global infrastructure. Now we had to think how to exploit it to the maximum. As always, it was crucial that we moved fast to protect our advantage. We might be the only internet company with a global network today, but in six months' time that might no longer be the case.

In normal circumstances, I would have handed this sort of project over to Luke Alvarez as our head of business development. But I didn't want to distract him from the more important job of launching the website. So on Edward's advice I turned to his old employer, the Boston Consulting Group. I asked him to arrange a meeting for me with his former boss Henry Elkington, head of BCG's European technology practice. The last time I'd met Elkington, he'd complained to me about all the people we had poached from his team. Now I figured we could pay him back.

BCG's London office, situated in a quiet back street just a few minutes' walk from Green Park, was blissfully cool and quiet after the chaos of boo. It seemed almost designed to encourage grand plans and, when I explained my ideas, Elkington was enthusiastic in a restrained, consultancy sort of way.

Over the next hour or so we discussed the possibilities. In building up our infrastructure, we had spent months dealing with tax and currency problems and now had an enormously attractive asset in know-how. A European company operating in one market would be able to gain instant access to the rest of Europe through our platform. So one idea was to establish joint ventures with bricks and mortar retailers like Marks & Spencer or the German department store chain Karstadt. Our platform was equally attractive to American internet companies looking to expand into Europe – our ready-made infrastructure would save them a fortune. Then there was the 'big brother' concept: we could offer a small European start-up – say, a pet-foods retailer in Germany – our regional platform and access to investors in exchange for a half-share in their company.

It was natural, I thought, that once boo had become operational, the young ambitious people who had helped to set it up would be looking for new challenges. The opportunity to run a business under boo's wing would give them a more important role and the company would benefit from their experience for a little while longer. I had an almost imperial vision. Edward and Charlotte and Luke were the generals that we would send forth to carve out unconquered internet territory.

But the first step was to consider what new product categories we could launch under the boo brand. If we could sell sportswear and fashion goods, why not other things as well? 'I'll put four consultants on the job at once,' Elkington said. 'We should have something to show you in a couple of weeks.'

Kajsa and Patrik both loved the idea.

'When can we tell investors?' Patrik asked, already thinking about how the plan would affect our valuation.

I hesitated. While the shareholders would certainly expect us to exploit the commercial potential of our platform to the maximum, they might be concerned that we were undertaking such an ambitious project before we had even launched.

'Not yet,' I said. 'It'll be more of a surprise if we tell them later.'

Exactly two weeks later, a few days after the staff party, the three of us and Edward Griffith headed over to BCG to see what they had done.

'Aaah, air conditioning,' Kajsa said, as we sank into the soft chairs in the lobby. Elkington arrived a few minutes later and, as he showed us into a soundproof meeting room, we chatted about the big news of the day – the death of John F. Kennedy Jr.

'It's the Kennedy curse,' Edward said ominously.

'No,' Elkington replied in a practical voice. 'It's just bad luck.'

Elkington's team had been working hard. They'd produced several mini reports that examined everything from the overall size of the market to profit margins for a wide range of products from furniture to electronic goods. They'd even bought some products from existing online stores to check the labelling in different countries.

'We've also interviewed some of the suppliers to see how they feel about working with internet companies,' Elkington said. 'The response was pretty good.'

A year ago, I thought to myself, they probably wouldn't have picked up the phone. Now they were too scared not to.

The consultants concluded that the most promising areas were toys and cosmetics. Although internet companies were targeting these areas in the US market, Europe was still wide open. Toys didn't really fit our image, but cosmetics, on the other hand, seemed to have everything. The products were small and expensive, they were sold all year round and weren't as prone to the vagaries of fashion as clothing – some of the biggest-selling perfumes in the world had been around for fifty years.

'It's a $6 billion market in the US and about $7 billion in Europe,' said Elkington. 'But right now, only about 1 per cent of total sales are online.' He glanced up briefly to check if the significance of this fact had sunk in. 'The really great thing about cosmetics,' he continued, 'is that most people are repeat buyers. Once you get them to your site, they'll keep coming back to you.'

Kajsa was enthusiastic. She had wanted us to think about cosmetics before Elkington's consultants had even begun their research. 'They're a lot like clothes,' she pointed out. 'The good stuff is really hard to find in some countries.'

I thought it was a great idea, too. The synergy with what we were already doing was perfect. 'Can you get your people to focus their research on this?' I asked Elkington.

'Sure,' he said. 'Whatever you want.'

We all knew it could still be months before there were any results from Project Champagne – as we called BCG's new research mission – but couldn't help daydreaming a little as we walked back to the office.

'If it's a separate business, we'll have to give it a different name, right?' Kajsa said.

'I guess so,' I said. 'Any ideas?'

She smirked. 'How about bootiful?'

There was one thing guaranteed to bring us back down to earth again. Technology. As we began to pull together the different parts of the platform, more and more bugs seemed to pop up. So many in fact that no one had any clear notion of when the launch date would actually be. All I kept hearing was 'two weeks', only to find that two weeks would go by and we were no closer than before. We were now a large company, with huge outgoings. It was vital that we start making money as quickly as possible. I discussed my worries with Luke and let him into the secret that we were looking for a new CTO. The question was what we should do in the interim. We needed someone who could examine all the technology issues and identify exactly what was holding us up.

We decided to talk to Viant, an American e-business consultancy. Troubleshooting was not something that Viant had done much of. It specialized in either helping to build e-commerce start-ups from the ground up or offering advice to larger companies such as Compaq or Charles Schwab. But Viant had just opened up a London office and its managers were very keen to help because we would be their first client.

When I told Steve Bennett that I wanted to bring in Viant to audit the platform, he was strongly opposed to the idea.

'It's the wrong decision,' he said. 'They'll only slow us down.'

'But all the investors are complaining,' I replied. 'We can't continue to have more and more postponements of the launch date. We need to show them that we've got a handle on this problem.'

Reluctantly, he agreed to co-operate. 'But they're not going to help us,' he insisted.

Technology had been a running concern for months now, but still felt more like a pip in the tooth than something we really had to worry about. It barely dented that summer's mood of bullish self-confidence, and it was all too easy to turn my mind to the pleasant prospect of launching boo.com in France.

'It's only a temporary space,' said Serge Papo, head of the newly opened Paris office, as he led us up the front steps of an imposing, Napoleonic-era building. 'We're looking for something better.' It was 20 July. We had chosen Paris Fashion Week as the ideal occasion for the launch, and had come over, together with Charlotte Neser and Paul Kanareck, for a two-day stay. It was a particularly significant trip for Charlotte, since she had recently been promoted to become vice-president of new markets, and the Paris office was the first opening that she had overseen in her new role.

The reason for Serge's concern about his new premises wasn't immediately obvious. There was nothing wrong with the location. It was on the Place Vendôme – one of the most upmarket addresses in central Paris – and directly across the road from the famous Ritz hotel. Once inside, though, the atmosphere was very different. The boo office consisted of a small, shabby-looking reception area with no receptionist, a meeting room that was bare apart from a large round table, and an open-plan working space, into which Serge's ten or so staff had been crammed. It was a miniaturized version of what we'd just left behind in London – right down to the faulty air conditioning.

'Hey, everyone,' Serge said, as we stood in the doorway. 'Here are Ernst and Kajsa.'

Opening an office in Paris was the first step in an aggressive global rollout we were planning over the next few months. We wanted to have offices in Amsterdam, Milan and Madrid by the end of the year. Charlotte had also begun research on Eastern Europe, the Middle East, Latin America and Asia. Now that we had established an infrastructure and a global network of offices, we had a model for opening further offices easily and cheaply. We had started with Paris because of its status as a major capital of fashion. A splash here would create a ripple effect that would get us noticed and written about in other parts of the world.

Charlotte had recruited Serge through Heidrick & Struggles' Paris office. She had been impressed by his instant feel for the boo brand and his wide range of contacts, which would help him to build a presence in France fast. He didn't have much management experience, but he was bright, energetic and well plugged into the youth culture of Paris. As a former DJ, he had spun records at some of the city's hottest clubs, like the Palace and Queen, and even produced a record that made it to number 9 on the Billboard dance charts. He was also known for having organized some of the first, and biggest, rave parties held in Paris back in the early 1990s. More recently, he had branched out into new media consulting and, when we hired him in late May, had been working on an electronic media project for Prisma Press, a publishing division of Bertelsmann. His brief from us had been to build an office in two months. It hadn't been easy. But somehow he had managed and now that it was open we wanted to give him a bit of support.

Serge had lined up two days of interviews with the French fashion press and what looked like just about every major newspaper and magazine in the country.

'OK. Let's go,' I said as we sat down for our first day of interviews at the round table in the meeting room. Ahead of us that morning were interviews with *L'Express*, *La Tribune* and *Le Journal du Dimanche*. There were as many more in the afternoon. Just before showing in the first journalist, Serge gave us a few words of advice. 'You have to be careful about the way you talk to these people,' he said. 'The French media is used to getting its own way. They think France is the centre of the world.'

'Just like the French people, then?'

'Right,' he said.

Our one taste of Gallic arrogance occurred during an interview with a journalist from *Le Figaro*. He kept asking questions about our finances, although we made it clear to him that for legal reasons this was not an area we could discuss in advance of our IPO.

Eventually, he got annoyed. 'I'm not happy about this,' he said, in French, as he was leaving. 'I don't know what I'm going to write about you people.'

Everyone else we saw found more than enough to write about. For all the talk that was going on about the internet, boo was still one of the first, and by far the biggest, start-ups operating in France. They loved the website prototype and were fascinated by our story.

'You guys are like the new Bill Gates,' said one woman. Kajsa started to laugh and had to leave the room.

By now we had done so many interviews that we could talk about boo.com practically in our sleep. But never before had we met so many journalists all in a row. By the time we had finished hours later, we were worn out from repeating ourselves.

'I feel like a message machine,' Kajsa said.

With all the interviews, there had been very little time to talk to staff. But I had arranged with Serge that we would take them all out to a restaurant in the evening and through our French PR firm he had managed to get us on to the guest list of the exclusive Man Ray restaurant and nightclub.

The Man Ray was about halfway down the rue Marbeuf, a side street off the Champs Elysées. Once a run-down cinema, it had been completely renovated a year or so earlier by its new owners, who included actors Johnny Depp and Sean Penn. It was always a pretty happening place, but it was obvious that tonight was special. There were barricades around the entrance and a posse of photographers was taking shots of people as they entered.

'Hey, it's Mark Baker,' said Kajsa, rushing over to give him a hug. 'What the hell are you doing here?'

Mark Baker, looking a bit like an ageing rock star with leather pants and long blond hair, was an old friend of Kajsa from New York. He was the part owner of Lotus, an almost absurdly hip Manhattan nightclub, but was probably better known for the celebrity parties he organized around the world. He was the ultimate socialite and a great guy to know.

'What's going on here tonight?' I asked.

'It's supposed to be for Puff Daddy's new album,' he said. 'But there'll be other stuff going on as well.' It was the last day of Paris Fashion Week, he explained, and Man Ray was one of the unofficial post-show venues. 'Don't worry,' he said, slapping me on the shoulder. 'It's going to be an awesome night.'

In the cavernous basement, it took us a while to make out Paul Kanareck and Charlotte sitting at a table with most of the Paris staff. Everyone was in high spirits.

'We thought maybe you had a better party to go to,' Serge joked as we sat down.

I smiled. 'No. We've just spent half an hour posing for the paparazzi.'

'Aaah. Of course,' he said, slapping his forehead. 'You and Puff Daddy, huh?'

I ordered a round of vodka and grapefruit as a welcome to all the new staff and over the next hour or so tried to get to know them.

I sat down between a tall Moroccan web designer called Farid Chaouki, whose previous job had been working on the special effects of *Titanic*, and Loic Prigent, chief editor of *Boom* France. Loic had made his name as a fashion columnist on the newspaper *Libération* and then worked at the TV network Canal Plus, writing scripts for fashion shows. In spite of his reputation as a savant of the fashion industry, he wasn't afraid to poke fun at it and he outlined to me his plan that *Boom* France would target the pretensions of the Paris cultural scene. Sitting next to Loic was Geneviève Gauckler, a freelance graphic designer who had produced record covers and designed the recent print ads for Jazz perfume. She had never worked for an internet company before and was eager to develop online skills. Quiet, almost Zen-like, every now and then she burst into fits of whinnying laughter as Loic cracked another joke.

Across the table from me sat *Boom*'s meticulous sub-editor, the beautiful Sibylle Grandchamp, and next to her the office manager Laure Quentin. For a moment I was convinced that I had seen Laure somewhere before, but then Serge's English girlfriend, Louise Barber, the French office's temporary marketing manager, pointed out that she was the spitting image of Miss Boo.

The conversation flowed back and forth around the table. I asked Serge what it was about boo that had made him want to join us.

'I liked the fact that you were trying to create a completely new brand, but I wasn't really sure at first,' he admitted. 'Then I came to London.' He whistled through his teeth. 'I couldn't believe it. There were people walking in the office with bare feet. I fell in love. I couldn't even sleep.'

As the conversation continued, the drinks flowed at a faster rate, Paul Kanareck seeing to it that no one ran out of vodka and grapefruit. After three rounds, he told the waiter just to bring the bottle. By now everyone was looking a bit woozy: they weren't used to this sort of behaviour. I noticed Loic furtively tipping his glass into a giant pot-plant. That plant will be dead tomorrow, I thought.

Shortly after 11 p.m. there was a sudden influx of people. Waiters pushed back tables. Lights were set up and a crowd gathered.

'What's going on?' I asked a passing waiter.

'It's a photo-shoot,' he replied. 'I think it's for American *Vogue*.'

We all picked up our drinks and stumbled over to watch. It was definitely worth the effort. There were models everywhere. Most of the big fashion designers had shown up, the stars of the *haute couture* shows that I'd been reading about all week. Quickly I spotted John Galliano, head designer for Christian Dior, who had aroused a sensation with his latest, Gothic collection. Standing some distance away was Alexander McQueen, who had caused some controversy this year – and saved a fortune in supermodel fees – by displaying his clothes on Plexiglas mannequins that rose through trapdoors in the floor. Sitting at a table near by was Karl Lagerfeld, with his trademark fan and grim expression. He was now at Chanel. His collection had included black dresses with cuffs made of curly white judges' wigs.

The designers were taking it in turns to be photographed by a charismatic, middle-aged woman who seemed familiar. 'Who's that?' I asked Kajsa.

She looked at me as if I were a moron. 'Annie Leibowitz,' she said. 'Only the greatest female photographer in the world.'

By the time the shoot wrapped up half an hour later, the party was really beginning to kick off. Puff Daddy, looking ultra cool in a white suit, was in the DJ booth mixing tunes. Johnny Depp, in jeans, black T-shirt and tinted glasses, stood in a corner with ex-girlfriend Kate Moss, who was laughing and knocking back champagne. It was difficult to spot anyone who *wasn't* famous. The entire A-list seemed to have turned out. If there had been a gas explosion that night, *Hello!* would have had to close.

Kajsa and Paul had struck up an unlikely friendship with an immaculately coiffured Ivana Trump, who was sitting with her teenage daughter, Ivanka. I sidled over to listen.

'You look amazing,' Kajsa said, admiring Ivana's dress.

'Tank you, Darlink,' said Ivana, with a smile that was all red lipstick and white teeth.

She looked a little confused as Paul gave a long-winded and rather drunken description of boo, but seemed to like the name. 'boo,' she said, turning to her daughter, who looked tired and bored.

'Can we go home now, Mum?' she asked in a whiny voice.

As the evening raced by, everyone got hammered. Our group had been joined now by Ascer, my old schoolfriend and drinking partner, and Tim Nicholson, a bearded and heavily built Englishman in his early forties who had been a member of the Gigastream team. A typical computer geek, Tim had no fashion sense whatsoever. Now he was dressed in grey trousers and a bright yellow shirt: he had probably gone into a shop and bought the first thing that had come into his head, but his 'look' was so strikingly spontaneous and off-beat that people thought he must be a fashion guru or at least a nightclub owner. Charlotte had asked Tim and Ascer to help her open the foreign offices. They were meant to be an advance SWAT team that would turn up in each market and prepare the groundwork before a country manager was hired. The two of them, along with Charlotte and Paul, were jumping around on the dance floor in an unpretentious English sort of way. In marked contrast, the French boo crew, although very drunk, managed to preserve an appearance of perfect poise. Was this something they were born with or did they have to take special classes?

I found myself dancing face to face with Gisele, the Brazilian supermodel. I remembered reading that she had been going out with Leonardo Di Caprio, but I couldn't see him anywhere tonight. In my fuzzy state I wondered whether she was now unattached. But after a brief conversation she drifted away and my chance was gone for ever.

Back at the bar, I was pondering where I'd gone wrong, when Kajsa wandered over. 'This place is starting to get out of control,' she said, laughing. She'd just been talking to Patrick Demarchelier, one of the world's top fashion photographers, when Kate Moss had walked past and, lifting up her top, said, 'Here. Photograph this.'

It was now around three in the morning. Paul and I decided to head outside for a breath of fresh air. The mob of photographers waiting by the barriers stirred as we walked out, but quickly put their cameras down again when they saw us. The air was heavy and warm, but it cleared our heads a little.

'You know,' Paul said, as we sat on the pavement, 'this is the only time I've been to a party and really partied instead of just sitting around drinking all night.'

I agreed. 'It would be great if Edward and Jay were here.'

'Let's call them,' Paul suggested.

Jay, in New York, listened to our incoherent rambling with barely concealed amusement. 'You guys are smashed,' he said. 'Have a drink for me.'

This seemed like a good idea, so Paul and I decided to head back downstairs. As we got up from the pavement, I noticed a commotion by the photographers and went over to see what was going on. It was a surreal sight. Tim Nicholson had stumbled outside and flung his arm around a departing Jean-Paul Gaultier. The designer, wearing his usual blue-striped matelot shirt, hugged him back. With flashes popping all over the place, he said, 'Zis is my special friend.'

I was going to die. Maybe I was already dead. I felt as if I had been fixed to the pillow by a large bolt through my forehead. I stayed absolutely still for about fifteen minutes, then slowly, very carefully, turned my head to the bedside clock. It was 10 a.m. Our first interview of the day, with Dominique Dupuich of *Cosmopolitan*, had begun a whole hour ago. Serge looked at me dolefully as I stumbled into the office with bloodshot eyes. Kajsa had yet to even arrive and he had had to cope singlehandedly.

Eventually Kajsa turned up looking even more ill than I did and what was left of the day seemed to take an age to pass, as an endless procession of journalists trooped in and out of the room. We ended up missing the last train and stayed an extra night. Completely exhausted, we arrived back in London early the next morning. I went straight to the office, where Edward made my extended hangover complete by updating me on our latest technology troubles. People were more desperate than ever to know when we would finally launch. 'It's like the First World War,' said Edward. 'The troops are waiting in the trenches to go over the top . . .' – he noticed the Fauchon bag I was carrying – 'while the officers have just come back from a spot of leave in Paris.'

The other big news was that Patrik had received responses to the letters he'd sent a month ago, asking investment banks to pitch for our IPO. Goldman Sachs, Morgan Stanley Dean Witter and Crédit Suisse First Boston (CSFB), the three leading banks in the internet sector, were all interested.

'I think we should line them up and decide which one we want,'

Patrik said, puffing up noticeably. 'It's called a beauty parade.' He had in fact already set this up. 'I've told them we'll be in New York on August the 6th.'

I would have preferred to hold back a little longer, at least until our technology problems were solved. I was also worried about J.P. Morgan's reaction if they found out, as they probably would. But Patrik's excitement was infectious. These were the same banks that had snubbed us a year ago. We were returning to Wall Street as conquering heroes. I was also curious to hear what their funding strategy would be. What kind of value would they put on our IPO? How much were we really worth?

The air felt warm and heavy when I landed in New York on the evening of 5 August. Patrik, his executive assistant Sarah Arundel and Paul Kanareck had come on an earlier flight, but were nowhere to be seen when I looked for them in the bar of the SoHo Grand. I decided to turn in early, conscious that we were flying out again the next evening. I needed the sleep.

The other three were waiting in the lobby when I came down the next morning. Patrik was wearing what looked like a new pinstripe suit and carrying a briefcase. This was a big day for him and he kept shuffling around impatiently, eager to get started. Paul, who had lost his luggage, was in a pair of khakis and a white shirt bought from the airport the previous day.

'You look like a dressed-down banker,' I said.

'That's the idea,' he replied.

The Morgan Stanley headquarters was in Times Square, which with its blaring horns and giant neon signs was at the epicentre of New York's brash activity but a handy place to keep tabs on the latest stock prices. This financial powerhouse had a secret weapon when it came to e-commerce: Mary Meeker, head of its internet research team. Meeker − whose monikers included the 'Queen of Wall Street', 'Oracle of the Net' and 'The Axe' (a name given to the top analyst in any sector) − inspired a near religious following among investors. It was Meeker who, a couple of years earlier, had advised clients to buy stocks in AOL, Compaq, Dell and Microsoft while they were still at pre-nosebleed levels. Her backing, I knew, would guarantee market support for our shares after our IPO.

The pitch took place on the 41st floor, with panoramic views of downtown Manhattan. There were three people in the small meeting room: André de Baubigny, the genial, permanently tanned banker we'd met on our first scouting trip in April 1998; Kirsten Feldman, the personable head of Morgan Stanley's retail division, and another banker called Lisa Clyde. The atmosphere was relaxed and informal. As Feldman passed a bowl of pretzels around the room, de Baubigny recalled the last time we were here. 'You and Kajsa kept giggling,' he laughed. The big joke was that now we had made it.

Only after the pretzels were finished did the discussion become serious. 'We're really impressed with what you've achieved in the past year,' de Baubigny said. 'We think we can help take you forward from here.' Morgan Stanley, he said, could help us raise more money, handle our IPO and meet any other needs we might have in the future. 'We believe in building long-term relationships . . .'

boo would have an entrée into an exclusive club. 'We only work with the market leaders or first movers in every sector,' Feldman pointed out.

Then came the trump card.

'Of course you'll meet Mary,' de Baubigny said offhandedly.

'Mary Meeker?' Patrik asked.

'Of course. She'll help you through the IPO process.' De Baubigny paused. 'When she supports a company, she has the total confidence of the market.'

Towards the end of the meeting, de Baubigny asked us who we were seeing next.

'Goldman Sachs,' I said.

The three bankers looked at each other and grinned. 'Ask them about 1-800 Flowers,' de Baubigny said. This online florist was one of the few internet IPOs not to have soared. It had listed on the stock market the previous day and immediately tumbled 13 per cent.

'Is Goldman their banker?' Patrik asked.

De Baubigny, still smiling, threw up his hands. 'Just ask them,' he said.

The cab drive to Goldman Sachs, just around the corner from Wall Street, took about 20 minutes. The interior was much the same as any other bank we'd seen – all glass, marble and polished steel –

but the people seemed different somehow. They were all just so . . . professional. Even the receptionist looked like an MBA. Everything was perfect.

There were more than a dozen people gathered around the table of a huge conference room. Our host was Lawrence Calcano, the ultra-smooth, all-American head of the bank's high-tech group. Calcano, in a sports jacket and casual trousers, was flanked by another Goldman heayweight. Lawton Fitt, in her mid-forties with sculpted hair, per-fect nails and a power suit, ran the bank's technology equity capital markets division. She had personally overseen more than 250 tech-nology IPOs in the past ten years, including Yahoo, eBay, eToys and, most recently, TheStreet.com. Also present were Walter K. Levy, a retired retailing guru brought in by the bank as a consultant on special deals, Fergal O'Driscoll, head of high tech in Europe, who had flown in specially from London, and an assortment of other experts from dif-ferent parts of the bank. They had even invited someone Swedish, for no apparent reason other than that he was Swedish. *'Hej,'* he said, when introduced. *'Hej,'* I replied. We didn't speak again.

Calcano first thanked us for dropping by. 'You must have a very hectic schedule,' he said. He handed us each a heavy folder and got started. The presentation, which began with a lengthy overview of Goldman's credentials, seemed calculated to lull us into a hypnotic state. Goldman Sachs was the 'dominant internet franchise', Calcano told us. It had worked with the leaders and pioneers. 'Our internet expertise is unsurpassed.' We were invited to look at a chart in our folder of Goldman's internet *keiretsu* – the Japanese term for a network of interconnected corporations. Goldman sat in the centre like the sun, while arrows fanned out to the companies in its orbit, America Online, Yahoo and eBay. The chart listed the names and direct phone numbers of the CEOs of each company. 'These are the sorts of people we talk to every day,' Calcano noted. Lawton Fitt then spent a few minutes explaining how Goldman had managed more internet IPOs than its two largest competitors combined – Morgan Stanley and Crédit Suisse First Boston. The impressive chart that served to illustrate this assertion reminded me of a similar one that Morgan Stanley had shown us a little earlier. Only then Morgan Stanley was top. But Lawton Fitt couldn't help me out of my confusion. 'It all depends on how you measure it,' she said, without elaborating.

Now the other bankers and analysts took turns to speak. They told us why boo would succeed – 'innovative technology'; 'low fixed costs and high margin potential'; 'explosive growth potential' – and gave a lengthy survey of the online retailing landscape. Finally, a good two hours later, Calcano rounded things off: 'Goldman Sachs is highly enthusiastic regarding the opportunity to become boo.com's long-term financial adviser,' he said. 'We have cemented our enthusiasm and commitment through an investment in the company.'

We were all overwhelmed, especially Patrik. This was an experience he would probably tell his grandchildren about. Even so, we managed to ask a few questions.

'What do you think J.P. Morgan will do if we hire you?' I asked.

'Don't worry about them,' Lawton Fitt replied. 'Goldman is the market leader. This sort of thing happens all the time.'

'Talk to StarMedia,' added Calcano. 'They worked with J.P. Morgan for a short while, but then saw it made sense to come over to us. I'll give you the number of the CEO, if you like, and you can speak to him yourself.'

Patrik saved the tough question until last. 'What happened with 1–800–Flowers?'

Lawton Fitt didn't even blink. 'It can happen to anyone,' she said. 'The markets are unpredictable. For all we know, it could be back up again tomorrow.'

After the Goldman Sachs experience, we felt in need of a quick drink and dropped into an Irish bar just off Wall Street.

'I feel like I've been brainwashed,' said Paul, knocking back a glass of wine.

'They had absolutely everyone there,' I said. 'They even brought in that old guy. What was his name? Walter K. Levy?'

'I kept wondering if his nurse was going to come in,' said Paul. '"That's enough excitement for today, Walter."'

Patrik, lost in his own thoughts, didn't join in the laughter.

'Even you must feel a bit brainwashed,' I said to him.

'Yes, but they were really great,' he replied. 'We have to get rid of J.P. Morgan immediately.'

'Do you remember last year, Patrik?' Now everyone wants to work with us. It's really strange.'

Patrik didn't answer, but a satisfied smile came to his lips.

The next bank we visited, Crédit Suisse First Boston, was, to some extent, an upstart in the internet field. Its reputation was based largely on the clout of its rainmaking technology head, Frank Quattrone, who had been poached, along with around a hundred members of his team, from Deutsche Morgan Grenfell a year earlier. The swoop had set Wall Street alight. It had also put a dent in CSFB's balance sheet, costing as much as $1 billion, according to some media estimates.

I was put out that Quattrone himself wasn't at the meeting. Instead we were greeted by Carlos Bhola, who headed a small deputation of bankers and analysts.

'We don't have much time,' I told them. 'We've got a plane to catch.'

'We'd better get started, then,' said Bhola.

CSFB had obviously been working on this for weeks. Each of us was given an enormous pitch document, ring-bound and beautifully presented. A banker and an analyst had been flown over from London especially for the meeting.

The pitch began with the usual self-promotional stuff. CSFB had handled the IPOs of Amazon, Netscape, Cisco and MP3.com. According to CSFB's calculations, it had done more IPOs, mergers and acquisitions deals and debt raisings than either Goldman or Morgan Stanley. By now, though, I had stopped paying attention to these charts.

What I liked about their pitch was its entrepreneurial flavour: the bank seemed less concerned about its own image in the market than Morgan Stanley or Goldman Sachs, and more ready to take risks and, if necessary, to move fast. boo.com wouldn't just be another deal, Bhola told us, it would be 'an event transaction'. We would get the full support of Shane Leonard, CSFB's London-based technology analyst.

To our surprise CSFB even attached a valuation to boo – something neither of the two other banks had done. Assuming our IPO was imminent and certain criteria were met, their estimate was a private-market valuation of $360 million, with an IPO valuation of

$690 million. If we hired CSFB, they would immediately begin raising money from private investors – or at least trying to – at the $360 million valuation. That was almost double our previous valuation. None of us said anything, but I felt the electricity in the air.

The dollar signs were still in our eyes when they led us out an hour later. But it was a tough decision. As the sleek, black Lincoln town car, whisked us off to the airport I thought of Paris trying to make up his mind about which of the three goddesses should have the golden apple.

10

WE NEVER DID CHOOSE A BANK. The appropriate classical allusion was not Paris all, but Tantalus in the Underworld reaching for the bunch of grapes that vanishes just as he touches it. Indeed, even while we were being praised and courted in New York, I knew that the whole trip was an impossible dream – that we should have been pleased if any bank was prepared to work with us at all.

The day before our departure, 4 August, Luke Alvarez and Edward Griffith had met with Viant to hear its verdict on our technology platform.

They came up to my desk afterwards. 'We need to talk about this somewhere quiet,' said Edward, his anxious expression hinting at what was to come. So the three of us went out to the boo coffee shop just a couple of minutes' walk from the office.

'OK,' I said, once we had sat down. 'What did they say?'

While Edward concentrated with unusual intensity on stirring the sugar into his coffee, Luke looked at me with a gallows smile.

'Well, basically, they think we're fucked,' he said. 'Those were the exact words: "You're fucked."'

'What's that supposed to mean?' I asked, staring at Luke across the table.

'They don't think we can launch.'

'At all?' I was becoming sceptical. Luke was prone to exaggeration when he wanted to make a point.

'What they said,' Edward interjected, 'is that we probably can't launch for quite a while.'

'Nine months,' Luke added. 'They think the whole way we've gone about building the platform is flawed. They think we should go back to investors, ask for more money, and start all over again.' He leaned back in his chair. 'Basically, they think we're fucked.'

As I tried to take this in, Edward and Luke took turns in explaining the details of Viant's initial findings. Systems architecture, the user interface, product data, the application development process – there were huge problems in pretty much all these areas. Our overall project management was a disaster too. We were now working with eighteen different technology companies who were scattered throughout the world. What they needed was a central architect – someone tough and disciplined who could co-ordinate what they were doing, but it was probably too big a job for any one person to handle – especially in such a tight timeframe. I was starting to wish we'd stuck with Ericsson all those months ago.

'The main problem is that we don't have any version control,' Luke said, pointing at the appropriate paragraph in Viant's two-page summary of their initial findings. Most early versions of a website, it noted, had bugs in them. The process of fixing these bugs, it went on, would sometimes create new ones. The only way of controlling this, and tracing problems back to where they'd started, was to work on the website in small, carefully documented stages. 'You need to build and test, build and test,' said Edward, who was reading over my shoulder. And in doing so, it was vital to have a central system of management in place to track the changes that were being made in all the software components, to create a central code base. But we had none. In fact, everyone – from the technology companies to our own tech staff – was tinkering with the website at will. 'We've got bugs everywhere,' Luke said.

The other 'critical area of technology risk' was content management. There were three databases that needed to work in concert, but the way in which they had been linked together meant that there was a circuitous updating process and no single 'boo view' of content information. Conflicts in hierarchy between the different databases were leading to product mismatches.

'It means you won't be able to buy anything,' Luke said. 'Either that or people will get the wrong thing in the post.'

I was shaken. This was the nightmare scenario. It would have been better to have been found naked in Hyde Park with a prostitute. For a second, I considered the possibility that we'd never launch. The company would have to be shut down, having already spent more than $30 million of other people's money. At the same time, though, I wasn't totally convinced by Viant's bleak outlook. 'They could be trying to scare us into thinking we need their help,' I pointed out.

Luke shook his head. 'I don't think so. They said they weren't sure if they wanted to work with us any more. They think it'll hurt their reputation.'

'Maybe they're trying to lower our expectations,' I added.

'Yeah, maybe,' he said, shrugging. 'I don't know. But we've got real problems and we really have to stop pissing around.' He glanced across at Edward, as if looking for support. 'The other thing they said is that Steve can't handle this.'

'It's not as if we haven't tried to sort this out,' I said. 'But we still haven't found a new CTO.'

'We can't wait,' Luke replied. 'He's just getting in everyone's way. He can't help us fix the problem.'

'But the whole tech team is behind him. Who's going to guarantee no one's going to drop a spanner in the works if he goes? Viant? You're telling me they don't even know yet if they want to work with us.'

Edward agreed with me. Unless Viant could guarantee the integrity of the systems, we had to hold on to Steve for now.

'OK,' said Luke. 'But if we're to turn this round, you need to let me have more authority.'

The plan that Luke went on to lay in front of me was ambitious, even by his standards. He wanted to project-manage the entire launch process. This meant mapping every single thing that needed to be done. Not just in technology, either – in all parts of the business, from marketing to logistics. 'We need to see how all the pieces fit together,' he said. 'It's the only way we can set a realistic launch date.'

I knew he was right. If things were even half as bad as Viant was suggesting, we'd have to tell the board members at once and inform all the shareholders. And when we did, we'd have to give them a deadline we could actually stick to. Our credibility was on the line. Even so, I wondered if Luke really knew what he was getting himself into.

'I can handle this,' he said, as if reading my thoughts.

OK,' I said. 'It's all yours.'

I was starting to wonder how we had ever believed we were only weeks away from launch. It was a mass delusion. We either hadn't seen, or had simply closed our eyes to, all the warning signs. So who was to blame? Was it the technology companies for making promises they couldn't deliver? Partly. Of course it would be easy to blame Steve Bennett, but when it finally came down to it, I realized with a sinking feeling, I had to take responsibility. As the CEO, my neck was on the line, anyway. I was the one that everyone would blame if the company didn't launch. But I knew that they'd be right too. Instead of focusing singlemindedly on just getting the website up and running, I had tried to implement an immensely complex and ambitious vision in its entirety. Our online magazine, the rollout of overseas offices, the development of new product lines to sell on our site – these were all things that could have waited until the site was in operation. But I had wanted to build utopia instantly. It had taken eleven Apollo missions to land on the moon; I had wanted to do it all in one.

Nor had I taken into account the huge pressure that this vision created. It was far ahead of the infrastructure we had to support it, but I'd banned all talk of failure or delays as defeatist. The result was that rather than reveal their worries people had preferred to ride blindly into the guns.

I wished now that *I* had someone in whom I could confide my worries. Hundreds of people turned to me for guidance, but to whom could I turn? I felt very alone. There was no wise old man to advise me – not even my old mentor Dag Tigerschiöld. I marvelled at my previous arrogance. Now I saw that I had been just a kid playing at business.

In New York, I had arrived at the SoHo Grand to find faxes in sealed envelopes waiting for me, from London, with progress reports of the unfolding crisis. On the morning of meeting banks eager to pitch for the business of the world's most exciting new company, I was issuing directives cancelling all leave and implementing a state of emergency.

Back in London, I talked to Steve Bennett, revealing the substance of Viant's report, but omitting their comments about him. Luke, I explained, would be heading our 'Project Launch', which I stressed would co-ordinate all aspects of the business, not just technology. I knew Steve wasn't going to be around much longer, but while he was it was vital that he persuade the tech team to co-operate.

We then formed an 'Operational Steering Committee', whose purpose was to galvanize the entire company into working towards the launch. Anyone engaged in any activity that didn't further this cause was to drop it and to refocus on something that did. This applied as much to our external partners as to our own staff. I asked Henry Elkington, for example, to switch the BCG team that had been researching future product lines to practical tasks that had some immediate application. Mike Brantjes, a former BCG consultant whom we had employed to open an Amsterdam office, was called back to London. The battle for boo had begun.

In the week that followed Viant's verdict, the scale of the challenge quickly became clear as Luke and his team compiled a rough list of the things that needed to be done before we could launch. Seven critical areas were identified: bug-fixing; business testing; technology operations; merchandising operations; order fulfilment; customer operations; operational resourcing. These headings were broken down into the specific tasks that they entailed. Over 700 were identified. Team leaders were then assigned to each critical area and told to produce their own micro-lists.

'Here's some light reading for you,' Luke said, plonking down a stack of papers on my desk one afternoon. The list of tasks had now swollen to more than 10,000. As I looked at the huge pile, an image flashed through my mind of Kajsa and me typing up our first, flimsy business plan. We never imagined it would lead to this.

For all his self-confidence, Luke and I both knew he needed lots of help. It was one thing to draw up project plans. But a lot of the hands-on work, especially in technology, would have to be handled by experts.

This was where Viant came in – if they would accept the job. Luke was terrified they'd refuse. 'Viant doesn't usually do this kind of work,' he said. 'They're strategy consultants. Not crisis specialists.'

A week after their last dramatic meeting, Luke and Edward sat down in the goldfish bowl again with Robbie Vann-Adibe, one of Viant's millionaire founders, and Michael Keany, head of Viant's newly opened London office.

I stayed away. I was pretty confident Viant wouldn't say no to a big fee. But if they did, I'd swing in and try to change their mind. It was a case of saving the heavy artillery until you really needed it.

Luke collared me afterwards. His mood was buoyant. 'They were really negative at the start,' he said. 'They said they'd already decided not to get involved.'

'So what happened?'

'I showed them the lists. I told them we knew we probably couldn't launch for quite a while. I think they were impressed that we're taking it so seriously.'

'So they'll help us?'

'Yeah. They don't want to lead the project. But they'll help.'

Viant confirmed all of this in an email later that afternoon. They were surprised by how in a week we had adapted to a situation that it would probably have taken a larger corporation months to address.

The term 'project launch' was now being whispered around the office. But most people had no idea what it actually meant. The official line, although hardly anyone believed it, was that we'd be launching any day. The best way to explain what was going on, I decided, was to hold a company-wide meeting. I asked Luke to write the invitation, which I then sent out by email.

Sent: Wednesday, August 18, 1999 6:36 PM
To: BooAll-UK
Subject: Project Launch and other irritants.

Have you found yourself asking these questions over the last few weeks?
* What is all this special project stuff that's happening?
* Why are all these wanker consultants wandering around?
* Do senior management ever do any real work?
* Are we ever going to launch?
If so, and even if not, come to a special lunch meeting on Friday

at 1pm PROMPT at the Cafe Royale, 68 Regent St to find out the answer to these questions and more.

We will tell you all about Project Launch, why it will make your life easier and how it will get us to launch.

Yours with thanks and appreciation

Ernst, Kajsa, Patrik

The Café Royale was only a short walk from our office and most people wandered over together in a long procession. We had booked one of the largest rooms, but there were still people standing against the back wall and sitting on the floor. It was so crowded that I put two of our human resources staff by the door to make sure journalists didn't try to sneak in. Similar meetings would take place that day in New York and at all our European offices. Project Launch was a global effort.

I had asked Paul Kanareck to prepare a morale-raising speech for me. At the top of the sheet of paper, Paul had jokingly suggested a few opening lines that might capture the momentous nature of the occasion: 'Friends, Romans, countrymen . . .', 'Four score and twenty years ago our forefathers . . .' That sort of thing. But as I stared at the packed gathering, I thought that I really ought to come up with something myself.

'I am an insect,' I began. It was rather an unconventional line. I had been thinking of Gregor in Kafka's story, 'Metamorphosis', the man who wakes one day to find that he is a beetle. Our predicament, it occurred to me, was similar. While we grappled with the technology problems, we were on our backs unable to move. Like Gregor, we had to try to turn ourselves over.

I paused to let the words sink in, but few people seemed to recognize the allusion. Most just looked at me in baffled silence, wondering what on earth their CEO could be talking about. The pressure must have finally got to him.

As I went on, I tried to simplify things. We were all playing our part in an effort to build something that had never been achieved before, something that would make the entire world sit up and take notice. In the process we had built up a community of extraordinary diversity and talent. You only had to look round the room to see that.

But now, just as we had hoped that the long weeks of personal sacrifice were over, we would have to roll up our sleeves again and dig in for one more effort. I told them how Kajsa and I had been in exactly the same situation when we were launching bokus.com. Just when we thought the hard work was over, the hardest work of all seemed to begin, as we struggled to overcome last-minute obstacles. It had been a painful experience, but also one of the most rewarding, as the dream finally became reality. In the coming weeks, everyone in this room would work harder than they ever had before, but they too would experience the exhilaration of making a dream come true.

There was a round of enthusiastic applause. Then, after a few words from Kajsa and Patrik, Luke took over for the more practical stuff. He had prepared a presentation that explained, in broad terms, what was being done. It ended with the news that everyone had been waiting for. 'Our new launch date,' he declared, 'is 1 November. And this time we're going to stick to it.'

As members of staff each helped themselves to a glass of white wine afterwards and talked about the weeks ahead, the mood in the room was buoyant. It was as if we had announced some great success, not a reverse that we had to overcome. The only note of uncertainty concerned the opening words of my speech. What did I mean by saying I was an insect?

'You have to think about it,' I said.

'Did you mean that like an insect we'll be dead by the end of the summer?' someone asked.

'I don't know what it means,' said someone else, 'but I'm proud to work for a company whose CEO can compare himself to an insect. It doesn't often happen.'

It had been a good afternoon, I thought, as I walked back to the office afterwards. Being on the brink of catastrophe had been turned into another grand adventure. Every now and then another boo person I passed on the way back congratulated me. I thought of a comment Jay had made a few days earlier. I was like one of those cartoon characters, who occasionally get blown up by dynamite or flattened by ten-ton anvils but always miraculously manage to pull themselves together again to fight another day.

★

The new launch date required some awkward adjustments. For the third time Kajsa had to put off an advertising campaign, which was embarrassing and costly. It was too late to postpone ads in some of the big US magazines like *Vogue* and *Arena* and, where we were able to rebook, we often lost our upfront payments. Even worse was the impact on grassroots marketing. Countless events had to be called off, and a totally new campaign thought out from scratch. We had had 'Here Comes the Summer!' and 'Back to School'. Now it was 'Presents for Christmas'.

Then there were our finances. How were we going to fund another three-month delay? Two days after the announcement of the new date Rachel Yasue and I sat down in the goldfish bowl to talk things through.

The KPMG accountant was still filling in as our chief financial officer while we continued to look for a permanent replacement. She may not have been the typical boo person, but she had turned out to be exactly what we needed. Since joining in mid-June, she had restructured our finance department from top to bottom. She'd got rid of all the financial contractors and doubled the number of full-time staff to twenty-five. We now had a new financial controller, Stefan Pregelj – who was so dedicated that I would find him working in the office every Saturday and Sunday – as well as a treasurer and teams for the payroll and accounts payable. After lots of heavy training sessions, everyone had finally started using the IFS accounting system. The result was that our financial accounts were more accurate and more up to date than they'd ever been.

We had originally expected the $22 million raised in our previous round to last until mid-October, by which time the website was supposed to have been up and running for a couple of months. At that point, we were due to go on a huge roadshow to raise an extra $60 million, which would take us through to our IPO in early 2000. This 'pre-IPO' round would now have to be delayed. But we'd still need more money. The only questions were how much and how soon.

Rachel had been working out ways of stretching the resources we already had to give us a little bit more time. In particular, she had been looking closely at the cashflow situation. One of her enormously successful initiatives had been to renegotiate payment terms with some of our technology suppliers. 'They're all on board now,' she explained. 'We don't have to pay them until the end of the year.'

'Good,' I said. 'What about the product suppliers?'

'They're a bit more complicated,' she said. 'But we're working on them.'

Rachel also had a plan to sell everything we owned – all our furniture, computer equipment and so on – and then lease it back. This would give us some more cash to play with. But it was only a stopgap. We were now burning an average of $10 million a month.

'What are we going to need to get us through to launch?' I asked.

Rachel took a second or two to think this over. 'No less than $12 million,' she said.

'OK. We'll go for $15 million.'

An hour or so later, Patrik, Kajsa and I had a conference call with Chris Bataillard at J.P. Morgan. I had already filled him in a week or so earlier on the broad details of Project Launch. Although concerned, he'd seemed relieved that we were finally getting on top of things. Now we needed to decide the best way to approach investors.

'If we're only raising $15 million, it doesn't really make sense to open a completely new round,' he said.

'So what do we do instead?'

'We only closed the last round a few weeks ago, right?'

We mumbled our assent.

'So now we just reopen it again. There's enough leftover demand and it means we don't have to come up with new documentation. You'll probably have the money in a few weeks.'

'What about the valuation?' Patrik asked in a guarded tone.

'It stays the same. That's the whole point. Everything stays the same.'

Patrik was silent. I knew what he was thinking. Before Viant had brought us back down to earth, he and I had talked about possibly doubling our valuation in the next round. It wasn't easy to let that go.

Bataillard sensed our hesitation. 'You haven't achieved anything since the last round,' he said. 'Actually, the story is a lot worse. You should be grateful the valuation isn't falling.'

★

We had booked a quiet back room at Home House with windows that looked out over a patio and a small garden. A tray of pastries and pots of coffee and tea had been laid out on the table. It was 11 September and we were about to begin our monthly board meeting. We had already got in touch with most of our shareholders to inform them of our launch delay. But it was only now that we had our first real opportunity to explain ourselves in person, since three of our most important investors had seats on the board.

We had decided to put on a show. Paul Kanareck and Mike Brantjes had worked through the night to put the finishing touches to a massive day-long presentation that would give a detailed account of the state of health of the company, as well as explain the technical problems and the measures that were being taken to solve them.

The three investors who sat on our board entered the room in single file.

Ahmed Kouther was the representative of the Saudi Arabian firm SEDCO. Stocky and conservatively dressed in a navy-blue suit, he was a former IT manager at National Commercial Bank, one of the biggest banks in the Middle East. He was likeable and often funny but also took his role as a board member very seriously. He was the only investor who had actually turned up to any of our previous meetings. He'd also shown the most concern in recent months about our constant delays.

After Kouther came Luciano Favero from 21Investimenti, the Benetton-family-controlled investment firm, who had the quiet, slightly inscrutable manner of an Italian bureaucrat. He said very little in English, leaving us and the other board members to wonder how much he understood of what was being said.

Last to enter was the ever-active Jean-Bernard Tellio from Arnault. I was a little surprised Tellio had even managed to turn up. For months now, he had been buying up stakes in internet companies all over Europe and the US. It can't have been easy to juggle all these commitments. After agreeing to invest $1.6 million in our last funding round, funds had accidentally been sent to us twice. Tellio had seemed unruffled when we told him. 'Oh, really,' he said, laughing. 'You'd better send one of them back.'

The three investors took their seats. It was a small audience, but their tickets had been very expensive. We were well rehearsed but nervous. Already we had given them a demonstration of the website at the office. Now the main part of the show was about to begin.

Kajsa set the scene by reminding the room of the reception boo.com had already received. A selection of quotes were projected on to a screen: 'boo.com a global fashion play,' noted the *Industry Standard*. 'The biggest, boldest bet in the short history of electronic shopping,' said the *Herald Tribune*. 'It's an incredibly ambitious strategy . . . that . . . others will be forced to follow if they want to survive,' said *Newsweek* magazine, in an article that had appeared just the week before. boo.com had proved its genius for capturing the limelight, said Kajsa, but all this attention had generated high expectations. Now was the time to show how we were going to fulfil those expectations.

I then gave an overview of the company. 'It has been an incredibly busy few months for us,' I began. 'We've signed up twenty-two suppliers now. We have an inventory of 11,000 products. We also have six offices around the world and plan to open more over the next year.' Then there were the first-rate customer service centres we had built, the enormous pre-launch traffic to our website and a marketing department that was the envy of every big company in the world. But our policy of complete honesty meant that there were also some awkward moments. A projected chart reminded the room of the launch dates that had come and gone: 3 May . . . 17 May . . . 14 June . . . 5 July . . . 16 August . . . The embarrassing procession ended with a large question mark.

The point was to show how we had recognized our mistakes and learned from them. 'Poor ability to predict,' I explained, 'inspired us to audit ourselves and to act.' A detailed account of Project Launch followed. It was the highlight of the presentation.

During the course of the day, key staff members and advisers turned up to speak to the meeting. Paul Kanareck, our master of ceremonies, stood discreetly by the door to usher them in at the appropriate moments from an adjoining room, where they waited nervously. Luke and Edward explained the complex organization of Project Launch, Rachel Yasue outlined the measures that had been taken to optimize the company's financial resources, Jay gave an overview of the situation in the US, Kajsa's new vice-president of marketing, Marina Galanti, talked about the measures that were being taken to build up brand awareness.

By far the most nervous member of our cast was Michael Keany, from Viant. His was only a small part, but like Harry Lime in *The Third Man* it was the most important in the entire show.

'Remember, this isn't just an ordinary start-up,' he said. 'I've never seen a company with such colossal ambitions. It's really the sheer scale of those ambitions that have caused them so many problems.'

He pointed out that boo.com hadn't even launched, but already had more visitors to its holding site than L.L. Bean, bluefly or Macys. If it had been a less high-profile site, the platform could have been tested quietly. But to date, boo had over 230,000 registrations. There was no possible way it could launch quietly, and a huge effort was required to ensure that the site didn't collapse under the pressure.

'Can you guarantee the website will actually launch when you say it will?' Kouther asked.

'I can't guarantee anything,' said Keany, 'but I think it's achievable.'

'We're investors in Viant,' said Tellio. 'They're a great organization.' At that moment he took another telephone call and left the meeting. A little later we saw him through the window talking business with Samer Salty, who happened to be sitting in the garden outside. It was perfectly in character, but annoying after all the effort we had gone to.

Luciano Favero merely commented that it was very important to have an IPO. I assured him that we were still on track to have one in the first quarter of 2000. Patrik then, to general approval, explained our plan to reopen the previous funding round and to raise an extra $15 million.

There was no applause, but as our small audience filed out afterwards, I was left with the overwhelming feeling that no one cared too much about what we did, as long as everything was under control.

Even before the board meeting, we realized that money wouldn't be hard to find. The first person Patrik had spoken to was Tom

Henderson at Eden Capital. Henderson then got in touch with Viant, and once he had satisified himself that this time we really were going to meet our launch date, he quickly agreed to invest another $7.5 million. Whatever glitches there may have been in developing the site, it was clear that fundamentally boo.com still represented an excellent investment opportunity.

To get the rest of the money, we planned simply to call existing shareholders. It would be quicker and easier than looking for new investors. But we decided not to turn people away if they were really interested in investing, and it was this attitude that brought us into contact with Lebanon's Hariri family. They were prominent figures in the Arab world and would soon become our biggest and most important shareholder. Their business empire was managed by Saad Hariri, and included Saudi Oger, one of the largest construction companies in Saudi Arabia, real estate, banking and, most recently, telecommunications and technology. Like so many others, the Hariris had been captivated by the almost limitless potential of the internet and had set up a special fund to invest in the new economy. Whenever it saw an attractive opportunity, this 'Millennium Fund' gave other individuals and institutions in the Middle East a chance to co-invest without their names being made public – a benefit that was considered to be of particular importance in a society that placed a high value on privacy.

The job of seeking out opportunities in the new economy had been entrusted to Saad's cousin, 25-year-old Nader Hariri. The internet, they and many others believed, was a field in which long years of experience could be more a hindrance than a help – that the younger you were the better you were able to keep up with the extraordinary openings that the digital revolution presented. Nader had been travelling to Paris some time in mid-July, when he saw Kajsa and me on the cover of *Fortune*. His curiosity grew as, over the next few weeks, he found our names appearing in lots of other newspapers and magazines. Impressed by what he read, he got in touch with J.P. Morgan and asked if he could meet with us.

Now a few weeks later I joined Patrik and Kajsa in a meeting room to prepare for the encounter. We were all curious to see what Nader would be like. I imagined someone young and arrogant, used to getting his own way, but when he was shown into the room I was instantly struck by how polite and unassuming he was. There was a gentle calmness about him. When he spoke, it was almost in a whisper. His appearance was equally understated. He was trim with short dark hair and wore a simple but beautifully cut brown woollen suit. With him was his adviser, Wissam Ariss, a former McKinsey consultant who did most of the talking.

Our presentation hadn't changed much in the past few months – first global internet company, multi-language, multi-currency website, 3D imaging, and so on. Nader nodded, smiled occasionally and asked a few questions. I asked Edward Griffith to come in and give a demonstration of our test website. It was risky, given the various difficulties, but we had to show him something, and there were now a few products on our test site that could actually be bought and shipped. The idea was to let Nader order something and then have it delivered to his home. We all gathered around a computer that had been set up for the occasion. But as soon as Edward got started, I realized it was a big risk.

'It's a little slow,' Edward said, after clicking about five times on a pair of running shoes. 'The tech team is probably working on the site right now,' he explained. 'That always slows it down.'

As the minutes ticked by, Edward tried clicking on different icons. He turned the computer off and back on again. Nothing seemed to work. It was very embarrassing, but Nader didn't appear to mind. He just watched patiently and smiled at our awkward jokes. Eventually we gave up.

'If you leave us your address,' Edward said, 'we'll order something later on and have it shipped to wherever you want.'

Nader agreed, even handing over his credit card details to pay for the item.

Luckily, the pair of running shoes Edward ordered showed up a few days later, and, over the next month, Nader dropped by our office for two more briefings, making it clear he would like to have an opportunity to invest the next time we were looking for money. So, when Chris Bataillard at J.P. Morgan started calling investors on 12 September, the day after our board meeting, we told him to call Nader as well.

Bataillard rang me that evening, just as I was heading home. 'Nader wants to meet Viant,' he said. 'If that goes well, he's offering $12 million.' The news was a shock. If we accepted, Nader's Millennium Fund would be our largest single shareholder.

As it turned out, though, we weren't able to accept such a large investment. Over the next few days more offers came in from existing shareholders, including Bernard Arnault of LVMH and 21Investimenti. The fact that we hadn't increased our valuation was obviously seen as an opportunity too good to be missed regardless of our launch problems. It was a chance for investors to buy more shares, at the same cost, rather than having to pay a higher price as they would have expected in a new funding round. When all the offers were counted, they added up to $23 million – much more than we needed. In the allocation of shares that followed, Nader as our newest investor was scaled down to $4 million. I hoped he wouldn't mind too much.

I was at my desk, feeling overwhelmed by the mountain of faxes and progress reports piled in front of me, when Patrik came by. 'Nader called,' he said. 'He's really upset.'

'Upset?' I had trouble imagining the softly spoken Nader throwing a tantrum.

'Well, disappointed. He really wanted to invest more.'

'What did you tell him?'

Patrik shrugged. 'I said too bad. That's the way it is.'

I cringed at the lack of diplomacy. Patrik's approach to dealing with investors had been getting very direct in recent months. One of his latest tactics was to set deadlines. 'You have an hour to make up your mind,' I heard him say on the phone to one indecisive investor. 'If we don't hear back from you by then, you're out.'

It might not have mattered much in the case of small, interfering VCs, but Nader Hariri impressed me as someone who could be the sort of constructive shareholder in the company that I felt we badly needed. So when Patrik had wandered off, I got on the phone to Samer Salty, who since leaving J.P. Morgan had become an increasingly valued source of advice – particularly when it came to dealing with Middle Eastern investors.

'What do you think we should do?' I asked.

'You should probably start by showing him a bit more respect,' he said. 'These people operate on a very personal basis. It's not just about money. It's about relationships. If I were you I'd call him up and apologize.'

I decided to go one step further. I asked Nader if Patrik and I could meet him in person.

'That's very kind of you,' he said. 'I'm at the Dorchester. Can you meet me here at 7 p.m.?'

'Sure. We'll be there.'

Patrik and I caught a cab to the hotel. I had invited Samer Salty to join us, but Patrik seemed annoyed when he saw him standing outside the hotel. 'Why is he here?' he said, in front of Salty.

'I asked him to come,' I said.

'Well I don't want him here.' He turned to Salty. 'You're not our banker any more. You're an investor now. There's no reason why you should be here.'

'Fine. I'll leave,' said Salty, taken aback and shaking his head at Patrik's bluntness.

'I'll call you later,' I shouted, as he walked away. Patrik better be careful, I thought. He was running out of friends faster than he could make them.

Nader was obviously one of the Dorchester's regular visitors. We asked for him at the reception desk and were straight away led to the Promenade, a splendid central lobby with gilded marble columns, potted palms and deep sofas. Nader greeted us and invited us to sit down with him at a tea table covered with an immaculate white linen cloth.

We spent the first few minutes chatting inconsequentially as we drank tea from Wedgwood china cups and helped ourselves to a plate of finger-thin salmon and cucumber sandwiches.

But the conversation soon turned to business. 'I have a very strong regard for what you are doing,' Nader said. 'I think your company could be like the Amazon.com for Europe.'

Patrik and I shifted in our chairs a little at the compliment and mumbled our thanks.

Nader took a sip of his tea and carefully put the cup down again. 'As you know, we are looking to invest a certain percentage of our fund in internet companies. But we want to make a significant investment.' He seemed irritated that we had turned his money down. We had built up his hopes and then dashed them at the last minute. It wasn't fair.

Up to this point, Nader had been talking in his usual quiet tone. Now he looked me straight in the eyes and said: 'We are the kind of investors who stick around. We will support you in every round, and also after the IPO. We are always there in the good times and bad times.'

I was thrown by his honesty. He didn't want to play games. This was important to him and he wanted us to know it.

'It isn't that we don't want to give you more,' I explained. 'But there was a lot of demand and we had to give priority to our early stage investors.'

Patrik nodded. 'And we don't want to take in more money at this valuation,' he said. 'It will dilute the existing shareholders too much. They won't let us do it.'

'The valuation isn't the main problem for us,' Nader said.

These were the magic words. Patrik's face lit up. I coughed. Suddenly we had an answer.

'We can probably increase your allocation a bit in this round,' I said.

'That's right,' Patrik added. 'Then maybe we can talk about opening a new round at a higher valuation.'

Nader looked pleased.

He had recently talked to Viant, who had given him positive feedback on progress on our technology platform. There seemed no major obstacle now in the way of our forthcoming launch. Here was a golden opportunity to invest before the IPO that would surely follow in a matter of months. With new technology stocks soaring, there was huge pressure on investors to grab such opportunities quickly. Everyone sensed that at some stage these stocks would hit the ceiling, but in the autumn of 1999 there still seemed to be a long way to go until they did. Investing in this sector was high risk, but very high reward. The start-up that went public and then saw its shares shoot up 300 per cent on the first day was beginning to be regarded almost as an everyday occurence.

Over the next few days, Patrik and I managed to increase Nader's allocation by an extra $1 million – having persuaded Eden Capital and Arnault to take a slight cut. This was more of a goodwill gesture than anything else, and it was only towards the end of September when we met Nader again at the Dorchester, this time for breakfast, that we discovered just how high he had set his sights.

Patrik and I agreed to meet outside the hotel at 8.30 a.m., so I decided to catch a cab straight from home rather than go into the office first. On a good day, the trip from Notting Hill shouldn't have taken more than half an hour. But this must have been national roadworks day. Everywhere I looked, there were huge holes in the road and groups of workmen standing around, smoking cigarettes. It was almost nine when my cab finally pulled into the forecourt. Patrik wasn't too put out as he had only just got there himself.

This time we were led into the Grill Room, a magnificent baroque dining room with tapestries on the walls and a ceiling inlaid with gold leaf. Nader was waiting for us with his McKinsey adviser.

After various pleasantries had been exchanged over toast and marmalade, Nader thanked us, on behalf of the Millennium Fund, for increasing their allocation. 'It was much appreciated,' he said. 'What we would like to do now is talk about how to move forward from here.'

Wissam Ariss explained that there was enormous pressure from other co-investors in the Millennium Fund to be allowed a larger allocation.

'We'd like to propose an investment of $15 million,' Nader said. After a brief pause to allow the figure to sink in, he added, 'Let's strike a deal.'

What he was essentially suggesting was that we open a completely new funding round for them alone. We weren't completely surprised. Patrik and I had discussed the possibility before the meeting. We'd agreed that other shareholders wouldn't mind, as long as the valuation was high enough. But our discussion hadn't got as far as deciding on what valuation to ask for. Now, it looked as if we'd have to make up our minds quickly.

'Obviously, we'll have to agree on the terms,' Patrik said.

'Of course,' Ariss said. 'This is what we would like to talk about.'

To buy some time, I gave a quick rundown of what the banks in

New York had told us when they had pitched for our IPO. So it hadn't been such a wasted trip after all.

Nader and his adviser listened patiently, but they wanted a number now.

Patrik duly obliged. 'We think a pre–IPO valuation of $450 – $500 million would be fair.'

This was based on the way the markets were going but was more than double the valuation in our last round. At the same time, it was a lot less than what we would be worth if everything went according to plan and we had a successful IPO.

Nader's eyes widened slightly, then he calmly turned to confer in a whisper with his adviser.

'That's much too high for us,' he said finally. 'We're prepared to go as high as $375 million. And we want a board seat too'.

'That's pre-money,' Ariss said, meaning our valuation would be $390 million once their investment was included.

It was at this point that Patrik and I realized that they wanted to do a deal right now.

'I think we need to talk about this outside for a few minutes,' Patrik said.

'The company is worth $390 million,' he said, outside the Grill Room. 'This is incredible.'

I had never seen him so excited. I understood, because I felt the same. If we could double our valuation in the space of a week, what would happen in the next few months?

'God,' I said, under my breath. 'Let's call Kajsa.'

Kajsa sounded equally shocked when I told her. 'What do you think we should do?' I asked.

'What do you mean?' she said. 'Go back in and say yes.' Kajsa was pleased, not just about the valuation, but that we wouldn't need more money for quite a while.

Patrik and I tried to compose ourselves before heading back inside. We had to remember that their valuation, although high, wasn't unreasonable – especially if you believed, as we did, that boo would be worth more than $1 billion within the next six months. They had also protected themselves by insisting on a 'ratchet down' clause, which meant that if the valuation fell in future rounds they would be given free shares to make up the difference.

Nader and Ariss looked expectant.

'We're happy with those terms,' I said.

Nader relaxed visibly. 'That's great,' he said. 'I'm looking forward to working with you.'

All things considered, it had been a pretty successful couple of months. In early September, we even finally managed to find a replacement for Steve Bennett after nearly five months of looking. Rob Shepherd was Scottish, in his late forties and had a lot of experience of handling big projects. He was CTO for BSkyB, a job that gave him responsibility for hundreds of people. Laconic and occasionally abrasive, he looked fit, had a deep tan and sounded a bit like Sean Connery. Edward Griffith called him the 'ice man' because nothing seemed to bother him. Shepherd attributed his composure to the fact that he'd survived the reign of Sam Chisholm, the difficult former head of BSkyB. 'If I got through that,' he said, in one of our early meetings, 'I can get through anything.'

After our problems with Steve Bennett, we were obsessively careful to get this new appointment right. 'I think he's been sitting in boardrooms and executive suites for too long,' Edward said, trying as hard as he could to think of some possible drawback. 'He might have lost touch with the people on the ground.'

So I asked him to take Shepherd on a tour of the office. Working for a start-up, especially one as chaotic as ours, was a lot different from working at a satellite television company like BSkyB. The tour had to be carefully conducted, since nobody outside senior management yet knew that we had any plans to get another CTO. If anyone asked, Shepherd was to pretend to be a consultant. There were so many of them running around our office by now that one more wouldn't raise any eyebrows.

'How did it go?' I asked Edward afterwards.

'He was completely at home,' Edward said. 'Nothing seems to disturb him.'

Then I asked Michael Keany of Viant to meet him.

'Don't worry,' Keany said. 'This guy knows his stuff.'

But before making a final decision, I asked Shepherd to meet me and Edward in the downstairs bar of the Meridien hotel. By now, Shepherd was well briefed on the state of our technology. He probably had a better idea of our problems than I did myself. But there were other issues that had to be cleared up. I had decided that, rather than fire Steve Bennett, I would try to find another role for him in the company. After all, the trouble had always been that he was doing the wrong sort of job: one that required more management skills than he had. In a purely research and development role, which is what he had had at Hewlett Packard, with his enormous technical ability he might suddenly become a very valuable asset. But there was another reason for keeping him. He was well liked by the tech team and I was terrified that some might quit or, even worse, sabotage our equipment if he were fired. But I needed to know how Shepherd felt about the prospect of having Bennett still around.

'Do you think you could work under those conditions?' I asked.

He stirred his drink with a swizzle stick. 'Listen,' he said, in his Sean Connery twang. 'I've been put in some pretty difficult situations before now. If you want me to manage this guy, that isn't going to be a problem.'

Edward looked on in admiration. He was totally sold on Shepherd now.

'I just want to make sure,' Shepherd continued, 'that when I come in, I'm clearly in charge.'

'Don't worry,' I said. 'You will be.'

The package we agreed with Shepherd was £180,000 a year, with an additional sign-on bonus. It was almost double what we had paid Steve, but that was the price of hiring a heavy hitter, especially at a time when new internet companies were starting up by the day. It was a simple case of supply and demand. The main thing, I realized with a sense of relief, was that our search was finally over.

Experienced soldiers say your first kill is always the hardest. Now I was getting some idea of what they meant.

Even before the negotiations with Shepherd had concluded, Edward Griffith and I had started to prepare for the looming confrontation with Bennett. We were both nervous as hell. This was an incredibly personal thing to do. We couldn't just send an email or hand the job to our lawyers. This would be just us and him. Eyeball to eyeball. I had no idea what to say, or for that matter, how Bennett would react. Even if he accepted another job within the company, the sudden loss of authority would be a heavy blow. He didn't seem the kind of person who would go on a psychopathic rampage. But who could tell? Maybe this would tip him over the edge. I could imagine the newspaper reports: 'He was a quiet man who generally kept himself to himself . . .'

Of course, I didn't really believe that Bennett would stick a knife in my back. I was more worried about how to contain the fallout that might result from his replacement. If we didn't do it exactly right, there might be further delays to our launch. If that happened, there was a good chance *I* would be fired.

I spoke first to Theresa Petrie, one of our human resources managers. She was hesitant. Firing executives wasn't her speciality. But she knew someone at Price Waterhouse Coopers who had done this sort of thing in the past. He agreed to meet me and Edward at the Meridien.

A well-built Englishman in his late forties, he seemed to enjoy the opportunity to share his knowledge. 'You need to be really clear and firm about what's happening,' he said. 'Have you worked out his compensation package?'

'Not yet,' I admitted.

'Well, make sure you do. You don't want to get drawn into a big discussion about it.'

I outlined my concerns about how the tech team would react to Bennett's dismissal. Would they follow him out the door? Would they jam screwdrivers into our circuit boards? After asking us a lot of questions about the key tech staff, their roles and personalities, he said, 'It sounds pretty unlikely to me. When you change leadership it isn't usually as bad as you think.' People might be angry, he added, but it was rare for them actually to do something about it. 'It helps that you've got someone to take over immediately.'

Edward then got on the phone to Tony Coleman, whom we'd just hired as boo's head of human resources. Coleman was a true veteran when it came to hiring and firing. His previous job had involved running the HR department for clothing retailer Gap International in San Francisco. Before that he'd worked at American Express. He hadn't formally started work for us yet, but he was happy to offer Edward detailed advice, even sketching out a sort of script for all the things we needed to say. There were a few key messages. Get to the point quickly and never talk about your reasons. Try instead to focus the conversation on how to move things forward. Don't get into arguments. Be sensitive, but avoid showing a sympathy that he might try to take advantage of. In case Bennett chose not to accept an alternative job, Coleman also suggested that we hire a career counsellor for him to consult after the meeting. It would help him cope with the shock and get him thinking about the future instead of the past.

As a final precaution, I asked Edward to tell Bennett's deputy, James Cronin, what was about to happen. James was close to Bennett and I was worried about how he would react. He knew more about our technology platform than anyone else in the company. If he chose to resign, it could set us back weeks.

'He was really upset,' Edward told me after taking James out for dinner. 'But I think he'll get over it.'

The morning of the execution was overcast but warm. Edward had called Bennett and told him to meet us at the Langham Hotel, just a short walk from our office, to go over some project plans. Bennett hadn't wanted to come at first. He was working from home that day and didn't feel like catching the train from Wales to London unless he absolutely had to. It was only when Edward insisted that he reluctantly agreed.

Edward and I got to the hotel around 8.30, half an hour before Bennett was supposed to show up. I wanted to make sure everything had been arranged properly. We had booked two rooms – one for us and one next door for the career counsellor. Everything seemed fine. So Edward and I took a walk around the block. By now, I was getting really nervous. My palms were sweating and I kept fiddling with a paper clip in my pocket.

'Do you think James called him last night?' I asked.

Edward looked uncertain. 'I don't know. I doubt it. But I guess he might have.'

I wasn't sure what I preferred. Was it better for him to be prepared, or taken completely by surprise? This raised another question. Had Bennett ever realized that the job was too big for him? Or had he convinced himself that everything was under control?

Either way, this would be tough on him. I imagined him going home and telling his wife. I wondered what he would say. 'He's going to be devastated by this,' I said. 'It's going to destroy his life.'

Edward tried to be supportive. 'You're doing the right thing. You're the CEO. You need to think about what's best for the company.'

It was now just before nine, so we headed back to the hotel. The rooms we'd booked were in the basement and when we got down there the career counsellor had already arrived. He appeared to be in his early fifties and was wearing a worn-looking hat that matched his dark suit. I said hello, filled him in quickly on what was about to happen and ushered him into the second room. 'Just stay here,' I said. 'We'll let you know when we're ready.'

Our room was small and windowless. On the table was a jug of water and a few glasses. We spent the first few minutes trying to decide where to sit. Edward thought we should face him. I wasn't sure. 'That's a bit intimidating.' In the end, we agreed Bennett should sit in the middle. Suddenly I realized that Bennett might be waiting in the lobby. Edward agreed to go up and take a look. He came back a few seconds later with Bennett right behind him.

'Hi, Steve,' I said, getting up awkwardly.

Bennett immediately knew something was up. It didn't take a genius to work out that we weren't here to discuss project plans. He looked very tense.

'Hi,' he said, sitting down slowly.

Somehow, I managed to remember the lines I'd been rehearsing and began blurting them out. 'I've called you here because I have made the decision that we need a new CTO.' I took a deep breath. 'The company is a lot bigger now than when we first hired you. I don't think any of us realized how much work the job would involve. Now we need someone who can take us to the next level –

someone very senior.'

Bennett was sitting stiffly in his chair, looking like he wished he was anywhere but here.

'We can probably offer you another job in the company if you want to stay,' I continued. 'But then we'll have to change some of the terms in your contract.'

At this point I turned to Edward, who seemed a bit surprised. 'Uhh. Yes,' he said, looking down at some notes he'd prepared. 'You'll keep your salary, but lose most of the share options. You'll also have to give up the car and the apartment.' He paused. 'If you decide to leave, you'll get a one-off payment equal to six months' salary.'

We waited to hear what Bennett had to say. When he spoke, his voice was shaking slightly.

'Can I ask why? Was it something specific?'

'Today isn't about why,' I said, sticking to the script. 'Today is about making sure you're OK and that you understand the financial and legal implications of what's going on.'

Bennett nodded quietly and sank into his chair. He looked sad now. 'I understand things haven't really been working out,' he said. 'It's a shame it had to come to this.' He chuckled softly. 'It's been a pretty crazy time.'

I was impressed by how he was handling it. But it only made me feel worse.

'We've hired a consultant to give you some advice if you need it,' I said.

Bennett looked surprised. 'Is he here?'

I nodded. 'You don't have to see him if you don't want to.' But he might as well, I thought, as the guy was costing us £400 an hour.

Bennett smiled. 'Sure. I'll see him.'

I think all three of us were relieved when the meeting was over. Bennett went back home that afternoon to think things through. At first, it looked as if he would take up our offer and stay in the company. He came back to the office a couple of times and even met with Rob Shepherd. But a few days later, he called me.

'I've decided I want to leave,' he said.

11

FOR A FEW WEEKS, the goldfish bowl was the nerve centre of boo.com. It was here that Luke had set up his operations room. Stuck up on the glass walls on long strips of paper, one above the other, were charts that represented the major issues that had to be addressed, with all the sub-areas of responsibility clearly defined. Order fulfilment, for example, was broken down into returns, supplier payments, invoicing, and so on. These subdivisions were themselves subdivided into still more component tasks. Timelines were clearly specified and, if they began to slip, marked with different-coloured lozenges according to the degree of urgency. Like a war room general, Luke, surveying progress on all fronts, could switch resources to tackle the most pressing matters.

One flimsy sheet of paper distilled a hugely complex organizational infrastructure in which hundreds of people might be involved. The returns, for example. All our European orders would be packed in Deutsche Post's warehouse in Cologne. Then if a customer in, say, Paris ordered a pair of shoes, a La Poste label would be stuck on the box so that it appeared as if the package had been sent from France. The package would then join a consignment of French-bound goods, all likewise labelled in the Cologne warehouse with French labels, and trucked across the border where it would join the French postal system. When the customer opened the box, inside would be a label with a French address to which the shoes could be returned if he or she no longer wanted them. From this French collection address, all the French returns would then be trucked back across the border to the Deutsche Post warehouse. Here the box would be opened, the shoes checked against a barcode and then entered into the computer system, alerting the finance department that the customer's credit card was to be refunded. It would then have to be decided whether the goods could be resold and whether they needed a new box. There were different collection addresses, labels, tax charges – and different currencies – for each of the European countries in which we had supply arrangements. Then there was our US warehouse in Kentucky . . . So just to make sure that the boo.com returns system was working, it was very easy – without Luke's charts – to lose count of all the issues that needed to be addressed.

While Luke focused on implementation, the operational steering committee decided the overall strategy, with senior members of the boo team taking responsibility for each of the major launch-critical issues. So Charlotte, temporarily putting aside her new job as head of new markets, oversaw the team responsible for order fulfilment; Jay, although he still had the huge US office to worry about, turned his attention to merchandising operations; Karl O'Hanlon led our bug-fixing drive; and Edward focused on technology operations. In regular meetings we would discuss the strategic requirements of the different areas of the company, then formulate the policy that Luke's team would put into operational effect.

The international character of the Carnaby Street office became even more marked as boo staff from the European and US offices came to London on extended launch-related missions. It's hard to convey the sheer overload of work. The reputation that boo was beginning to get for extravagant parties and high living masked the reality of a company that had always expected a superhuman degree of commitment and effort from its workforce. On this occasion we cancelled the holidays of virtually the entire company and people worked not only late into the night but at weekends as well. The staff had long come to terms with the fact that boo.com meant a 24/7 lifestyle, but now it was 25/8. It wasn't unusual in these few weeks – perhaps especially among the tech team who were in the front line – for someone to come in at 7 a.m. on a Tuesday morning, work at the office almost continuously through two days and two nights, return home late on the Thursday to snatch the few hours of sleep that by now had become a physical necessity – only to be back in the office the next day and probably over the weekend too.

To understand this kind of total devotion to a cause you probably had to be in Britain in about 1940, when car factories were turning out aeroplanes or tanks overnight. There was something exhilarating about the speed with which our new launch mode could sweep away problems that before had seemed to require months to solve.

Through September and October, 'launch-critical activities' was the phrase on everybody's lips. Most of these activities involved procedures that could be of mind-numbing dullness and soak up a colossal number of work hours. Few jobs were bigger or duller or more vital than unravelling our product data. When Project Launch began, there were 4,000 different products sitting in our warehouses. But of these, owing to errors in data entry and the discrepancies between the databases, only 100 items could be successfully ordered. The unenviable task of sorting this out was given to Cherry Freeman, a 23-year-old who had been hired back in March to manage business development. Soon she had integrated the data entry teams and copy-writers with some new technical recruits into a product group of fifty. They would spend the next six weeks reading through the thousands of products to ensure that they were consistent between the different databases, checking, testing and fixing the technology and making sure that all this information was accessible in different languages. For the team, it must have quickly dispelled any illusions they might have had about the glamorous world of the internet start-up. As day and night they pored over long print-outs that snaked over their desks and on to the floor, they were engaged in the equivalent of proof-reading the telephone directory.

Their contribution was just one of the countless unsung but vital 'back end' activities that formed the bulk of Project Launch, but as the date of the launch approached, people's minds switched more and more to the smaller 'front end' fraction that would finally dictate what the world made of boo.com. It wasn't fair, but first impressions would be critical in determining whether people wished to return to the site.

In its report, Viant had commented that our site was cluttered and hard to use. While the user interface achieved 'a high "cool" factor', there was 'nothing yet in place to create an indispensable site for [boo's] target audience'. So Kajsa and Niclas Sellebråten pulled together from our offices around the world a crisis creative team of designers, copywriters and translators to simplify the graphics and the thousands of links throughout the site.

Perhaps inevitably as the public face of the company, Miss Boo quickly became the chief cause of concern. For the past few months she had been sporting a red ponytail and looked like a high school cheerleader, which wasn't nearly good enough for the cool, urban image we had been trying to create. She seemed barely old enough to order milkshakes in the local diner let alone hang out in downtown bars. So the design team tried to make her more sophisticated by giving her different hair. But none of the styles they experimented with, from white dreads to black Afro, was quite right. The trouble was that she almost seemed to be trying too hard. As Kajsa put it, 'She's so cool, she's really uncool.' It was difficult to know what could be done. 'Maybe she should change her hair all the time,' Kajsa said, 'like every three months. She's such a fashion victim that she's always on top of what's going on.' One way or another, it was clear that we needed some expert advice. So we booked the world's top hair-stylist, Eugene Soulemain, whose clients included top Hollywood actresses and fashion houses like Prada, Louis Vuitton and Hussein Chalayan. For a few weeks, while she waited for Eugene to fit her into his busy schedule, Miss Boo sat bald but beautiful in a quiet corner of Niclas's Macintosh.

But it wasn't enough that she should just look cool. She had to talk cool too. A journalist called Lucy Ryder-Richardson wrote some lines for her, but the style was thought to be too European when the point of Miss Boo was that she was the kind of girl who felt at home all over the world. So at the beginning of October we brought the New York style commentator Glenn O'Brien over to London for a couple of days to make her hip but transatlantic. Glenn had begun his career working for Andy Warhol at *Interview* magazine and went on to be variously a comedian, poet, author and copywriter. Michael Skidmore had known him at Barneys, where Glenn had been creative director for advertising.

Glenn reworked Miss Boo's lines on the site to make them more universal, but also provided a profile of Miss Boo that our copywriters and translators could use to develop her character in the future. As she had to seem equally convincing in Swedish, Finnish, Danish, German and French, the trick was to write lines that were cool but not too idiomatic to prevent easy translation:

How old are you Miss Boo?
None of your business, but I'm legal, I'm a registered voter, and this is my natural hair colour.
What's your background?
For somebody two-dimensional my background is remarkably deep. I've been educated in all the best stores and television commercials. I have a degree in taboo violation. I've been around the world many times, I went around it today in fact, and I speak seven languages including English and American.
Do you like boys or girls?
Naturally.
What are your measurements?
Don't get fresh with me. How big is your screen?

It was hardly Chekhov, but it was fun and provoked a huge thirst among the copywriters and translators to know more about Miss Boo. Where did she come from? What did she read? What programmes did she watch on TV? There were endless debates, but Keith White, a project manager in the creative department who had previously worked for Wieden & Kennedy, got as close to capturing her spirit as anyone: 'She's truly global. There are people who are always changing, but they have a personal style. They can fit in Paris and the next day take an overnight train and be somewhere else and take the Concorde to New York and not make a big fuss of it. Miss Boo is someone who can be one minute on the Concorde, and the next taking the subway uptown.'

Top of our list of priorities was speed. More than any previous form of communication, the internet in 1999 depended on people's patience. Websurfing was an oddly inappropriate word for the common internet experience, which was really one of standing in queues. You had to wait to log on, you had to wait to get to a site, and then you had to wait again while that site downloaded. The more ambitious the site, the more it was likely to challenge the axiom that all good things come to those who wait – and no site was more ambitious than boo.com. Byte-hungry graphics, animation, sound, multilanguage functionality – all contributed to increasing the download time. It was taking more than four minutes just to download our home page, which hardly suggested that we were serious about addressing the needs of the 'cash rich, but time poor'. No matter how worthwhile the wait might prove to be, few people in practice would bother.

A lot of the problem could be solved by eliminating bugs and simplifying the source code. It would be like turning a winding gravel road into a motorway. But the sheer volume of traffic that the site was likely to attract would then quickly clog it up again. The part of the site that would bear the brunt of this traffic would be the e-commerce engine that processed all the interactive requests made by visitors to the site. In my early meetings with Interworld at the beginning of the year I had stressed that we needed a system that was capable of coping with 10,000 simultaneous users. But the attempts to customize the engine to our requirements had the effect of turning a racing car into a double-decker bus. Bits were bolted on all over the place, which – in the words of James Cronin who tested the engine by simulating real users – made the site 'like shopping in treacle'.

James suggested that we bring in Phil Harman, an expert from Sun Microsystems' performance testing lab in Manchester. After a week of tinkering with the site, Harman suggested that the quickest way of speeding everything up was to buy more hardware. It would also be a lot more expensive, but, like someone calling out a plumber to fix a leak on a Sunday, we didn't really have much choice.

Our e-commerce engine had sat on two Sun servers, each with four processors. After Harman's visit, James bought five more Sun servers, each with ten processors. The bill ran to almost £1 million. But we soon discovered that even this massive increase in the number and capacity of our servers was not enough to cope with our huge and extremely complicated database. Rather than waste any more valuable time on elaborate testing, I encouraged James to order the biggest machine that Sun could give us.

We were certainly doing our bit to cement Sun's reputation as the leading supplier of hardware to the internet industry, and at one point its president, Ed Zander, sporting a massive Rolex watch, dropped by our office to pay his respects.

Nicknamed the 'Starfire', the E-10,000 server was capable of holding sixty-four processors and cost £1.3 million. It wasn't the sort of thing that you could buy over the counter. Usually, it had to be ordered long in advance and carefully tested by a team of Sun specialists. We were lucky when one became immediately available after a big multinational client of Sun cancelled their order. It was now sitting at Amsterdam airport, waiting to be flown back to the US. When James showed me a photograph of the monster, I was astonished that you could actually transport it by air. Sprouting industrial-strength cables on all sides, the hulk of metal seemed to be a throwback to that age before the PC when computers were giant contraptions that you could walk inside. It was so heavy that when it was installed in our data centre in London's Docklands, Sun had to send construction experts to check that it wouldn't crash through the floor. But at least now I was confident that when the e-doors opened, we would be ready for the stampede.

As we accumulated ever more expensive bits of hardware, I began to worry about security. It was a source of pride that boo was a relaxed, informal company where people were free to come and go as they wished, but our very openness made us extremely vulnerable. What was to stop some madman wandering off the street and taking an axe to our server room?

I explained my concerns to Paul Kanareck, and asked him to find a security firm. After an afternoon of thumbing through the Yellow Pages and getting companies to fax us their details, Paul handed me an impressive list of credentials from a company called Task International. Its chairman was Sir Jeremy Moore, commander of the British land forces during the Falklands War. Task sounded reassuringly blue chip and elite. Its assignments had included providing bodyguards for Middle Eastern royalty and training Russian SWAT teams in hostage rescue. Protecting boo, I thought, would be a doddle.

A few days later, after an inspection of our office, Task's CEO Paul Slaughter, who was a former detective sergeant, and an ex-army officer, John Bartaby-Russell, briefed us on our security needs.

As they took their seats in the goldfish bowl, they wore grave and concerned expressions. 'You've got yourselves in a pretty dangerous situation,' Slaughter warned us. 'You don't have any access control to the building, and a lot of transient staff with hardly any restrictions on where they can go.'

'We've got an open culture,' I explained.

'I understand,' he said. 'But security is a serious issue.'

We agreed to the installation of CCTV cameras and also accepted their recommendation to hire a detachment of ex-Gurkhas to protect the premises 24 hours a day. Specialists in jungle combat, these Nepalese soldiers had over the past 200 years built up an awesome reputation as one of the most feared fighting units in the British Army. Their motto was: 'It is better to die than to be a coward.' But when our twelve guards took up their posts a few weeks later, immaculately turned out in dark blue blazers and beige trousers, what struck me most was their quiet courtesy and good humour. Under the command of ex-sergeant Chandra Gurung, they were a formidable but reassuring presence.

One of the very few distractions from Project Launch was an important announcement that Nike made towards the end of September. Charlotte and I had made the long pilgrimage to the court of the mighty sportswear company a couple of months earlier. They were of enormous significance to us not only because they had 30 per cent of the sports shoe market in the US, but also because we admired their brand so much. It would be a partnership made in heaven, but although they had their own website, Nike.com, they had been hesitant about getting involved in other internet ventures. They said they wanted to see how our launch went first, before considering a supplier agreement with us. But now to our dismay they were announcing a joint venture with the internet sporting goods retailer Fogdog. In return for the right to sell Nike products, Fogdog – whose president, Tim Joyce, had previously been a senior executive at Nike – would offer Nike a sizeable equity stake in the company.

Now that we could see a competitor out there, the notion of 'first mover advantange' suddenly took on real meaning and the importance of getting our site up and running as quickly as possible really came home to us. It wasn't simply a matter of supplier relationships, but also the need to meet our revenue targets so that we stayed on track for our IPO. Our whole future financing depended on this.

In the meantime I emailed the vice-president and general manager of Nike.com, Mary Kate Buckley, whom we had met when we were in Beaverton, just to remind her that in the new chapter of e-commerce about to open Nike could do a lot better than Fogdog.

Dear Mary Kate,
We read with great interest the news of your new relationship with Fogdog, which we clearly recognise as a major milestone in the development of your online strategy. It appears we came to Portland with the wrong presentation under our arms. We should have brought our shareholder structure and investment bankers instead. We are completely confident that this is a market in which we will rapidly consolidate the number one position – given our aggressive global launch, and branding that has already captured media as well as consumer attention.

We are about to open the site to the hundred of thousands of customers who have already registered with us. Once we have given you the opportunity to test us by ordering some of your competitors' merchandise (!) we should, our busy schedules withstanding, meet to compare notes.

We would be delighted to entertain you here in London, where we can demonstrate some of our infamous Swedish hospitality – which I regard as far more enticing than 12 per cent of our equity.

A few days later Mary Kate sent a tantalizing email in reply:

Dear Ernst,
I am one of your hundreds of thousands of pre-registered customers and look forward to testing your service and continuing our dialogue thereafter (I'm always looking for any excuse to come to London).

Until then I wish you the best of luck for a successful launch (and many sales thereafter).

It was like sixteen-year-olds flirting, I thought to myself, as I printed off a hard copy of Mary Kate's email to show around the office. So began a concerted campaign over the next few months to win Nike's heart.

Any doubts we may have had about the effectiveness of Project Launch were removed when we made an important date on time. 5 October 1999 was the day of the 'soft launch' of boo.com, when the site was opened up to a limited number of 'friends and family' that included employees, investors, suppliers and business partners. We had set up a special domain address for the occasion: www.vodkagrapefruit.com. For the first time our website would be accessible on the internet for anyone with the right password and user name. Over the month of October we intended gradually to scale up our controlled community to reach over 10,000 potential customers, who would be encouraged to make purchases with a massive discount of 50 per cent off everything on the site and, in return, to fill in a detailed questionnaire. The significant volumes running through the system would enable us to conduct detailed scenario testing and compile preliminary statistics from the feedback.

Paul Kanareck and I spent the day leading up to the midnight launch in Munich. For some time now Christoph, our country manager for Germany, had been complaining to me about the need for better communication with the local offices. Project Launch had tended to encourage over-centralization, as the offices around the world fell under the sway of Luke's goldfish bowl and found more and more of their staff seconded to join crisis teams in London. An important part of putting the company on to an operational footing would be to encourage the local offices to think for themselves again.

The Munich staff were obviously appreciative that their CEO had made the effort to come out to listen to their concerns, but as they pleaded for greater freedom to apply a German perspective to addressing the needs of German consumers, I couldn't prevent some of my thoughts slipping away to what was happening back in London.

After leaving the office at about nine, we had dinner with Christoph. Afterwards Paul and I went to a Cuban bar to sit out the time until the soft launch, every now and then ringing Edward Griffith in London for one more progress report. There had been some hitches. The building had been without power for much of the day.

'It's bloody London Electricity,' Edward explained. 'They're digging up cables on Carnaby Street.' The tech team got round the problem by running extension leads through our windows to the office next door, which hadn't been affected. 'We're almost there,' Edward said. 'I'll ring you back when we're ready to go.'

But now there'd been no word for about an hour. The soundtrack to *Buena Vista Social Club* had started to play on the bar stereo for about the third time and the vodka–grapefruit toasts to vodkagrapefruit.com were beginning to pile up.

I rang Edward again. 'What's happening?'

'More bugs,' he replied in a weary voice. 'We're fixing them now. I'll ring you back.'

On the wall above our table was a picture of Fidel Castro haranguing a crowd. Just now he seemed to be grinning at our capitalist pretensions. Maybe we had chosen the wrong bar.

This had better work, I thought. Earlier in the day emails had been sent out to all investors and suppliers, inviting them to visit the site. To let them down again would really test their patience.

'It will be OK,' said Paul, sensing what was on my mind. 'It doesn't have to be perfect.'

Half an hour later my mobile rang. I snatched at it.

'We're live,' said Edward. 'It looks OK, but it's pretty slow.'

'That's all right,' I said, adopting Paul's attitude. 'We can fix that.' The most important thing right now was that we had stuck to a deadline at last.

It was only after I'd put down the phone that I realized it was now past midnight. It was my birthday. I was 29.

There was a celebratory atmosphere in the office when I got back the next day. We now had a live, fully functioning website, with about 1,000 products on it – well short of the 4,000 in our warehouse, but with the continued efforts of Cherry Freeman's product data team the number was creeping up every day. Nader Hariri sent over ten enormous trays of chocolates to congratulate us on our soft launch.

The overwhelming feeling was of a lucky escape. Only a few weeks ago, in the aftermath of the Viant report, things had seemed so bleak that we had doubted if we would ever see this day. But now, whatever difficulties the next few weeks would bring, we knew that boo.com was finally on its way. At lunchtime I went out with Kajsa, Paul, Luke and Charlotte to the Gaucho Grille, a newly opened Argentine steak house where you could order steaks by the gram. For my birthday, Paul gave me a film poster of *The Magnificent Seven*. 'They were seven – and they fought like seven hundred!' declared the tagline.

In the office posters went up to announce '25 Days to launch boo.com'. The countdown had begun. The major activity in the days leading up to the launch proper would be testing and metrics – testing not just the site itself, but the supply chain. The only way we could be sure that our system was capable of standing up to real life was to see it in operation in as many different circumstances as possible. We did our best to supplement the information that was now beginning to pour in from 'friends and family' with a few experiments of our own. It was like car manufacturers testing the family saloon by dropping it off a cliff.

Tony Barsham who had recently left KSA to join boo and Karl Wills, our head of logistics, devised special lists of people who lived in challenging places. 'Do you know anyone in Gdansk?' they would ask. 'How about the Peloponnese?' I began to think of some of my Nordic poets who lived on remote Arctic islands. Maybe they'd appreciate some North Face mountain gear. People were encouraged not only to order items but also to send them back, and to let us know when they received the refund on their credit card. Shopping became not just a pleasure but a duty. There was an enormous sense of satisfaction in seeing boo.com on your credit card statement when you knew that every purchase helped to build the company.

All sorts of issues that we could never have anticipated quickly emerged. In Portugal, we discovered that every package needed a serial number stamped on it by hand; for some reason, which I still don't understand, an electronically printed one was not good enough. In Canada, returns were taxed when they were sent back across the border to our US warehouse. So we hired a broker who was able to clear the goods for us and avoid the extra tax. In Britain, Parcel Force left our packages stranded at Coventry airport for two days when its staff went out on strike. So we gave the contract to DHL instead. They were expensive, but reliable. In this way we solved a lot of the teething problems ahead of the launch.

At last we could put the boo crew in the call centres through their paces. The first callers were a couple of teenage girls in France – probably an investor's daughters – who didn't have a computer connection and wanted to know how they could order from the site. As we knew that the volume of questions generated by friends and family alone wouldn't be enough to keep the crew fully occupied, we organized 'soak tests', during which everyone in all of our offices around the world would ring and email the call centres over a two-hour period. In the quiet times, we had the crew surf the site looking for bugs. Why was it, for example, that anyone who read the 'terms and conditions' page got thrown back to the front of the website? And why did people logging into 'Club boo' suddenly find themselves looking at Swedish web pages?

As we entered the last week of October, the results from the tests began to flood in. A summary of the questionnaires revealed a number of technology problems that still had to be sorted out, chief among them the slowness of the site. But on the whole, the response was very positive. Our call centre staff were informative and efficient, our distribution worked well, with products often arriving on people's doorsteps in less than five days, and many visitors praised the design of the site. We also had our first customer statistics. In the week ended 23 October we received 528 orders, valued at $51,538. The three top-selling brands in order of sales were Helly Hansen, North Face and DKNY. Everybody got a buzz out of the fact that we were actually making money now and tracked the figures closely.

The hunger for statistics offered irresistible scope for amusement. When Christoph came over to London just before the final launch, he showed how serious he had been about good communication between the local offices by calling up Annica in Stockholm to update her on the latest figures. Ascer was with him to record the conversation on minidisc for posterity.

'Annica, have you looked at your orders? Sweden is doing extremely well. France is very poor. It's like 1. Germany's 2, UK's 15, and you're close to 300. It's unbelievable.'

Ascer now joined the conversation, which Christoph had put on the speaker. 'Hello, Annica. You know, the US is only 11.'

'But this is fantastic! Where can I see this?' Annica said.

'Go into www.intranet.boo.com,' said Christoph.

'Yes?'

'Then you go into "boots". And then you go into "customer search". And then you enter the day's date. And then you'll see it and you're going to love it. You can see each and every customer.'

'Boots . . . Customer search . . .'

'Have you got the selection page yet?'

'Yes.'

'OK. Well, on the left hand side you can see "order date". Put in "one" because it's today.'

'Then, I do "search"?'

'Yes . . . Wow!' Christoph said.

'What's happening?'

'We're watching your sales here, Annica. It's really amazing on this screen, because here we're connected to the IP Server and you can see them popping up.'

'Yes,' added Ascer. 'Really cool.'

'But I can't see this screen,' said Annica. 'I wish I could see what you're seeing.'

'You should have heard Serge,' said Ascer. 'He was so excited when we told him. Just to see all the customers, and their names and addresses . . . But haven't you found the screen yet? Under "customer country", click "Sweden". There's a long list – you'll have to scroll a lot.'

'No. I still can't find it.'

'Annica,' chipped in Christoph, 'it's 313. Another order has just popped up.'

'Great! But I can't see it.'

'But what's this?' said Ascer. 'Another one, and it's your name. Annica, did you just make an order?'

'No.'

'Strange. It's your code here. Have you given your password to someone?'

'No.'

'There are two orders in your name here . . . This is really strange . . . because actually – it's all of them. You just click on a customer and then it pops up and it says Annica Mattsson. But you really should check this because your name is popping up all the time.'

'It's me who is making all the orders?'

'Yes.'

'Oh, my God!'

'What are your credit card details? Have you shopped with your Amex or your Visa?'

'My Visa.'

'That's what it shows.'

'But you haven't bought 300 things, have you?'

'Of course not!'

Ascer and Christoph finally grew tired of the game when Serge at the Paris office was brought into a conference call to help Annica find the fictitious screen.

'Realistically, you only have about three orders,' admitted Christoph, 'and it's not always you.'

'You're horrible, you guys,' said Annica.

'They're sadistic bastards,' Serge agreed.

When Ascer wasn't playing practical jokes on Annica, he spent much of his time overseeing the refurbishment of a large office on Regent Street that we hoped to move into as soon as possible after the launch. While we focused just on getting the site up and running it was necessary to put up with any discomfort or inconvenience, which included the gross overcrowding of the Carnaby Street office.

But as the launch date approached, it became important to encourage, and plan for, an operational, rather than a crisis, environment. It was one thing to build a company, quite another to run it efficiently. So with the help of the BCG team and Tobin Ireland – who had joined from McKinsey in July – I tried to make sense out of the statistics that were now pouring in and, on the basis of what we were learning about the operation of vodkagrapefruit.com, to map out the post-launch tasks. Before we had had to create an infrastructure; now we had to figure out how people could work most effectively within that infrastructure: we had to change the culture of the company from aggressive start-up to mature retailer.

Since Project Launch had begun, everyone had been too busy to give the subject much thought, but I could sense a vague unease about what would happen once the launch had taken place. So I made it a priority now to outline what their permanent roles would be, with Tobin Ireland working out detailed job descriptions for all the key management positions of the future.

A key part of this quest for operational normality was to work out an 'issues manual'. Staff needed to know the chain of responsibility and the appropriate responses for every possible scenario. The point was to instil the reflexes of sound business practice into an organization that had not been in existence long enough to acquire them through experience. The issues that the manual covered ranged from the very minor to the dramatic, starting with the launch itself. What if the launch were late? 'Don't issue a press release regarding further delay,' the manual advised, 'but if press call, issue a holding statement saying we are not worried. "Work we had planned is taking longer to complete" rather than "we have come across a technical hitch".' What if a supplier or business partner withdrew from a relationship with boo.com? 'If a supplier drops off, and it comes out in public, tell honestly the reason why, but try to get a friendly statement from that supplier, or another supplier who is still with us. We should still be very positive about the supplier who has left.'

The need for formulating coherent responses to such situations was underlined by a perceptible change in the attitude of the media to us. After our previous over-optimistic predictions about our launch date we were determined not to make ourselves hostages to fortune again and deliberately kept the new date a secret. But it only left the press free to conclude that we had disappointed expectations.

WHERE IS BOO.COM? a headline in the *Industry Standard* demanded on 17 September. 'The company has alternately described its launch date as early June, late June, late July and, most recently, late August or early September.' A similar piece followed in the *New York Post* soon afterwards. No one had turned nasty yet, but the new coolness made it clear that we had to be ready to explain ourselves.

Our manual had even anticipated Miss Boo as a possible issue. What were we to do if she were criticized for perpetuating negative stereotypes of women? What if consumers disliked her? But perhaps the question we ought to have asked was: What if we couldn't get her hair right? Eugene came over to London shortly after the soft launch and spent a day in the Carnaby Street office getting to know Miss Boo. He then flew to New York to work on her hair with our 3D designer Calder Martin.

When Kajsa showed me the results with an exasperated smile a few days later, I found myself amazed by how many things you could do with hair. Miss Boo's long locks now flowed down over her shoulders, striped red and black like a tiger, and on top of her head, in a sort of grid system of partings, sat four tight corkscrew curls that reminded me of those huge iron springs you see in electricity substations. People might look like that on some planet in a galaxy far far away, but it wouldn't do for Earth's first global sports and fashion site. In a hurried compromise, Miss Boo ended up having a ponytail again, although now it was black with a more sophisticated fringe.

'We won't offend anyone with that,' said Kajsa. But there was a frustrating sense of having expended huge energy to get hardly any distance at all. It seemed to set the tone for the last few days before the launch. We were entering Zeno's paradox mode: the harder we tried to cover the remaining ground, the more tasks there seemed to be for us to do.

On 27 October, I sent the following email to staff:

Hi everyone,
    After 10 months of incredible work and effort we are there. The full launch of boo.com has now been officially set for next

Tuesday, 2nd of November, 1999 at 10.00 a.m. (GMT).

As many of you appreciate the site has already been open since the beginning of October with real orders going through, and a lot of them too! As of today we will be dramatically expanding the password community generating enough volume to ensure that Tuesday is not a shock to our systems, this will include the global employee list of Sun Microsystems and the investment bank J.P. Morgan, our advisers (circa.100,000 people who will only be able to access the site from their offices).

Just prior to next Tuesday we will also email all the 350,000 people who have pre-registered at the site, informing them of its impending opening.

This is going to be an enormously challenging and demanding last few days and it is important that everyone remain calm and focused. Tuesday will be really, really exciting but let's make sure we get there with our minds and bodies intact.

I'm greatly looking forward to sharing this incredible moment with all of you next week.

Take care and good luck,

Ernst

We were in microtime now. Launch meetings were taking place not every few days or so, but every few hours. On the eve of the launch, which slipped back one day to Wednesday, the steering committee gathered for one more meeting in the relaxed surroundings of the Meridien hotel. The consensus was that on the whole we were in good shape. We had delayed the launch by one day to allow for a final round of bug-fixing. There were still a few more bugs to fix, but as the effect of attempting to patch them was usually to introduce new ones, we decided that it would be safer to leave them. 'Most people won't see more than 25 per cent of the site,' Karl O'Hanlon pointed out. 'Even if there are twenty bugs, they'll see five of them, and of those five bugs they'll blame three of them on their browser. In fact, most people will get more bugs from their browser, anyway.'

The biggest disappointment was that one of our last-minute bug-fixing attempts had upset the purchase path for Macintosh users. It meant that they could view the site but their orders would fail if they tried to buy anything. Journalists were among the biggest users of Macs, so there was a risk of some negative media coverage – but as they usually expected everything for free anyway, I didn't think this was necessarily such a problem.

The day itself began early for Kajsa, with a 6 a.m. visit to CNN's London studio to do an interview on the morning 'World Business' slot. She then joined us in the office for the very last meeting of the steering committee. The launch itself was now scheduled for 8 a.m. There was really very little that could be said. If we weren't ready now . . . It was more a case of buoying each other up for the day ahead.

'We've had an email from Nader of Millennium,' reported Charlotte, 'saying the best of luck for the best ever dot.com site.'

I listened to the various progress reports, then repeated a warning that had become a familiar refrain in the last few days. 'There's probably going to be lots of problems, but it's very important that we don't panic and keep everyone calm.'

As 8 a.m. approached the office rapidly began to fill up. Trays of croissants and Veuve Clicquot-Ponsardin were set out for an office-wide champagne breakfast.

Someone had rung up the speaking clock. 'The time sponsored by Accurist will be 7.57 and 10 seconds . . .' But in the best tradition of launches, there was a last-minute postponement. James Cronin still had a few important checks of the system to run.

While our new CTO Rob Shepherd stood by James hunched over his computer screen at the far end of the office, the rest of us partied.

Chris Bataillard from J.P. Morgan turned up with an Irish banker called Brian Crawford. Kajsa explained some of the changes we'd made to the site in the past few days. 'It's a bit faster now.'

'That's good,' said Bataillard. 'I was trying to get in on Sunday night on an old machine and it was just crunching along. I can't wait to see it.'

Patrik had added a festive note to his usual sober appearance by wearing a dazzling gold tie. Kajsa's younger sister, Tove Leander, who had been weaving her way through the boo crowd with a video camera interviewing people for the occasion, asked him how many people he thought would visit the site.

'Well, Karl thinks we're going to have a million visitors today.'

'How do you feel? Are you excited?'

'Very excited. This is a moment I will remember for as long as I live.'

Edward stood by the whiteboard, wiping clean the last list of problems to solve. It was very strange. For the first time in two years, there was absolutely nothing to do. We were in the eye of the storm.

But we could always watch TV, and shortly after 8 a.m. as many people as could fit in piled into the goldfish bowl to see Kajsa on CNN. Outside, it seemed like the rest of the 200 or so people in the building were pressing their noses against the glass. So this is what the fish feel like, I thought.

'The web's global shopping mall has just gotten bigger,' announced one of the two CNN co-presenters. 'boo.com will today launch its urban sportswear site, with a virtual sales assistant and technology that lets you examine even the stitching on the clothes.' The room erupted with cheers and clapping. In the atmosphere of champagne-fuelled revelry it was like watching a jousting tournament in which our champion – dressed in an orange sweatshirt with the boo.com logo – was more than holding her own. When a presenter interrupted Kajsa's explanation of boo.com's attractions as a global business, Kajsa, to huge cheers, interrupted back to make one final point about 'free delivery and free returns'. The conversation then turned to the prospect of an IPO. 'Are people going to have a chance to buy your stock at some stage in the future? Is that something you're thinking about?' But with a finality that would have had Skadden Arps applauding, Kajsa kicked the issue firmly into touch: 'We first have to launch this company and make it a healthy company, and then we might think about things like that.'

As we rejoined the party and knocked back more champagne, the tech team were still working away. 'We could have spent another half an hour in bed,' said someone. But at last Rob Shepherd signalled that we were ready to go. All at once about 200 people converged on the tech end of the office. If we had been a ship, we would have capsized. Christoph was with us in London, but Charlotte set up a conference call with all the other country managers and put them on the speakerphone. 'Hello, Serge . . . Hi, Jay . . . We're seconds away.'

'I think James should switch it on,' said Kajsa.

'No, I think Ernst should,' replied James in his quiet and unassuming way.

'I could pour champagne over it,' I suggested. 'Or crash a glass in the screen.'

James then explained that whenever a major change was made to the system, an entry had to be made in a log file. 'So what shall we put? What would you like to mark this point?'

'At last,' someone suggested.

'Carpe diem,' said Luke.

'Carpe diem,' said Kajsa in affirmation. 'OK. Carpe diem.'

James typed in the words, then leaned back in his chair, pointing to the button I had to press. 'Hit there.'

I looked up at the sea of faces. 'So I'm going to hit it now, then. I hope nobody is going to die. And I think it's going to be a great day.'

The whole office began a countdown: 'Seven . . . six . . . five . . . four . . . three . . . two . . . one . . . zero.'

I pressed the button to the accompaniment of deafening cheers and whistles.

At 8.59 and 18 seconds on Wednesday, 3 November 1999 boo.com finally came into the world.

'Let's go and shop,' said Luke.

But the real work was just about to begin. 'Back to the guns,' I said.

12

OUR WEBSITE WAS open to the world; the orders were flowing, the money had started to roll in. Through the combined effort of several hundred people we had finally achieved our goal – to transform boo from an exciting idea into a living, breathing internet company.

We should have felt wonderful, and we did, at first. But once the effects of the champagne had worn off and everyone had slowly returned to their desks, a heaviness began to settle over the office.

We had braced ourselves for disaster and dreamed of triumphant success. In the end, we got neither. Things worked, but not as well as we might have hoped. There were plenty of visitors to the site, but not the tidal wave of traffic that we had expected. By the afternoon, when the first statistics began to come in, we knew that the figure of a million some people had talked about was a complete fantasy.

'By three o'clock we had 25,000 visitors,' reported Luke. 'Of which about eighty were orders. So that's a quarter of a per cent conversion rate. It's lower than we expected, but not terrible. Let's say we have 50,000 visits by the end of the day, that means we have 1.5 million visits a month, which puts us by a long way number one in apparel on the web.'

'Excellent,' said Charlotte.

'Great,' I added. 'Now we can really focus on the problems and improve the conversion rates.'

But behind the positive words we all felt an aching disappointment. I had long known that launching such a pioneering site would be only the first step to eventual perfection, but it still frustrated me not to have come closer to our ideal straight away.

On day two, we found out what the papers made of our début.

'The site is a wonder of hypermodern flash illustration with sound and moving images and special effects,' wrote *Expressen*, one of the biggest dailies in Sweden. 'boo.com is fun to look at, you stay longer than you planned for and you want to come back.' The *New York Post* commented with similar enthusiasm: 'The hype is true; boo.com is the hottest looking e-tailing site ever.' But after these two reviews we struggled to find any encouraging comments.

The *Financial Times*, which six months ago had brought boo.com triumphantly into the open, ran a pursed-lipped news report that, oddly, devoted more space to our past difficulties than to the launch itself. 'boo's management were tripped up by integrating the various software systems. The anachronistic paper-based stock control systems of some smaller suppliers complicated matters further. Problems also emerged in ring-fencing differential pricing across Europe . . .' The piece had the tone of a respectful obituary.

But the report that left the bitterest taste that day was James Ledbetter's in the *Industry Standard*: 'It is that rarest of treasures – a warm, cloudless day in England,' began his glowing account of boo.com back in May. But now, in a dark and dull November, he greeted our launch with petulant bile.

In a step-by-step account he described the tortuous, 81-minute process he went through to complete an order, beginning at 2 p.m. Pacific Standard Time: 'I'm told that boo.com, one of the year's most anticipated e-commerce sites, is finally up for consumer use. That makes it almost six months late, but since I've been a boo believer for this long, I figure I'll check it out.' So he ordered a pair of black Converse high-tops. 'It costs $41 plus tax. That's pretty hefty, but hey – it's convenient, right?'

Then at 2.35 p.m. after an attempt to place an order:

There's a problem: my order has been erased. I try to start back at the beginning . . . But when I enter my user name and password, I get transferred to a page that says 'loading'. And I stay there. I go back to the first page again, and I notice a warning: 'If you use a Mac, you may experience some problems, so please be patient, we are fixing them.' I do use a Mac, but this is truly irritating: I've been patient with this site for six months already. Anyway, my colleague has a ThinkPad, and boo.com caused his machine to crash altogether, so I guess I'm lucky.

Finally, at 3.21 p.m., after repeated calls to the customer service centre, he received confirmation of his order: 'Eighty-one minutes to pay too much money for a pair of shoes that I'm still going to have to wait a week to get? The first time I wrote about boo.com, everyone wanted to know what the name meant. Now I know: It's the sound a reviewer makes.'

Et tu, Brute, I found myself thinking as I read the piece. The first time James Ledbetter wrote about boo.com he had noted, correctly, that we were 'adamant about not being a "discount" site'. But now that had all been forgotten. It was easy to smart at the injustice of it all, but I knew that James Ledbetter was an example of something we were going to have to come to terms with pretty quickly. The media built you up; and they tore you down. We had to be either heroes or villains; there was no in-between. The Mac problem certainly hadn't helped. We were almost setting ourselves up as targets for a largely Mac-based profession. In the next few days we were going to learn a lot of lessons, but this was one of the first: you can't afford to joke about journalists.

Somehow, with grim resolve and fixed smiles, we managed to get through that second day. But after one last progress meeting, our frayed tempers finally snapped.

To avert the tidal wave that we had feared would drown the system, we had imposed a news blackout prior to launch day itself. Our plan was then over the next 24 hours to alert by email, in staggered stages, the 300,000 people who had registered with the site. At 3 a.m. on the morning of day two, it came to Scandinavia's turn. A member of the tech team sent out the email – which had been written hours earlier by our vice president of global marketing Marina Galanti – without checking that it was correctly formatted first. The result was that thousands of recipients across Scandinavia received not an irresistible invitation to shop on the web, but gobbledegook.

It was just one of those cock-ups. The poor guy in the tech team had probably been sitting at his screen for the past 30 hours, but we were too tired and emotional ourselves to be sensible about it. So when Luke Alvarez foolishly brought up the subject again with Kajsa and me at the end of the day, his attempts to be conciliatory had the opposite effect of igniting our suppressed rage.

'I know you were frustrated this morning about what happened with the direct marketing, but it takes time to solve five months of chaos, and the only way we're going to get through this shit is to keep calm and make people, particularly like Rob Shepherd who are new, feel supported.'

How long were we going to keep on blaming people who weren't around any more, I thought to myself.

'I don't agree,' I said aloud. 'It's Marina and it's Rob. They can't play tired or blame someone else. They need to take responsibility.'

'What happened was a big fucking mistake,' added Kajsa.

'Sure, it was a big fuck-up,' replied Luke. 'But we probably made the wrong call about sending it out at all.'

'It's unbelievable that they can't handle a thing like that,' said Kajsa.

'But in the end, the guy was exhausted,' said Luke. 'It was three in the morning and he pressed the wrong buttons.'

'So Marina and Rob should have been there at three o'clock in the morning with him,' Kajsa retorted. 'I don't care how they do it, but they should do it right. We're paying them a lot of money. I think it's totally unacceptable. Did you see the email?'

'Yeah, I got one,' said Luke.

'What's the point of having a senior management team,' I said, 'if they don't manage?'

At this point, Marina of all people dropped by with another email that shouldn't have gone out.

Kajsa looked at it, then raised her eyes to the ceiling. 'This is getting worse and worse! Marina, you should really make a very detailed plan of exactly how you're going to deal with this. I want it on paper.'

Marina, usually calm and ultra-professional, was shaking.

Kajsa's sister stood in the corner of the goldfish bowl recording the increasingly heated conversation with a camcorder. We had asked her to record the historic days of boo.com's launch. We had told her she could film everything. 'We're an open company.' But even for boo.com there were limits.

'Turn off the camera,' I told her.

The real arguments were just about to begin.

On the third day, we began to get things back into perspective again. We had achieved our main goal, which was to get the site up and running. The sales figures may have been disappointing, but they were directly related to the various glitches. And the single most important factor in sorting them out was having launched, since the direct consumer feedback would teach us valuable lessons about the actual use of the site that it would have been hard to anticipate earlier.

The key problems were slow download times, the Mac-users not being able to make purchases on the site, more bugs to fix and a fraud detection system that was so stringent that it rejected the orders of people with web-based email accounts. But now that we were open, we could systematically begin to eliminate these problems one by one. Each day the site would get better and better. The priority now was to adapt to the routine of running a disciplined retail business.

In this new phase of the company's growth different skills were needed. The aggressive pioneers had to make way for the administrators. Of our senior staff, Luke was the person most visibly affected by the switch. In the crisis weeks leading up to the launch whole swathes of the company had reported to him. But now he had to cede control of his tech staff to our new CTO Rob Shepherd, and the fifty-strong product data team to Tobin Ireland, whom I had appointed chief retail officer. Having won the war for us, Luke had to say goodbye to his army and return to his old job.

I had only to look at my brand new organizational structure chart to see that some diplomacy would be required. As chief retail officer, Tobin was responsible for the complete end-to-end retail process, from buying merchandise to dealing with the customer – in other words, running the shop. No fewer than four vice-presidents reported to him – the VPs of Global Merchandising, Commercial Retail, Product Catalogue and Customer Operations. Luke, as head of business development, was on the same rung of the organisational ladder as Tobin, but had only been a vice-president himself, if a senior one. He felt that the title did not give due credit to his importance. Not only was Tobin chief retail officer, but Rob Shepherd was chief technology officer and Edward chief of staff. None of these people were senior to him, so soon after I had announced the new structure, he said to me, 'I see you have all these chiefs and the chiefs have vice-presidents under them. I want to be a chief too.'

'Fine,' I said. 'But you can't be chief business development officer. It's too cumbersome. You need to come up with another name.'

Eventually, we changed his title to chief development officer, although it made him a chief with very few Indians.

The organisational changes ushered in a new age of office politics. I had hoped that we would be spared this, but it was an inevitable part of our growth. While my announcement of Luke's new role contained no hidden agenda, the same could not be said of Marina Galanti's 'promotion'. Our former vice-president of global marketing, I announced, would henceforth be Senior Advisor to the CEO for a six month period. 'This will involve Marina reporting to me on how to focus the business for upcoming marketing opportunities, as we guide our external agencies world-wide in the development of our strategy and brand for the oncoming year.' In other words, her contract for her role as the vice-president of global marketing had been terminated.

It wasn't that she was doing a bad job. On the contrary, she was supremely capable, with the skills that most large corporations would pay handsomely for – indeed, several already had. Before she came to boo, her high-powered positions had included being head of international PR for Benetton Group and head of global marketing for Body Shop International. The trouble was that most awkward problem of all – through no fault of her own, she did not 'fit in'.

It was a natural function of her ability that, as head of marketing, she should wish to control marketing and PR throughout the group. But this centralizing instinct was at odds with the more equal relationship we had intended between our different local offices. Friction grew between Marina and the country managers, who didn't like interference in what they considered to be local issues. Marina, quite correctly, felt that they were young and inexperienced and needed guidance, but she was not prepared to give it in a way that respected their autonomy. Even so, we might have seen our way through the difficulties had it not been for a personality clash between her and Kajsa. Much more egalitarian and low key by nature, Kajsa found it hard to cope with Marina's assertive manner, while Marina, for her part, resented reporting to someone who was not only younger than her but also not prepared to defer to her great expertise. Kajsa had looked upon Marina's appointment as a way of relieving herself of some of the heavy marketing burden, but in the end their failure to get on served only to double her stress.

The two were constantly rubbing each other up the wrong way, and a large part of my time was spent trying to patch up the differences between them – while Charlotte, in her role as vice-president of Europe and new markets, had to work equally hard smoothing the feathers that Marina had ruffled in the local offices. Finally we had to accept that their differences were irreconcilable – and Marina left shortly afterwards.

In the new operational environment, the spotlight was now on Tobin Ireland. Quiet, patient and methodical, he was the steady hand inculcating a more rigorous and balanced view of our business. An early collision with Michael Skidmore served as an example of the sort of discipline he sought to impose.

Skidmore was hoping to reach an agreement with the suppliers Burton, who specialized in clothes for winter sports, and wanted to make a commitment to stock their snowboards to clinch the deal.

'We're not a hard goods company,' Tobin pointed out.

'Then they'll not go with us,' said Skidmore.

'I don't think that's true,' replied Tobin. 'I've been in shops that have Burton gear, which don't have snowboards.'

'Let me tell you,' said Skidmore, raising his voice, 'they will not go on the internet with us if they think we're not going to carry their snowboards. Because they're a legend. They're a cult.'

'We're not a hard goods business,' insisted Tobin.

'But we're not going to be doing hard goods; we just want to buy *their* hard goods.'

'We can't distribute snowboards.'

'Why can't we?'

'Because we don't have the right boxes.'

'We should figure out a way to make it work, because otherwise we're going to lose the line.'

'We either do hard goods or we don't,' said Tobin. 'Because from a physical operation point of view we need to build up a capability to distribute them.'

'What capability?'

'Bigger boxes.'

'Is that *all*?' said Skidmore in disbelief that Tobin could be raising such apparently trifling objections.

'Then there are storage locations.'

'We don't need to buy a ton. Don't make it sound like it's complicated.'

'Maybe we don't want Burton at the moment,' said Tobin.

Skidmore shook his head with contempt at such a philistine suggestion. 'This is where you know *nothing* about fashion,' he snarled. 'Oh yes, we want them. This is like saying to Giorgio Armani, "Giorgio, I love your stuff, but I don't like your suits. And I'm not going to buy your shoes." Do you understand? You've got to buy it as a collection.'

But Tobin was implacable. 'It won't work. It would be cheaper to buy the boards and give them away internally within the company.'

This was the sort of firmness the company needed now. I wanted to maintain the hunger of a start-up culture, but combine it with a procedural competence. The watchword was 'stabilization'. In the run-up to Christmas, Tobin and I would have long meetings poring over countless details completely at odds with the perceived glamour of a dot.com. Quite apart from the senior management meetings that took place every Saturday, there was rarely a weekend when he and I wouldn't also be working through long checklists covering virtually every aspect of his enormous responsibilities.

As we grappled with the myriad needs of a fully operational global retailer, we began to appreciate the full complexity of what we had created. Rather awed by this huge machine, I wanted to do everything that could be done to get us back on track after the delayed launch, and, whether it was with Tobin or other members of the management team, I was extremely persistent in pushing them to meet the goals we had set for ourselves. If this attitude created enormous pressure, people accepted it, I think, because they could see that I expected every bit as much of myself. With hindsight, maybe we worked too hard. My idea of relaxation was to come in on a Sunday and, in the quiet of a near-empty office, catch up with issues there had often been no opportunity to think about during the week. Then I would slip out in the early evening for a movie and a burger – perhaps the only time I could truly call my own. It was not a lifestyle that anyone could sustain indefinitely.

Shortly before Project Launch we had hired as vice-president of human resources Tony Coleman, who had previously been human resources director at Gap International. He began to put a more mature organizational structure in place, hiring people with more operational experience, as well as a commercial director who would act as a kind of all-seeing store manager.

It was time for the grey hairs, not only within the rank and file of the company but at board level too. It still bothered me that there was no one on the board to whom I could turn for advice. What we needed, Tony advised, were a few non-executive directors who would probably have full-time positions as senior executives of other companies but would attend our board meetings to offer the benefit of their practical experience. Tony pointed out that even if these individuals did nothing at all they could still have 'trophy' value: their association with the company would attract finance from potential investors. But I hoped that we could find people who really would bring to the board substantial expertise in a relevant field and guide a very young management team on operating a large and complicated business. It seemed to me a shortcoming, which we ought to have tackled long before now, that we could have nominees on our board backed by great business names like Bernard Arnault and the Benettons, yet not benefit from their companies' accumulated knowledge and experience. It would have been fantastic, for example, if the managing director of the LVMH Group, Myron Ullman, with all his hands-on experience, could have sat on our board. But our nominees were mostly ex-bankers in their early thirties who had little practical experience of having run a business.

By far the most important position to fill was that of chief financial officer. Rachel Yasue was doing a great job as an interim CFO, but was costing us a fortune and would have to go back to KPMG at some stage. We had been interviewing candidates ever since Patrik had stepped down more than five months earlier, but getting nowhere. In our desperation to find someone we hired a new recruitment company, switching from Heidrick & Struggles to Korn/Ferry. But the problem, as Anthony Harling went to some lengths to point out, wasn't Heidrick & Struggles at all but Patrik. His insistence on retaining overall responsibility for financial strategy and dealing with the investment banks scared any promising candidates away. No one would take such a senior position unless they had full control over these areas.

'You need to do something about Patrik!' insisted Edward, who had been helping in the hunt for a CFO. Both J.P. Morgan and some shareholders, in a more veiled way, were making the same point. Co-founder or not, Patrik, who was hanging on as executive chairman without a properly defined role, was unfinished business that I would have to tackle sooner rather than later.

In the meantime I briefed Tony Coleman on the situation and together we worked out a plan for minimizing Patrik's interference with our hunt for a new CFO. The idea was that Tony and I would interview the candidates first without Patrik's knowledge. Once we had found someone suitable, we would tell them that they should regard Patrik's intervention in financial matters as temporary, since another role was being worked out for him.

Just before the launch we had a lucky break when Mohsen Moazami, a consultant at Kurt Salmon Associates whom I'd met in LA over a year ago, paid a visit. Over lunch at the Circus he confided how impressed he was with what we had achieved in a year, and listened sympathetically as I related the troubles we had been having in our hunt for a CFO.

'I think I can help you,' he said over lunch at the Circus, and he gave me the name of Dean Hawkins, a 38-year-old Australian who had been a banker for UBS in Switzerland and then joined Adidas as its chief financial officer in 1996. This was the major league. Adidas was one of the world's biggest sporting goods companies, with profits of more than $300 million a year.

We lined up a meeting with Hawkins at Korn/Ferry's New York office on Park Avenue. 'Just remember,' said Coleman before we met him. 'You don't "interview" senior people like this. You have "discussions" with them.'

Although still relatively young, Hawkins had greying hair and carried himself with the sort of gravity typical of seasoned executives. He spoke slowly and deliberately; his eyes were probing and intelligent. 'I've seen you before,' he said, after we'd shaken hands.

'Oh,' I replied, caught a little off balance.

'Yes. We were on the same plane to Nuremberg once. You were two seats in front of me.'

Nuremberg was the city to which you flew to get to Herzo-genaurach, the small town where Adidas was based. It was also the home to Puma, a sportswear brand that I had visited some months earlier.

Hawkins had joined Adidas soon after handling its IPO while still a banker at UBS. Although he had been appointed as CFO, he told me, he had been closely involved in all parts of the business, from brand management to logistics. I was highly impressed. He had detailed knowledge of retail operations and the needs of a global business, but he was also a deal-maker who, in the Adidas flotation, had proved that he could lead a strong finance team.

A week later, we met again in the Meridien Hotel in London. In our 'discussion' his questions were as searching as mine. He wanted to know what sort of CEO I would be. It was important to him that we should have a close working relationship. He also made it clear that once he had steered us successfully through our IPO, he wanted to move over to the operational side. One of the reasons he wanted to leave Adidas was because he had just missed out getting the chief executive's job. We discussed the possibility that after the IPO he might become my chief operating officer and, ultimately, even my successor one day. The prospect in particular of having a COO had considerable attractions, as for some time now I had felt that there were too many people reporting to me: a strong COO would allow me to devote more of my time to the overall vision of the company and building strategic relationships.

If only we had found this guy earlier, I couldn't help thinking. We seemed to complement each other perfectly. I had the vision, he had the grasp of details and figures. In fact he was the bean counter we had been looking for all along. But much more than that, he offered the attraction of solid achievement at the highest level. We had plenty of brilliant people like Luke, Jay and Tobin, but they were too young and inexperienced to come anywhere close to matching Hawkins's track record. It was like bringing a battleship into what had previously been a fleet of nippy but lightly armed frigates.

Hawkins in turn was impressed with boo.com. He had read the copious articles about us and was amazed that we had managed to establish such a powerful brand in little more than six months. Considering that we had yet to sign up the really big names, he also thought that our early revenue figures were promising. 'I can probably help you convince Adidas and Nike to come on board,' he said. 'Then your sales will really ramp up.'

Our headhunter in New York had warned him that Patrik would be a temporary inconvenience, so I was delighted to hear a few days after the Meridien meeting that Hawkins was still interested, as long as we could agree financial terms. The proposed package of £280,000, plus pension and share options, put all our other salaries to shame, including that of Michael Skidmore, but Hawkins would have been worth it at twice the price. I couldn't wait for him to begin.

It was two weeks after the launch. Confident that everything was now stable, Kajsa and I were just about to set off to to speak at a conference in Venice. Over the last few months we had been flooded with such invitations. They were so time-consuming that usually we had to say no, but every now and then we would attend an event that seemed particularly interesting. I couldn't resist, for example, an invitation to speak at Oxford University: having hosted so many celebrity visits as a student organizer, it was fun to be the guest for a change.

The Venice conference was put on by MicroStrategy, a provider of internet-related software. Founded by MIT graduate Michael Saylor in 1989 when he was only 24, it had grown into one of the largest software companies in the world, with over 2,000 employees. As they had also agreed to pay for Edward and Paul to come along too – both of whom had worked hard and deserved a holiday – we were happy to say yes. The Venice location, it occurred to me, also meant that we would be able to drop in on the Benettons.

Kajsa and I set off a day ahead of the others. Speeding across the lagoon in a water taxi from Marco Polo airport, I watched the floating city looming towards us out of the dark. Our boat swept past Santa Maria della Salute at the mouth of the Grand Canal and drew up alongside the Gritti Hotel on the opposite bank. It was the greatest arrival in the world.

The next morning, Kajsa and and I set off for Ponzano to see Alessandro Benetton of 21Investimenti. The meeting had been set up by Esther Galan, my new 'super PA'. Good humoured and dedicated, she became an indispensable part of the boo team. Her formidable command of personal logistics meant that there was now hardly a minute of my day that need not be constructively occupied. It seemed as if I had only to open my eyes to find myself at an important meeting across the ocean or in an informal tête-à-tête with an investor like Alessandro.

Like the Benetton Group itself, 21Investimenti occupied a villa in the countryside near Ponzano. Although smaller and less ostentatious than the Villa Minelli, it was an impressive building with high wooden ceiling beams and paintings by Italian masters on the walls. After a brief tour, Kajsa and I settled down in Alessandro's office.

It had been almost a year since our last encounter and we spent the first few minutes chatting casually about each other's lives. Alessandro was in the process of building a new house and Kajsa had some tips for him on architects. I couldn't help noticing a huge collection of large silver and gold cups displayed along the walls.

'I'm president of our Formula One team,' Alessandro explained.

'Michael Schumacher,' I said approvingly as I examined the names on one of the trophies.

'We work only with the best people,' said Alessandro.

'A shame about his move to Ferrari.'

'Yes, but we discovered him.'

Kajsa and I then guided him through boo.com's first two weeks of

business. The pre-launch hype had generated some absurd expectations, yet we were able to demonstrate a solid start. By the end of the
first week, 609 orders had been placed, at a value of $64,000 with 96
per cent of these orders being delivered on time. Since then our sales,
and perhaps even more significantly our conversion rate – a crucial
indicator of future performance – had day by day climbed steadily.
The three top-selling brands in Europe were Helly Hansen, Fred
Perry and Royal Elastics; in the US, New Balance, North Face and,
once again, vindicating Michael Skidmore's faith in them, Royal
Elastics. The first week's traffic of 228,248 visits propelled us to the
top of the list of internet apparel sites. Or almost. Gap may have been
marginally ahead, but would quickly be overtaken.

We explained to Alessandro that we could look forward to even
more rapid progress once we had sorted out the remaining technical
problems. The most urgent was the continuing disruption to the
purchase path for Mac-users, although more embarrassing on this
particular occasion was a tiny, but lethal glitch that had for most of
the first two weeks made it impossible for Italian customers to place
orders.

'It's only just been fixed,' I had to admit to Alessandro. 'We've had
one order so far. For $5.'

'Well, it's a start,' said Alessandro and, tactfully changing the subject, he outlined ways in which he and boo.com might work more
closely together in the future. 'We could help you with PR when
you launch in Italy,' he said. 'We also have some outlet stores across
Europe where you could sell some of your old stock if you want.'

In the afternoon we picked up Paul and Edward from the Gritti
Hotel and took a water taxi to the conference, which was taking
place in the magnificent medieval hall of the Scuola Grande di San
Giovanni Evangelista.We climbed the stairs from the quiet courtyard
and turned a corner to find an audience of more than 500 people
from around the world waiting for us, each wearing headsets to allow
for simultaneous translations. It felt more like the United Nations
than a technology conference.

Overwhelmed by instant stage fright, we quickly backed out again and spent the few minutes that remained before we were due to speak in a near-by café trying to calm our nerves. 'This is what it's all about, guys,' said Paul. 'You're going to have to do a lot more of these. It's better to face your demons now.'

Back in the hall again Kajsa and I chose not to stand at a podium, but – with the informality that people now recognized as a distinguishing characteristic of boo – sat at a table on the platform and took turns speaking as we guided our audience through the story of boo.com from its conception less than two years before in Stockholm to its recent launch. Attaching his laptop to the hall's projection system, Paul then demonstrated some of the wonders of the website.

At the Q&A session afterwards, we were faced with a sea of hands. It seemed like everyone in the hall had a question to ask, whether it was about our approach to branding, Miss Boo or how we built the platform. The moderator had to cut us short to keep to the conference schedule, but outside the hall a crowd of conference-goers and journalists flocked around us, fighting one another to get in more questions and to press business cards into our hands.

'We should have brought along the Gurkhas,' said Paul, as a microphone was thrust into his face. We gave quick prearranged interviews to the *Corriere della Sera* and two other Italian papers, and then we were off, still pursued by a pack of reporters. They continued to swarm around as we made our way to the jetty where the taxi boat was waiting for us. Only when it had whisked us out into the lagoon were we able to relax again.

'Fame!' said Paul. 'You'd better get used to it.'

The magic of boo had invested us with a strange magnetic quality. When we sat down for a few early evening drinks in the hotel bar, again we were surrounded by conference-goers who wanted to get to know us. I found myself talking to Hillary Hedges, who worked for a VC firm called Arts Alliance and was on secondment to lastminute.com.

The biggest problem of the evening was doing up my bow-tie for the dress dinner that took place at the Palazzo Pisani Moretta. I had refused to buy one of those clip-on ones and struggled with the loops.

'At this rate we'll miss the dinner,' said Paul, as the short length of ribbon resisted all my efforts to turn it into a bow.

Only after some last-minute assistance from Hillary Hedges was I finally successful.

At the entrance to the palazzo, attendants in eighteenth-century costume handed out glasses of champagne. We walked up a grand staircase lined with coats of armour and full-length portraits of Venetian aristocrats.

'They're really splashing out,' Edward said.

'They can afford it,' I replied. Over the past year, MicroStrategy's shares had soared 1,000 per cent, pushing the company's value to more than $3.5 billion.

We were to dine in the magnificent Sala della Musica on the second floor, which was ornately decorated in baroque style with heavy silk curtains, mirrors and murals. A magnificent buffet awaited us, with steaming silver platters of whole turkeys and ham on the bone. The four of us helped ourselves to food and then sat down at a crowded table. Soon a French journalist, who had been sitting some distance away, felt compelled to pick up her heavy antique chair, lift it several feet around the edge of the table and cram it in between Kajsa and me. It seemed an ungainly way to get an exclusive.

Even Michael Saylor himself dropped by at one point to congratulate us on our presentation: he looked fabulously all-American in a dinner jacket with glittering gold buttons and a pin-on red bow-tie. As Saylor move on to another table, Edward leaned over and whispered to me, 'You realize this guy's worth billions.'

It wasn't until about 1 a.m. that we made our departure. The wine was long finished and we had even managed to polish off a couple of bottles of vodka. When we got outside, we waited in the rain for a water taxi, then wandered arm in arm through the back streets of Venice, accompanied by our fan club of nine or ten other people, until we came to the Antico Martini, on the Campo San Fantin. My final memory of the night is of Paul and Edward singing 'Let It Be', as they stood soaking wet on a karaoke stage.

The time had come for another round of financing, and this time we were keen to focus on 'strategic' investors that could provide not only money but also complementary business expertise. About a month before the launch we had received a promising approach from Federated Department Stores, the giant US owner of more than 400 stores, including Macy's and Bloomingdales. Federated, like other big 'bricks and mortar' businesses, had been racing to build an internet presence. It had recently spent $1.7 billion on the purchase of Fingerhut, a major catalogue and internet retailer of consumer goods in the US. A stake in boo would give it a foothold in Europe and bring us the benefit of its enormous direct retailing expertise

The financial terms being discussed – an investment of $10 million at a pre-money valuation of $410 million – were extremely attractive, and in late November a few days after our return from Venice, a day-long due diligence session took place at Home House.

The Federated group included two Fingerhut executives, Ted Osborne and Mark Nelson, and Richard Grigson, a representative from their bank, Morgan Stanley, who specialized in fashion and retailing. Edward co-ordinated the presentations from our senior management team, and reported back to me through the day on what appeared to be encouraging progress. In the evening, Kajsa, Patrik and I joined the group for drinks.

It was an occasion that required careful stage management, since some time ago we had arranged a dinner that evening at which our prospective CFO Dean Hawkins would meet the three founders. It seemed the best way of finally introducing Patrik. In the informal setting, we had a better chance of making sure that he did nothing to frighten off Hawkins, who had verbally agreed to join us but had yet to sign a contract.

My plan was to have drinks with the Federated delegation in one room, then to excuse myself along with Kajsa and Patrik and to slip into the room next door for dinner with Hawkins, leaving Edward, Charlotte and Tobin to take the Federated delegation to dinner at Mezzo on Dean Street, where I would join them at about eleven in the evening. In the alcoholic haze, I calculated, they would hardly know we had been gone.

The drinks session went well. The Federated executives had been impressed by the presentations during the day and even had positive things to say about our glitch-plagued technical platform. Their banker Richard Grigson soon felt at home gossiping with Kajsa about the five Fendi sisters, Paola, Anna, Franca, Carla and Alda, who were famous for their differences of opinion but had recently managed to see eye-to-eye long enough to sell a majority stake in their company to LVMH and Prada. Then, as I explained that I would have to excuse myself for a couple of hours to take a senior candidate out to dinner, Grigson happened to catch sight of Dean Hawkins walking down the corridor.

'Is that your candidate?' he asked, eyebrows raised.

I nodded, unable to suppress a smile.

'If he's the guy I think he is, it will be fantastic for you.'

This particular encounter hadn't been stage-managed, but it was the most telling touch of the evening.

The dinner with Hawkins could only really be awkward. I had done what I could to limit the damage by reminding Patrik earlier in the day that as CFO Hawkins would expect to have complete control of dealings with bankers and investors.

'Sure,' said Patrik. 'But we'll have to work very closely together.'

I didn't want to risk a confrontation by pushing the issue, and in any case Tony Coleman had rung Hawkins to warn him beforehand. 'Whatever Patrik says this evening, don't worry about it,' he told him. 'We'll sort everything out before you start.'

Sure enough, halfway through the dinner, Patrik said to Hawkins, 'We should meet soon for a one to one to talk about how we're going to work together.'

Without even blinking, Hawkins replied, 'I'm pretty busy. I'll have to check my diary and get back to you.'

If only we had met this guy a long time ago.

The successful conclusion of the Federated deal seemed only a matter of time. 'I left extremely impressed with what you had accomplished,' commented Ted Osborne in an email to me on 30 November. 'It was a pleasure writing my due diligence report. I wish I could say that for every due diligence I go on.'

While we waited for the formalities to be completed, we turned our attention to moving into our larger office at Chesham House on

Regent Street, one floor of which had been completely refurbished. With two or three people now sitting at every desk in the Carnaby Street office, the move was long overdue.

Before Kajsa had found Chesham House, which was less than a hundred metres away from where we already were, I had briefly considered renting the former London Stock Exchange building. It would be the perfect place to hold our future IPO party and, with amenities that included the vast trading floor, a gym, canteen and auditorium, was almost three times as large as the Carnaby Street office and only a little more expensive. But staff were so hostile to the idea that I quickly dropped it. Bang in the middle of the conformist City, it stood for everything boo had been trying to escape from.

The big move to Chesham House took place over the weekend of 10–12 December. It was a huge logistical exercise that involved moving everyone except the tech and customer service departments, who would stay on in Carnaby Street until the refurbishments to our other floor in Chesham House were completed. As tons of equipment shuttled back and forth in orange packing crates between Carnaby Street, Regent Street and our temporary office in Holborn, now completely vacated, it was in fact not just one move but four: Carnaby to Regent Street, Holborn to Regent Street, Holborn to Carnaby, and, as everything was rearranged within the original office, Carnaby to Carnaby.

As nearly the entire UK company gathered together on one floor, at Chesham House, for the first time I got a sense of just how large boo had become. There was more than enough space now for us to indulge ourselves with corporate comforts and also plenty of meeting rooms so that we no longer had to rush out to cafés or to Home House. But while Patrik chose to have his own office, I took a desk in the corner of the main open-plan floor. Now it was actually possible to walk around without climbing over people. There were even some spare desks that people from our other offices like Jay Herratti could use whenever they were in town.

But the thrill of that first day in Chesham House was marred by a sudden hitch in our negotiations with Federated. Their vice-chairman, Ron Tysoe, who had initiated the talks with us a couple of months earlier, asked for a conference call that afternoon with

Patrik, Kajsa and me. Usually laid-back and charming, this time he launched into a barrage of questions about our sales, the number of website hits and our technical difficulties.

'Is something wrong?' I asked.

'We're a bit worried about your burn rate,' he admitted. 'Your sales figures too. They seem a bit on the low side. You've only just launched, and it would be useful to have some more visibility on your sales trends.'

The conversation ended with him promising to get back to us soon. It was an ominous development, but I tried to put it out of my mind as I set off for a quick shopping expedition with Paul Kanareck. The boo Christmas party was taking place the next evening at the Eve Club on Regent Street. The theme was glamour and I needed something to wear.

'This is how you shop,' I said to Paul as we marched into the Paul Smith shop on Westbourne Grove. 'You go in, you make your decision in two minutes, and you pay.'

Five minutes later, I walked out with a blue velvet suit.

'If only the boo.com website were as quick as that,' joked Paul.

Back in the office, I was busy showing off my new suit to Edward when I got a call from Brian Crawford, the banker who had stepped into Samer Salty's shoes at J.P. Morgan.

He sounded tired. 'I just got off the phone with Ron Tysoe at Federated,' he said. 'They want to wait.'

'How long?'

'They want to see how things go over Christmas. I think they're still keen. They're just being careful.'

I was deeply disappointed. We had lost control of the situation. It was now impossible to know when, or if, Federated would come back. My most immediate concern was our financial situation. We urgently needed $20 million to get us through to February, of which half was supposed to have come from Federated and the other half from existing shareholders. I couldn't help wondering how share-holders would react to this unexpected turn of events. It wouldn't take long to find out. Our board meeting was scheduled for the following morning.

★

The highlight of the boo Christmas party was a première of the 'boo movie', an edited version with music of the camcorder footage that Kajsa's sister had shot before and after the launch. Every member of staff received their own videotape copy as a Christmas present. I left early at 1 a.m as I had to be up in time to catch a flight to Amsterdam where we were obliged to hold at least a few of our board meetings since boo had been registered as a Dutch company for tax reasons.

The Amsterdam office, at 540 Singel, had finally been opened by Mike Brantjes a couple of months earlier in a small modern building that overlooked a canal in the heart of the city. It was another miniature version of Carnaby Street, with an open-plan area off which a meeting room had been improvised by putting up a glass partition. For the board meeting, several Ikea desks had been pushed together to make a long makeshift table.

Among the board members who began to shuffle in shortly before 1 p.m. were two important new faces. Over the past few weeks, Nader Hariri of the Millennium Fund had backed up his promise of hands-on support with several visits to our office and regular calls of encouragement. He had also recently invited us to dinner at Mosimanns, an exclusive private restaurant in Chelsea, so that we could meet his cousin Saad Hariri, who was in overall charge of the family's business interests. 'We are more than an investor,' Saad declared in summary of the Hariri business approach. 'We are your partner.' François Tison, the new representative for Bernard Arnault, added to the board's stock of ex-bankers, but was a refreshingly energetic presence. He seemed to be in as continual a hurry as his predecessor Jean-Bernard Tellio. With hardly any pause for reflection he would express his forthright views on almost any given issue. Little more than thirty-years-old, he brought the average age of the boo board down to lower than that of its managment team.

The dominating issue on that particular day was inevitably Federated's postponement of their investment decision until after Christmas. I knew that if we were going to ask shareholders to make up the $10 million shortfall we would need to offer compelling proof of our achievements. So I had asked Tobin Ireland, Rob Shepherd and Rachel Yasue to deliver presentations to the board on what were presently the three key areas of the business: sales, technology and finance.

After an upbeat overview, I gave the floor to Tobin. Although the number of visitors to the site was lower than had initially been expected, he was able to demonstrate a rapid and continuing improvement. In the six weeks since launch, we had made $353,000 and our conversion rate had doubled. The average order value of $115 was $30 more than we had forecast, which meant that our distribution costs were much cheaper than we had anticipated in our business model. We were also well placed to make the most of the Christmas season. With the blessing of our suppliers, we had cut prices on all products by 15 per cent in the three weeks leading up to Christmas, and would be operating our customer service centres around the clock with the exception of Christmas and New Year's Eve. Perhaps most impressive was our supply chain. By the second week of December, 90 per cent of our US orders, and 97 per cent of our European orders, were being dispatched on time. Tobin concluded with a brief look at future developments that would help to accelerate sales growth. These included the introduction of a low-bandwidth site in February and a customer loyalty scheme in March.

Rob Shepherd then offered a typically level-headed explanation of the technology situation. He was the sort of person who never promised more than he was confident of being able to deliver, and the board found him an immensely reassuring presence. The chief problem continued to be impaired access for Mac-users. The tech team would work to resolve the issue as quickly as possible, but also expected to achieve a 50 per cent reduction in download times by the end of January and to release the new version of the site in April.

Rachel Yasue's presentation on finance set the scene for the big discussion of the meeting. Strenuous efforts had been made to reduce the cost base, but, she concluded, the company would still need $20 million to take it through to the next round. What we currently had in the bank would last at the most a couple of weeks.

Chris Bataillard explained the situation with Federated and made the proposal that the existing investors should provide the full $20 million.

It did not go down well.

'It's very easy for you to come back to us all the time,' snapped Tison. 'But why haven't you come up with other options? You're the company's financial adviser. That's your job.'

Bataillard, struggling to maintain his composure, replied, 'This isn't necessarily something we can control. You have to remember that the launch was delayed and the company has had some bad press.' He also pointed out that the millennium bug was making many potential investors put off their decisions until after the New Year.

Tison, looking unconvinced, polished his glasses agitatedly. 'This really isn't good enough.' He had a valid point. The Nasdaq had just closed at its fifty-fourth record high this year. Even with all of our problems, it was hard to believe that a bank like J.P. Morgan didn't have other investors on stand-by.

The bad-tempered discussion that followed would have become more so if everyone hadn't been in such a tearing hurry to leave. Richard Ely of Skadden Arps and Tim Gordon of Ernst & Young were made to feel little more welcome than a pair of door-to-door salesmen as their presentations pitching for the IPO were quickly curtailed and they were asked to leave. As the discussion returned to funding strategy, several other matters were postponed until the next meeting.

It was finally decided that J.P. Morgan should at once get in touch with boo's eight largest shareholders to gauge their interest in making a further investment. As an added incentive, boo's pre-money valuation would be lowered to $285 million. This was around $100 million less than the level at which the Millennium Fund had invested just a few months earlier, and I couldn't help glancing across at Nader. It was obviously not the sort of thing he wanted to hear at his first board meeting, although the 'ratchet down' clause he had negotiated came into effect and the Millennium Fund got more shares.

Schiphol is just about my favourite airport in the world. It is the only one I know that has an airside casino. For the nervous passenger I can think of no better place to relax. Once you have exposed yourself to the whims of the roulette table, the odds of surviving your flight seem reassuringly stacked in your favour. In the few minutes I had to spare I had time to win on the red, then on the black, then to bet everything on my favourite number: 11. As the wheel spun, I reflected on the large part that luck seemed to play in the boo.com story. The presentations of Tobin, Rob and Rachel, which had converted the health of boo.com into exact units of measurement, were really the nearest we had come to certainty that afternoon. They showed a company that was putting all the fundamentals in place, that had weathered the precarious early stages of its existence and was now moving fast along the road to eventual profit. But how far we would get along that road depended finally on the decisions of people over whom we had no control.

Over the coming few days, as the investors made their minds up, I was glad for the distraction of a Christmas tour of the boo offices. The first leg of my journey, on the same afternoon as the board meeting, was to New York. I was there only the week before, meeting Mary Meeker, the Queen of Wall Street.

Early the next morning Jay came over for breakfast at the SoHo Grand and together we took a taxi to the office. A lot had changed in the past few months and the once empty, unrenovated loft was now teeming with more than a hundred people. Huge floor-to-ceiling windows overlooked the Hudson River, and the main open-plan area had been divided up into oak and brushed-steel cubicles. The overall effect was light, cool and modern.

Jay was clearly proud of what had been created. 'Look at them all,' he said. 'If we grow any more, we'll have to find a new space.'

The chief topic of conversation was the poorer than expected performance of boo.com in the US. So far, only 20 per cent of our overall sales had come from the US, instead of the 40 per cent that we had forecast. It was an example, Jay said, of the vital need to iron out the remaining technical glitches. US consumers were too impatient and demanding to put up with such problems. If the site wasn't working perfectly, they wouldn't shop. Neither of us had any time for complacency, but we could at least console ourselves with the thought that everything possible was being done to fix things. If only it was as simple with investors, I thought, as I told Jay about the board meeting. With them, you just had to sit back and wait.

In the evening, boo's New York Christmas party took place at Automatic Slims, a West Village bar that Jay had rented for the evening. I chatted to Scott Messing, Vanessa Rolfo, Gretchen Hyden and Sara Dworkin about the latest gossip in the US office, and soon found myself surrounded by some of US boo's prettiest girls.

'Be careful,' said Jay. 'I don't want to have to cope with a scandal.'

'Don't worry. We have good lawyers.' The vodka and grapefruit juice kept flowing until people were either dancing on the bar or quietly passing out. At one point someone noticed a boo ad that was by chance playing on a small TV suspended above the bar. There was a deafening cheer, that seemed to echo on and on for hours. The night wound up with me helping to carry a comatose 200 kilo homeboy who worked in our customer service centre to a taxi.

'The poor guy put away a lot of vodka and grapefruit,' said Jay. 'Americans aren't used to so much alcohol.'

'No,' I disagreed. 'You need to train your people better.'

The call finally came the next day – a voicemail from Chris Bataillard that I picked up late in the evening. 'It's looking pretty good,' he said breezily. 'I think we're going to get the money. There are just a few conditions. I'll send you an email.'

The 'few' conditions turned out to be a two-page list. Many were simply a formalization of things that we had anyway been promising – such as the resolution of the technical issues, the reduction of our burn rate and also a commitment that we, the founders, would invest $3 million of our own money in the funding round.

But two conditions stood out. The first demanded that we appoint a 'high quality non-executive chairman' before the end of January. And the second – in case there was any doubt about the first – stipulated: 'Patrik Hedelin to be responsible for neither the finance area nor contact with existing or potential shareholders.' Together they amounted to an ultimatum for his dismissal.

It was hardly a surprise. Since Patrik had stepped down as CFO, the complaints about him had grown. It was not just J.P. Morgan, but also several of our shareholders. They were fed up with his hard-hitting manner, his ambiguous position as chairman and the difficulty he seemed to have supplying them with clear information. I knew we had to deal with the situation, but I didn't like this very underhand method – even if in many ways it made my job a lot easier.

Early the next morning I rang Bataillard. 'I've read the email,' I said.

'Good. What did you think?'

His tone was a little hesitant. We had talked about Patrik often enough, but he still wasn't sure whether he could assume my collusion.

'Where did all these conditions come from?' I asked.

'We just made a list of everything that shareholders said to us. You shouldn't worry too much about most of them.'

He paused before continuing. 'The key thing here is Patrik . . .'

'Yes. I guessed that.'

'It's gone too far. Just look at what happened with Federated.'

'What do you mean?'

'Patrik called them too many times, and confused them with the way he presented the numbers.'

'Are you saying that's why they pulled out?'

'No. But I'm sure it didn't help. There's only one thing worse than having a high burn rate, and that's not knowing what it is.' I should have a friendly word with Patrik, he suggested, and persuade him to leave quietly.

'What if he's not prepared to go?'

'Then you don't get the money. Look, we'll help if we can,' he went on. 'But this is really something you have to face.'

My next call was to Kajsa.

'Hmm,' she said, trying not to sound too pleased. 'Do you think they already had this planned before the board meeting?'

'Probably. I don't know.'

'Well it's a pretty good way of solving this. I know it isn't very nice, but it had to happen sooner or later, right?'

'What am I going to tell him?'

'Just say that the shareholders are demanding it. It's not your fault. He can't blame you.'

I spent the next few hours agonizing over what to say to Patrik. I would have liked to have been able to work out some sinecure position in which he could do no harm, but there was nothing that wouldn't have seemed an obvious insult to him. As I had to catch a flight that afternoon to Munich, where I was supposed to have dinner with Christoph and his team, I decided to put the call off until the next day.

I rang him first thing at his home in Stockholm, where he was spending the weekend, as usual.

'I think we're going to get the money,' I said. 'But there are some conditions.'

'Oh?' Patrik sounded like he had just woken up.

'It's probably best if I fax them to you,' I said. 'Then maybe we can talk.'

I faxed the list from the hotel lobby, then sat down in the breakfast room to wait for his call. It didn't take long.

'What kind of a list is this?' he said. 'This is the most unprofessional thing I've ever seen.'

I told him what Bataillard had told me – that these were the conditions that the different shareholders had demanded.

But Patrik clearly didn't believe it. 'No,' he replied. 'Those J.P. Morgan bastards are behind this. They've been wanting to get rid of me for ages.'

It was a flawless assessment of the situation. I wasn't sure what I could add, so I just let him continue to rage against the bankers.

'This is typical of them,' he shouted. His tone became defiant. 'We don't have to agree to this, anyway. We can fight them.'

'I think we need to talk more about this when I get back to London.'

'OK,' said Patrik. 'But I'm going to call the shareholders. I'll find out what's going on.'

The next morning, I caught an early flight to London. I got into our new office to find the packing crates gone, all the desks in place and the staff already working away as if they had been there for ever. It wasn't the boo way to drag things out, I thought to myself, as I marched into Patrik's office for a final showdown, but he had other ideas. He thought that we were going to make a last stand together.

'I think Nader is on the bankers' side,' he said. 'We probably can't count on him. Tison is neutral. But a lot of the other shareholders don't know what's going on. Have you spoken to anyone?'

'A few,' I said, feeling uncomfortable. 'I think most of them agree with the conditions.'

Patrik was unconcerned. 'Don't worry about it. They'll give us the money. They have just as much at stake as we do. The only people pushing this are the bankers.'

'Maybe they started it. But a lot of the shareholders feel strongly about this as well. I don't think we can just ignore them. We really need the money.'

Patrik's expression slowly began to change. Defiance turned to confusion and then disappointment. For the first time he realized that he did not have my support.

'When Dean Hawkins starts as the CFO, you won't be able to deal with investors anyway,' I continued. 'It doesn't make sense to have two people doing that. We're also going to need a proper chairman at some point.'

Patrik hadn't slumped to the ground yet, but it felt like rattling off bullets. I tried to assume a more magnanimous tone. 'Maybe we can find you another role,' I said.

'No. If this happens, I'm going to . . .' His words trailed off. 'It's not that I mind so much. I need to spend more time with my family, anyway. I just don't see why we should let those bankers push us around.' He looked away. 'I need to think about this.'

'OK,' I said. 'Let's talk later.'

But over the next few days Patrik and I were both in and out of the office so much that we didn't get a chance to speak again before the Christmas break. On 23 December, I returned home to Lund determined to make the most of a much-needed holiday. For just a few days I hoped to be able to relax with my family, catch up with old friends and forget about boo.com. On that first night, as I walked through the town centre to meet a few of my friends at a bar, I felt as if I were back at university again, once again studying for the degree I never completed. I passed the Academic Society, where I used to put on talks by celebrity guests, and recalled the wild dinners there to which they would be invited afterwards. Maybe one day soon, I thought, the Society would invite me to give a speech. I half expected fellow members of the student union to come running down the steps when suddenly the shrill tone of my mobile snatched me back to the present.

It was Ahmed Kouther from SEDCO: 'I just spoke to Patrik.'

'What did you say?'

'I made it clear that the shareholders don't think he's the right person to be dealing with investors. Then we had an argument. I refuse to be spoken to like that.'

I felt like dropping the phone down a drain.

The next time it rang, it was Patrik.

'OK, then,' he said. 'I've thought about it. I'll step down. But it will be on my terms. We'll just say that I want to spend more time with my family . . .'

As he would remain a co-founder and a board member, there was no reason why this decision should seem a particularly dramatic event. It all sounded fine.

'OK,' I said. 'I'm glad we could sort this out.'

'But there are a few things I want in return,' Patrik continued. 'I want to restructure the board. And I want to kick J.P. Morgan out. That's the most important thing. I want them out if it's the last thing I do.'

'Patrik . . .'

'This time we definitely need to work with Goldman.'

'Patrik, I don't care. Do whatever you want. Let's speak after Christmas, OK?'

'OK.'

'I'll give you a call tomorrow.'

'Good.'

I hung up and switched off the phone.

13

PATRIK WASN'T THE ONLY PERSON who wanted to kick J.P. Morgan out. None of the board members had forgotten the Federated fiasco. While in all other respects their patience with Patrik had run out, they were only too keen to embrace the idea that Goldman Sachs should handle boo.com's IPO. The possibility was quickly raised again and soon after my return to London we received a mandate letter in which Goldman outlined the way it might work with us.

In a conference call on New Year's Eve the Goldman Sachs team, led by their retail specialist Jennifer Moses, proposed a scheme whereby they would lead the IPO in the second quarter of 2000. Before that, however, they would work with another bank, BancBoston Robertson Stephens – who also took part in the conference call – to secure a pre-IPO funding round of $40 million.

The day before, Paul Kanareck had emailed the bank an overview of our post-launch performance and our financial forecasts. It was the business equivalent of a school report. While the early technical problems had hampered us, we had none the less demonstrated that all the fundamentals were in place. 'boo has had a difficult first term but shows enormous promise,' would have been a fair summary of the progress.

With a marketing and PR spend of only $22.4 million we had managed to create a worldwide brand. The ground had been laid for rapid expansion and, with our website now working reliably, an aggressive campaign to enlarge our customer base. The site had launched in 18 countries with 22 brands in November, and would be operating in 31 countries with 40 brands in time for the spring/summer season.

We had figures for only 50 days of trading, but already they suggested exponential growth. Our conversion rate, for example, had crept up from 0.25 per cent for our first week to 0.98 per cent for the week ending 19 December. Our financial model, now under the careful supervision of our head of financial planning Ruth Prior, had been adjusted in the light of the real figures and offered an enticing snapshot of the future. Our turnover was forecast to rise from $100 million in the financial year 2000/01 to $1,350 million by 2003/4. The vital dynamo for sales would be heavy investment in marketing to drive traffic to the website – the figure estimated for 2003/4 was $106.4 million, well over four times the amount we had originally spent to establish the brand. Our losses, which were predicted to peak at $102.3 million in 2000/01, were of course heavy, reflecting our high start-up cost, but we expected to break even very early with a forecast profit of $51.9 million in 2003/04. From that point onwards, investors could expect the returns on their investment to rise sharply.

Both the management team and the core shareholders felt that the fundamentals of the business paved the way for an extremely successful IPO and expected fierce competition between the three banks to manage it. We decided that they should all make a formal pitch in the new year. Needless to say, J.P. Morgan were not expected to win, but it was only fair that they should be given the opportunity to compete.

Almost as momentous as the prospect of our IPO was the coming of the new millennium. I spent the evening quietly at home in Notting Hill, watching the fireworks from my rooftop terrace with a few Swedish friends and relatives.

Shortly after midnight I received a call from James Cronin, who, in a typical display of self-sacrifice, had agreed to watch over our website and make sure it wasn't stung by the infamous Y2K bug.

'Everything's OK,' he said. 'Happy new millennium.'

'No bugs, then?'

'No more than usual.'

'You should go and have some fun,' I told him

'We're cracking open a few bottles here,' he said.

As I watched one more rocket soar into the night sky, I felt a brief sense of satisfaction and pride. It had been an incredible year, easily the most exciting in my life. In twelve months we had conjured out of nothing a global company that now employed over 400 people. Decades of experience that would normally take a lifetime to amass had sped by in fast-forward. I couldn't help feeling that if only I had known what I knew now when we first set out, we would have launched much earlier and have had a successful IPO some time ago.

A huge amount had been achieved, but the sheer pace of events meant that many mistakes had been made too. We should never have tried to manage the development of the technology platform ourselves; it caused massive disruption to our efforts to focus on becoming the retailer we actually were. With hindsight, even our hugely successful attempts to generate publicity for the company seemed misguided; the sheer scale and positive tone of the early coverage invited a backlash when the company failed to launch on time.

But these mistakes, it seemed to me, offered tremendous opportunities for improvement. The key for the year ahead was not to regret them, but to learn from them. Having weathered the various crises, I felt that we were now in a fantastic position to cement a stable and secure future. Since October, several senior executives had joined the company, improved versions of the website were soon to be released, and now the banks were about to pitch for our IPO. boo.com may have been built in the twentieth century, but it would really come into its own in the twenty-first.

One of my first tasks of the new millennium was to tell Chris Bataillard that J.P. Morgan would have to pitch for the IPO alongside Goldman Sachs and Robertson Stephens. It was a difficult call to make, because over the past months I had developed a close working relationship with Chris. Whatever troubles we may have had with J.P. Morgan, Chris himself had believed in us from the very beginning and remained one of our strongest supporters. He often visited the company and his personal commitment was unquestioned, but I felt that he lacked the support he needed within the bank – especially from the US side of the business – to attract powerful new investors.

The shareholders' hardline attitude left me little room for

manoeuvre, but Bataillard's astonished reaction served only to strengthen the feeling I had of having committed some small act of treachery. 'I can't believe you're telling me this!' he said. 'If we had known we couldn't do the IPO, we would never have taken you on as a client.'

My suggestion that J.P. Morgan might be able to play some ancillary role seemed only to rub salt in the wound

Bataillard chuckled quietly. 'You must be joking,' he said. 'There is absolutely no way we're working under Goldman. If we're not the lead bank any more, then we don't want to be involved at all.' None the less, he agreed that the bank would pitch for the IPO.

We decided that the three banks should make their pitches to the board by conference call on Thursday, 6 January. It was vital that the issue be settled as quickly as possible, since the $17 million we had finally raised in the last round would run out by 10 February.

Gathering together so many people in different places all at once was a complicated enough task in itself. It was made even more difficult by the need continually to include and exclude the banks from the call. The only way to ensure that they could deliver their pitches in private was to organize a tight schedule, in which the banks would take it in turns at a specified time to join the conference call, with each of them using different pin numbers to gain access. 'I feel like I'm working for the CIA,' said Paul Kanareck, who was given the task of organizing the event.

At about 5.45 p.m. Christopher Heather, the company's group legal counsel, joined me and Kajsa in the conference room. Extremely dedicated, Christopher had begun at boo in April 1999 and built up a small legal department of four or five people.

As we stared at the plastic three-cornered speaker in the middle of the table, it felt a bit like talking to a spaceship; the distant-sounding voices of the investors seeming to belong to aliens from another planet.

'Hello, François . . . Nader . . . Luciano . . . Ah, Patrik . . .'

Patrik had only just returned to Sweden, but was still a board member and, officially, also executive chairman of the company until 10 January. With his loathing for J.P. Morgan, he certainly didn't want to miss the *coup de grâce*.

We were a little late in getting started because Ahmed Kouther, calling in from Jedda, kept getting disconnected. When he finally did get through, he couldn't hear us.

'Hello?'

'Hi, Ahmed. We're all here,' I replied.

'Hello? *Hello*?'

Shortly after six, Jennifer Moses and her team were patched into the call and began Goldman Sachs's half-hour presentation. I still had memories of their previous pitch in New York, which had left us with the impression of being courted by the most powerful bank in the world. Since they had also been so bullish about the prospect of working with us over Christmas, I expected an extremely polished performance. But the only part of this second presentation that could have been predicted was the flaunting of their world-beating credentials – Goldman, 'the Dominant Internet Franchise'; Goldman, the sun at the centre of the internet *keiretsu* . . .

Otherwise, it seemed less a pitch than a veiled declaration of their reluctance to be involved.

'It's important to make sure you're completely ready before setting off down this path,' Jennifer Moses said.

'What does that mean?' François Tison asked.

'Look, don't get me wrong,' she said. 'We like the story. But it would help if you had a bit more of a trading history.'

What had caused them to change their tune? I wondered. They had had our figures since Christmas. If they were having second thoughts, they ought to have told us before the board meeting.

'Maybe we could do the private placement and then IPO on a smaller exchange to start with,' she suggested. 'Like Stockholm.'

There was a shocked silence. For a long while the spaceship ceased to emit any voices – just a shout from someone's child in the background – as the board members in their various cities from Paris to Jedda mulled over this humiliating suggestion. The idea of listing our shares on any exchange other than the Nasdaq was inconceivable to us. boo was a global internet business and needed access to global investors. I wondered what Patrik made of the great Goldman Sachs now.

'How's it going?' asked Edward when I wandered out of the conference room between presentations.

'Goldman Sachs have gone nuts,' I said. 'They want us to do our IPO in Stockholm.'

It was with considerable nervousness that at 6.30 p.m. I welcomed Steve Schweich, the managing director of Robertson Stephens's European operations, to the conference call. After all, the bank had been highly recommended by Goldman Sachs. So maybe, they would be singing the same song too. But to my relief, Schweich put in an aggressive, highly convincing pitch for our business.

'The market appetite for big internet stories like this is enormous,' he said. Robertson Stephens had just successfully raised close to $60 million for a Swedish e-tailer named LetsBuyIt.com. 'We were actually turning investors away.' The bank also had one of the most respected retailing analysts in the market, Lauren Cooks Levitan, whose support would prove invaluable in attracting investors.

At seven it was J.P. Morgan's turn to make their presentation. Bataillard vigorously defended the bank's record to date. The difficulty in bringing investors on board in the last round had been caused by the various problems that had followed the launch, he said, but the bank believed that most of those issues were now being resolved. Aware of our doubts about the support of some people within the bank, Bataillard went out of his way to stress the support of J.P. Morgan as a whole. The senior management of its equities division, he assured us, was prepared to devote *all* its resources to executing an IPO in the second quarter.

As Bataillard ran through what the bank had achieved for boo.com, I could detect a hurt pride and a determination to hold on to a company that the bank had done as much as anyone to bring into the world. There was a sense of renewed commitment, which impressed everyone except Patrik.

When Bataillard pointed out that in the past year J.P. Morgan had raised $100 million for boo.com, Patrick snorted loudly: 'We raised most of that ourselves. You haven't brought any new investors in since last April.'

Surprised to hear Patrik's voice, Bataillard recovered quickly. 'Well, we've said what we're prepared to do. The rest is up to you.'

In light of the Goldman Sachs débâcle, J.P. Morgan need hardly have fought so hard to hold on to us. In the subsequent board discussion, their experience and the long-term relationship they had built up with us were the crucial factors in deciding that they should continue to be our bank. But we had also been hugely impressed by Robertson Stephens, and Ahmed Kouther suggested that they should be asked to work in a supporting role to J.P. Morgan. The effect, we hoped, would be for the two banks to spur each other on in a friendly rivalry.

One of Patrik's last acts as executive chairman of boo.com was to sign the board meeting minutes confirming the appointment of J.P. Morgan as the lead bank in the IPO. It hadn't gone the way any of us had expected, and he had to admit that his champion Goldman Sachs had let us down badly.

Preparation for our pre-IPO funding round got under way soon afterwards with a 'kick off' meeting in the great hall at J.P. Morgan. The aim was to produce an updated version of our private placement memorandum within the next week so that we could start meeting investors in late January.

A boo team led by Edward and Sarah Arundel hammered out the details of the memorandum with the bankers. Jay Herratti also came over from New York for the week to help out. I dropped by the J.P. Morgan offices a couple of times and caused a little controversy when I criticized the bankers' use of English. 'Ernst is such a perfectionist,' commented Lorcan O'Shea, one of the J.P. Morgan bankers. 'He always wants to bring in a team of writers from *The Economist* to make sure it reads well.'

But by and large the memorandum was making good progress, and I was pleased to be able to turn back to the job of running a company again. The great new project of the year was the complete overhaul of our website. Every department had been asked to contribute ideas to the development of Version 2, and encouraged to be as bold and innovative as they wanted to be. The merchandise team suggested dozens of new features that would improve the way products were displayed; the logistics team argued for a more effective means of tracking and tracing products; the marketing team came up with ideas for new promotions; and so on. But what was most exciting was the way these different departments worked together, learning what proposals were feasible within the framework of the company as a whole. As web designers sat down with people from, say, the merchandise department or finance, there was an exhilarating sense of new ideas being sparked off through the interchange. This was the spirit of boo.com at its best – people from different disciplines and backgrounds working together to perfect a shared vision.

In the midst of all the planning, it was good every now and then to get a reminder of what boo was finally all about: happy customers. In the new year, Tobin circulated the following message around the company:

Dear everyone at boo!!!!!
RE: ORDER ID 215482 – SUSAN JONES
I just wanted to drop you a quick line to say how absolutely fantastic I thought your service was. I ordered a Helly Hansen new brand bubble jacket from you on this Wednesday evening, and it arrived here first thing Friday morning – that is what I call fantastic service!

I really cannot believe how quick and easy the whole process was, how quickly you responded with your order confirmation e-mail and then how quickly the product arrived – I just wanted you to know you have one extremely impressed, grateful and extremely extremely satisfied customer here! . . .

I have to admit to myself and my boyfriend being extremely cautious in ordering anything from the internet and even more cautious in giving our credit card number, but you have completely put a whole new faith into this system for us both and [we] shall definitely have no hesitation in using your company again and also recommending you. THANK YOU and happy new year to you all!

Susan Jones – a very satisfied miss boo!!

We were all extremely extremely proud. 'Who is this Susan Jones?' I asked. 'Is she related to anyone we know? Give her a discount on the next five orders!'

One casualty of our efforts to put in place a more streamlined retail operation was Michael Skidmore. His flair was beyond doubt, but it was often difficult to know how to accommodate it. No one, for example, could figure out how we would ever manage to sell 200 Antarctic sleeping bags – it was tempting to send them all to Susan Jones. As we sought to widen our customer base, we needed a team that could buy in a more disciplined and strategic way. In the new year we brought in Maryann McGeorge as vice-president for commercial retail. Previously senior vice president of merchandise operations at the Venator Group, which owned the huge sports shoe retailer Foot Locker, she had a quarter of a century's retail experience and had been responsible for 6000 stores. Then almost immediately afterwards we hired as our vice-president of merchandising Ed Whitehead, who had over twenty years of merchandising experience with companies that included Nike, Calvin Klein and Polo/Ralph Lauren. Caught between this Scylla and Charybdis, the only way out for Skidmore was a generous settlement. I felt very sad to see him go. He may have been the oldest member of the senior management team by some way, but he epitomized boo's youthful exuberance. Now we needed to buckle down.

Early on the morning of Tuesday, 11 January the first draft of the private placement memorandum was emailed to me by Jeremy Grant, an analyst who had stepped into Felix von Schubert's old job at J.P. Morgan and inevitably been nicknamed by us as the 'New Felix'. The memorandum put forward a bold vision of how 'the first truly global e-tailer' planned to take a big share of a market that was worth $100 billion a year and still growing. We now had a robust, tried and tested platform that would enable rapid expansion into new markets. 'In simple terms boo.com aims to revolutionize e-commerce, driving it away from the predominant trend of discounting grey market products to an environment that accommodates the retail of premium products.' Any potential investor reading the memorandum, I thought, would quickly realize that here was a company that had put the critical development problems of its start-up phase behind it and was on the verge of reaping huge rewards in an explosive growth of sales. As I scrolled through the pages, I felt a tremendous sense of anticipation for what lay ahead. In just a few days' time we were going to be meeting Adidas and Nike. Agreements with these two giant suppliers would be further confirmation of the extraordinary progress we had made.

Then, in the afternoon, I received a call from Rory O'Sullivan, head of Robertson Stephens's internet division in Europe. He must have received his copy of the memorandum, I thought. In the past few days he had been so friendly and helpful that in my buoyant mood I half imagined that he had rung up to congratulate us.

But now his voice was sombre. 'Hi, Ernst,' he said. 'I'm afraid we've got some bad news.'

'Oh?'

'We've decided that we're not prepared to go ahead. We feel very uncomfortable about the idea of an IPO in the second quarter. It's too early.'

In my brief tenure as CEO of boo.com there had been many shocks, but this one was off the scale. 'What's the problem?' I asked.

'Basically, our retail analyst, Lauren Cooks Levitan, doesn't think institutional investors will go for it yet,' O'Sullivan said. 'She thinks you need more revenue momentum. There has to be strong evidence that your sales are growing at a steady rate and that the business model is actually working.' Cooks Levitan also felt that before proceeding with a pre-IPO round, we needed to sign some more big suppliers and Dean Hawkins, who was due to begin as our new CFO at the beginning of February, needed to be fully integrated into the business for at least a couple of months.

'We're really sorry,' said O'Sullivan, 'but this process is analyst-led and we can't move forward if she doesn't support it.'

'Look, we've got to talk to her,' I said, still having trouble believing what I was hearing. 'Can't you set up a meeting? She hasn't even spoken to us yet.'

'Sure. I can do that, but I don't think it will make a lot of difference.'

I rang Brian Crawford at J.P. Morgan immediately afterwards to discover that he had already heard the news. 'I think we need to talk,' he said. 'I'll be right over.'

By the time he arrived, about an hour later, it was already dark outside and the office was emptying. I had asked Jay and Edward to join the discussion in one of our small meeting rooms.

'Can you believe they did this?' I said. 'They only pitched to us a week ago. They had all the figures.'

Crawford shifted awkwardly in his chair. 'Actually, Ernst, the reason I came over is to let you know that J.P. Morgan don't want to proceed with this, either.'

None of us spoke. It was beginning to feel like Act V of some lost Shakespeare tragedy.

He looked embarrassed. It wasn't his decision. J.P. Morgan's research analyst Tom Wyman, he explained, felt that the public markets would not view an IPO favourably at this stage in the company's development, and the bank's equity team felt the same.

'How can you do this?' I said. 'You promised you would complete the funding round by 10 February.' I was close to panic and very upset, but there was no point in getting angry. Crawford was just the messenger. We had to face the facts fast and deal with them. Why were we so surprised? I wondered. The last year had been a whole series of unexpected hurdles. Why should they suddenly disappear now?

'What the hell am I supposed to say to the shareholders?' I asked.

'Well, you're going to have to think about some alternative funding proposals.'

'You mean ask them for more money again?'

'Yes.'

'How are we to put it to them? You've got to help us rationalize this somehow. What do we have to do to convince you that we're ready for an IPO?'

I knew that we had to act immediately. Crawford agreed to go back to his office that night and help us to draft a letter to the investors. It wasn't until about 10.45 in the evening – after many calls and emails going back and forth between the J.P. Morgan and boo offices – that we finally had a version that everybody was happy with.

In the letter I explained the banks' decision and stated the conditions that needed to be met before J.P. Morgan and Robertson Stephens would be prepared to support an IPO: the new CFO had to be fully integrated into the business; a signed supplier agreement had to be secured with either Nike or Adidas; there had to be clear evidence of further revenue momentum; the promised improvements to the website had to be in place; and we had to meet our projected targets for the first quarter of 2000. It was a daunting list, but served to spell out the steps that would get us back on target. I knew that it was vital to have a concrete plan of action to keep the board members behind us.

I went on to call for an emergency board meeting to reassess our funding plans. I promised that we would forward detailed projections of the company's burn rate under different operational assumptions: 'Specifically we will prepare a scenario of a restructured business which is able to deliver on business targets while operating on a radically lower cost base.'

Once we had finished the letter, Edward, Jay and I stayed on to discuss exactly what our restructuring 'scenario' would entail. At some point a banker from J.P. Morgan's New York office, Alexander Fuchs, who had been involved in putting together the private placement memorandum, stopped by and stayed most of the evening. This was the nearest bankers came to being doctors. I half expected him to be wearing a stethoscope. 'You've got to get your burn rate right down,' he advised, 'and cut your staff by 50 per cent. This is your last chance to get your cost structure in shape.' His point was that because of the five months' delay in launching our site, we had a very high burn rate which our early revenues did not support. As it would take some time to ramp up revenues, it was vital in the interim to address this imbalance if we were to avoid scaring investors off.

After chatting to Fuchs about what our proposed restructuring would actually involve, we drafted an agenda for an emergency meeting of boo's management team the next day. It was an attempt, like the letter, to map out a positive way forward, and the Powerpoint document that Jay and Edward prepared ran through all the issues with a surreal detachment. I leafed through the pages: couched in the usual management consultant's phrases, they seemed so calmly expressed that for a moment I wondered whether there had been any crisis at all.

'Cost savings opportunities exist everywhere,' the document declared:

Marketing, Creative, Boom
Business development
Human Resources
Retail, Supplier Management
New Markets
Logistics, Content Management, Customer Service
Holding, Travel
Legal, Finance

Underneath this list was the boxed comment: 'Finding waste is not likely to be difficult.'

The one thing eerily absent from the entire document was people. The can-do language concealed the fact that each line of the list represented a handful of people's jobs to be scrapped. Add them up, and the total was a sizeable chunk of the company. It was extraordinary to think that it was only that morning that I had been going through the memorandum for our pre-IPO round of funding. There was one sentence I could recall reading with particular pride: 'boo.com believes that a key asset of its high-growth strategy is the strong culture and working lifestyle that has already developed throughout its worldwide organization.' Well, that was about to take a dent. In the space of one day our glorious schemes for expansion had vanished in a puff of smoke.

The next day I put the principal shareholders in the picture. They were as shocked by the news as I had been, but promised their broad support. I then called an emergency meeting of senior executives, at which attendance was compulsory.

'I'm guessing either that someone died, or we're getting taken over,' Luke quipped as he entered the room. 'Which is it, Ernst?'

'Neither,' I replied. 'But the news isn't good.'

Also present were Kajsa, Edward, Jay, Charlotte, Tobin, Tony Coleman, Rob Shepherd and Rachel Yasue.

I started by explaining what had happened the previous day. 'The banks just think it's too early,' I said. I then made it clear that we still had the backing of our shareholders, but in order to meet the banks' conditions for an IPO we would have to reduce our burn rate to an absolute minimum.

'I know we've already been trying,' I said, seeing some confused expressions. But now it's a matter not just of shaving costs, but making proper strategic decisions.'

There was a long and profound silence – as if someone really had died.

'I know this is going to be tougher than anything we've all been through, but we must keep calm and not get it out of proportion,' I continued. 'The simple story is that boo is not ready to go to the markets yet. We must do all that we can to make it ready.'

Still no one said anything. I was beginning to wonder if anyone ever would again. The financing of the company was not something that most of the management team would normally ever have to think about. Now they had to address it in a very direct and cruel way.

Finally, Tobin Ireland spoke up, voicing the thought that must have been on everyone's minds. 'What's the real trouble here? Is it delivering the milestones you mentioned? Or are there some fundamental problems with the business?'

'It's really a combination of the two,' I replied. 'We've got to focus on our core business and ensure it makes those milestones on time. But it's also about our ability in the longer term to run an efficient cost-controlled business. We have to prove that we can.'

I felt a huge sense of relief now that the full situation had been confided. The worst thing was uncertainty. Once people knew what they were up against, usually they had the strength to cope with it.

Slowly the room came back to life, as the discussion switched to the measures we would now have to take to restructure the business. It was a grim and painful discussion because now we were talking about people's jobs, but we were focused and united again.

'What sort of numbers are we talking about?' asked Tobin, who as chief retail officer was in charge of something like 200 people.

'We've got to think in terms of the absolute minimum necessary to operate our core business,' I said.

'Then we're going to have to define very carefully what our core business is,' warned Tobin.

We agreed to set up a small task force of senior executives to organize the restructuring process. It would receive input from a few handpicked managers, but otherwise its existence would be kept a complete secret from the rest of the company.

'We have to do this quickly,' I said. 'We have to have a plan we can present to the shareholders at the beginning of next week. Is that possible?'

'It's tough, but possible,' said Rachel Yasue.

'Then we have five days.'

I can't remember whose idea it was, but as a dark counterpart to Project Launch – the last crisis that the senior management team had faced together – Project Paunch was well named. Then we had established a command centre in the goldfish bowl at Carnaby Street; now, here in Chesham House, we established one in Patrik's office, which had conveniently just become available. I couldn't help but think of all the other offices and desks that would soon be empty, and wondered whether perhaps it wouldn't have been better if we had all stayed at Carnaby Street.

To prevent panic within the company it was vital that no one knew what was going on. Documentation concerning Project Paunch was restricted to the project office, which was kept locked at all times. If anyone asked what we were up to, they were to be told that senior management was engaged in 'budget planning'. And if any new manager was brought into the project, they had to receive clearance from me personally.

Our first priority, in just a day, was to identify the key business assets and then to produce a list of 'touchables' and 'untouchables'. To facilitate this process, a couple of staff from the finance depart-ment – sworn to secrecy – would supply a breakdown of costs across the business and analyse the savings that any proposed cuts represented. All potential savings would then be reviewed over the weekend, and the final decisions settled on Sunday evening in time for presentation to the board the following day.

A lot of savings could be made in a relatively painless way. Travel costs, for instance, could be reduced by the introduction of video conferencing; staff wages could be frozen; and initiatives, such as expansion into new markets, postponed. But they were not enough in themselves, and the most dreaded category of potential savings was of course the 'headcount reduction'.

'Everyone needs to take responsibility,' I warned. 'We're not going to survive unless we make tough decisions.'

But although every member of the senior management team knew that job-cuts were essential, they naturally shrank back from making them in their particular area. Over the next few days they would come to me with proposals for cuts, and repeatedly I would send them back again and again to cut further. I knew that I had to be tough for them – that I had to bear some of the load of their guilt. But there was no one I could turn to for comfort myself, no one who had been through this situation and could tell me how far it was really necessary to go. I knew I had to be cruel to be kind, but only much later would I discover that I had not been nearly cruel enough. It is one of the hardest things for an insider to judge the degree of such cuts. The likelihood is that unless he is by nature heartless, he will always err on the side of leniency. Just as I was pushing my management team to cut, cut, cut, I needed a powerful chairman with the necessary distance from the situation who could push me. It was a role that a more experienced board of directors might have fulfilled, but mine, I knew, would simply accept whatever I recommended.

By far the toughest decision was *Boom*. While most departments would lose at least some staff, it was decided that the whole magazine had to close. It had been an important part of our branding strategy, but had failed to work as well as we had hoped. The very spirit of freedom with which it had been conceived tripped it up in practice. In each country where boo operated there was a separate *Boom* team with its own editor. All these teams operated under the loose central co-ordination of Kate Alvarez in London, but lacked a strong editor-in-chief. The result was that there were constant arguments about what percentage of the magazine content should be local and what percentage global. The inability of the teams to agree not only compromised the effectiveness of the magazine but also turned out to be a time-consuming distraction for the managers, who tried to settle the disputes when they should have been attending to our core business.

Kajsa had made various attempts to solve the problem. First she promoted Kate Alvarez, but there was uproar from the local editors, who refused to be answerable to someone who had always been on their level. Then just before Christmas she hired Alex Marashian, formerly of *Colors* magazine, as editor-in-chief, and asked Mike Brantjes, the head of our Amsterdam office, to develop a business plan. Alex was successful in getting everyone to work together to produce a unified vision, and the first edition under his guidance was due to be put up on the site in a few weeks.

But even if many of *Boom*'s problems had been sorted out at last, most of the senior management team felt that, because it wasn't bringing in sales directly, it could not be justified as an essential part of our business, and that supporting it also took up the valuable time of our design and tech teams. Kajsa argued strongly that in terms of building the brand and attracting visitors to the site it was the most powerful marketing tool we had, that our site would look soulless without it, 'just a place to sell stuff'. But its marketing value was impossible to quantify, and 'a place to sell stuff' was the thing that at this point in boo.com's development the bankers and the investors most wanted us to focus on. Closing the magazine was the single most effective way in which we could signal to them that we were serious.

But it was hard for Kajsa to accept after having worked so hard to put the magazine on the right footing. There was also a degree of guilt. From the outset *Boom* had been Kajsa's brainchild. The notion that art and commerce could be mutually supporting – that we could create a loyal customer base through a magazine that had its own independent validity – appealed enormously to her. But in the end it had failed to work out as she had hoped, and now, just when she was convinced it was finally about to prove its worth, she had lost the chance to vindicate herself. Past history would have caused her to look on the situation with a certain sense of doom, because a similar thing had happened when we sold bokus, as KF had decided to close down that site's online magazine.

'Do we really have to do this?' she asked when we met on Friday afternoon in Patrik's old office to discuss the various cuts.

'We do,' I said, to general agreement from the others in the room.

'Can't we slim the magazine down somehow? Why do we have to get rid of it completely?'

'Look,' said Luke. 'It means firing my sister. This is hard for all of us.'

'Kajsa, it's too late,' I said. As much as I sympathized with what she was saying, I also thought it crucial that as a founder she send a clear message to the other managers about her commitment to cutting costs. 'Everyone thinks *Boom* should go,' I said. 'If we don't do this, we're endangering the business.'

But Kajsa was not won over. She threatened to resign, stayed because she didn't want to be accused of shirking her responsibility as a co-founder of the company, and only finally went along with the changes because she had the whole management team against her.

Three days later, on Monday, 17 January, we delivered our estimated cost reductions to the board. Over the next year our proposed cutbacks would save us $27 million. In total, 131 staff would lose their jobs. Besides *Boom*, most of the job cuts would be made by scaling down the customer service teams and streamlining the local offices. The figure represented over a quarter of boo.com's total workforce.

The meeting went better than we could have expected. The board approved our restructuring plan and also J.P. Morgan's revised funding strategy: the bank now planned to raise $50 million from new and existing shareholders and then go straight to an IPO in the second quarter.

We had come through yet another crisis, but it was impossible to feel happy. As the meeting broke up and our board members rushed off to catch their planes, I thought: This is the day that we lost our innocence.

The period in boo history that followed will be looked back on as the Golden Age of euphemisms. Our longed-for IPO was back on track, but it could be easily derailed again if the cutbacks were perceived by the media and the financial community as a crisis. So we contrived to present the firing of staff that was to take place on Tuesday, 25 January as a normal part of retail business. If anyone asked, they were to be told that it was simply a routine 'post-Christmas capacity reduction'. We had worked out several other similar phrases, although none had such a festive ring. What boo was undergoing, for example, was a 'shift from a development to an operations business', and our 'robust and automated infrastructure' was now 'fully operational and not labour-intensive'. But what none of us could face was the reality of breaking the news to staff. They were our friends, after all, most of them our own age.

Suddenly we realized just how very young we were. Of the senior management team, most of us were still in our late twenties and early thirties and had never had to do anything like this before. So it was almost with desperation that we turned for guidance to our head of human resources, Tony Coleman. In his early forties, he possessed the experience that we so badly needed. A small man about the size of Napoleon, he assured us that he had sacked a whole army of people before. He knew what had to be done. The day before, we sat down with him for a final strategy session. Immediately he took charge, pulling his chair close to the table and making sure everyone was silent before speaking. 'This is always a tricky process,' he said, with a grave expression. 'But if we handle it right, we can get it over very quickly.'

The textbook procedure, he explained, was to tell everyone simultaneously in separate rooms. 'You don't want people finding out before it's their turn,' he said. 'The important thing is to tell them quickly. You shouldn't spend more than ten minutes with them at the most. And, above all, keep your feelings to yourselves. Your sympathy isn't going to help them. Everything you say must be kept on a strictly professional level.'

Kajsa grimaced. 'God, that's so corporate. I don't see why we have to be that cold.'

'People who have just lost their jobs don't need your sympathy,' Coleman said. 'They don't care. They just want to know the facts.'

'Maybe if they work in a bank,' she countered. 'But these are our friends. We can't just throw them out.'

'What happens after we've told them?' Luke asked, looking equally upset.

'They have to go home and think about it,' Coleman replied.

'Straight away? Can't they even pick up their stuff?'

'Yes, but they can't turn on their computers.'

'Why not?'

'Staff who have been dismissed in these situations have often been known to attempt minor acts of sabotage or send out dirty emails.'

'Who cares if they do send dirty emails,' protested Charlotte. 'It's a basic human dignity to allow people to go back and take stuff off their computers.'

Coleman was impassive. 'I've done this lots of times before,' he said. 'I know what I'm talking about. If anyone wants to retrieve files from their computers they make an appointment to come in a few days later.'

There was a sense of uncomfortable collusion in something that we instinctively felt was wrong, but we knew we had to put the best interests of the company first, and, however inhuman Coleman's approach may have seemed, it was very difficult to argue with its logic. We had to get this over with as quickly as possible and move on. 'The key thing,' he told me, 'is to protect the morale of the people inside the company and to make sure that they want to stay.'

The sky was bright and clear when I woke up the next morning, in stark contrast to the way I was feeling. On my way to the office, Nader Hariri called me on my mobile to wish me good luck for what he knew would be a dreadful day. As I entered the office, I felt a strange sense of dislocation. I couldn't believe that the people I passed on the way to my desk were so unaware of what was about to happen. It seemed almost indecent that they should be in such a sunny mood.

Close examination of a few more than usually sombre faces might have suggested that this was not going to be a normal day. Luke, who couldn't keep still, was pacing nervously about the office. Kajsa didn't even bother to hide her distress. She had already threatened to resign, and it was still entirely possible that she would be the first job loss of the day. She had never agreed that the dismissal of the *Boom* team was the correct thing to do and resented the fact that she was expected to break the news to them.

'Can't you talk to them instead?' she asked.

I shook my head. 'You're their manager,' I said. 'They'll be even more upset if you don't tell them.'

Tony Coleman, who looked like an undertaker in his dark suit and needed only a top hat to complete the picture, started the proceedings promptly at 10 a.m. He had staggered the meetings over the length of the morning so that he could personally be present at as many of them as possible.

With a mixture of guilt and relief, I watched as Kajsa walked briskly off to dismiss her staff. They had been gathered into three rooms, according to their different job descriptions. With Tony Coleman at her heels, she walked into the first room, fired the people there, walked into the next room, fired the people there, and then into the third. It was all over in about fifteen minutes.

Shocked, angry and ashen-faced, the *Boom* team and other members of Kajsa's staff trickled out of the building. Kate Alvarez was in tears. The Gurkhas had been detailed to watch over them to make sure that they left the premises straight away and didn't take any company property. It was all very corporate, very correct and very brutal.

I had only two staff of my own – Esther Galan and Paul Kanareck – and didn't personally have to dismiss anyone, but as CEO I felt the greatest responsibility for all the sackings, and sitting at my desk quietly while my management team had to take part in the blood-letting made me feel even more ashamed. Tony Coleman, who organized the day, may have become the focus of people's anger, but he was only carrying out my orders.

The grim scenes were repeated in boo's other offices. Staff turned up to work in New York to find waiting for them alarmed voice mails from their friends in Europe. Jay spent the entire day in a meeting room laying off more than thirty people. As soon as the US *Boom* team heard what was happening, they instantly got in touch with James Ledbetter and the whole story was on the *Industry Standard* website by noon.

The obvious anger of the *Boom* journalists only served to increase Kajsa's sense of guilt. In the evening she rang up everyone she had fired in the London office and said how sorry she was. She told them to come back in whenever they liked, and to stay as long as they liked. But it was too late. Whatever Tony Coleman may have said about looking after the staff who were staying on, after that day boo.com would never be quite the same again.

The magazine stood as the symbol of what had gone. While it may not have contributed in any obvious way to the core business, none the less it was the voice, soul and spirit of boo. But while I regretted that in our inexperience we had listened as much as we did to Tony Coleman, as terrible as Project Paunch had been, I knew that what we had done was necessary. If we had lost the confidence of the banks and the investors, we would have lost the whole company.

Our attempts to gloss over what had happened were futile. The newspapers knew that something was up. 'There's trouble in e-paradise,' declared the *Guardian*. As far as they were concerned, our restructuring marked not the end of our troubles, but the beginning. 'Is boo's boo-boo a sign of bigger problems?' asked the *New York Post*. The Swedish newspaper *Dagens Industri* even went so far as to say that boo was 'struggling for survival'.

Suddenly, everything we did was made to fit the story. The fact that we had recently begun an end-of-season sale offering up to 40 per cent discounts was taken as a sign of our desperation, although every premium store did the same thing to sell out their old stock before they brought in the new collections for the spring and summer. Perhaps it was because we never closed, but it had never occurred to people that the retail calendar might apply to an e-tailer too.

Under the onslaught our instinct was to batten down the hatches. The most awkward hurdle was an appearance Kajsa and I were due to make, just a week after the mass firing, at First Tuesday, the forum for aspiring internet entrepreneurs. They were expecting an audience of 800. It had been arranged a long time ago and it was very late to cancel, but even so, Financial Dynamics, the PR firm we had engaged a few weeks earlier to help with our IPO, advised us not to turn up.

'It's a terrible idea,' said the firm's CEO Nick Miles. 'There are going to be people there asking some very tough questions. You don't want to be crucified in public.' His idea was that both Kajsa and I should succumb to a nasty bout of flu. There was a lot of it going around at that time.

We both felt petrified at the prospect of making our first appearance at First Tuesday in these circumstances, but knew that it would be too obvious that we had something to hide if we didn't. So we decided to brave it.

As we arrived together with Paul Kanareck at Lord's Cricket Ground, where the event was to take place, I wondered if we weren't doing a very stupid thing. Here we were knocking on the door of the lynch mob when perhaps we should have been running fast in the opposite direction.

'There's still time to catch a taxi to the airport,' joked Paul.

'Yes. Let's go to Brazil,' I replied.

The media were out in force that night. While the First Tuesday audience gathered in a large room, chatting and drinking wine, Kajsa and I did a couple of TV interviews at the back of the next-door conference hall where we were due to speak. At least, I thought, they would give us a taste of the sort of questioning we could expect.

Predictably, the reporter of the CNBC business channel started off by raising our end-of-season sale. Were we backtracking on our no-discount policy? No, I insisted, we were just doing what every big retailer in the world did as a normal part of its business.

'So basically you're saying to me there is no problem?'

'No.'

'No problem at all.'

'No.'

At that point the needle of a lie detector would probably have shot up, but viewers of CNBC would have noticed just the hint of a smile. The CNBC reporter was smiling too, obviously not believing a word.

'Some people have speculated that internet companies are now getting their comeuppance,' she continued. 'In other words that the problems that you are experiencing have to do with the fact that there are too many internet companies in the internet space. Do you agree with that?'

What did I have to say, I wondered, to convince her that we really had no problems? Gamely I tried to explain how what was happening at the moment was simply a natural process of traditional retailers beginning to move into a sector that had previously been dominated by West Coast technology-focused start-ups. I didn't say anything about boo.com. It seemed a safely general answer, with no mention of problems at all.

But in one more example of the strange disconnection between her questions and my answers, she asked, 'So is this all going to push back your IPO?'

'Well, that's a leading question,' I answered. 'I think the most important thing for us to do is create a healthy company.'

Of course we really did have problems, but they weren't the problems the media thought we had. Sometimes it could be a very frustrating game. We had tried to put the best face on a very painful time. We knew that our restructuring was too complicated a process for the media – which depended on simple, dramatic stories – to present with accuracy. But our stonewalling left them free to jump to their own conclusions.

After the interviews, we went up on to the platform and waited nervously for our trial to begin. As I watched the audience trail in from the drinks session next door, I hoped that the wine had put them in a benign mood. But Kajsa and I thought it was safer to stick to water.

We decided to launch the evening with a pre-emptive strike. I even took advantage of some particularly good sales figures for the day before to indulge in a little bit of theatre. 'Let me get the hot issue out of the way,' I said in a preamble to our speech. 'boo has never revealed any financial information and has been seen as very secretive. This has fuelled speculation about targets, burn rate and our valuation. So if you promise that you won't ask any more questions about our finances, I'll give you some numbers.' After a pause, and a murmured assent from the audience, I took a piece of paper from my pocket and read what no one could deny were pretty impressive figures – although the 40 per cent discount had of course made a big difference. The gross order value of goods sold that day was $83,063. This came from 1,078 orders. The number of visitors viewing the site was 36,381, and the conversion rate was 2.96 per cent. I also mentioned that Crédit Suisse First Boston Retail Group had ranked boo.com number one among ten pure e-tail sites, including Amazon.com, in speed and accuracy of orders delivery and processing returns and the website's ease of use and unique features. We then moved quickly into our speech in which we described how boo.com got to be what it was today and outlined our plans for the future.

A large contingent of boo people had shown up. Encouraged by Paul, they made sure to give us a particularly enthusiastic round of applause. After a terrible month, it seemed a sign that the boo spirit might be flickering back to life again. Nader Hariri and Samer Salty were also there, as well as Dean Hawkins, our new CFO, who had begun to work for us that week. So much had happened in the past month that I couldn't help but wonder what he must be thinking.

During the question and answer session afterwards – or the 'interactive mode', as our host described it – the questions may have been tough, but we always found it easier to speak to people directly as it was possible to build up a rapport. One person asked if the figures I had quoted were representative, given the fact that they came during the first week of our sale. There was nothing for it but to put up the stone wall again. I reminded him of the understanding on which I had revealed normally confidential information and said that I could make no comment. 'Should we tell him to leave?' I asked the audience, making a joke out of it. Another person asked about the recent job cuts. Was this the first sign that the internet sector was heading for trouble? 'To say it is the end of the industry is crazy,' replied Kajsa. 'In a maturing business this sort of thing is natural.'

We did our best to suggest that it was business as normal, yet at the same time didn't conceal the fact that there had been mistakes. 'We have always been very ambitious and wanted to do everything in one go,' I said. 'We have been over-optimistic in some areas.'

In spite of some pretty challenging questions, the audience was by and large on our side. After all, they wanted to get e-commerce companies off the ground like we had done and we were there to tell them how to do it. Once the 'interactive mode' was over, people flocked round us and pressed business cards into our hands.

But the more important test was the wider response to our fortunes beyond the walls of Lord's Cricket Ground. Two days later, an article in the *Financial Times* by Caroline Daniel, who had attended the evening, summarized the opinions of industry insiders.

Our technologically sophisticated site had expected too much of users, the article suggested, but we now seemed to be doing everything we could to tailor our ambitions to the real world:

> Mike Ross, chief excutive of Easyshop, an online lingerie retailer, said: 'This will be a great site in two years' time. But it is better to build a site for the lowest common denominator to appeal to the widest possible market.'
>
> boo is learning from these criticisms. Later this month, it will launch a lower bandwidth version of the site, and rebuild the whole site in April. In spite of the European difficulties there has been good feedback in the US, where e-commerce is more established.
>
> Kimberly Greenberger, an associate at Crédit Suisse First Boston, said boo's website rated in the top five of sites it surveyed in the US over Christmas. 'This was very surprising given the publicity surrounding the delayed launch.'

We had weathered a lot of hostile press comment, but the feeling after First Tuesday was that people were now prepared to give us the benefit of the doubt. We had braved the gauntlet and survived.

14

WE WERE ON THE RUN. In the past trouble-filled few weeks it had been a recurring fantasy, which now at last Kajsa and I were making come true. Behind us, lay the Pacific Ocean; ahead Highway 99 twisting up into the mountains through the snowy blackness. The windscreen wipers, switching rhythmically back and forth as they pushed aside the thick wedges of snow, induced a hypnotic calm and I would have been happy if our driver just carried on for ever. Inside this bubble, we were safe. No phones to answer, board meetings to attend, or money to beg. Abdication of responsibility, I thought to myself – I could get a taste for it. I tried to recall my last free weekend – certainly, not this side of the millennium.

It was early March, a month since our appearance at First Tuesday. In a promotional tour of North America, Kajsa and I had just spent the last two days in a Toronto internet café that Jay Herratti had hired demonstrating our website to journalists and showing off our spring collection and some of the new brands that we had recently signed. On Sunday evening we would be flying down to San Francisco and then Los Angeles for more meetings, but now we had a glorious day and a half to ourselves, and had chosen the ski resort of Whistler, British Columbia, as a convenient spot to relax en route.

'We could continue driving,' I joked to Kajsa, 'and live incognito as Eskimos. No one would ever find us out here.'

'Still, it hasn't gone so badly,' said Kajsa.

The tour seemed to be generating a real buzz. As Jay put it, 'Every time you two go on the road, we get about a million hits.'

We could also cheer ourselves with the recent sales figures. In our first trading period, 3 November to 31 January, boo.com had achieved net revenues of $0.7 million; and now, in February alone, the net revenues were also $0.7 million. It was just a tiny fraction of what we expected to achieve eventually, but we had still generated significantly more sales in our first few months after launch than most of the major US e-commerce start-ups, including giants like eToys and drugstore.com or competitors like Fogdog – and far more than other UK players like lastminute.com. The fact that the average basket value in Europe was $110 – $25 more than our original forecast – was also a powerful endorsement of our business model: after the first generation of discount e-tailers, the next generation of e-commerce would involve consumers prepared to pay premium prices online, affording a high margin for the company. There was the comforting sense of turning a corner. We were beginning to take off.

'Wouldn't it be nice not to have to deal with crises all the time,' said Kajsa. 'To have the sort of business where we can just run the business.'

'And even have a weekend every weekend,' I added. Just a few more thickets to work through, I thought, and then surely we would be in open country at last.

Soon Kajsa nodded off and I found my thoughts slipping back over the events of another turbulent month.

It had begun with the arrival of our new chief financial officer, Dean Hawkins. It had been a much-longed-for day, but I knew that I had a lot of explaining to do. The last time I had spoken to Dean was before the mass firings when we were still expecting J.P. Morgan and Robertson Stephens to secure a pre-IPO round of $40 million by 10 February. Since then things had changed a little.

I hadn't wanted to say anything until Dean arrived because I thought it would be much easier to take him through the situation when he was actually in the office. I knew he could hardly have missed all the media coverage of our problems anyway. But now I realized that we would have to work very hard to make him feel comfortable and, in an effort at reassurance, I took him out to lunch at the Circus with Nader Hariri. It passed off reasonably well. Nader said he was delighted that Dean had come on board and assured him that the Millennium Fund would give the company its full support. We also explained that the original pre-IPO round had been cancelled and that instead the company would raise $50 million from new and existing investors before going straight to an IPO.

But soon afterwards Dean went through the finances and was shocked by what he discovered. He had always impressed me before as a calm person, but now, as we spoke about the situation in his office, he seemed to be almost in a state of panic. 'You have debts, you have creditors, you have only $500,000 in the bank! I can't believe that you didn't tell me about any of this!' He went on to accuse me of misleading him. He said that he had only taken the job on the understanding that the $40 million would have been raised by the time he arrived.

I was surprised that someone of his experience should have so little awareness of how unpredictable raising finance could be, but then, I reflected, that was the difference between working for a long-established corporation with deep pockets like Adidas and a company which, however high its profile may have been, was still a start-up.

I conceded that I ought to have kept him informed, while assuring him that the money from the investors would be coming any day now. But it wasn't enough.

'I can't trust you,' said Dean.

A heated argument followed, in which he said he was seriously thinking of resigning. He had so little faith in me, he said, that the only way he could imagine staying was if he had effective control of the company.

I knew we would have to act pretty quickly to calm him down.

'The main thing is to make sure he stays,' said Nader when I told him how Dean had reacted.

The arrival a day or two later of $10 million committed during the funding round seemed to have the desired effect, for at the weekend Dean invited me to his house in Richmond for the afternoon to discuss the situation. 'Maybe I over-reacted.' he said. 'I've done some more thinking and. I'd like to stay if I can be chief operating officer.' This didn't bother me at all, because it was the sort of role that I had envisaged he would eventually play. In the friendly conversation that followed we agreed that we would be a great team: Dean would take responsibility for marketing, retail and finance while I focused on technology, corporate communication, HR and legal issues as well as the overall vision. At last he had been won round, I thought. The only thing we had to agree now were his terms.

Why was it, I wondered as our car climbed higher into the mountains, that so many of the biggest boo events seemed to happen at the weekend? It was exactly a week after my visit to Dean's home that Edward Griffith rang and asked if he could meet me at the Global Café in Golden Square. As soon as I saw him, I could see in his eyes that something was wrong.

He wanted to set up a company of his own, he told me. He had hoped he would have a chance to do so under the aegis of boo itself when, with the help of Henry Elkington, we had initiated Project Champagne. But nothing had come of that and instead, as we brought in more and more senior people like Rob Shepherd and Dean Hawkins, he felt increasingly remote from the centre of things. At Christmas he had been promoted to vice-president of strategy and corporate planning, but it was too much of a back-seat job for someone who wanted to lead teams and manage big projects. The company had grown too big for him, he said. His fondest memories were of the very early days when we were just a handful of people doing everything ourselves.

On a personal level his resignation shook me badly. Dean Hawkins's departure would have been far more damaging, but I had always known the score – he belonged to the modern new breed of corporate executive whose loyalty to the company tended to be as negotiable as salary and equity. Edward, by contrast, was family; he had been through thick and thin with us. It was yet one more warning that as we grew larger we risked losing the spirit that had orginally inspired us.

Our car now passed into the Whistler valley. I looked at my watch. It was midnight. The weekend had begun. For the next 24 hours, I promised myself, I would not think about boo: I would put all my efforts instead into enjoying myself. I wondered if I still remembered how.

That Friday night we had been driving through some of the most breathtaking scenery in the world, but in our wintry cocoon had seen nothing. The next morning as I drew open the curtains of my room, I felt like a child unwrapping a birthday present. Sunlight poured in. My eyes ached as they adjusted to the dazzling expanse of snow. In the distance a lake, a pine forest and looming into the sky the majestic bulk of the Blackcomb and Whistler mountains.

It was 8 a.m. I hurried downstairs, this time not to attend the usual early meeting but to make the most of the slopes. After a buffet breakfast, we hired our ski equipment from the hotel concierge and caught the ski lift to the top of Blackcomb Mountain. The warmth of the sun, the pure mountain air, the sheer sense of speed and space made my spirits soar. When we could enjoy such peace, why were we always putting ourselves in such stressful situations? The worries of the last few months seemed trivial, even illusory.

We skied miles and miles, breaking only for lunch at a café near the top of the slopes, where we sat with our skis outside on wooden benches relaxing in the sunlight. At dusk we returned exhausted to the hotel and, sitting by a large fireplace, reminisced about the last few years – the poetry festival, our publishing company, bokus and now boo.com. This was the overview of our lives that the sheer pace of events had prevented us from taking before. Like trekkers standing on a mountain summit, we could look back along the valley and see the long way that we had come. It was wonderful to be able to chat to Kajsa not about some task that urgently needed to be done but just about our lives in general. As boo had grown, such conversations had become increasingly rare. A gulf had opened up between us. She had a big marketing department to run, while, as CEO, I spent most of my time with other senior managers. She also had to cope with the conflict between boo and her personal life. In the office she had little time for casual conversation because there was always a pressure to get home to spend time with her young daughter Alva.

After dinner we retired early to rest our aching limbs and to enjoy a deep, restorative sleep. When I met Kajsa at breakfast early the next morning, I felt like a science fiction hero who had just stepped out of an energizer machine. I was ready to take on the world, looking forward to another half-day of skiing but also eager to get back to work. The mental space that our break afforded had even enabled me to get round to thinking about the terms we would offer Dean

Hawkins as our new COO. After a large breakfast of coffee, pancakes and maple syrup, I scribbled down an offer on a sheet of paper and faxed it to Dean at his home in Richmond. I would be seeing him on Wednesday in Portland when he would join Tobin and me for a presentation to Nike, and I wanted to outline a basis for discussion:

A quick note about your new compensation package. Let's continue talking on the phone and in Portland on Wednesday.
Company valuation in 2–3 years 1 billion.
Base: 1.25% of equity post IPO
exercise price 3.98   value $8.5m
Additional to the above you will get an extra bonus of equity if the company can float within a certain timeframe.
IPO before end of June, 1.25% of equity post IPO
exercise price 3.98
IPO before end of September, 0.625% of equity post IPO
exercise price 3.98 per cent

No explanation of the detail was required for it to be obvious that he could expect to become fabulously rich in a few months' time if our IPO went ahead as planned. As I went to endless trouble trying to make him happy enough to stay, I had taken to thinking of Dean as one of those expensive signings who when they arrive at their new football club sit on the bench for weeks without scoring any goals. But no footballer I knew, in any league around the world, could hope to receive a compensation package like this. It reflected just how very badly we needed him. For the way the game was going now we risked being relegated to a lower league and losing a fortune. The almost continual difficulties we had been having in our relationship with banks and shareholders underlined the importance of having him in place to work out a prudent financial strategy, but also his retail background with Adidas meant that he could exert immense influence with suppliers. The sooner I could get him on the pitch properly motivated the better.

After an early lunch, Kajsa and I set off back down Highway 99 to Vancouver and caught an early evening flight down the coast to San Francisco, where we checked into the Hotel Monaco on Geary

Street. We were in high spirits, looking forward to catching up with Jay the next day for the second part of our tour. Newly invigorated and suntanned, we wondered if he would notice the difference.

But waiting for me outside my door the next morning, along with a copy of the *San Francisco Chronicle*, was a fax from Dean Hawkins. After the euphoria of the past two days, reading it was like slamming into a brick wall.

He could not accept my offer, he wrote, and as time was now dragging on he would have to be 'very direct'. He then set out his terms for staying at boo.com and made it clear that he was 'not really expecting to enter a negotiation'. He wanted to have an immediate option for 2 per cent of the company to be based on the post-IPO shareholding structure of the company and with an exercise price of $5 million. He also wanted a second option for 2 per cent if boo was floated on the stock market before the end of June 2000, or 1 per cent if it was floated before the end of October. Then with his usual thoroughness he outlined a vesting schedule – the period over which he would be able to sell the shares – and a contingency plan against the possible buyout of boo.

Dean was obviously going to be very expensive, but at the same time I couldn't help being a bit impressed. He had shown just the grasp of financial detail we needed. As one of the key conditions that J.P. Morgan had set down for proceeding to the IPO was that Dean should have fully integrated himself into the business, there was really no choice but to accept his terms – although it bothered me that they were so disproportionate to what any other senior executive in the company was receiving. The situation had its absurd aspect. However useful Dean might be in the future, the most important thing now was simply that he should stay, that everyone should realize he was ours.

Getting Dean to stay had been an extremely difficult affair, but at least, I thought, now it was over. But I was wrong. Two days later, while Kajsa flew back to London to attend the opening of an exhibition at the National Portrait Gallery called 'Business Leaders of the 21st Century', at which our portraits were to be unveiled, I moved on to Portland. I met Dean and Tobin together briefly in the evening. Then the next morning, Dean joined me for an early breakfast in our hotel before we set off for Beaverton to see Nike with Tobin, and our new head of merchandising, Ed Whitehead.

'I've decided I want to leave,' he said.

It was my turn to be shocked. 'Have you really thought this through?' I asked.

'I've had a really good offer from Chello,' he said, 'which I'm going to accept.'

Chello was a multibillion-dollar broadband ISP in Holland with which boo had been discussing the possibility of a strategic partnership. They were hoping to go public in May and were looking for a new CFO to handle the flotation.

Before I had a chance to recover from the shock, Tobin Ireland walked into the room.

'Let's talk about this back in London,' I said to Dean and we changed the subject to Nike.

Tobin looked excited and a little apprehensive. 'This is a really big deal for us,' he said, not realizing that an even bigger deal had just fallen through. I was now kicking myself for agreeing to do the PR tour. I should have stayed in London until Dean's contract had been resolved.

'It's really odd my meeting Nike like this after having worked for Adidas,' said Dean. Apparently the rivalry between the two companies was so intense that their two CEOs had never met and refused to talk to each other.

I found myself desperately hoping that at the Nike meeting we'd make some miraculous breakthrough and that the immediate offer of a supplier agreement would persuade Dean to change his mind. But Mary Kate Buckley was still playing hard to get, and the recent headlines certainly wouldn't have encouraged her to consider us a good match.

In our presentation we decided to take the honest approach, even quoting some of the negative press and then explaining the true situation. One headline that would have disturbed Nike was 'boo.com in distress sale': like all full-price retailers, we explained that we had end-of-season sales to clear product. Another was 'boo.com is running out of cash': we had just secured another significant private round of funding, we told them, and were also considering some strategic investment deals.

From that point onwards, the story we had to tell got more and more impressive. After taking them through our fast-growing sales figures, we talked about recent improvements to the site which showed beyond doubt that we had put our early technology problems behind us. Speed had increased by 50 per cent; we had launched a lower bandwidth site a month ago; we had enormously simplified the purchase path; and we were well on the way to launching Version 2 in the second quarter of the year. All the hard data from the site in operation proved that our business model was working.

But the reason why they should really love us was our brand. 'If you have a body, you are an athlete,' Nike's co-founder Bill Bowerman famously said. This definition, which lay at the heart of the Nike brand, sat well with boo's identification of the urban active lifestyle as the dominant mass market aspiration. boo's brand positioning was neither sports nor fashion but a fusion of the two.

Nike was impressed. I was confident that we would win them over. Dean, I knew, would be a lot more difficult, but I was determined over the next week, back in London, to have a go. After all, in those heady days when the Nasdaq had pushed the bubble to its limit, I had every reason to be confident in my powers of persuasion.

Indeed, in this fairy-tale time even the British prime minister was listening to me. On 16 March, I proudly went along to a meeting at Downing Street to brief Tony Blair on e-commerce in Europe ahead of a EU summit in Lisbon. The Dutch prime minister Wim Kok was there too. Paul Kanareck had arranged for some of the Swedish media to take photographs when I emerged from No. 10. It would drive some welcome traffic to the website, I thought as I smiled for the cameras, yet at the same time I reflected on the irony: here I was advising the Prime Minister when I had to return to the office to deal with a possibly fatal blow to the company.

Somehow, over the course of the last few weeks, while Dean had continued to haggle over his terms, we had managed to raise $28 million of our $50 million pre-IPO round. There were various understandings that would have accounted for the remainder – Nader in particular had worked hard to find new investors, several of whom had made provisional commitments to take shares in the company. But now that Hawkins was determined to leave, such undertakings would quickly melt away. With the Nasdaq over twice what it had been a year ago, there was an uncomfortable sense of a jackpot eluding our grasp.

The lesson of the last few weeks was the very painful one that however awful things seem to be, they can always get a little worse. I had finally resigned myself to Dean's departure and refocused my efforts on minimizing the damage that it would cause. But if he had arrived with bad grace, his departure was even worse.

'I expect some sort of leaving package as compensation,' he said when I dropped by his office to talk about the matter.

I raised my eyebrows. He'd hardly even arrived.

'You have to realize,' he went on, 'that this whole experience has put me in a very difficult position. I have my reputation to think of.' He then asked for a settlement of six months' salary.

With hindsight, I clearly should have kept him informed of developments before he arrived to work for us, but I had done nothing formally wrong, and, in any case, our past differences were settled when we later agreed that he should become COO. Far from being damaged by his association with boo, it seemed to me that he had profited from it enormously, finally using his position as our CFO as a stepping stone for his job with Chello. But the last thing we wanted was for him to walk out and then bad-mouth us. What would that do for investor confidence?

'I don't think you have any case at all,' I replied, 'but you know that especially in the present situation, the most important thing for me is to preserve the goodwill of this company. So I'll have to accept if you sign a confidentiality agreement. But I want you to know that I feel very uncomfortable about this and under normal circumstances I would fight it.'

'I understand,' he said, 'but you need to understand me too.'

It was true that he had had a rough ride. He had suddenly found himself in a situation that he would never willingly have accepted. He was also uncomfortable with the pressure shareholders were putting on him to do a quick IPO when he didn't think we were ready for it – he himself would have preferred to bring in a big strategic investor. But I didn't think that the undoubted stress of coping with all this was worth six months' salary. Giving it to him was one of the bitterest decisions I've ever had to make in my life, but I knew I had to take it if the company was to survive.

I was almost beginning to long for the good old days with Patrik. In seven weeks, boo.com had moved from a promising situation to the brink of disaster. We needed a committed CFO working hard to sort out the company's difficulties, not one that we had to beg to stay. It would have been better if he had left instantly.

The only way I could find to come to terms with the situation was to seek refuge in black humour.

'Do you think we should get the Gurkhas to take care of him?' I asked Paul Kanareck shortly after our group legal counsel, Christopher Heather, had drawn up Dean's confidentiality agreement. 'It would save us a lot of money.'

'Well, that's what they're trained for.'

The funny thing was that the business itself was continuing to go from strength to strength, yet it had always been that intangible thing, confidence, that mattered the most, and, like dogs smelling fear, the senior executives could sense the unease. When shortly afterwards Luke Alvarez announced his resignation, I almost felt like asking him why he had taken so long to make up his mind.

The only bright spot of news that March was the dismissal of the unpopular Tony Coleman after it was discovered that he had put false information on his CV. I talked to Christopher Heather about what we ought to do and a few days later we put our plan into operation. While Paul Kanareck briefed Chandra Gurung to have the Gurkhas wait close by in case there was any violence, Christopher and I marched straight into Tony's office and sat down. We told him that he was suspended for two weeks pending the results of an internal investigation. Meanwhile he was to hand over his company mobile and Palm Pilot and leave the building at once. He was not even to switch off his computer. With five or six Gurkhas, I personally escorted him down to the street. Contrary to our fears, he went very quietly, presumably lost in admiration at the execution of a textbook suspension and stunned to be receiving a taste of his own medicine at last. Two weeks later, faced with the alternative of having his contract terminated, he resigned.

As we struggled to close the funding round, I asked Jay Herratti to come over from New York to help cope with the growing crisis and in particular to help us in the hunt for funding. I then called an emergency board meeting for 5 April to address the issue. Rachel Yasue, who must have begun to feel a bit like a yo-yo, was back again as our interim CFO.

It had never been easy getting all of our board members in one place at the same time and this latest meeting was no exception. The only people in our conference room that Wednesday afternoon besides Kajsa and myself were Christopher Heather and Rachel Yasue. The others all attended by speakerphone.

The mood was tense. First, Rachel explained our financial situation. J.P. Morgan's attempts to raise $50 million from the existing shareholders had been only partly successful. Most of the $28 million received in the course of the last two months had already been spent on the payment of long-standing debts. The remaining $22 million was urgently needed just for the company to be able to continue functioning, never mind proceed to an IPO. A heated debate ensued in which the as-ever-forthright François Tison placed the blame firmly on J.P. Morgan. 'They've promised to raise money for the company three times now and they haven't done it,' he said.

Luciano Favero from 21Investimenti grunted in agreement. 'We're going to write them a letter to complain,' he said.

'OK,' I replied. 'But that doesn't change the situation. I think we have to start thinking about other ways of getting the money together.'

'Like what?' Tison asked.

I suggested that the board members themselves should call the shareholders who were still hesitating to put up more money and put as much pressure on them as they could. 'They need to realize that this is a serious situation.'

'Then I think we have to find some way to show them that we're all committed to sorting this out,' said Tison. 'It's time we found out what J.P. Morgan is prepared to do. They could probably put up $10 million. That's nothing for a big bank like them.' Such a gesture from our own bank would act as a vital vote of confidence in the company.

I reminded Tison that I had actually suggested the same thing to J.P. Morgan some weeks earlier, but that their equity division had rejected the idea, arguing – against the colleagues of theirs who had been advising us – that our valuation was too high.

Tison bristled. 'Then how the hell can they advise other people to put money into this company?'

It was a good point and the meeting closed with the decision that I would urgently raise the issue with J.P. Morgan again.

'I thought we had already been through this,' said Brian Crawford when I rang him that same afternoon. 'I can't make decisions like this anyway.'

'Then you need to put us in touch with whoever does make the decisions, and you need to do it now.'

A conference call was arranged for two or three days later with Preben Prebensen, J.P. Morgan's head of investment banking in Europe. Tison and Favero took part, to exert maximum pressure.

'It's time you showed some commitment!' declared Tison after running through the bank's various failings over the last few months.

'We've already done that,' replied Prebensen, making the point that J.P. Morgan had taken all its fees in shares. He also said that we were losing sight of the fact that the bank's advisory and investment businesses operated independently.

'Well you need to make an exception this time,' I said. 'It doesn't have to be a lot of money. But this is really important for the company.'

Tison was more direct. 'It's your reputation on the line as well if this company goes bust,' he said. 'You should think very carefully about that.'

Prebensen sighed. Here he was, one of the most senior executives in a major Wall Street bank, being bullied by the investors in a start-up. 'I'll have to get back to you,' he said.

I couldn't forget Tison's comment at the board meeting that $10 million was nothing to a bank like J.P. Morgan, but Brian Crawford's call the next day quickly brought me back to earth. 'OK,' he said. 'We'll give you $1.3 million.' This figure represented a pro rata addition to their current shareholding. It seemed less a vote of confidence than one of pity – we were a case deserving of charity.

With the sudden departure of three senior executives and the continuing struggle to complete the current round of financing, rumours about the health of the company multiplied. Dean Hawkin's departure in particular, so soon after he had arrived, caused enormous worry, especially within the management team. In an effort to restore morale, I called a meeting of the entire London staff. The last time there had been such an event, we had gathered in the Café Royale. But in this new climate of cost-conscious austerity, we had to look for a more modest venue. After ringing around, Esther Galan discovered that if we could convene and close our meeting before the start of the early afternoon matinée, we would get an excellent rate from the Odeon, Leicester Square. So we arranged to meet there at 8.30 a.m. on 10 April. It was something of a come-down, but we had to be philosophical.

'Do you think we can afford to have coffee and croissants?' I asked.

'I don't see why not,' replied Esther. 'If everyone has one only each.'

Jay and Paul had helped me to draft a speech and I arranged to meet with Paul early on the day itself for one last run-through. I got to the office at 7 a.m., as we had agreed. When, after half an hour, he still hadn't shown up, I tried his mobile to find that it had been switched off.

Extremely put out, I set off for the Odeon at 8 a.m. This was one time, I thought, as I passed through the garish cinema foyer, with its popcorn and confectionery counters, when I could really have done with some support.

Grabbing a styrofoam cup of coffee, I marched into the auditorium and joined Kajsa, Esther and Jay in the front row of the stalls. After they had wished me good luck, Jay stood up and clapped his hands to get everyone's attention. As I went up onto the stage, I could sense that people were expecting grim news, and I took some comfort from the thought that what I had to tell them would probably come as a pleasant surprise. When I turned round, I was struck by the vastness of the auditorium. Our 250 staff, huddled in the first few rows of the stalls, looked strangely vulnerable in the gaping darkness of a theatre that could accommodate over 2000.

'Good morning,' I said when everyone had finally settled down. 'I've called this meeting today because I know many of you have expressed concerns about some of the difficulties we've been having lately, and I'd like to try to convince you that our business is in better shape than it has ever been, and that we have some great opportunities to look forward to.'

I ran through our achievements – launching the world's first global e-tailing platform, convincing over forty of the world's top brands to sell their merchandise through us, building a powerful marketing machine, improving the speed and performance of the site. As a pioneer we had made just about every mistake that could be made, but we had come through this difficult time to become one of the leading online e-tailers.

The ambitious nature of the company meant that it had consumed a large amount of capital and its future funding was bound to be a challenge. But our investors were extremely supportive, and because of the company's reputation as the leader in its sector we would continue to attract support.

I then turned to the recent high-profile resignations. 'The people *are* the company,' I declared, 'and every person leaving is a loss. But we all know that the best people work at boo and it's only natural that we should be a target.'

Indeed, our head start in European e-commerce and our high profile meant that we were really *the* target. With the dot.com boom now at its zenith, head-hunters clogging up our switchboard had become an unpleasant fact of life, and they had some powerful incentives to offer. It wasn't uncommon for people to double their salaries as well as receive massive sign-on bonuses.

'We wish good luck to those who choose to leave, but shall continue to do the best we can to make people want to stay,' I continued. 'Those who do stay will have chosen a leader, a famous brand and a company that has now gone through the bumps and is poised for success.'

I apologized for not having made more of a personal effort to communicate developments within the company. The mad non-stop round of meeting investors and suppliers had made it difficult, but I promised that from now we would have regular meetings like the one today.

'Be humble and honest,' Paul had written on the draft speech. Well, I had done my best.

The whole point of the meeting had been not to suggest a crisis, but to give an overview of the enormous progress we had made. So after I had finished, presentations on key aspects of the business followed. Rob Shepherd spoke about the improvements that had been made to the website and the forthcoming Version 2, while Brian McCarter spoke about our brand positioning. We all knew what boo meant, but like many of the best things in life found it very hard to put in to words. Now at last we had worked out a coherent statement. boo, Brian explained, was an authority on contemporary style. People looked to boo.com, for its knowledge and expertise. boo was a collection. Every single item on the site had been selected for a reason and told a piece of the boo.com story. boo was a resource. People came to the site not just to buy but also to explore and learn.

As Brian waxed lyrical, I was amazed but also alarmed by how much passion you could pack into a three-letter word. 'boo reflects a way of life that is all about curiosity, creativity, energy and truth . . .' If we weren't careful, I thought, we'd be taking on the Scientologists next, and it was with some relief that I listened to Brian explain that boo could also be 'irreverent, playful, fun and sexy'.

It was a pretty good pep talk, but the biggest round of applause that morning was for Sara Dworkin, whom I introduced as our new head of HR. We hadn't announced Tony Coleman's dismissal, but everyone knew what Sara's appearance meant.

In the foyer, on the way out, I bumped into Paul. He had overslept and arrived halfway through the meeting. 'How could you do this to me?' I said. 'It was my most important speech. I should probably sack you if you weren't so loyal.'

Paul, who had had almost no chance to recover from weeks of round-the-clock effort, could only yawn in agreement.

★

'We will support you,' Nader Hariri had promised in the Dorchester more than six months ago when he had first become an investor. 'We are always there in the good times and bad times.' I don't think he could have expected the bad times to have been quite as bad as they were now, but he was true to his word. Over the next few weeks, as the two of us met virtually every day at the Dorchester to discuss the latest progress with shareholders and other potential investors, Nader was always quietly reassuring. 'We'll get through this somehow,' he said.

The walk from Regent Street through Mayfair to the Dorchester operated as a kind of pressure valve, releasing the enormous tension that built up in the office. It was a chance just to relax and reflect a little. In the calm surroundings of the Dorchester, I could talk openly with Nader, without having to speak in the usual guarded terms for the sake of employee morale or investor confidence. I was able to be myself, knowing that Nader wanted to do whatever he could to help and that he believed as much in boo as I did.

Earlier in April, he had tried to introduce us to some new investors in Paris, and now, as it began to seem unlikely that the other existing shareholders would come up with the money needed to complete the round, he devoted himself full time to trying to find a solution. The biggest frustration for him was the lack of unity among the core shareholders. In the blinkered pursuit of their own narrow agendas, they seemed unable to agree an approach that would be in the best interests of the company – and ultimately themselves. The key it seemed to him was to find some framework that would allow the shareholders to co-operate constructively. So he introduced us to Wasserstein Perella, a US investment bank that the Millennium Fund had worked with in the past. Wasserstein was known mostly for handling mergers and acquisitions, and a couple of months before it had acted as an adviser to Time Warner in its $160 billion merger with AOL. But it also had a reputation for handling crisis situations.

Soon after our staff meeting at the Odeon, Nader and I went along to the firm's office in St James's Street and met one of their senior bankers, Ken Buckfire, who was usually based in New York. He was the investment banking equivalent of a green-beret. When the bullets were flying and everyone was running for cover, he would be sent in to sort things out.

'Yeah, you've got problems,' Buckfire told me. 'But I've seen a lot of companies in much worse shape than this.' He promised to think about potential solutions, but also to look at the company's complicated shareholder structure. As important a priority as finding new investors was to get the ones we already had to work together properly. 'Don't worry,' he said. 'We'll find the answer.'

Our struggle for funding had not been helped by a long slide in the value of the Nasdaq technology index since reaching its high point on 10 March. The question on everyone's lips was whether the internet bubble had finally burst. Friday, 14 April 2000 brought the resounding answer, as the Nasdaq plunged 355 points, or nearly 10 per cent, the worst one-day fall in the index's thirty-year history. To compound the misery, the Dow Jones Industrial Average had fallen 616 points and all the commentators were expecting a bloodbath when the markets opened on Monday.

By grim coincidence, a board meeting had been arranged for the very next day to review our progress in finding new investors. In the circumstances, it was a pleasant surprise that anyone had even bothered to turn up. I entered the meeting room to find Nader Hariri and Luciano Favero already there.

In the light of the morning's headlines, nothing really needed to be said. We all knew that the battle for funding had now turned decisively against us

Rachel Yasue then made the seriousness of our situation even more plain with her report on the latest state of our finances. 'We have hardly any money left in the bank,' she said. 'We're going to need at least $4 million to meet all our commitments and to fund the business for the next two weeks.' She also pointed out that we had about $20 million of outstanding debts, of which more than half was already overdue.

At this point I invited Samer Salty to address the board. Concerned about our precarious position, he had spoken to contacts at Morgan Stanley about possible investors, and they had put him in touch with the Texas Pacific Group.

'Most of you have probably heard of them before,' said Samer Salty.

I didn't know about the others, but I certainly had. Texas Pacific was an American private equity firm that had just been involved in the largest leveraged buyout ever seen in Europe with the near-$6 billion acquisition of Britain's Punch Taverns and the pubs division of Allied Domecq. In buying up underperforming businesses, it took an aggressive and unsentimental approach. A few months earlier, for example, it had bought Bally, the 150-year-old Swiss shoe and fashion accessory company. In a matter of weeks it had shut 100 stores and fired 500 staff. But it was hard to argue with their previous results. When in 1996 they bought Ducati, the Italian motorcycle manufacturer, it had been on the verge of bankruptcy, but only three years later Texas Pacific were able to sell shares in the company at a 400 per cent profit.

Although the terms of any investment were still hazy, Salty explained that Texas Pacific had said that it might be prepared to invest around $50 million by the end of the week. 'But it will be on a low valuation,' he said.

'How low?' François Tison asked.

'Something like $20 million to $25 million.'

It was an index of how far our fortunes had fallen. boo was now worth less than when we had first gone out to investors with nothing more than a business plan.

Luciano Favero was the first to break the shocked silence. 'That's ridiculous!' he said. At such a valuation, Texas Pacific would benefit from a 'wipe out' round in which it would swamp the shares of the existing shareholders.

But however humiliating, we had no choice but to talk, and the meeting resolved that Salty should ask Texas Pacific to put its offer in writing for consideration at a second board meeting the next day. In the meantime, to ensure that we had the short-term funding to continue in business, Brian Crawford from J.P. Morgan was asked over the next 24 hours to make one more approach to existing shareholders. They were to be told that without the money, there was a strong likelihood that the company would have to cease trading. We hoped that this would finally make the difference.

With his usual calm Crawford added 'Get $4 million' to his 'To do' list, but it was a difficult enough task during normal banking hours let alone at the weekend. The biggest crises, I began to realize, were when absurdity became routine.

The meeting broke up with a warning from Christopher Heather: 'You should all be very aware,' he said, 'that the company can only keep trading if there's a reasonable prospect of being able to continue to raise funding.'

The words were chilling, but as grave as our situation was, I still felt confident that a solution would be found. However half-hearted the other investors may have been, both Bernard Arnault and the Millennium Fund had shown themselves determined to do what they could to put the company on a satisfactory financial footing. While Millennium had the most to lose financially if boo went bust, I sensed that Arnault was more concerned about the broader implications. A few months earlier, Arnault had created an investment company called europ@web in which most of his internet investments, including boo, were now held. His plan was to sell a chunk of europ@web through an IPO within the next few months and he was understandably anxious to avoid anything that might shake the confidence of an already jittery internet sector. Then waiting in the wings were Texas Pacific and Wasserstein Perella, with the formidable Ken Buckfire working hard to find a structure that would unlock funds from the present shareholders as well as attract new ones. I had also talked to Chris Bataillard, who had now left J.P. Morgan but promised to do whatever he could to help from the outside. One possibility he had raised was that we should work with Flemings, a British merchant bank. He had contacts there and felt that if J.P. Morgan were dragging their feet they had the sort of aggression we needed to organize a quick IPO. It had seemed only a remote eventuality, but in just a few hours I would come to wish that I had listened to him more carefully.

The next day, after lunch, I was browsing the stalls at Portobello Market in an attempt to take my mind off the meeting due to take place that night when Brian Crawford rang me on my mobile.

'Any luck with the fund-raising?' I asked.

'Well, actually something else has come up that we need to talk about first.'

'What's happened?'

'We've decided that it's inappropriate for us to be involved in this process any more. We think that you should look for a more suitable adviser.'

'What are you saying? Don't tell me you're quitting now.'

Crawford hesitated. 'I'm sorry, but the general feeling is that there's very little we can do to help you. Your chances of going to IPO are very low now. You saw what happened in the markets last week. Even if it bounces back, people are going to be a lot more selective. You should probably talk to Flemings. Chris has already updated them on your situation.'

'So I guess that means you won't be investing the $1.3 million, either?'

'I'm afraid not,' said Crawford. 'Look, this wasn't my decision.'

'I know,' I said. 'But that doesn't help me right now.'

It wasn't just the impossibility of proceeding to an IPO. J.P. Morgan was also worried about the implications of a deal with Texas Pacific. Before it could take place, shareholders would have to agree on a valuation and, as they had all invested at different levels, the bank would have the difficult task of mediating between them. Its job had been to advise us, not to be the ringmaster it increasingly seemed to be becoming. It wasn't mentioned, but the bank must also have worried that some of the shareholders who had invested at a very high valuation might consider suing them.

'Jesus,' said Kajsa when I called her to break the news. 'Can it get any worse?'

As I headed into the office that afternoon, François Tison called. He had received an email that Brian Crawford had sent to all the board members outlining the bank's decision.

'Have you seen it?' he asked, sounding livid.

'Yes.'

'Is it for real?'

'I'm afraid so.'

'I cannot believe it,' he replied. 'I'm sending a reply. They're not going to get off so easily.'

Tison's email, which he copied to me and the rest of the board, didn't hold anything back: 'I think it's absolutely outrageous that you would advise us to seek another adviser at 2 p.m. on a Sunday afternoon . . . This is a severe blow to the company, maybe the final blow, and I am very sad, not to say upset, to see it coming from you.'

Tison might have been the most outspoken, but his feelings were echoed by all our board members, who rang me one by one to express their annoyance and frustration.

That evening Nader brought along some extra firepower to the meeting. Over the last few weeks he had kept his cousin Saad up to date with developments. Convinced now that the situation had become desperate, Saad, in consultation with the board of the Millennium Fund, decided to send the Fund's close advisor Ali Kolaghassi to London to help out and find a solution. A tough but reassuring presence, Ali was an expert in restructuring and generally stressful situations. As usual, we struggled to set up the various links to the conference call, and people talked over each other as they strained to hear often faint or echoing voices. I wondered what Ali made of the chaos, but at least the issues at stake were simple.

Item number one on the agenda: $4 million, which we needed at once if we were to continue trading. One by one, I asked the investors if they were prepared to put up any more money, and the usual poker game followed in which they looked to Arnault and the Millennium Fund, the two lead investors most heavily exposed, to protect their investment. It had been a depressing feature of the whole disastrous round. The attitude of the smaller investors was that in any crisis the big players would always stump up because they had the most to lose. The big players, for their part, became increasingly insistent that the other investors should share the risk. A waiting game then ensued, in which a problem that might have been solved easily at an early stage escalated into a major crisis.

François Tison, who was calling from a party in Paris, had stepped out on to a balcony to join our meeting. We could hear the rain driving down and the occasional peal of thunder. Quickly, as if he were without an umbrella to shelter himself, he said, 'We can probably put up another million, but I must check with Arnault first.'

I looked across the table at Nader and Ali Kolaghassi. 'We need to talk about this,' said Nader. The two left the room. I drew a series of intricate doodles on my pad while we waited in silence. Five minutes later they came back in.

'OK,' said Nader. 'We'll put up the other 2 million. But we want to be closely involved in working out any solution.'

There was an almost audible sigh of relief as the meeting now turned to Texas Pacific's written offer, which their European managing director, Abel Halpern, had faxed to our office earlier that day. 'I should stress,' Halpern wrote, 'that we will view issues such as valuation with extreme discipline and scepticism. As such we will be quite inflexible once we have developed a firm view and will not be interested in entering a protracted process of negotiation.'

After the meeting, I took Nader and Ali aside to thank them for all that they had done. Without them, the company would certainly not have survived the weekend.

'Now you understand how difficult it is to make a decision with our shareholders,' I said to Ali.

'Nader warned me,' he replied. 'But I had no idea it was this bad.'

After the last 48 hours it was of course a triumph just to be alive, but when I broke the news to the senior management team the next day they were understandably dismayed.

'It's a terrible idea,' said Tobin Ireland. 'These people are asset strippers. They'll come in and tear the company apart.'

It was a view that everyone else shared. But once I had explained that we could no longer hope for our existing shareholders to bail us out again, they realized that there was little alternative. Texas Pacific would put an end to boo as we knew it, and probably fire the entire management team, but it was the most realistic chance we had of saving the business.

Shortly afterwards Jay and I met some Texas Pacific executives to arrange a due diligence meeting later that week. Tobin was shocked to discover that one of them had been an old Mckinsey colleague of his called Huw Phillips. 'Do you expect me to humiliate myself by presenting to a former colleague who is then going to come in and tell me what to do?!'

I was worried whether Tobin was going to turn up for our presentation and indeed whether we were doing the right thing talking to Texas Pacific at all. I was reassured when Richard Grigison of Morgan Stanley, who were hoping to advise Texas Pacific in any buy-out deal, dropped by the office on the same day. 'They're good guys,' he said. 'They may be tough, but they understand fashion too.'

Two days later, executives from both Texas Pacific and some of the companies it had invested in turned up for the due diligence session.

I had expected humourless number crunchers, but was taken aback to find as friendly and relaxed a bunch of people as you could hope to meet. Even Huw Phillips seemed charming. It made me eager to meet their managing director, who had written such an uncompromising letter to our board. Perhaps his bark would turn out to be worse than his bite.

'Oh, Abel's coming along later,' I was told.

If the Texas Pacific team had managed to surprise us, we certainly surprised them. They had expected an uncertain, defensive performance from a company on its knees. Instead, we spoke with the confidence of a team that had already spent many of the previous weeks rehearsing and gathering together information to present for our IPO.

After giving a brief introduction and sitting through the early part of the presentation, I slipped out of the room to attend to other matters. Burning with curiosity, I also did some websurfing to find out what I could about Abel Halpern. What I read was pretty impressive. Not only did he have a Harvard MBA, but he had also worked as a trade union organiser in Las Vegas. He had even served an internship in Sheffield with the British National Union of Miners. It seemed an appealingly unusual career path. As one article put it, he was 'a poacher turned gamekeeper'.

Then, suddenly, without any warning, there he was himself.

'Ernst,' said Jay, 'Meet Abel Halpern.'

I looked up to see looming before my desk an extremely large man in his early thirties with big round glasses and an immaculately cut designer suit.

'Abel would like a quick word with us,' said Jay.

'Sure,' I said, and we went into one of our small meeting rooms.

Halpern got straight to the point. 'I don't want to waste your time or mine,' he said, 'so I'll tell you exactly what I think. You have two assets: your brand and your back end logistics and fulfilment platform. We aren't really interested in the brand. But we think we can probably do something with the other bits.'

It was strange. I knew exactly what sort of company Texas Pacific was, but this verdict still surprised me.

'If we're to invest,' Halpern continued, 'a good chunk of our money is going to go on paying off debts. We're also going to have to do a lot of restructuring to make a profitable business out of this. You have really good people, young creative people, but most of them are going to have to go. You need to think, can you run this business with fifty people? If we come in, we'll need to do some radical things.'

It was beginning to sound very nasty indeed, but once again Halpern managed to surprise me.

'So what I'm saying is that we'll only do this if you're prepared to accept a zero valuation.'

Jay was open-mouthed. 'Zero? You mean nothing? You're saying this company is worth nothing?'

'I'm saying those are the only terms that we'd accept.' But he pointed out that the present shareholders could potentially get some return on their investment in a couple of years or so once boo started making money. 'You and your shareholders need to be prepared emotionally to deal with this. If you are, then we can keep talking. 'If not, there's no point in taking things any further.'

As soon as Halpern's army of executives had trooped out of the office, I rang Nader and Tison. 'What am I to tell them?' I asked.

'We'll have to think of something else,' said Nader calmly.

Tison's reply was as robust as ever: 'Tell them to go to hell!'

15

WE OWED ABEL HALPERN a favour. While I disagreed with his estimate of the company's worth, his other advice, unpleasant but sound, gave us the sort of shake-up we badly needed. If we were to make the company attractive to investors, then we had not only to restructure it, as we had done back in January, but also to rethink the entire business – to rationalize how in cold commercial terms we could exploit it to the maximum. The lesson of Texas Pacific was that nothing was sacrosanct.

So after we told them to go to hell, Jay and I went to Canaletto, an Italian sandwich bar on Beak Street and, over lunch, planned how we would rework the company. Now that we had been forced to think about it, we realized that it was really two businesses in one. There was boo.com the international e-tailer of sports and designer clothes; but then there was the technology and logistics platform that could ship products anywhere in Europe or the US within five days.

This second part wasn't a business yet, but there was every reason why it should be. The platform was capable of handling upwards of 15,000 orders a day and could feasibly be modified to cope with a far greater figure, but at present we were using only a tiny fraction of its current capacity. We could sell our spare capacity to retailers who were looking for a ready-made global retailing platform.

It was an idea that we had already toyed with the previous year in our discussions with Henry Elkington and his consultants at Boston Consulting Group, but our notion of two distinct companies took it one step further: boo.com, the retailer, would become the first customer of this new e-commerce distribution business.

In an extraordinarily productive afternoon we even came up with a name for the new company. Having previously called our plan to find new investors Operation Swordfish, we decided to go for a variation on a theme.

'Let's call it Dolphin,' Jay said.

'Why?'

'Because Dolphins are intelligent. They're also friendly, and if this is the plan that's going to save us, we need to name it after a friendly fish.'

'Dolphins are mammals,' I pointed out.

'Who's going to invest in a company called Shark?'

'OK,' I agreed. 'Dolphin it is.'

The management team responded enthusiastically to the idea, embracing it as a radical but obvious answer to our difficulties. They had become used to having to lift themselves for one new trial after another just when they might have hoped to find some stability at last, but this plan in its very boldness had the feel of a break-through solution.

Yet for all the euphoria, there was a realization that implementing it would involve more pain for the company than ever before. What was the absolute minimum required to run the two companies? This was the unpalatable question that provided the starting point for our discussions. If our plan was to be attractive to investors, then both new companies would need to be pared to the bone. boo.com, the international retailer, for example, would sell in eighteen countries but operate from a single London office.

The restructuring, which we called Operation Catfish, would involve the shedding of more jobs than we had imagined in our worst dreams. Dolphin, the state-of-the-art technology and fulfilment provider, would at the time of the split have about 110 staff, and the new boo.com just 70. But the fact that we had engineered for ourselves a rescue scheme that seemed to be of obvious attraction to investors bolstered everyone's morale. We felt that we were in control of our own destinies again.

All we had to do was stay alive long enough for the plans to come to fruition. We were like the crew of a crippled submarine who have to lie in their bunks and not use up the oxygen. The emergency measures imposed to eke out our cash flow included a halt to all travel, marketing expenditure and new commitments of any kind.

This challenge to our ability to keep the business moving forward somehow helped us to appreciate the enormous asset we had. When the site had first launched, the various teething problems had put us on the defensive. We couldn't help feeling uneasy about what visitors might find, and knew that the various glitches would counteract the effect of our marketing campaign. But six months on, we had ironed out the difficulties to create a superb site and an overall shopping experience that was in itself our greatest advert. Customers were impressed not only by the site but also by the style and speed with which the products they had ordered were delivered. We knew that we had only to persuade people to buy from boo.com once for them to want to come back on subsequent occasions. So we devised a scheme to encourage that all-important first-time visit. For a week over Easter, customers who shopped on the site would receive electronic coupons worth £20 off future purchases. As it was technically a promotion rather than a discount, we didn't need clearance from suppliers.

By far the most effective means of advertising the scheme turned out to be not expensive online banners or newspaper advertising but emails, of which over 220,000 were sent out over the week of the offer:

Subject: £20 Off? Try It On

Hi there,

What would you do with £20 from boo.com?

Grab a new back pack and head for the hills? Snap up some sandals and cruise to the beach? Whatever you decide, you'll get it for £20 less at boo.com.

How does it work? All you have to do is go to boo.com and shop. When you get to the checkout, look for the 'promotional code' box and enter this code: BCAD0001.

PS: Know anyone else who knows a good deal when they see one? Forward them this email.

On the first day of the offer, Thursday 20 April, we had over 4000 orders – ten times as many as normal – and at one point so many people were visiting the website at the same time that we had to lower the 'velvet rope' briefly to restrict access to the site. The success of the scheme was a tribute to the ingenuity and teamwork of our technology, marketing and retail departments, but above all served to prove that the best ideas are free. The emails, at negligible cost, generated over 70 per cent of the orders.

The offer generated many times our daily average of orders and proved to be an excellent dry-run for Dolphin. There was an enormous thrill in seeing the powerful machine we had built operating at full stretch. In those difficult days, it lifted the spirits of not only the company but also our backers. Nader would ring me several times a day to keep up with the number of orders. At one point, James Cronin told me, we were peaking at around three a second. It was like taking a high performance car on to the autobahn and putting your foot down.

Best of all, the voucher scheme provided Deutsche Post with a direct demonstration of Dolphin's potential, and we spoke to them as a potential strategic investor in our new idea. It appealed to them as providing a perfect synergy with their own business, encouraging the growth of cross-border delivery. 'This is exactly what we've been looking for,' enthused Dr Martin Raab, head of corporate development. We also presented the idea to managers at Kingfisher, the giant British retailer, who seemed equally intrigued. As both companies, clearly impressed, went away to consider the idea further, it was like the old days in which we had stunned investors and suppliers alike with our extraodinary prototype. Here was an example of the power of a good idea to change fortunes.

But the real confirmation that we had been thinking along the right lines came when we discussed Dolphin with Tom Henderson of Eden Capital.

'Now you're talking,' he said.

Eden was one of the shareholders who had so far held back from making any further investment in the company, but our new business model suddenly made us an attractive proposition again. Henderson was smart; he knew that there would be a demand for Dolphin because in recent months Eden had invested in several other e-commerce startups which would have benefitted from just such a platform. The scale of financing Henderson suggested we aim for was $30 million to clear boo.com's debt and to split the company in two and then $50 million for each new company.

Meanwhile, Wasserstein Perella, the bank Nader had introduced, found a promising new shareholder structure which involved bringing in a venture capital firm to head up a consortium of investors. Episode 1 had been created only a couple of months earlier with $100 million to invest in UK start-ups. One of the two founders, Simon Murdoch, had set up Bookpages, the internet book-seller that Amazon bought in order to get a footing in Britain. The shared background was encouraging.

Jay and I met Murdoch's colleague Richard Tahta at Wasserstein Perella's office on St James's Street in the week before Easter. Also present were Nader and Ali and Howard Covington, the CEO of Wasserstein's UK operations. The hope was that Episode 1 would be able to provide a cohesion and purpose to the wider shareholder base that had previously been missing.

A small and bald man of about forty, who spoke very fast, Tahta defied the conventional idea of a saviour. We listened politely to his battery of questions, but felt that it would have been a more constructive meeting if he had shown a little more interest in listening to us. Can you take me through the logistics structure? . . . What are your percentage returns? . . . What's your customer acquisition cost? The inquisition was disconcerting, but the desperate hunt for investors over the last few weeks had given me an almost instant recall of such figures.

The following week, on 26 April, we received a letter of intent from Episode 1 offering, subject to due diligence, to invest $50 million for an 80 per cent stake.

Our board meeting the next day brought home the timeliness of the offer. As usual, Rachel Yasue began the meeting with an update of the financial situation. It was only the support of the Millennium Fund and Bernard Arnault that kept us afloat. They had just advanced $2 million and $1 million respectively, with another $4 million on the way. About $2 million a week was needed to keep the company going, but a whole army of creditors would still need careful juggling. Our ad agency, BMP, had just filed a statutory claim for £2.1 million; our credit insurance for marketing had been withdrawn; and UPS had refused to distribute any more packages unless it was paid in full.

Christopher Heather, like a doctor checking the pulse of a patient on the critical list, then gave what had become his customary assessment of whether we were legally permitted to trade. On this occasion, he had brought along Peter Bloxham of Freshfields law firm for a second opinion.

Back in February we had appointed Freshfields to advise on our IPO. The meetings at their Fleet Street office had begun with Mark Trapnell, a corporate finance lawyer, on a high floor with an impressive view of St Paul's Cathedral. But as our IPO became derailed and we found ourselves mired in financing difficulties, we retreated to Bloxham's insolvency division in the basement. Now the joint verdict of the two lawyers was that, thanks to the interest of both Episode 1 and Eden Capital, we were still very much alive.

The meeting ended with an anxious letter from senior management asking to be kept posted on board decisions. The sort of nerves required to carry on the business in the teeth of such adversity reminded me of the early days of LeanderMalmsten, but now we had not a handful of employees and creditors to worry about, but hundreds. There had been little time in the last couple of years to indulge my passion for poetry, but now one very famous poem came to mind: 'If you can keep your head when all about you/Are losing theirs and blaming it on you;/ If you can trust yourself when all men doubt you,/But make allowance for their doubting too;/ . . . you'll be a Man, my son!'

They were useful words to remember whenever I walked from my desk through the open-plan area of our office to the boardroom in one direction or to the adjoining meeting-rooms that had become known as the War Room in the other. Locked away in these rooms, a handful of boo's senior executives struggled with the crises and discussed rescue plans that we knew would involve mass redundancies. As we went back and forth, we were in full view of the rest of the staff and had to be careful not to allow our expressions to betray any anxiety. For the sake of company morale and staff confidence, however precarious our future seemed, it was vital that business should carry on as usual.

'Hello Everyone,' began one of my staff letters written at about this time. 'After much hard work and perseverance on behalf of HR and the payroll managers, I am happy to report the following promotions and job shifts resulting from the Performance Review.' After listing names, I then went on: 'I look forward to the pleasure of delivering many more announcements of this nature as people continue to develop within the company. Congratulations to everyone listed below and good luck in your new jobs!'

The day after the board meeting, Jay, Paul, Christopher Heather and I went over to Freshfields first thing in the morning to discuss the terms of the Episode 1 offer with Mark Trapnell. It was good not to be heading down to the basement for a change. We set up a conference call with Wasserstein Perella and discussed how we would develop the letter of intent into a proper shareholder agreement.

About an hour had gone by when Paul's mobile rang. He walked out of the room to take the call but quickly came back in again. 'Time out, everyone. We have something we need to deal with.'

He handed me his phone. It was Tobin calling from the office.

'What's the problem?' I asked.

'You have to get back here right away,' he said. 'This is absolutely crazy. There are people marching through the office, throwing their weight around, upsetting everyone and basically taking over the place.'

'What people?'

Tobin was in such a state that it took some time after we had rung him back and put him on the speakerphone to calm him down and work out what was going on. I had said a day or two earlier that Murdoch and Tahta could drop by to see the office and that Tobin and Charlotte would show them around. But there had been some misunderstanding and they had turned up with several other people, expecting to be able to start their due diligence straight away. Among this unexpectedly large party were managers from two small start-ups EZshop and brandfever.com. Both these e-commerce apparel companies were direct competitors of boo. Not only were Murdoch and Tahta refusing to sign our non-disclosure agreement, but they were also insisting that EZshop and brandfever.com should be allowed to take part in the due diligence process.

'I don't know what to do,' Tobin said. 'They kept talking about how they were here to "save" us.'

'What did you say?' I asked, uncomfortable to be having this conversation in front of our lawyers.

'I told them there was no way I'd show them anything until I had spoken to you.'

'OK. Put them on the speakerphone,' I said. 'Let me talk to them myself.'

Murdoch and Tahta then came on to the speakerphone. As I began to ask them about what was going on, Tahta lost his temper. 'For fuck's sake, we're here to save your company. You're in no position to be picky about this. We haven't got time to mess around.'

'I understand,' I said. 'We want to move this along as quickly as possible too. But you have to realize that we're all under a lot of stress right now. If we're going to work together, then it's important that you show some respect to my staff.' I also explained the need to do things in an agreed way. 'When we get people in for due diligence we prepare everything very carefully. This is how we operate.'

They agreed to sign their own non-disclosure agreement and we worked out a proper timetable for due diligence. But it was still a humiliating situation which required boo management to hand over confidential information to people they perceived to be direct competitors. Afterwards I complained to Wasserstein Perella, and, much to Tahta's credit, he later rang me up to apologize for the chaotic morning.

As the entire management team had been on edge for weeks, I knew it was only a matter of time before one of us was pushed over. Back at the office, I called a meeting at the end of the day to go through what had happened that morning. Just before Christopher Heather and I entered the meeting-room, Tobin came to me and said he was going to resign. It was so sudden there was no time to take it in. I just continued on into the room, with Tobin following behind. Then as if I hadn't heard, he repeated it, this time to the entire management team.

'I've decided to leave and I think you would all be wise to consider your own positions as well,' he said, to general astonishment.

It actually hadn't been the first resignation that week. Rob Shepherd had told me that he intended to leave to join Chello, the same company that had hired Dean Hawkins. But our technology platform was no longer such a critical issue, so I was able to be philosophical. Tobin, on the other hand, had been a lynchpin on whom we had relied heavily. Up until this moment the tight kinship of the inner circle – the sense that we would all go down together if necessary – had seemed the best guarantee that we would finally get through, but if Tobin left that would all fall apart.

There was a long reproachful silence. Then Charlotte, on the verge of tears, said: 'I can't believe you're doing this now. I thought we were in this together.'

'I'm sorry,' Tobin said. 'I've been taking legal advice . . . and, well, I have to think about my reputation.'

Jay shook his head. 'Isn't it a bit late to start worrying about that? If this company goes bust, your reputation is going to be affected whether you leave now or wait until the end.'

Tobin looked down. 'I've made my decision.'

But there was a sense that already he was regretting it and wanted somehow to win back our approval. When the meeting broke up, he suggested that we should all go for a drink.

'What a good idea,' I said.

'No thanks,' said Charlotte.

Once everybody had left the room, she began to cry. Jay and I went back in to try to comfort her. 'Come along for a drink,' we said. 'You'll feel better.'

Tobin's resignation was very disappointing, but I couldn't really blame him. After all, I had brought him in to operate the company, not to help carve it up. I had admired his discipline, method and patience, but these qualities, which were great in peacetime, were less helpful in a war. Even so, he had held up remarkably well. As chief retail officer, he had borne the brunt of our difficulties. He had more people reporting into him than anyone else, all wanting to know what was going on, and had also to handle angry suppliers – some on the point of bankruptcy themselves – demanding to be paid.

For someone by nature honest and straightforward, it must have been extremely difficult to assume the poker face that had in the last few weeks become an occupational necessity. He hated to pretend that things were all right when he knew they weren't, and, although he had always been one of the most loyal members of the management team, he struggled with the idea of being at the mercy of Texas Pacific and now Episode 1.

Among the many emails waiting for me that day was Tobin's formal resignation letter:

Dear Ernst,

It is with regret that I confirm in writing my decision to resign from my position as chief retail officer effective immediately.

   If the board or investors wish to make me an offer to stay and fully participate in the current transaction process then I am willing to consider any offer in writing from them that is presented to me by Tuesday May 2nd, 2000.

Yours sincerely,

Tobin Ireland

How much did he pay his lawyer for this? I wondered. Its tone of corporate self-interest was so contrary to the spirit of our situation that only an outsider could have thought it up. It made me feel more sorry than angry. Here was Tobin desperately trying to follow the prudent path when the ground had long ago given way beneath him.

But over the weekend he had second thoughts. He came up to me first thing on Monday morning. He had over-reacted, he said. If it was all right, he'd like to stay. 'No problem,' I said. 'I know it's been very difficult for you, but you've done a fantastic job. Now let's fight to save the company.' And from that moment on, he fought tirelessly. Indeed, my most notable memory of this period was how adversity brought out the best in everyone. There were plenty of opportunities to abandon ship. Headhunters were circling like vultures – even I was offered a job by a financial company that was looking for an entrepreneur to build up its internet presence. Politely, I declined. Whatever happened, I was going to see this through to the end, but I was heartened to discover how many other people were prepared to join me.

After Episode 1's stormy visit to the office, I met up with Richard Tahta over the weekend to discuss his impressions of the business. We stopped off at a Starbucks before heading back to the office with our cups of coffee. This time his questions left me with the impression that he was daunted not only by the sheer complexity of the business but also the prospect of managing such a disparate set of investors. A few days later, he rang to say that Episode 1 had decided not to proceed.

Nader and Ali who had worked so hard to bring about such a deal were particularly disappointed. They suggested that now we should move ahead to a rights issue without a consortium. Wasserstein meanwhile found a potential executive chairman, who might at least provide some guidance to the shareholders in the absence of a strong lead investor. David Simmonds, who had formerly headed the Somerfield supermarket chain, came into the office to discuss the possibility, but eventually declined for much the same reasons as Episode 1 had.

In any case, a much more appealing opportunity now presented itself. Tom Henderson of Eden Capital, who had been busy analysing our plan for splitting the company into two businesses, called with an offer to invest a substantial sum for a majority stake in Dolphin if he was happy with the due diligence outcome. But we still had to work out what would happen to the retail company, boo.com, in which Eden Capital had little interest. Nader and Ali Kolaghassi met with Henderson to try and plan a way forward.

Meanwhile our attempts to carry on in a very difficult situation won not admiration but mockery from the media. When at the end of April we issued a report on worldwide retail trends, the *New York Post* found it too good an opportunity to resist: Under the headline, 'AILING BOO.COM FINDS THE SECRET TO E-TAIL SUCCESS', it wrote: 'When the going gets bad – like when top-level management begins walking out faster than the click of a mouse, when mass firings are necessary to cut costs, when technical snafus impede the use of the Website – it's not necessary to look for ways to watch the bottom line. Just let the employees loose to perform a global e-commerce trend report, as the crew at struggling e-tailer boo.com did.'

This sort of stuff was best ignored, but one article that we couldn't ignore appeared in the *Wall Street Journal Europe* on 3 May: 'Shareholders in boo.com Group Ltd. are seeking a buyer for the Internet retailer of trendy sports clothing, having decided it has few prospects of raising additional funds.' It then went on to give a detailed account of our plight. In terms of PR, this was about as bad as it could get. The piece could not only undermine our efforts to raise more money but also cause panic within the company. So on the same day I sent an email to staff to quell the growing fears:

> As you may have noticed, the *Wall Street Journal Europe* has made mention of boo.com's current fund raising efforts, putting those in the context of the current mood in the marketplace. You should know that this article does not provide a comprehensive picture of our current fund raising efforts, and that in fact we are considering a number of different options for the future of the company.
>
> With all this in perspective, it is key to recognise that we are still a few weeks away from finalising any new investment, and whilst we now have some money in place, we need to be extremely cost conscious when taking on any new commitments or expenditure, whilst continuing with business as usual. Accordingly this belt tightening will be a challenging time for us. However, what we are going through at the moment is no different to what most other companies in this sector are currently facing, and one that we are far better positioned to get through.

But the very precariousness of our situation seemed to concentrate minds to our advantage. Once the core shareholders realized that they had finally reached the abyss, with considerable persuasion from

Nader, Ali and Tison, they found the long-absent consensus to step back from the edge. For weeks they had been arguing over what the valuation of the company should be in any new round of investment. Now, as a prelude to a $30 million funding package, they agreed on the humiliatingly low valuation of $20 million. Still, it was a lot better than zero.

I was jubilant and wasted no time – in another email on Friday 5 May – sharing the news with staff:

Dear all,

We have today reached agreement on a new round of investment – with a substantial sum being committed by the core shareholders . . . This substantial investment demonstrates their ongoing commitment to us.

You may know that in the process of finalising this round we have entered into discussions with a number of people to look at potential strategic opportunities. As we proceed with normal business we will continue to explore these avenues to ensure that we maximise the value of boo to our employees, shareholders and suppliers.

I appreciate that speculative press articles and rumours can be unsettling (they are to me as well). boo, like other internet companies, is being targeted by many journalists at the moment – hopefully this will shortly pass. These are tough times for the internet sector and all of your hard work and commitment have contributed to the good shape we are now in.

I'll keep you updated on developments and if you have any questions on this please talk with your managers or come and discuss it with me.

Regards,

Ernst

It was a great way to end the week. But the roller-coaster ride was far from over. On Wednesday 9 May, at a board meeting to discuss the funding package, it was agreed that it should go ahead on the basis of our restructuring plan. But now that we seemed to be alive again, the realization came home that we would have to sack half the company. Kajsa, who still found it difficult to come to terms with our first restructuring, had been deeply depressed at the thought of having to go through it all again. She abstained on a vote on the issue and broke down in tears, threatening to resign if we went ahead. Sacking so many people, she argued, would be tantamount to destroying the company anyway.

'What are we going to do about Kajsa?' Nader asked after the meeting. 'If she resigns, we're not going to get the deal.'

So I tried to win her round. But although she agreed not to quit for the sake of the company's future, she remained adamant that the path we were taking was not one that she approved of. The recent developments had left her feeling scared and dejected.

The board's decision in favour might have seemed an end to the matter, but the objection was raised that we couldn't take such a course of action until the investors had finally committed the money, and at a board meeting the next morning the decision was reversed.

The final plunge began on Sunday 14 May. In an article that made our funding plans public for the first time, the *Sunday Telegraph* reported on a last-minute hitch: 'One of the two main investors who was expected to inject the vital funds last week is said to have stalled, while the other, thought to be Bernard Arnault, the French businessman, is only prepared to put up more cash if others match him. Unless the issue can be resolved this weekend, the group is expected to call in administrators within days.' Even worse, the piece reported that if boo.com did receive the funding, it was still expected 'to shed more than half of its 400 staff and close most of its offices around the world'.

There was an avalanche of voice-mail messages from journalists wanting to know my reaction to the piece. Instead of answering them, I headed out into the warm spring sun to join Charlotte and a couple of her friends for a drink in the Ladbroke Arms pub. The media onslaught was something we would all just have to get used to and stop worrying about.

'You look really calm,' said one of Charlotte's friends, Simon

Walker, in an unsubtle attempt to extract some information.

I just smiled.

When I got back to my flat, however, I couldn't avoid a phone call from a young journalist from the *Financial Times*. It turned out to provide a much needed moment of light relief. She had read the *Sunday Telegraph* piece and wondered what was going on. I said very little but somehow managed to persuade her that, whatever she may have read in the *Telegraph*, our funding plans were still on course.

'So when's the IPO?' she asked.

If only more journalists were like this, I thought to myself, and was pleased to see her article in the *FT* the next day under the headline: 'BOO.COM NEAR TO INJECTION OF £30M FUNDS'.

But it was otherwise a dismal Monday. The biggest source of comfort for some time had been the knowledge that Eden Capital was eager to invest in Dolphin. For the past week their advisers PricewaterhouseCoopers had been reviewing the Dolphin business concept. And once Eden finally committed, I knew that the other shareholders would have a framework for progress and would be able quickly to settle their remaining differences. Only the day before, I had spoken to Spencer Skinner, the independent consultant to Eden Capital who was leading their research into Dolphin. He had sounded very positive, but now I was just about to get a rude shock.

As I made my way towards Notting Hill Gate that morning looking for a taxi, I switched on my mobile to find a long string of messages. Sandwiched between a friend who was getting married and yet another journalist was Tom Henderson. His voice was flat. 'The answer is no,' he said. 'I'm afraid it's too complicated.'

Just at this moment a taxi drew up and I jumped in. My stomach churned and I pushed down the window. Had I heard right? I skipped through the messages again. 'The answer is no . . .'

No, I thought. Not no again! Not after we've come this far. It seemed as if someone up there really wanted us to fail. All the investors had been waiting to hear from Eden Capital before finally deciding whether to commit themselves to the rights issue. This would kill it.

I phoned Tom from the office. 'I got your message,' I said. 'I'm not sure what you meant.'

Tom sounded uncomfortable. 'Ernst, I'm sorry. I spoke to my people at PricewaterhouseCoopers.' He paused. 'They think there are going to be problems adapting the technology for Dolphin.'

Then there was the general mayhem that was occurring in the internet sector. Two of his other internet investments were on the verge of collapse. boo.com was just one crisis too many. 'I'm really sorry,' he repeated. 'I know this is a bad time for you . . .'

I called Kajsa, who had already been in despair over the restructuring. 'This is terrible,' she said. 'What will the shareholders do?' This was the big question now, but it was impossible to pretend that there were any attractive options left out there that might galvanize their support. Kingfisher and Deutsche Post still had a notional interest in Dolphin, but the chance of them making up their minds in time to make any difference was remote. I then held a senior management meeting and called the core investors. They would have to go away and reconsider their position, they said. The discussions were brief and funereal. I knew then that fortune had taken a fatal turn against us, but I knew too that if we were to have any chance at all we had to keep fighting.

The ironic thing was that our figures were continuing to get better and better. Gross sales in the month to 14 May were $500,000. Another indicator of how well we had established ourselves was the fact that 40 per cent of our business came from existing customers. This was a very good sign. If they bought once, they would come back again. But no one by this stage was interested in figures.

Later that morning I sent an email to staff. Aware of the anxiety everyone must be feeling, I had recently been making extra efforts to communicate, even though I knew that the things that everyone really wanted to know had to be kept secret:

Dear all,

I realise there has been a lot of speculation about boo in the papers that must be very unnerving for everyone, myself included. I am unfortunately still unable to update you as we are continuing to work hard to finalise the financing. I also appreciate this is not the best way of communicating to you, but I don't think there is much value in having a company meeting until I have definitive and concrete answers to give you. I will be certain to update you all immediately with any news. In the meantime I hope I can rely upon your ongoing discretion with anyone outside the company – as it is in all of our best interests to try and control the negative perception currently circulating about us.

Finally, given the beautiful weather, cool afternoon drinks are on me this afternoon at 3:00 p.m. at Midas Touch, 4 Golden Square. I look forward to seeing you all there!

Thanks again for your patience,

Ernst

As we waited through Tuesday to hear from the investors, the only amusing moment came with a proposal from someone in Sweden who wanted to use the boo platform to sell ice-cream machines. I wondered how that would go down with PricewaterhouseCooper. We decided we had to try to come up with some ideas that would revive the rights issue. In the evening we drafted a letter to be emailed to all the shareholders first thing the next morning. Then we'd call them – and anyone else for that matter who might be able to help:

Dear Shareholder,

I am writing to inform you that boo.com Group is currently facing a serious financing crisis which, if not resolved within the next 12 hours, would force me to act in accordance with UK law and to file for bankruptcy by midnight tonight. I am making one final attempt to save the company and I am asking for your contribution to a Rights Issue . . .

First thing on the morning of Wednesday 17 May, Kajsa, Charlotte, Christopher Heather and I took our seats in the War Room and began making calls. It was the last determined effort to save the company. There was a general feeling of incredulity that we should be resorting to such desperate measures when the business itself was continuing to go so well.

As about $7 million of the funding package that the core shareholders were now re-considering had already been made over to the company, our target to carry on in business was $20 million.

The first three numbers we dialled were routed through to tinny-sounding voice mails, and the fourth disconnected. The next number on the list was Lucien Toutounji, the representative of a company called Whitehall, incorporated in Liechtenstein and with an office in Giza, Egypt. Last September, I recalled, Whitehall had invested $500,000. The only contact we'd had with Mr. Toutounji since then was via the Egypt-online emails he sent every few months, asking for progress reports.

A woman's voice answered, but I couldn't understand the guttural sounds. It took a few awkward seconds to establish that she spoke a little English.

'I . . . mother-in-law,' she explained helpfully. 'Meester Toutounji out.'

We tried the number again half an hour later. This time, the only sound we got was the screeching of a fax.

'Wow, you guys must be really stressed!' said Nashat Masri, of Foursan Technology Partners, a new Jordan-based venture capital fund that recently gave us $4.4 million.

'Yeah, it's been pretty stressful,' admitted Christopher, looking across the table at us with a pained expression. He paused just long enough to be polite. 'Did you . . . uh . . . get our fax this morning?'

'Yeah. I've just been looking through it,' Nashat said.

'So what do you think? Can you help?'

'I'm not really sure until I speak to the investors,' he replied. 'But I'll call you back as soon as I have an answer.'

The answer arrived half an hour later. He'd love to be able to help us, he said, with that strange cheerfulness, but . . .

And so our morning might have continued had Tison and Nader not agreed to commit $4 million each on condition that by the end of the day we had reached the $20 million target. It persuaded a few other people to say yes.

We'll make it, we thought, but by the afternoon the total was sticking obstinately on $12 million.

Then just as I wondered what we could do next, my mobile rang. It was Tobin. He sounded breathless and as though he was walking through an airport.

'It went pretty well,' he said. 'They said they're going to think about it.'

'Who said? Who's going to think about it?' I asked, momentarily confused.

'Zara. I mean the Jazztel guys . . . You know. Listen, I'll call you back in a minute. I'm just going through customs.'

As I waited, it all came back to me. Tobin and Jessica Ordovas, our manager for Spain and Italy, in an epic instance of clutching at straws, had caught the first flight in the morning to Madrid. It was Jessica's idea to call her brother, the executive assistant to Martin Varsavsky, one of Spain's most successful entrepreneurs. Varsavsky ran Jazztel, a Spanish telecoms company. 'I can't promise that Martin will see you,' Jessica's brother had said. 'But if you get over here I should be able to set you up with his advisers.'

He was true to his word, Tobin explained when he called back a few minutes later. Over lunch with the advisers, he and Jessica had given a presentation on boo's latest sales figures and calmly asked for several million dollars – by the end of the day. The advisers explained that Varsavsky himself was unlikely to be interested, but that they also had connections with Zara, the Spanish retailing chain, which had been thinking about developing an online presence. How boo it would be, I thought, if we were saved like this.

'They're going to call the CEO for us,' said Tobin.

His enthusiasm was infectious and made us think of other people we could try. As we launched on a flurry of renewed calling, James Cronin joined us in the room. He had already won the boo award for lateral thinking with his plan to sell the company on eBay. He registered Miss Boo as the seller and even sent a followup email to one of eBay's vice presidents. 'This is not a joke,' it read. 'We really will do this.'

But as the afternoon wore on with call after call receiving the same negative response, we began to realize that we probably wouldn't make our target. Christopher sent out a fax to the shareholders to update them on our $12 million total so far and to remind them that time was running out.

At 5 o'clock I made a conscious effort to switch over to a way of thinking hard to adopt after years of encouraging everyone to banish failure from their minds. What if we didn't get the money? How were we to break the news to staff? What about the press? I still hoped for a last-minute miracle and had Esther Galan postpone a board meeting scheduled for 6 until 8 p.m. to buy a little bit more time. But we still had to prepare for the worst.

I slipped out of the room and called David Bick, who had replaced Financial Dynamics as our PR adviser after the IPO had fallen through and had been invaluable in the crisis.

'We should give an exclusive to the *FT*,' he said. 'Let them have your side of the story before it's too late.'

All that day we had been besieged by the media. But it was nothing compared to what would ensue if the company went under. David knew that it would be a nightmare for all of us and that the last thing we would want to be thinking about was fighting off the press. So his idea was that one complete interview with the *FT* would save us from having to make any further comment. All the other newspapers could then quote from the *FT*. But there was a catch. I would have to do the interview *before* the board meeting at the end of the day or risk missing the deadline for the next day's issue. If boo was somehow pulled back from the brink of collapse, the *FT* would have to pull their story.

I asked David to set up the interview, then spoke to Rachel Yasue, who called her KPMG colleagues in corporate recovery – the polite phrase for liquidators. Both they and the insolvency lawyers at Freshfields were invited to attend the board meeting. Just in case, I told myself. Just in case.

In the taxi to David Bick's City office where the interview was to take place I took a call on my mobile from Kajsa wishing me good luck. We'd had so much bad luck recently, I thought to myself, that surely it was only fair that the odds should now turn in our favour. It still wasn't too late to have a happy ending. I imagined all the possible eleventh-hour rescues from Bill Gates developing a sudden interest in fashion to Eden Capital having second thoughts. As the taxi pulled up outside David's office, I half considered sending it around the block again – anything for a little bit more time.

I entered David's office a little after 6 to find Caroline Daniel and Thorold Barker already waiting. *Two* journalists, I thought to myself. This must be a very special story. It was hard to know who looked the more stressed. I was about to lose a company; they had the scoop of the year – the world's first big internet collapse – but hardly any time to make their deadline. Pleasantries were limited to Caroline's comment that I was wearing the same Paul Smith suit I had worn exactly a year earlier on the cover of *Fortune* magazine as CEO of one of the world's coolest companies.

It was small comfort, but at last I was able to speak with complete openness, which didn't make their job any easier because they had so little time to take in all the financial details that suddenly I was releasing with casual indifference. 'We have been too visionary,' I said. 'We wanted everything to be perfect, and we have not had control of costs. My mistake has been not to have a counterpart who was a strong financial controller.'

Halfway through, Thorold hurried off to write the story for the front page. His deadline was 7.30. Caroline continued to ask questions for a more detailed inside piece but soon had to rush off too. It was raining heavily that day. Later I learned that when she got back to the *FT* office and her colleagues saw her wet notebook, they asked her if it was because of my tears. I like to think that a few might even have been her own. She had been one of the journalists to follow the boo.com story almost from the beginning. Over the past year she had seen it through all the triumphs and the disasters. She certainly had her scoop now, but she must have filed it with very mixed emotions.

Usually our board meetings were just a handful of people huddled around a speakerphone. But on this occasion I had invited everyone in the management team who had been involved in the fund-raising effort. I wanted the board to have the very latest update on the situation, but also I thought it was important that the people who had tried so hard that day to save the company should be there to hear the final verdict. There was still the unspoken hope that the $12 million would be enough, that Millennium or Arnault would step in to make up the difference.

But when I arrived back at the office, I also found waiting outside the boardroom a stiff and awkward-looking group of lawyers and liquidators. They were far less welcome.

'You can come in,' I said to Phil Wallace, who was heading the team of liquidators from KPMG's corporate recovery department, 'but I'd be grateful if everyone else could wait outside.' We filed into the room slowly, getting in one another's way as we took our seats. Kajsa and I were sitting at opposite ends of the table, with Christopher, James and Charlotte taking up positions on either side. Then Tobin, back safely from Madrid, entered the room, followed closely by Rachel Yasue.

As usual, it took a while to patch in the board members attending by phone. Then, after a brief welcome, I handed over to Christopher Heather, who described in detail the fund-raising attempts of the day. 'We now have commitments totaling $12 million,' he said. 'I know that's not quite enough, but we're not far off.'

James Cronin then told the meeting about his promising contacts with some big retailers who were interested in the Dolphin idea of selling their products on boo's platform. 'If we just had a little more time, we could sign up some more of them . . .'

'You've had two months to try and save the company,' said François Tison's voice over the speakerphone. There was a mixture of frustration and sadness in his tone. He had tried hard to find a solution. There had been so many hopes, yet in the end still no viable framework that Bernard Arnault and the Millennium Fund could push to the other investors.

Then Jessica Ordovas stood up and, without having been invited to speak, made an impromptu intervention. 'We haven't heard back from Zara yet,' she said, her voice shaking. 'But there's still a chance that they'll be interested.'

There was silence.

'I'm not part of senior management. I'm here representing the employees,' she continued in a tone that was half pleading, half defiant. 'I just want to say that I think most of our staff would work for 48 hours without pay if they thought there was any hope of saving the company.'

But soon there was nothing left for management to add that hadn't already been said often before, and it was time for the board members to have their say.

Ken Baird, a lawyer from Freshfields, explained the legal procedure if they were unable to commit the necessary funds. They could either make boo insolvent, which would effectively mean closing it down; or they could put it into administration. The latter option would involve liquidators running the company to extract some value, but would require investors to put up some more short-term cash. The consensus was that the company should liquidate, but first the board members had to make up their minds once and for all about whether to provide the money we needed to carry the business forward.

There was a long silence on the line. Christopher Heather looked stunned. 'I hope everybody understands what this means,' he said. 'If you don't put up more money, this company will go bust. That means you will lose everything.'

A muffled cough from the speakerphone was the only proof that anyone was listening. Christopher was so upset that he had to leave the room for a few moments.

At this point, I realized that there was nothing else to do. 'Can I ask you all to confirm whether or not you will to put up any more money?' I asked. At least now they would have say something.

One by one each board member answered no. Finally it was Nader's turn. I knew that it was irrational to expect that he could rescue us on his own, but I couldn't help having the thought.

There was a long pause.

'No,' he said finally.

'Well, that's it, then,' I said. 'We are going to have to put the company into liquidation.'

While everyone else around the table slowly got to their feet, I remained for some moments motionless in my chair. Kajsa and Christopher hugged each other. Tobin put his arm around a distraught Jessica.

Someone passed me a phone. It was Nader. 'I'm really sorry we couldn't help,' he said. It was a nice gesture and went a little way towards easing the resentment I felt right now towards our investors.

But even now it wasn't over. If you're in a plane crash, that's it. You're dead. This was like surviving the crash, then spending the next day crawling through the jungle. First, we had to call the heads of all the foreign offices to explain the situation. The liquidators from KPMG, who were now in charge, insisted on monitoring the calls, issuing strict instructions as to what could and couldn't be said.

Charlotte got hold of Annica in Stockholm. She would have liked to have broken the news gently, but with a liquidator listening in had to speak with a forced formality. 'As you know, we have been trying to raise money for the past month. This has been unsuccessful and this evening the board has decided to file for liquidation.'

'So what happens now?' asked Annica.

Before Charlotte could say anything, the liquidator interrupted. 'boo.com's company structure means that each of its foreign offices are legally separate entities,' he said.

'So what am I supposed to do?' Annica replied.

'The London company owns the website and everything you've been selling, so if I were you, I'd follow our example and file for liquidation.' After a brief silence, he realized that he would have to try to make things more simple. 'Do you have any money left in your account?' he sighed.

'Yes.'

'Well you might want to use it to get a lawyer.'

Once all the country managers had been told, we began the massive job of trying to call something like 200 employees before they read the news in the papers.

Jessica came up with the idea of a pyramid system. Call five people each, then tell each of them to call five people, and so on.

Quite a few of them we could tell personally. A bewildered huddle of people who had stayed in the office to work late gathered around as we emerged from the boardroom with our defeated expressions. People were shocked, some crying.

James Cronin returned to the office in Carnaby Street to shut down the website. We'd been told that boo's brand would be worth more to a buyer if we kept the website running, but we obviously couldn't have people buying products any more. So James came up with a compromise that would allow web-surfers to browse the products, but freeze the site at the point of purchase. As I watched him leave, my thoughts slipped back to 8.59 on the morning of Wednesday 3 November 1999, when Kajsa had invited him to press the button that would launch boo on the world – and how he had said no, that I should. He couldn't have known then that it would be he who would have to switch it off.

Kajsa and I slipped into a side office with Dina Cholack, our head of PR, to draft a press release with the lawyers. After weeks of always having to choose our words carefully, we put down the unvarnished truth. Ken Baird insisted on taking a look before we sent it out. 'You've got to be careful,' he said. 'What if one of these investors is thinking about buying the company?' But apart from one small word change, he cleared it to be sent off to the newspapers that night as we had written it:

Ernst Malmsten and Kajsa Leander, joint founders and major shareholders of boo.com, the active streetwear online retailer, have issued the following personal statement:

'We are deeply disappointed that it has been necessary to ask KPMG to become liquidators of the company.

'The senior management of boo.com has made strenuous efforts over the last few weeks to raise the additional funds that would have allowed the company to go forward with a clear plan. This plan involved a restructuring of the retail operations, the development of an e-fulfilment business using our unique advanced technology and operations platform, and the identification of strategic partners. It is disappointing to both the management and staff alike that we were not able to bring this plan to fruition particularly against the background of steadily-improved trading.

'It will be of little consolation to our staff, but we wish to thank them for their fortitude, patience and commitment. They have had to endure weeks of media speculation about the business and had continued to apply themselves with great enthusiasm despite these adverse circumstances. Recognition should also go to our suppliers who have maintained their support for us throughout this difficult period. We thank them for this.

'We believe very strongly that in boo.com there is a formula for a successful business and fervently hope that those who are now responsible for dealing with the company will be able to recognize this.'

Epilogue

A LONG DAY IS NEARLY OVER. It's been one of the worst days in my life but I don't want it to end, because I know that when it does I will have to try to make sense of it and I'm not sure that I can bear to do that right now.

The *Financial Times* have been told that they can run the story. A press release has just been sent off to all the newspapers and agencies. There's nothing else left to do. For the first time I feel helpless. A handful of people stand by their desks looking bewildered and lost.

'Let's go for a drink,' I suggest.

'My head's splitting,' says Kajsa, 'I'm sorry.'

Only Charlotte and Tobin agree to come along, more for my sake than because they really want to. Everyone's too tired, too sad.

All the pubs have shut long ago, so Home House, the boo home from home, is the obvious place to go. Charlotte and Tobin bring with them several plastic carrier bags that they've hurriedly stuffed with important files. As we stand outside the office waiting for a taxi, we look as if we've just raided the place.

At Home House, I push my way past the happy, smiling faces of the successful London crowd and order three vodka and grapefruit juices at the bar. The horned bison's head mounted on the wall stares at me dolefully. People recognize me. I expect to see expressions of shock, sympathy or even glee on their faces, but it's obvious that no one yet knows.

They'll read about it in tomorrow's papers, but for a little longer we're still their equals, as safe as Cinderella at the ball. I even play with the idea that it hasn't really happened at all, that I'll go in to the office tomorrow morning, say hello to Esther and Paul and tell them about the terrible dream I had last night.

As I put down their drinks, Charlotte and Tobin each give me a weak smile as if to say, 'Do you remember?'

Yes, I remember. Here in Home House we used to hold our early management meetings every weekend, here we hosted the Global PR Summit, when we thought we were on top of the world, here we unveiled Project Launch. The scene of all our triumphs and disasters – what better place to bring down the curtain?

In our state of shock, Charlotte, Tobin and I say very little, just savour the bitter taste of the grapefruit juice. Then Charlotte's mobile rings. It's her friend Leslie. Charlotte tells her what has happened and briefly passes the phone to me.

'I'm so sorry . . .' says Leslie.

After about an hour, we leave and say goodbye on the deserted street outside.

In the taxi on the way home, I find it difficult to sit still because of my anxiety. I ring Kajsa. Our short conversation is desultory, but full of unexpressed feeling. We agree to meet at the office early in the morning – only a few hours away now.

I climb the familiar stairs to my flat, let myself in and sit down on the sofa. Although in Lund it's about 3 in the morning now, I ring my parents, the only people in the world to whom I can confide everything and expect unconditional help.

'It's a catastrophe,' I lament. 'I'm finished.'

They're shocked, but try to offer comforting words.

'Nobody is dead. It's just a company, not a human being,' my mother says.

'Think of it as a Harvard MBA,' suggests my father.

I then switch on my mobile and listen to an endless stream of voicemails from journalists around the world. About three or four of them are from the same woman on the *Wall Street Journal*: 'I've heard that you've had a secret press conference tonight. Please can you ring me back?' Her voice contains a silent reproach: how dare I not be around to answer questions on one of the biggest stories to break for weeks.

I'm just about to switch off the mobile again when there's a message from Jay: 'This is just to say thank you. It's been great to work for you. No matter how it ended, it's been an amazing ride.

I've learnt a lot, and if we were to do it all over again, I wouldn't hesitate for one second. I feel very proud of what we've achieved. You should too.'

The message briefly dispels the awful sense of defeat, but it's a transient feeling. I try to sleep, but can't, and hate the thought of what I will wake to. Anxiety grips me as I think how this day will affect the people who have worked for boo. Not only will they lose their jobs, but they can't even be paid for this month. They believed in boo's future, they spent months of their lives working long days and nights, but now, because of my failure, they will get nothing in return. What can I tell them? How can I ever make amends? I think of the investors. I used to joke about all the trouble they caused, when would they ever leave us alone? They will now. I think of all the money boo has burned through. Not my money, I remind myself with a wave of guilt and shame.

I can't control my panic, my sense of fear. I switch on every lamp in the flat to dispel the darkness. I ring Jay in New York. There's nothing very much to say, but I need to talk. Afterwards, I drift off to sleep for half an hour or so where I'm sitting on the sofa and then wake up feeling feverish. I switch on the TV. It's about 3 or 4 a.m. now and I watch the first news reports. 'The pioneering sports and fashion site boo has collapsed...'

After all the self-reproach, the biggest feeling I have is of trying in vain to unravel a ghastly puzzle. Why should boo fail now when everything was working so well? As the sky begins to lighten, I get up from the sofa, take a quick shower and put on a new shirt. I regain some courage like a condemned man preparing to face the long walk to the guillotine. I took my chances and now I must pay the penalty. I call a cab and on the way to the office stop off at a newsagent in Soho to pick up a copy of the *FT*. There's a big photograph of Kajsa and me on the front page.

The newsagent recognizes me. 'Better luck next time,' he says.

At the office, I exchange a sorry smile with one of the Gurkhas on his rounds. Otherwise the place is totally deserted except for a lone figure bent over a computer. Kajsa hears me come in and turns round.

She gets up and we embrace.

'What are we going to tell everyone?' I ask, stumped for a solution for perhaps the first time in my life. I'm not sure I can face them.

'Don't worry,' says Kajsa. 'We'll think of something.'

'How long have you been here?' I ask.

'About an hour. I couldn't sleep. Every time I tried, I kept on having the same nightmare. Being chased by journalists and cornered outside the office.'

'Are you sure it was a dream?' I say. 'Look at this.' And I drop my copy of the *FT* on her desk.

'BOO.COM COLLAPSES AS INVESTORS REFUSE FUNDS,' reads the headline. 'Online sports retailer becomes Europe's first big internet casualty.'

I switch on my computer and check my emails. One is from James Cronin:

From James Cronin
Sent: 18 May 2000 00:46
To: Senior Executive Committee
Subject: site order taking

Dear All,

I've just broken the site (in an inelegant way by stopping the order process step working). Nobody will be able to move from the checkout to the purchase path. So we won't be taking any more orders.

boo's closed.

Our last customer was Cindy Dodson. She ordered:
The North Face Ridge 9.5 Grey
Fred Perry Rib & Jersey Panelled Dress 12 Navy
Basket size $159.

See you in the morning.

Index